Believing Ancient Women

Intersectionality in Classical Antiquity
Series Editors: Mark Masterson, Victoria University of Wellington and Fiona McHardy, University of Roehampton

This series focuses on the intersection of gender and sexuality, in the Greco-Roman world, with a range of other factors including race, ethnicity, class, ability, masculinity, femininity, transgender and post-colonial gender studies. The books in the series will be theoretically informed and will sit at the forefront of the study of a variety of outsiders – those marginalised in relation to the 'classical ideal' – and how they were differently constructed in the ancient world. The series is also interested in the ways in which work in the field of classical reception contributes to that study.

Editorial Advisory Board
Patty Baker, Alastair Blanshard, Susan Deacy, Jacqueline Fabre-Serris, Cristiana Franco, Genevieve Liveley, Mark Masterson, Amy Richlin, Carisa R. Showden

Books available in the series
Women in the Law Courts of Classical Athens, Konstantinos Kapparis
Exploring Gender Diversity in the Ancient World, edited by Allison Surtees and Jennifer Dyer
Marginalised Populations in the Ancient Greek World: The Bioarchaeology of the Other, Carrie L. Sulosky Weaver
Age, Gender and Status in Macedonian Society, 550–300 BCE, Elina M. Salminen
Believing Ancient Women: Feminist Epistemologies for Greece and Rome, Megan E. Bowen, Mary H. Gilbert and Edith G. Nally
Toxic Masculinity in the Ancient World, Melanie Racette-Campbell and Aven McMaster

Visit the series web page at: edinburghuniversitypress.com/series-intersectionality-in-classical-antiquity

Believing Ancient Women

Feminist Epistemologies for Greece and Rome

Megan E. Bowen, Mary H. Gilbert and Edith G. Nally

EDINBURGH
University Press

Edinburgh University Press is one of the leading university presses in the UK. We publish academic books and journals in our selected subject areas across the humanities and social sciences, combining cutting-edge scholarship with high editorial and production values to produce academic works of lasting importance. For more information visit our website: edinburghuniversitypress.com

© editorial matter and organisation Megan E. Bowen, Mary H. Gilbert and Edith G. Nally, 2024, 2025
© the chapters their several authors 2024, 2025

Grateful acknowledgement is made to the sources listed in the List of Illustrations for permission to reproduce material previously published elsewhere. Every effort has been made to trace the copyright holders, but if any have been inadvertently overlooked, the publisher will be pleased to make the necessary arrangements at the first opportunity.

Edinburgh University Press Ltd
13 Infirmary Street
Edinburgh EH1 1LT

First published in hardback by Edinburgh University Press 2024

Typeset in 11/13 EB Garamond by
IDSUK (DataConnection) Ltd

A CIP record for this book is available from the British Library

ISBN 978 1 3995 1205 3 (hardback)
ISBN 978 1 3995 1206 0 (paperback)
ISBN 978 1 3995 1207 7 (webready PDF)
ISBN 978 1 3995 1208 4 (epub)

The right of Megan E. Bowen, Mary H. Gilbert and Edith G. Nally to be identified as the editors of this work has been asserted in accordance with the Copyright, Designs and Patents Act 1988, and the Copyright and Related Rights Regulations 2003 (SI No. 2498).

Contents

List of Illustrations vii
Acknowledgements viii
List of Contributors x

1. **Believing Ancient Women: An Introduction and Feminist Epistemological Field Guide** 1
   Edith G. Nally, Mary H. Gilbert and Megan E. Bowen

2. **'For you know how we cared for you': Sappho and Queer Epistemology** 30
   Erika L. Weiberg

3. **En-gendering Knowledge with the Oceanids in *Prometheus Bound*** 48
   Mary H. Gilbert

4. **Women's Complaints about Violence at Athens: Zobia and Aristogeiton** 68
   Fiona McHardy

5. **Bodies of Knowledge: Diotima's Reproductive Expertise in the *Symposium*** 82
   Edith G. Nally

6. **Monumental Presence and Absence: Approaching the Material Traces of Historical Women in the Classical World** 102
   Patricia Eunji Kim

7. Plautus's *Truculentus* and Terence's *Hecyra*: Patriarchal Authority and Women's Credibility 121
Serena S. Witzke

8. Incidental Women in the Letters of Cicero 138
Kristina Milnor

9. Signifying Dido: Constructs of Race and Gender in Augustan Rome 156
Shelley P. Haley

10. But She Didn't Complain: Ovid's Leucothoe, Rape Myths and Hermeneutical Injustice 169
Megan E. Bowen

11. 'Feebly fighting back': *Stuprum* in Eumolpus's *Pergamene Boy* 185
Debra Freas

12. The Viability of Feminist Stoicism: On the Compatibility of Stoic and Feminist Epistemology 202
Chelsea Bowden

13. What Everyone Knows: Hermeneutical Injustice in the Medieval Iphis 221
Jessica Hines

14. Religious Authority and Classical Reception in Baroque Rome: Martha Marchina's *Musa Posthuma* and Feminist Epistemologies of Care 242
Erika Zimmermann Damer

15. 'Grey' Rape on the Silver Screen: Rapes of Enslaved People in Mass Media about the Ancient World 262
Anise K. Strong

Selected Bibliography 280
Index 319

Figures

6.1 Sharon Hayes. *If They Should Ask*. 2017. Cast concrete, steel, and acrylic lettering, 9.5 × 10.3 × 8.7 feet. Rittenhouse Park, Philadelphia, PA. Monument Lab. Photo by Steve Weinick/Mural Arts Philadelphia. Courtesy of Monument Lab. 116

6.2 Sharon Hayes. *If They Should Ask*. 2017. Cast concrete, steel, and acrylic lettering, 9.5 × 10.3 × 8.7 feet. Rittenhouse Park, Philadelphia, PA. Monument Lab. Photo by Steve Weinick/Mural Arts Philadelphia. Courtesy of Monument Lab. 117

6.3 Philadelphia residents activating Sharon Hayes's sculptural installation, *If They Should Ask*. 2017. Cast concrete, steel, and acrylic lettering, 9.5 × 10.3 × 8.7 feet. Rittenhouse Park, Philadelphia, PA. Monument Lab. Photo by Steve Weinick/Mural Arts Philadelphia. Courtesy of Monument Lab. 119

Acknowledgements

First and foremost, we owe a huge debt to the contributors to this volume. It has been a pleasure to collaborate and learn from such an exceptional group of scholars. We owe them special acknowledgement not only for their brilliant contributions (and at times patient guidance) but also for agreeing to participate in a project that germinated during the second year of the coronavirus pandemic, a time when so many faced unprecedented challenges. We also believe it is important to acknowledge that much of the work of compiling the manuscript began amidst news of a number of mass shootings, including the racially motivated Buffalo massacre, and concluded just after the release of the *Dobbs* v. *Jackson Women's Health Organization* decision. We appreciate our contributors' endurance and commitment to this project while navigating the psychic, social, political and physical tolls of these tragedies.

Megan would like to thank Kevin Vahlbusch and David and Magdalena Bowen for their steadfast support. She is also grateful to Leo and Ophelia Bowen for their inspirational curiosity and persistent joy.

Mary would like to thank Jessica Hines, Richard Hutchins, Scarlett Kingsley, Desirée Melonas and Erika Weiberg for their suggestions, germinative conversations and enthusiasm for the project. She would also like to thank the students in her Sex, Gender and Power in Antiquity classes, and two students in particular: Madeleine Grabarczyk, who worked on the index, and Claire LeSar, who contributed the artwork on the book's cover. She is especially grateful to Alan Gilbert for reading her work at every stage, his daily care of their family and devotion to their son, Harrison.

Gwen would like to thank her colleagues at the University of Missouri–Kansas City for their support of her research, especially Clancy Martin for his unwavering encouragement and advice about publishing and Michelle

Smirnova for her suggestions and uplifting friendship. Gwen's deepest gratitude also goes to her mother, Edie Nally, for generously spending her hard-earned retirement looking after her grandchildren and to Benjamin Jasnow for introducing her to the co-editors of this volume so many years ago, for being her lifelong guide to classical antiquity, and for being a truly devoted husband and unparalleled caregiver to their children Iris and Hazel.

The co-editors would also like to thank one another for their commitment, hard work, humour and grace. Our lives have changed a great deal from the inception of this volume through its completion. Nevertheless, from the first phone conversation in the wake of Christine Blasey Ford's testimony, where we developed the idea for a panel on feminist epistemologies at the 2021 Society for Classical Studies, to the countless emails and texts we exchanged while in the throes of copyediting, we worked together tirelessly and in unison, learning from one another and developing new, cross-disciplinary approaches. This volume is a testament to our collective efforts and longstanding friendship.

Finally, we would like to thank Fiona McHardy for advising our proposal in the preliminary stages and steering us towards the Intersectionality in Classical Antiquity Series at Edinburgh University Press (EUP), along with Mark Masterson, series editor, and Nancy Rabinowitz, former series editor, for their enthusiasm about this project and for lending us their expertise from its genesis. Our thanks also go to Rachel Bridgewater, our editor at EUP, for her patience and flexibility. We are grateful for the comments of our anonymous readers, for our copyeditor, and to all who have worked behind the scenes to bring this volume to press.

List of Contributors

Chelsea Bowden is an assistant professor of philosophy at Denison University. Her research interests are in Hellenistic philosophy, particularly the Stoics and Pyrrhonian Skeptics, and in contemporary issues in ethics of belief and epistemology. Her current research focuses on questions concerning ancient and modern conceptions of good intellectual agency and intellectual virtue.

Megan Elena Bowen received a PhD in classics from the University of Virginia in 2018. She specialises in Roman literature and culture and has published on prayer and sexual violence in Ovid's *Metamorphoses* (2020). She is especially interested in issues related to gender and power in ancient texts and their reception.

Erika Zimmermann Damer is an associate professor of classics and Women's, Gender, and Sexuality Studies at the University of Richmond. She is the author of *In the Flesh: Embodied Identities in Roman Elegy* (2019) and co-editor of *Travel, Geography, and Empire in Latin Poetry* with Micah Myers (2021). She publishes on Roman elegy, Horace, Ovid and Roman graffiti. Her interdisciplinary work spans feminist intersectional thought, classical literature and its reception, cultural studies, epigraphy and material culture.

Debra Freas is a visiting lecturer at Wellesley College. Her research interests include narrative theory and race in the ancient novel, the reception of Greek tragedy, sexual violence in Latin poetry, and language pedagogy.

Mary Hamil Gilbert is an assistant professor of classics at Mississippi State University. Her research focuses on Greek and Roman drama, classical reception in early modern France, and women and gender studies. She has published articles and chapters on Aeschylus, Euripides, Seneca and the early modern French tragedian Jean Racine's reception of Greek and Roman drama, including 'Policing Women's Anger in the Roman Tragedy *Octavia*' (forthcoming), 'Je sentis tout mon corps et transir et brûler': Sublimating Ancient Sexuality in Jean Racine's *Phèdre et Hippolyte* in *The Routledge Companion to the Reception of Ancient Greek and Roman Gender* (2022), and 'Engaging Ancient Tragedy: Troy Falls Again in Jean Racine's *Andromaque*' (2018). She has also translated Anyte of Tegea's animal epigrams into English (2020).

Shelley P. Haley is the Edward North Chair of Classics Emerita at Hamilton College (USA). Her BA is from Syracuse University, and she received her PhD in Classical Studies from the University of Michigan. In 2021, she served as president of the Society for Classical Studies, the first African American woman to do so in the Society's 153-year history. Widely acclaimed as an expert on Cleopatra, Haley's current research centres on recovering the constructions of race and gender in ancient Rome by applying the theoretical framework of critical race feminist theory.

Jessica Hines is an assistant professor of English at Birmingham-Southern College whose work explores the intersection of sexuality, religion and the emotions in the medieval and early modern world. Her current monograph, *Identifying Pity: Chaucerian Poetics and the Suffering of Others*, argues that analysis of medieval pity discourse is essential for understanding long histories of misogyny, racism and class violence. Her research has been supported by grants from the Huntington Library and the Rhodes Information Initiative and has appeared in *Exemplaria*, the *Journal of Medieval and Early Modern Studies* and *Religion & Literature*.

Patricia Eunji Kim, PhD is an art historian, curator and educator based in New York City. She is assistant professor at New York University and senior editor and curator-at-large at Monument Lab. She is also a George Gurney Fellow at the Smithsonian American Art Museum. Dr Kim engages with art-historical and archaeological methods to explore questions of gender, race, power and memory in antiquity and the present. Her current monograph project is the first book-length study on the visual and material culture of Hellenistic queenship from the fourth to second centuries BCE – a corpus of materials central to a show she is guest-curating at the Cincinnati Art Museum. Dr Kim also brings her perspectives as an art historian of the ancient eastern Mediterranean and western Asia to bear on the most pressing social, cultural and political issues that we face today. Among others, she has written about and curated exhibitions on environmental temporalities, feminist ecologies and transnational memory cultures. Recent publications include *Timescales: Thinking across Ecological Temporalities* (2020) and *The National Monument Audit* (2021).

Fiona McHardy is professor of classics at the University of Roehampton. She is author of *Revenge in Athenian Culture* (2008) and has co-edited five volumes: *Women's Influence on Classical Civilization* (2004), *Lost Dramas of Classical Athens* (2005), *From Abortion to Pederasty: Addressing Difficult Topics in the Classics Classroom* (2014), *Revenge and Gender in Classical, Medieval and Renaissance Literature* (Edinburgh University Press, 2018) and *Diversity and the Study of Antiquity in Higher Education* (2023). She is currently writing a book on gender violence in ancient Greece.

Kristina Milnor is professor of classics and ancient studies at Barnard College. She is the author of *Gender, Domesticity, and the Age of Augustus* (2006; winner of the Goodwin Award for Excellence from the American Philological Association) and *Graffiti and the Literary Landscape in Roman Pompeii* (2014). She has also written articles on Plautus, Sulpicia, Livy and Barbie ™. She is currently at work on a book tentatively entitled *The Gendered Lives of Roman Money*.

Edith Gwendolyn Nally is an assistant professor of philosophy and an associate faculty member in the Classics program and the Race, Ethnic, and Gender Studies Department at the University of Missouri, Kansas City. She specialises in ancient Greek philosophy, epistemology and feminist philosophy and is the author of several articles and chapters on Plato's erotic philosophising, including 'A Case for Platonic Love' in *The Philosophy of Love and Sex* (forthcoming), 'Philosophy's Workmate: *Erōs* and the *erōtica* in Plato's *Symposium*' (2021) and 'The *Telos* Problem in Plato's *Symposium*' in *Wisdom, Love and Friendship in Ancient Philosophy* (2021).

Anise K. Strong is an associate professor of history at Western Michigan University, specialising in Roman history, global histories of genders and sexualities, and reception studies. Her first book was *Prostitutes and Matrons in the Roman World*; she is currently working on her second book on the representation in modern mass media of ancient Mediterranean women's desire and power.

Erika L. Weiberg is an assistant professor of classical studies at Duke University. She researches and teaches Greek language and literature, with a focus on Greek poetry, gender and sexuality, and theory and reception. Their first book, which is forthcoming, is titled *Demanding Witness: Women and the Trauma of*

Homecoming in Greek Tragedy. Demanding Witness investigates how the trauma of female characters is represented and received in four Greek tragedies about a warrior's homecoming.

Serena S. Witzke is a visiting assistant professor of classical studies at Wesleyan University. Her research interests include ancient comedy, gender and sexuality in antiquity, and classical reception. She is interested in social hierarchies and how they affect ancient women and men, particularly the ways that subaltern figures (women, enslaved persons, non-citizens) work to benefit themselves by negotiating the power structures that limit them. Publications include 'Violence against Women in Ancient Rome: Ideology versus Reality' in *The Topography of Violence in the Greco-Roman World*, 'Gendered Patterns of Recognition in Menander's *Sikyonioi*' in *EuGeStA*, 'Gender and Sexuality in Plautus', forthcoming in the *Blackwell Companion to Plautus*, and 'Ethics in Roman Comedy' for the *Antiquity* volume of *A Cultural History of Comedy*.

CHAPTER 1

Believing Ancient Women: An Introduction and Feminist Epistemological Field Guide

Edith G. Nally, Mary H. Gilbert and Megan E. Bowen

As suggested by the title *Believing Ancient Women*, this volume takes recent global movements to address inequities in credibility as its impetus. For instance, studies have found that in US law courts women expert witnesses who are cross-examined are perceived as 'less confident, trustworthy, likeable, believable, and credible' than their male counterparts.[1] In healthcare settings, women typically report more pain than men but receive less treatment.[2] Deficits in perceived credibility also routinely endanger maternal and foetal health; the US CDC's 'HEAR HER' campaign, part of the organisation's response to high maternal mortality rates, urges 'partners, friends, family, co-workers, and providers – anyone who supports pregnant and postpartum women – to really listen when she tells you something does not feel right'.[3] This credibility deficit is especially visible in cases of sexual violence. Police officers in both the US and UK routinely overestimate the frequency of false rape allegations.[4] Similar attitudes pervade media coverage and societal opinion. As demonstrated by the #MeToo and #BelieveWomen movements, it can take scores of women coming forward with similar accounts for their claims to be taken seriously.[5]

---

[1] Larson and Brodsky 2010.
[2] Lloyd, Paganini and Brinke 2020. Race and ethnicity have also been shown to affect pain intervention: see Pletcher, Kertesz, Kohn and Gonzales 2008.
[3] Barfield 2022.
[4] Tuerkheimer 2017. For the UK, see McMillan 2018.
[5] On the epistemic significance of the #MeToo movement, see Freedman 2020.

Feminist epistemologists have pointed to the credibility deficit as a particularly clear instance of how epistemic concepts – which are often treated by academics as highly steadfast notions, beyond the pale of social and political interference – are in fact shaped by systems of domination and subordination.[6] Credibility is, however, only one among many epistemic concepts that are sensitive to power relations. As such, the case studies included in this volume address a variety of epistemic concepts from Greco-Roman antiquity and its reception. All use feminist epistemological theories to demonstrate how a range of epistemic notions are impacted by social and political identities and their intersections. To succinctly illustrate the spirit of this project, we begin with two cases not analysed elsewhere in the volume. These cases, though admittedly too brief to do justice to both the identities and the epistemic views they express, nevertheless serve to motivate this project. Each demonstrates how exploring the intricate ways that systems of power infiltrate the epistemic realm promises to uncover rich and fertile ground for future scholarship about the classical world and its reception.

Ischomachus's wife: In the discussion of household roles in Xenophon's *Oeconomicus*, Socrates enquires about how Ischomachus's wife was educated. What did she know from her upbringing and what did her husband have to teach her? Ischomachus's reply addresses his wife's epistemic standing: 'And what knowledge (ἐπισταμένην) could she have had, Socrates, when I received her? She was not quite fifteen when she came to me, and before that time she was under constant supervision, seeing, hearing and speaking as little as possible (ὅπως ὡς ἐλάχιστα μὲν ὄψοιτο, ἐλάχιστα δ' ἀκούσοιτο, ἐλάχιστα δ' ἔροιτο, 7.5–6)'.[7] Save for a basic knowledge of weaving and a docile temperament, he claims, she came to him largely *without* knowledge, a *tabula rasa* upon which her husband inscribes her wifely duties. What is especially noteworthy is how Ischomachus's wife's subordination extends to her epistemic life (at least as reported by her husband); she learned what she learned, knows what she knows and believes what she believes as governed by the highly restrictive gender norms of fourth-century Athens. Her lack of knowledge, experience and confidence – held up as an ideal by the men discussing her – are all symptoms of the way in which her society exerts control over women, reinforcing and perpetuating male domination. But the education of Ischomachus's wife does not stop there. Ischomachus eventually entrusts her with the tutelage of an enslaved woman. It will be a pleasure, he claims, to pass on her domestic knowledge, to make the enslaved woman who was originally ignorant (ἀνεπιστήμονα) into someone knowledgeable (ἐπιστήμονα), and in so doing, double the enslaved woman's worth (7.41). He also promises her the pleasure of rewarding those enslaved people she finds particularly docile and helpful

---

[6] On credibility, see Fricker 2007 and Medina 2013.
[7] Translations are our own unless otherwise noted.

(σώφρονάς τε καὶ ὠφελίμους) and of punishing (κολάσαι) any enslaved person who reveals themself to be trouble (πονηρός). In this way, Ischomachus invites his wife to enjoy some of the 'perks' of the patriarchal system, provided that she continues to increase the value of his property. His 'generosity' is eventually rewarded by his wife's adoption of a man's style of thinking (ἀνδρικὴν τὴν διάνοιαν), a quality praised as particularly impressive (10.1). Ischomachus's wife, who came to him a blank slate in her youth, is now fully transformed into an agent of epistemic domination herself; not only has she had the lessons of her oppressors inscribed upon her, she now inscribes them upon others.

A concept familiar to feminist epistemological theory, namely 'epistemologies of ignorance', helps us understand Ischomachus's wife as both *victim* and *perpetrator* of epistemic domination. Whereas traditional epistemology largely concentrates on the production of knowledge, assuming that ignorance is simply a lack thereof, feminist epistemologists argue that ignorance is often much more complex, the result of social and political forces which sustain and perpetuate collective unawareness of liberatory ways of thinking.[8] Philosopher[9] José Medina, whose project concerns contemporary white supremacy, argues that 'collective ignorance may not be of one's choosing', still '[o]ne's participation in the collective bodies of ignorance one has inherited becomes *active*, because one acts on it and fails to act against it, whether one knows it or not, and whether one wills it or not'.[10] In this way, Ischomachus's wife, despite clearly inheriting her belief system from her oppressors (first her parents and then her husband), nevertheless becomes an *active* agent in perpetuating the enslaved/free hierarchy within her household. Still, Medina writes: 'different agents have different *kinds* and *degrees* of responsibility with respect to particular injustices depending on their (quoting Young) "*position* within the structural processes" that produce those injustices'.[11] In this way, Ischomachus's wife's epistemic responsibility might be of a different kind and degree than that of Ischomachus. This is not to excuse her as an active agent but merely to suggest that she likely fails to recognise or resist the systems of dominance in which she participates, in part because elite male Athenians maintain the collective ignorance of women of her class. The methods by which they do so are on display in Xenophon's dialogue, where a group of elite men openly discusses Ischomachus's methods for instilling in her the values of the patriarchy. Once again, the purpose of recognising that Ischomachus's wife's

---

[8] See, for example, Sullivan and Tuana 2007; Medina 2013; Maguire 2015; Fricker 2016; Fricker and Jenkins 2017; Tanesini 2020.

[9] Throughout the introduction we list the general academic focus of important thinkers both in order to illustrate the cross-disciplinary nature of feminist epistemological theorising and in the spirit of being a field guide for future research.

[10] Medina 2013.

[11] Medina 2013: 160, quoting Young 2006: 126.

ignorance is maintained by her oppressors is not to excuse her as active participant in grotesque institutions like slavery but to show that she has less control over her ignorance than her oppressors. A central tenet of Medina's project is that paying this kind of fine-grained attention to the sources of ignorance will be necessary for dismantling the systems which produce it.

Vibia Perpetua: At another end of antiquity, Vibia Perpetua (c. 182–203 CE), an African woman living in Roman Carthage, wrote a surviving prose account of the time she spent in a Roman prison that numbers among the very few extant women-authored ancient texts. In the short portion of the text generally attributed to her hand (sections 3–10),[12] Perpetua recounts a series of visions she experienced in the days leading up to her martyrdom. These are full of vivid, sensual language, which communicate her heightened physical, bodily experiences (for example, 'I saw a ladder', *video scalam*, 4.4; 'I stepped on [the snake's] head', *calcaui illi caput*, 4.7; 'I chewed the bit of cheese', *buccellam ... manducavi*, 4.9). Yet it turns out that Perpetua is giving far more than a report of her own, first-hand, subjective religious experience; she also claims authoritative, God-given knowledge with which to interpret these visions and their meanings for the past, present and future. We see this in the fact that she uses first-person forms of verbs of knowing to bracket the descriptions of her visions – she employs first-person forms of *cognoscō* twice, of *sciō* three times and of *intellego* five times. In the first instance, at her brother's request, Perpetua agrees to ask God for a vision on the grounds that she knows she can speak with him: 'and I, because I knew (*sciebam*) that I communicated with God . . . promised him I would do so' (4.2). After describing the experience of the vision, she marks the end of her description and the beginning of her interpretation with a second claim to know: 'we understood (*intelleximus*) that there was going to be a martyrdom' (4.10). In similar fashion, she marks the beginning and ending of her second vision of her late brother Dinocrates with epistemic claims, saying both that she knows (*cognovi*) she is capable of praying on the boy's behalf (7.8), and later, that she understands (*intellexi*) that her prayer-vision was successful (8.4). Finally, after recounting her third and final vision, in which she becomes male and fights a gladiator amidst a throng of cheering supporters, she returns to a more sobering style, this time doubling down on her identity as a knower: 'and I understood that I was going to fight against the devil, not wild animals; but I knew that victory would be mine', *et **intellexi** me non ad bestias, sed contra diabolum esse pugnaturam; sed **sciebam** mihi esse victoriam* (10.14).[13] In short, the spectators of her execution may see animals (*bestias*), but Perpetua claims there is something more sinister lurking beyond the physical bodies of these creatures. Likewise, the

---

[12] See Gold 2013 and 2018.

[13] This is the penultimate sentence of her narrative; she closes by asking a witness of her coming martyrdom to record it as they see fit.

spectators may see Perpetua die in gruesome fashion, but she glosses this apparent loss as a real victory. By closing her short account in this way, Perpetua correctly foresees the vast potential for future misunderstandings that martyrdom entails and works to wrest control of the narrative of her coming death through her authoritative epistemic claims.

Feminist epistemologists like the philosopher Lorraine Code have written about stereotypical associations of women with experience and sensation. Code introduces a case where both doctors and nurses, the former mainly men and the latter mainly women, were asked to testify about a contentious malpractice case: the doctors were asked questions about what they knew whereas the nurses were asked about what they had experienced. Rather than being treated as authoritative, knowledgeable and generally capable of assessing a situation objectively, women are commonly treated as able only to report what they themselves have subjectively experienced. And yet, Code continues, 'experience in our society is considered second-class as compared to knowledge'.[14] The association of women with their own subjective experiences, bodily sensations and emotions dates back to antiquity (as Chelsea Bowden discusses in Chapter 12 of this volume). Feminist historians of philosophy attribute the stereotypes of male, disembodied, objective reason and female, embodied, subjective experience back to Plato and Aristotle.[15] Interestingly, however, in Perpetua's writing, we find a subtle reappropriation and inversion of these stereotypes. She routinely uses her experiential and sensuous visions to bolster her claims to authority. Furthermore, her authority is not over the merely subjective or experiential domain; her visions give her access to matters of objective fact (for instance, that she will be executed and not pardoned). In this way, Perpetua embraces experiential knowledge as a mark of her spiritual authority, reappropriating the stereotype of the embodied female experiencer and dissolving the boundaries between so-called 'subjective' and 'objective' claims to know.

Though a great deal more could be said about how social and political forces intersect with epistemic concepts in both the example of Ischomachus's wife and Vibia Perpetua's prison diary, we have included these brief sketches to illustrate a simple truth well recognised in the field of feminist epistemology: the epistemic realm is not immune to systems of power. In fact, the central tenet of all feminist epistemologies, if indeed there is one, is that social identities – gender, sexuality, race, ethnicity, class, citizenship, nationality, language, religion, age, ability and so forth – matter to knowledge formation and the study of epistemic concepts. This view runs counter to a long philosophical and scholarly tradition of taking such concepts, especially standards like knowledge, justification and truth, to occupy an impartial realm separate from prejudice and other social distortions. Feminist

---

[14] Code 1991: 222.
[15] Lloyd 1984. See also Jaggar 1989: 151–2.

epistemologists have demonstrated that this is not so; knowledge, justification, truth, evidence, rationality, objectivity, authority, expertise, opinion, perception and so forth are routinely shaped by social and political injustices. What someone knows or is perceived as knowing, who the authorities on a subject are, how credible an account is, what evidence seems pertinent, and what conclusions are most rational are all sensitive to systems of domination and oppression.

A major reason that feminist epistemological theory has grown so rapidly in theoretical circles is that it promises to expose injustices at the root of our systems of thought. Feminist epistemologists often challenge seemingly unassailable facts about the life of the mind, many of which have been perpetuated as such to systematically exclude women, people of colour and other oppressed groups from academic and other dominant spheres of discourse (science, media, politics and so on). Feminist epistemological theory promises to break new ground in which before unheard, ignored and suppressed groups might find space to express their unique epistemic stories. This volume aims to employ the central insights of feminist epistemological theory in the study of the classical world to the same end, in order to investigate how epistemic concepts from Greco-Roman antiquity and its reception intersect with social identities, past and present, and in so doing reseed the field of classics with oppressed, ignored and otherwise systematically marginalised voices.

A FEMINIST EPISTEMOLOGICAL FIELD GUIDE

'Epistemology', as it has traditionally been understood, refers to the study of knowledge. In philosophical circles, however, the term has been stretched well beyond its original meaning to denote the study of a broader range of concepts related to cognitive success and failure, including knowledge, understanding, wisdom, belief, disbelief, assent, dissent, opinion, ignorance and the varying conditions that produce these states, such as justification, evidence, proof, objectivity, testimony, intellectual ability, intellectual virtues and vices, reason, rationality and irrationality, among others. Feminist epistemology is a growing field within many academic disciplines, and feminist epistemologies are unified, if at all,[16] by the view that social and political identities – especially sex, gender, sexual orientation, race, ethnicity, class, ability, age, status, nationality and their intersections – are significant in the formation and study of epistemic concepts.[17]

---

[16] See Smith 1997, responding to Hekman 1997.
[17] Feminist epistemology might be better cast as a species of social epistemology, which addresses, among other things, questions about the social and political nature of knowledge production, knowledge networks and collective knowers. Many of the seminal texts in feminist epistemology, especially standpoint theory (to be discussed below), are by sociologists and political theorists. See, for example, Smith 1974; Hartsock 1983; Collins 1990.

Because a major goal of this volume is to inspire and guide future feminist epistemological interpretations of ancient texts and cultures, the remainder of the introduction briefly outlines some of the more common feminist epistemological interventions. A few notes are first in order. It is regrettable that we primarily engage with English-language theories. This is a major limitation, as there are robust non-English-language epistemic traditions which might be brought fruitfully to bear on classical sources. In addition, the taxonomy of views offered here is incomplete. Many of the seminal feminist epistemological works are from the late 1980s, 1990s and early 2000s.[18] While the field is over thirty years old, it has grown exponentially in the past ten years. Google Scholar indexes over 27,000 results for 'feminist epistemology', with more than 15,000 from after 2010.[19] Since a complete survey of this literature is beyond the scope of this (or perhaps any) volume, our aim is instead to provide some key points of entry into this vast and growing literature.[20] Furthermore, isolating particular feminist epistemological approaches, as we do below, is highly artificial; most of the views that we introduce as distinct interpretative stances have significant theoretical overlap. Nevertheless, for clarity, we adopt this artifice. Finally, we envision this volume in dialogue with recent trends in scholarship about women in antiquity, in particular, the substantial literature on narrative authority and its relationship to gender,[21] the culture of sexual violence and victim-blaming in antiquity,[22] women and religious authority,[23] and the gendering of knowledge about bodies.[24] In each of the following sections of the introduction, however, we focus almost entirely on precedent works in classical studies which make use of feminist epistemology; largely for reasons of space, we have left out a great deal of classical scholarship that, though it is generally consistent with feminist epistemological theorising, does not engage with it directly. The individual chapters that follow do a much better job of situating their particular projects within the relevant classical scholarship.

---

[18] See Poole 2021 for some medieval and early modern precedents.
[19] 'Google Scholar: Feminist Epistemology', 18 August 2022, https://scholar.google.com/scholar?q=%22feminist+epistemology%22&hl=en&as_sdt=0%2C26&as_ylo=&as_yhi=.
[20] Other useful field guides include Grasswick 2018; Anderson 2020; Poole 2021. For a good entryway into the most recent literature, see the PhilPapers index of the topic: https://philpapers.org/browse/feminist-epistemology.
[21] See especially Wyke 1994; Greene 1998; Spentzou 2003; Kahane 2005; Fulkerson 2005; Spentzou 2003; Stevenson 2005.
[22] See especially Richlin 1992 and 2017; Rabinowitz 1993 and 2011; Deacy and Pierce 1997; James 1997, 2003 and 2016; Omitowoju 2002; Witzke 2016.
[23] See especially Staples 1998; Dillon 2003; Kraemer 2010; Strong 2016.
[24] See especially Dean-Jones 1994; Flemming 2000; King 2002; Richlin 2014.

Feminist standpoint theory

A common thread within feminist epistemologies is known as 'standpoint theory'. Standpoint theory, sometimes talked about in the language of 'situated' or 'differentiated' knowers, contends that an epistemic agent's identities have significance for the formation, use and study of epistemic concepts. More specifically, different 'standpoints', especially those acquired by non-dominant or marginalised knowers, can result in privileged access to certain facts or values unavailable to the dominant culture. Standpoint theory has roots in the writings of W. E. B. Du Bois, who introduces the idea of a 'double-consciousness' between his own lived experiences as a Black man striving for self-actualisation and an awareness of the racist constructs through which his oppressors perpetually view him.[25] Karl Marx is another predecessor to standpoint theory, in that he thinks the proletariat can break out of their 'false consciousness', or the set of beliefs about their economic, social and political lives as perpetuated by a capitalist and aristocratic society. By developing 'class consciousness', by coming to be aware of these beliefs and their causes, the underclass can begin to transform society. In these ways, standpoint theory – though not yet feminist – is born out of early racial and economic justice movements.

Distinctively *feminist* standpoint theory first arises in the women's movements of the 1970s and '80s.[26] Seminal works include the sociologist Dorothy Smith's 1974 development of 'the standpoint of women' in her critique of male-dominated sociological practices[27] and political scientist Nancy Hartsock's Marxist feminist project, which argues that women, because they have historically been tasked with childrearing and caregiving, occupy a 'privileged vantage point on male supremacy'.[28] Because of the nature of caregiving work – especially the relational, concrete, bodily and continuous nature of their labour – Hartsock argues that caregivers are in a unique epistemic position to detect the inadequacies of male-dominated, capitalist societies. The sociologist Patricia Hill Collins is another seminal thinker in this movement. She expands the field of feminist standpoint theory by considering the unique positionality of Black women and draws attention to the way white feminisms have failed to take Black women's lived experience into account.[29] Collins argues that 'African-American women have not only developed a distinctive black women's standpoint, but have done

---

[25] Du Bois 1903. See also Nardal 1932 [2002] and Anzaldúa 1987 and 2015.
[26] Poole 2021.
[27] Smith 1974.
[28] Hartsock 1983a: 284.
[29] Collins 1986 and 1990. See Haley 1993 for an early application of Collins's work in the field of classics.

so by using alternative ways of producing and validating knowledge'.[30] The white, male, Eurocentric knowledge validation processes by which scholarly institutions grant and credential epistemic authorities work to suppress and alienate Black women's knowledge. Collins outlines an alternative knowledge validation process, which is evident in the epistemic norms – norms like the importance of experience, dialogue, expressiveness, emotion, empathy and accountability in assessing a speaker's commitment to a claim – that have arisen out of necessity, and often survival, within communities of Black women.[31] More recently, standpoint theory has grown to include queer,[32] trans,[33] non-Western,[34] Indigenous[35] and disability-centred[36] approaches, among others.[37] While some of these interventions might seem to fall beyond the scope of feminist standpoint theory, we believe that a truly intersectional account will attend to the ways that different social locations overlap, interact and compound in oppressive societies.[38] For this reason, we find these approaches essential to realising the aims of this volume.

Feminist standpoint theory, then, is shorthand for a number of different theses.[39] First, as we have seen, standpoint theorists accept that there is *situated knowledge*, that a person's social location has epistemic significance. Feminist philosophers of science have been careful, however, to point out that accepting the existence of situated knowledge does not entail that there is no hope for universal truth or transcendent understanding; instead, situated knowledge entails only that there is no singular objective, detached, unemotional, value-neutral standpoint, or what has sometimes been called 'the view from nowhere', from which

---

[30] Collins 1990: 202.
[31] See also Mills 1988.
[32] See Hall 2017. Bailey 2021 gives an overview of standpoint theory as it applies to queer studies.
[33] Transgender 'autoethnographies' are perhaps a more familiar term in sociological research. See, for example, Nordmarken 2014. De Vries 2015 discusses the standpoint of transgender people of colour. For a discussion of the value of first-personal transgender theorising (arguably a defence of the value of transgender standpoint[s]), especially in discussions of the metaphysics of gender, see Bettcher 2018.
[34] See, for example, Narayan 1989.
[35] See, for example, Nakata 2007: 213–16.
[36] See, for example, Garland-Thomson 2016 and Silvers 2013.
[37] See, for example, Martinez 1996 and Hurtado 2003 on forming a Chicana feminist epistemological standpoint. Medina-Minton 2019 considers age, especially whether there is a unique child's standpoint.
[38] Crenshaw 1991. See also Smith, Smith and Frazier's 1977 *Combahee River Collective Statement*.
[39] The first three of these theses are taken directly from Toole 2019.

one can investigate the world.[40] Second, as has already been hinted at, feminist standpoint theorists tend to posit some variety of *privileged access*, or the view that there are facts and values available only from non-dominant social locations.[41] A common example is of sex-specific bodily processes; for instance, womb-bearing persons who have gestated babies will have privileged access to the pain and discomfort of gestation. Third, feminist standpoint theorists, following the notion of consciousness-raising in both Du Bois and Marx, believe that standpoints are largely acquired or earned. Philosopher Briana Toole writes: 'one is not epistemically privileged in virtue of occupying a particular social location. Rather, epistemic privilege may be achieved through the process of consciousness-raising'.[42] Occupying a standpoint is not the result of mere social difference, but also of an *earned awareness*. Fourth, many feminist standpoint theorists, following the philosopher Sandra Harding,[43] also accept the *strong objectivity* thesis, or the view that marginalised or outsider standpoints are, due to their privileged access, uniquely poised to offer critiques of dominant narratives, ultimately resulting in a more accurate, and less distorted, belief system (hence the name 'strong objectivity').[44] For example, the strong objectivity thesis would hold that the above-mentioned gestator's standpoint is of greater epistemic value than those who have not had the experience of gestation when it comes to critiquing, developing and implementing more just childbirth practices.

In some ways, applying feminist standpoint theory to classical studies is new in name only. *Feminist Theory and the Classics*, the revolutionary volume of feminist interpretations edited by Nancy Rabinowitz and Amy Richlin, is bound together by the view that the identity of the interpreter matters.[45] For example, Shelley Haley's contribution to that volume uses her experiences as a Black feminist to rethink Cleopatra's treatment by the field of classics, and Richlin's chapter grounds her pessimistic literary stance in the violence she witnessed friends who are women endure in contemporary society.[46] That volume as a whole has a

---

[40] Haraway 1991 discusses 'the view from nowhere'. Haslanger 1995 addresses the failure of the subjective/objective distinction. For a good summary of the literature on objectivity, a great deal of which overlaps with feminist philosophy of science, see Anderson 2020.
[41] See Tuana 1993: 283.
[42] Toole 2019: 600.
[43] Harding 1992, 1995 and 2015.
[44] Harding 1992 is in dialogue with a view often termed 'feminist empiricism'. Feminist empiricists hold that scientific systems, despite their claims to objectivity, produce socially situated results. See, for example, Longino 1990; Nelson 1990; and Anderson 1995a. For an overview of this literature and its relationship to standpoint theory, see Intemann 2010.
[45] Rabinowitz and Richlin 1993.
[46] Haley 1993: 23–43 and Richlin 1993a: 714–18.

similar aim to this one, to expose how institutions in the field have systematically excluded diverse viewpoints. As Rabinowitz puts it: '[w]hat is construed as the avoidance of any special interests in reality reflects one special interest group's attempt to maintain its authority and control'.[47] She goes on to suggest that what has been touted as the objective philological stance, a stance that claims to avoid theoretical musings in favour of dispassionate linguistic information, is in fact a method of institutional control, maintained to mute and exclude outsider voices. While feminist standpoint theory appears by name in that work only a handful of times, it is nevertheless clearly present as a guiding principle, both in its methodology and its aims.

There have, of course, been many other publications that take identity as an important maker of meaning with regard to the discipline of classics and the Greco-Roman world.[48] The myth of the objective philologist, however, remains nearly ubiquitous in every subfield of the discipline, a point to which Dan-el Padilla Peralta returns as he reflects on a racist assault against him and his identity as a knower at the 2019 meeting of the Society of Classical Studies.[49] Citing some central insights from feminist standpoint theory, Padilla Peralta denounces the discomfort white classical scholars, even the most well-intentioned ones, experience at the idea that his Black identity is a scholarly asset:

> The most maddening aspect of [the] episode was in some respects the most predictable. Seeing as no one in that room or in the conference corridors afterwards rallied to the defence of blackness as a cornerstone of my merit, I will now have to repeat an argument that will be familiar to critical race scholars of higher education but that is barely legible to the denizens of #classicssowhite. I should have been hired because I was black: because my Afro-Latinity is the rock-solid foundation upon which the edifice of what I have accomplished and everything I hope to accomplish rests; because my black body's vulnerability challenges and chastises the universalizing pretensions of color-blind classics; because my black being-in-the-world

---

[47] Rabinowitz 1993: 29.
[48] Chae 2018 and Umachandran 2020 explore ways the discipline of classics is hostile to people of colour. See also Dean-Jones 1994; Wyke 1994; Greene 1998; Staples 1998; Flemming 2000; King 2002; Dillon 2003; Spentzou 2003; Fulkerson 2005; Kahane 2005; Stevenson 2005; Kraemer 2010; Richlin 2014; and Strong 2016, among others.
[49] As part of a 2019 SCS panel entitled 'The Future of Classics', Padilla Peralta presented a paper about the field's complicity in systemic injustices facing the publication process for women and people of colour. During the question and answer session that followed his talk, independent scholar Mary Frances Williams publicly suggested that he obtained his faculty position at Princeton University because he was Black. For more on the incident, see Poser 2021.

makes it possible for me to ask new and different questions within the field, to inhabit new and different approaches to answering them, and to forge alliances with other scholars past and present whose black being-in-the-world has cleared the way for my leap into the breach.[50]

Padilla Peralta here expresses the strength of his unique epistemic standpoint. Part of his argument is that identity as a Black man strengthens his scholarly perspective; he has earned awareness and privileged access to questions and answers unavailable to white scholars. The epistemic resources accessible to classicists as a whole are, therefore, expanded and strengthened by his inclusion, and the inclusion of other marginalised voices, in the field.

In this volume, feminist standpoint theory is deployed first – following Rabinowitz, Haley, Richlin and Padilla Peralta – as a first-personal interpretative method. In keeping with her earlier work, **Haley (Chapter 9)** employs a Black feminist standpoint and critical race feminist theory to connect an account of violence against a woman of African descent in the *Acts of Peter* to the racialised-gendered treatments of Vergil's Dido and Livy's Sophoniba. Haley proposes that the concept of racialised gender helps to locate the origins of such anti-Blackness and misogynoir in the Augustan age, thereby revealing the epistemological framework which enabled similar attitudes to flourish in later periods. A second, and somewhat novel, way that the volume employs feminist standpoint theory is as a critical apparatus for re-examining marginalised perspectives represented, imagined or distorted by ancient sources. For example, **Weiberg (Chapter 2)** argues that the complex nexus of desire and embodiment presented in Sappho's poems is best understood as expressing a queer standpoint that resists gender binaries. **Gilbert (Chapter 3)** demonstrates that the chorus of Oceanids in *Prometheus Bound* occupies a decentred standpoint with respect to other Greek gods that allows them to play an important, underappreciated role in the knowledge production of the play. **Nally (Chapter 5)** argues that, in Plato's *Symposium*, Diotima argues from the standpoint of a caregiver to reveal something about *eros* that the dominant group, the elite Athenian pederasts, fail to consider: the best form of *eros* manifests not merely as a desire to pursue and possesses a beloved but also as the impulse to perpetuate and nurture what one loves. **Witzke (Chapter 7)**, expanding on Richlin's groundbreaking book on the topic, explores how the outsider standpoints of Plautus and Terence, both non-citizens lacking wealth and privilege, give them privileged epistemic access to critiques of the customs, morality and injustices of the citizen elite.[51] **Bowden (Chapter 12)** considers, among other things, how Stoic epistemology is inconsistent with feminist epistemological

---

[50] Padilla Peralta 2019.
[51] Richlin 2017.

conceptions of situated knowledge and privileged access. **Zimmermann Damer (Chapter 14)** reflects on her experiences reading with the Martha Marchina Group during the coronavirus pandemic and identifies in Marchina's poems a maternal/caregiving standpoint from which she challenges the worldviews of both her classical predecessors and contemporary scientific advances.

Anti-atomism

A second major strand of feminist epistemic theorising is its critique of a powerful and engrained orthodoxy about epistemic agency, known as 'atomism' or the 'atomistic knower'. This orthodoxy, which we have already partially addressed above, has been perpetuated by Euro-Anglo-American academic traditions and treats knowers as 'atomistic' in the sense that knowledge is stereotypically identified with disembodied, objective reasoners rather than their embodied, subjective experiences.[52] The thought is that knowledge results from sufficient rationality, no matter an epistemic agent's social location. To this extent, atomism treats knowers as entirely fungible; anyone with properly functioning rational capacities and access to the same evidence can develop the same insights.[53] Feminist standpoint theorists reject this outright, since it appears that some facts and values are only available via the first-hand experience of marginalised knowers.[54]

But there are further dimensions of this atomistic orthodoxy against which feminist epistemologists have argued. For example, many have borrowed a critique from social epistemology, a field sometimes taken to be the genus of which feminist epistemology is a species,[55] that knowledge is rarely if ever produced by a single individual. Instead, knowledge production can often be a long, collective endeavour. Linda Martín Alcoff has suggested that were we to take this tenet of social epistemology seriously, we would be less obsessed with notions of justification, warrant and evidence – the means and methods of atomistic, individualist epistemology – and would instead turn to an altogether different epistemic agenda:

> [W]e would need a more complicated understanding of the epistemic interrelationships of a knowing community; we would want to understand the relation between modes of social organization and the types of beliefs that

---

[52] However, interventions in trans theory reveal that this lived, bodily experience is itself subject to social and historical construction, such that lived, bodily experiences are not always uncomplicatedly available to the experiencer. See, for example, Salamon 2010.
[53] Grasswick 2004; Kukla 2006; Toole 2019.
[54] Code 1991.
[55] Grasswick and Webb 2002 and Grasswick 2018.

appear reasonable; and we would need to explore the influence of the political relationship between individuals on their epistemic relationships.[56]

Taking this suggestion seriously would completely transform our epistemic (and academic) lives; rather than maintaining the myth that individuals can single-handedly justify their own narrow claims to know, a myth that scholars and teachers routinely perpetuate, we would instead begin to evaluate knowledge claims as relations among knowers and their communities.[57]

Another deeply problematic facet of atomism is its insistence that objective knowledge is produced by dispassionate reasoners. As we have already seen, taking objectivity as an epistemic goal is problematic for excluding valuable subjective standpoints; but the demand for objectivity also works to discredit emotional and sensuous modes of investigation and expression, which are historically associated with women and other non-dominant groups. The Euro-Anglo-American tradition privileges the epistemic norms associated with elite white male institutions: the ideal investigator occupies the 'view from nowhere', being not only objective and fungible, but also unemotional, disembodied, impersonal, public-facing and therefore fully rational.[58] By contrast, women and other marginalised people are stereotyped by epistemic institutions as subjective, emotional, embodied, personal, private-facing and generally irrational.[59] Feminist philosophers of science have identified these stereotypes as a chief source of discrimination against women in science and other academic institutions. It is commonly held that scientific investigations (which other academic disciplines routinely mimic) should be as value-neutral and undistorted as possible; thus, investigators who are thought incapable of maintaining these standards have been routinely excluded. Susan Bordo traces the philosophical origins of these stereotypes to the dualist (mind–body) theories of antiquity and the early modern period.[60] Alison Jaggar locates their origins in the positivist mandate that 'truly scientific knowledge must be capable of intersubjective verification'.[61] Jaggar further contends that atomism's

---

[56] Alcoff 2008: 709. See also Goldberg 2011 for epistemic labour.
[57] For an overview of key topics in social epistemology, see Goldman and Whitcomb 2011; Schmidt 2017; Fricker, Graham, Henderson and Pedersen 2019.
[58] See Mignolo 2010 on Castro-Gómez 2007 for the assumption that there could be a detached, neutral observer, absent geopolitical or racial ties. See also Lugones 2010 for discussion of this view in decolonial feminist theory.
[59] Collins 1990 and Alcoff 2008 write about white, male epistemic institutions. Bordo 1987; Jaggar 1989; Rooney 1991; Code 1991; and Shotwell 2011 identify gendered (and, though to a lesser extent, racialised) epistemic stereotypes within these institutions.
[60] Bordo 1987.
[61] Jaggar 1989: 152.

rejection of emotion hurts us all; since emotions can and should play an important role in careful observation and evaluation, the myth of objectivity deprives knowledge communities of important observational and evaluative tools.

Whether or not the dichotomies perpetuated by atomism are ever true is a different matter. It is one thing to reject atomism for perpetuating the myth of objective investigation that alienates women and other marginalised groups historically thought to violate this ideal; it is another thing, however, to contest the existence of gendered or otherwise identity-differentiated modes of thought or expression. Take for example, so-called *feminine* cognitive styles, or the view that certain ways of thinking or abilities might be gendered feminine.[62] This is not an essentialist view, as it is consistent with these supposed gendered differences being entirely socially constructed.[63] For example, Elizabeth Anderson writes that:

> [I]t is seen as masculine to make one's point by means of argument, feminine to make one's point by means of narrative. Argument is commonly cast as an adversarial mode of discourse, in which one side claims vindication by vanquishing the opposition. Such pursuit of dominance follows the competitive pattern of male gender roles in combat, athletics, and business. Narrative is a seductive mode of discourse, persuading by an enticing invitation to take up the perspective of the narrator, which excites one's imagination and feeling. Its operations are more like love than war, and thereby follows a mode of persuasion thought more suitable for women.[64]

Other proposed feminine cognitive differences include relational, as opposed to rule-based, reasoning,[65] teaching tools that grow out of caregiving, like modelling, dialogue, practice and confirmation,[66] and particularistic/contextual, as opposed to universal/abstract, reasoning.[67] Whether any of these proposals hold is very much up for debate; yet the general approach of looking at whether and how identity affects cognitive differences is highly consistent with the anti-atomistic critique and with the general aims of this volume.[68]

---

[62] This terminology comes from Anderson 2020. See also Gilligan 1982; Noddings 1988; and Simson 2005.
[63] As we see it, the existence of feminine cognitive styles is consistent with the social construction of sex and gender.
[64] Anderson 2020.
[65] Gilligan 1982.
[66] Noddings 1988.
[67] Simson 2005.
[68] Though we do not address other identities here, ethnicity, race and nationality have also been studied as markers of cognitive style difference. See, for example, Shade 1982; Tomes 2008; Zmigrod 2018.

Again, there are scholarly precedents within classical studies that address the atomistic epistemological stance. Rabinowitz's critique of the objective philological stance is very much a critique of the atomistic knower; the careful philologist's constant retreat to purely linguistic analysis as a mode of knowing that exists in the abstract logical sphere, apart from lived or identifying experiences, is a way of systematically devaluing and rejecting those experiences.[69] Moreover, in a later publication, Rabinowitz makes the case for breaking free of the masculinist assumed scholarly stance, one that pretends to disembodied universality (again, the atomistic knower), in favour of adopting one's own, socially positioned and therefore more fully transparent, way of analysing literary texts. As it stands, she continues, much of classical scholarship is written from a particular social location, without acknowledging it:

> Much classical scholarship has in fact been interested, but it has not acknowledged that partisanship. For instance, in the debate of the status of women in antiquity, men made comparisons to the treatment of women in their own era and geographical location; thus in defending Greece, Kitto [1925] and Gomme [1951] were defending themselves. Similarly, political interests arguably shaped scholarship about slavery in antiquity. What about the relationship between Platonic studies and nineteenth-century male homoeroticism? [Dowling (1994)]. Feminist theory and postmodern theory in general hold that to acknowledge one's position and the consequences of that position for one's reading or interpretation is responsible behavior, not self-indulgence.[70]

Rabinowitz's point is that the pretence to atomism in classical scholarship, the pretence to distanced and therefore objective scholarship, is utter artifice; and like most artifice, it aims to obscure its own failings. By contrast, making space for scholarship in the personal voice, making room for lived experiences in the field of classics and beyond, though not a way of ensuring objectivity, is at the very least a more honest way of reading and interpreting.

Contributors in this volume advance the anti-atomistic critique in a variety of ways. For example, following Rabinowitz's call to the personal voice, some of our contributors make use of autobiography in their interpretative projects: See especially **Haley (Chapter 9)** and **Zimmermann Damer (Chapter 14)**. Other contributions address anti-atomistic themes within ancient sources. For example, **Weiberg (Chapter 2)** posits Sapphic sensuality as a type of 'knowing otherwise' that defies static expressions of identity binaries; **Gilbert (Chapter 3)** claims the chorus of Oceanids in *Prometheus Bound* exhibits feminine cognitive styles, especially in their gentle but persistent questioning of Prometheus

---

[69] Rabinowitz 2001.
[70] Rabinowitz 2001: 193

even when they disagree with him; and **Zimmermann Damer (Chapter 14)** argues that Martha Marchina's Latin poetry rejects classical themes and scientific advances in favour of a matrocentric, caregiver and experiential perspective. **McHardy (Chapter 4)**, though somewhat indirectly, advances the social epistemological critique of atomism by exploring communal knowledge processes, like gossip and hearsay, by which marginalised groups are able to influence public opinion and, ultimately, infiltrate the Athenian justice system. **Nally (Chapter 5)** addresses Plato's somatophobic attitudes in the *Symposium* and argues that, while some have seen this as indicative of his commitment to atomism – to an identity-less knower – Diotima's speech nevertheless casts her gender as epistemically significant. In particular, her epistemic and ethical conclusions are sensitive to the experiences of *erōs* on reproducing women. **Bowden (Chapter 12)** argues, against recent trends in feminist interpretations of Stoicism, that Stoic epistemology is largely inconsistent with feminist anti-atomism. Because the only significant features of the Stoic epistemic agent are certain fungible capacities (for example, the capacities for *phantasia* and *katalepsis*), social identities like gender, race and class appear epistemically irrelevant. The ideal Stoic epistemic agent also pursues knowledge autonomously, rather than through group knowledge production practices.

Epistemic injustice

A third major thread running through feminist epistemological theorising is the study of epistemic injustice. Philosopher Miranda Fricker introduces the term 'epistemic injustice' to refer to forms of discrimination that impact someone's 'capacity as a knower'.[71] She defines two varieties: the first is *testimonial injustice*, which 'occurs when prejudice causes a hearer to give a deflated level of credibility to a speaker's word'. Fricker gives the now well worn example of Tom Robinson in Harper Lee's *To Kill a Mockingbird*. In the novel, Tom is a Black man falsely accused of sexual assault by a white woman in 1930s Alabama. Although he testifies to his own innocence and the physical evidence supports thinking that he could not possibly have committed the crime, Tom is nevertheless convicted by the all-white jury. This is a literary example of testimonial injustice, since the jurors form their opinions based on bigoted stereotypes rather than the evidence before them. The philosopher José Medina identifies this fictional account as a straightforward case in which the 'social imaginary' creates a credibility deficit in a marginalised group, while affording an unjust excess of authority to a privileged group.[72] The philosopher Kristie Dotson furthers Fricker's categorisation of testimonial

---

[71] Fricker 2007: 1.
[72] Medina 2013.

injustice by detailing two common forms of 'testimonial silencing': 'testimonial quieting', whereby a speaker is denied authority as a knower, and 'testimonial smothering', whereby a speaker's account is shaped by coercive social forces.[73]

The second variety of epistemic injustice identified by Fricker is *hermeneutical injustice*, which occurs when 'someone has a significant area of their social experience obscured from understanding owing to prejudicial flaws in shared resources for social interpretation'.[74] Fricker gives as an example the administrative assistant Carmita Wood's experience of being sexually harassed at work, despite living in an age where there was not yet a term for (or even a clear conception of) sexual harassment. Wood and others were at a loss to describe what exactly had happened to them. Fricker writes, 'Carmita Wood suffered (among other things) an acute cognitive disadvantage from a gap in the collective hermeneutical resource'. This disadvantage was not, however, the result of mere bad luck, not like an as-yet-undiscovered medical diagnosis. Instead, carefully maintained systems of power and oppression deterred Wood and women like her from speaking out about their shared experiences. It was not until they gathered together that the phrase 'sexual harassment' was coined, defined and eventually prosecuted. Of course, hermeneutical injustice occurs not only where there are voids in the available conceptual resources, but also when the conceptual resources are so badly *distorted* so as to hinder their application.[75] The philosopher Katherine Jenkins has, for example, identified such distortions in her work on the epistemology of rape, where victims often fail to identify their experiences as 'rape' given false narratives about how rapes are perpetuated (that is, by strangers, under overwhelming physical force, and so on).[76]

Fricker's labelling of these forms of epistemic injustice, while exceedingly influential, should not occlude the fact that thinkers preceding her by decades (or centuries) had described similar phenomena. The feminist theorist Vivian May points out that Black intellectuals like Sojourner Truth and Anna Julia Cooper discussed how Black women were routinely subject to epistemic silencing and testimonial discreditation by white men.[77] Similarly, Collins, who is clearly addressing testimonial injustice, albeit without the label, writes that 'power relations shape who is believed and why'.[78] What is more, others have pointed out that Fricker's categories are not exhaustive of all forms of epistemic injustice. Dotson argues for a third variety not addressed in Fricker's two-part framework, *contributory injustice*, which occurs when dominant groups privilege one

---

[73] Dotson 2011.
[74] Fricker 2007: 147–75.
[75] See Mason 2021.
[76] Jenkins 2017.
[77] May 2014: 97–8.
[78] Collins 1990: 270.

set of hermeneutical resources over others.[79] Dotson argues that marginalised groups often develop alternate bodies of shared hermeneutical resources that are systematically excluded from dominant narratives. One suffers a contributory injustice when a dominant/powerful person refuses to take these alternative resources seriously. Relatedly, the philosopher Louise Rexzy P. Agra has written about the *epistemic paralysis* that strikes marginally situated knowers when dominant knowledge systems exclude them, thereby incapacitating that group's epistemic abilities within dominant discourse.[80]

Another category of epistemic injustice that has been widely discussed arises out of Eurocentrism and coloniser epistemologies: for example, the literary theorist Gayatri Chakravorty Spivak identifies *epistemic violence* in the ways that colonising regimes actively silence and destroy the knowledge systems of colonised peoples.[81] Similarly, the sociologist Boaventura de Sousa Santos addresses *epistemicide*, or the intentional destruction of Indigenous knowledge communities, especially in the Global South by Western domination.[82] Furthermore, feminist theorist Chandra Talpade Mohanty argues that 'Western feminist discourse' has routinely appropriated the knowledge systems of 'third world women'[83] and the sociologist Anibal Quijano writes about the way that Eurocentric colonisation dominates 'knowledge and the production of knowledge under its hegemony'.[84] These are arguably a form of what philosopher Emmalon Davis dubs 'epistemic appropriation', which occurs when 'epistemic resources developed within the margins gain uptake with dominant audiences', despite being 'overtly detached from the marginalised knowers responsible for their production'.[85] A number of theorists have also identified the related concept of 'epistemic exploitation' that occurs when the onus of explaining and educating a dominant culture about injustices suffered by an oppressed group falls to members of that group.[86]

A further form of epistemic injustice of enormous relevance to this volume is one that we struggled to find clearly identified in the feminist epistemological

---

[79] Dotson 2012 argues that Fricker's view, by contrasting testimonial and hermeneutical injustices with epistemic luck, is itself guilty of contributory injustice.

[80] Agra 2020.

[81] Spivak 1988.

[82] Santos 2016.

[83] Mohanty 1984. The term 'third world women' is not ours.

[84] Quijano 2000.

[85] Davis 2018 gives as examples of this phenomenon the appropriation of Harriet Taylor Mill's ideas in John Stuart Mill's *On Liberty*, now believed to be largely authored by Taylor Mill, and Harriet Beecher Stowe's appropriation and caricaturisation of Sojourner Truth's enslavement in 'Sojourner Truth, the Libyan Sibyl'. See Podosky 2021.

[86] Berenstain 2016; Davis 2016; Spivak 1999; Lorde 1984; and Holroyd and Puddifoot 2020.

literature. It will, however, be immediately familiar to anyone working in a historical field: women and other marginalised groups were and are, for much of Euro-Anglo-American history, systematically under-represented, especially as authors/creators but also in some respect as subjects, in the dominant, widely disseminated and 'canonical' corpus (that is, literature, philosophy, history and art, among others). The products of their intellectual and creative toil have been ignored, suppressed, or otherwise excluded from the elite-sanctioned catalogue of 'great works'. This is the case during many periods of Greco-Roman antiquity. In much of the surviving literature, there is an utter paucity of first-personal evidence about marginalised groups; what we do have is filtered through elite, male authors. In other historical periods, however, larger numbers of sources exist but have been relegated to the fringes, as, for example, is the case with women writing in the medieval, Byzantine and early modern periods.[87] For these periods, it has taken revisions of what was considered important, authoritative and/or canonical to elevate these sources and bring them into wider circulation (although much work remains to be done outside of the academy to, for example, put the name recognition of Marie de France or Anna Komnene on par with that of Geoffrey Chaucer). Another important aspect of this type of epistemic injustice is that women and other marginalised groups have not only been excluded from the canonical bodies of evidence but from what are considered the 'masterpieces' or 'works of genius'.[88] Whether these exclusions are a new form of epistemic injustice is up for debate: they might be thought of as merely the wide-scale result of many testimonial and contributory injustices, something like mega-contributory, mega-testimonial silencing. Furthermore, many of these exclusions are likely related in important ways to epistemicide, though not all are the (direct) result of colonialist forces. However, given the centrality of this type of exclusion to our work and to classical scholarship more generally, we think these phenomena need a clearer label: we dub these cases forms of 'evidentiary injustice'. Evidentiary injustice occurs when the intellectual products and first-personal accounts of marginalised groups are suppressed or excluded *en masse* from the received bodies of evidence, or relegated to the fringes, due to a perceived lack of importance or relevance.

Since, as we have seen, epistemic injustice comes in many, disparate forms – forms which are being more clearly identified all the time – it will be best to adopt something like Kidd, Medina and Pohlhaus Jr's fuller account of epistemic injustice, as including all:

> forms of unfair treatment that relate to issues of knowledge, understanding, and participation in communicative practices. These issues include

---

[87] See, for example, Waithe 1997–2001 and Gertz 2012.
[88] There is contemporary research showing that women are still stereotypically disassociated with so-called 'brilliance fields'. See, for example, Bernstein 2015.

a wide range of topics concerning wrongful treatment and unjust structures in meaning-making and knowledge producing practices, such as the following: exclusion and silencing; invisibility and inaudibility (or distorted presence or representation); having one's meanings or contributions systematically distorted, misheard, or misrepresented; having diminished status or standing in communicative practices; unfair differentials in authority and/or epistemic agency; being unfairly distrusted; receiving no or minimal uptake; being co-opted or instrumentalized; being marginalised as a result of dysfunctional dynamics; etc.[89]

This definition has the benefit of being expansive rather than exhaustive, allowing for the future identification of as-yet-illuminated epistemic injustices that remain occluded by our current hermeneutical limits (limits which are no doubt the product of dominance and subordination within contemporary feminist and social epistemological thought).

In addition to identifying different varieties of epistemic injustice, feminist epistemologists have also addressed its roots and causes. One common view is that epistemic injustices, along with entire systems of oppression, arise from *active ignorance*. Studies of what are sometimes called 'epistemologies of ignorance' examine how powerful groups build and maintain their epistemic norms to intentionally obscure information that challenges their social and political ideology. As philosopher Marilyn Frye, who is writing about white supremacy in the women's movement, puts it:

Ignorance is not something simple: it is not a simple lack, absence or emptiness, and it is not a passive state. Ignorance of this sort – the determined ignorance most white Americans have of American Indian tribes and clans, the ostrichlike ignorance most white Americans have of the histories of Asian peoples in this country, the impoverishing ignorance most white Americans have of black language – ignorance of these sorts is a complex result of many acts and many negligences. To begin to appreciate this one need only hear the active verb to 'ignore' in the word 'ignorance.' Our ignorance is perpetuated for us in many ways and we have many ways of perpetuating it for ourselves.[90]

Frye proposes that ignorance is not passive. It is a choice that dominant groups have whether to acknowledge the experiences of those less powerful (as is the case of the exclusion of women of colour by white feminists).[91] Choosing to stay unenlightened

---

[89] Kidd, Medina and Pohlhaus Jr 2017.
[90] Frye 1983.
[91] See also Ortega 2006 and Bailey 2008.

is what the philosopher Gaile Pohlhaus Jr labels 'wilful hermeneutical ignorance',[92] which, much like Fricker's hermeneutical injustice and Dotson's contributory injustice, occurs when 'dominantly situated knowers refuse to acknowledge epistemic tools developed from the experienced world of those situated marginally'.[93]

While some forms of ignorance appear to be a matter of *choosing* to remain in the dark, others appear more psychologically complicated (though no less *active*). For example, the philosophers Philip Olson and Laura Gillman explore ignorance in 'unconscious habits that inform our mental schemas, our social interactions, and our physicality'.[94] Others have examined forms of ignorance that are perpetuated by entire epistemic systems (though no less composed of active individuals).[95] For example, the philosopher Nancy Tuana details the practices that perpetuate mass ignorance surrounding the female orgasm in the scientific literature.[96] The queer theorist Eve Kosofsky Sedgwick examines how ignorance is 'harnessed, licensed, and regulated on a mass scale for striking enforcements, perhaps especially around sexuality'.[97] These mass, carefully maintained systems of ignorance, Sedgwick continues, are on display in the US legal system's treatment of rape (ignorance of a victim's lack of consent is a potentially exonerating plea), AIDS patients (it was initially legal for employers to fire people with AIDS so long as they claimed ignorance of the evidence that AIDS is unlikely to be transmitted in the workplace), and anti-sodomy laws (as Justice Harry Blackmun wrote in dissent of the Supreme Court upholding these laws: 'Only the most willful blindness could obscure the fact that sexual intimacy is a sensitive, key relationship of human existence, central to family life, community welfare, and the development of human personality').[98] Furthermore, this mass-maintained ignorance appears to perpetuate the very sort of binary thinking – homo/hetero, private/public, natural/artificial, among others – that Sedgwick (along with future generations of queer and trans theorists) aims to dismantle, as it creates false consciousness and forces false choices about our desires, sexuality, gender, relationships, bodies and so forth.[99] The philosopher Charles Mills has written about intentionality in systems of mass ignorance. What he dubs 'white ignorance' occurs both intentionally, as when those with straightforward racist motivations maintain

---

[92] Pohlhaus Jr 2012.
[93] Dotson 2012.
[94] Olson and Gillman 2013.
[95] See Pitts 2020 on the role of individual self-knowledge in structural patterns of ignorance.
[96] Tuana 2004. See also Tuana 2006 on the women's health movement as an epistemic awakening.
[97] Sedgwick 1990: 5.
[98] *Bowers* v. *Hardwick* 478 U.S. 186 (1986) (Blackmun dissenting opinion).
[99] See, for example, Fricker and Jenkins 2017, who address ignorance as it contributes to hermeneutical injustices in trans experiences.

false beliefs about non-white groups, and less intentionally, as when there is mass 'social suppression of the pertinent knowledge'.[100]

Medina has further identified the roots of active ignorance in 'epistemic vices' like epistemic arrogance, laziness and closed-mindedness.[101] Medina's work, like many in this sphere, is not merely descriptive but ameliorative: he advocates for a form of 'epistemic resistance' through the habituation of epistemic virtues, like epistemic humility, curiosity/diligence and open-mindedness. Furthermore, he argues that we have an epistemic duty to overcome active ignorance via 'beneficial epistemic friction in interactions with significantly different epistemic others'.[102] If we were to take this suggestion seriously, then knowledge production would take place through a kind of 'guerrilla pluralism' in which our epistemic differences are in constant combat, eventually resolving in epistemic equilibrium. In short, rather than avoiding, minimising or rejecting views that are different from our own, Medina envisions open and, if need be, jarring exposure to these views.

Classicists have marshalled the literature on epistemic injustice to address injustices within the field of classics itself. For instance, Yung In Chae draws on Fricker to explore her own disciplinary experiences and those of other people of colour in the field, and Mathura Umachandran explores methods for ameliorating systematic epistemic injustices within the discipline.[103] Classicists have also employed the framework of epistemic injustice to unveil biases inherent to extant literary and material culture from the ancient world. Serena Witzke uses the framework of epistemic injustice to dismantle long-standing harmful pedagogical practices and encourage students to get beyond the 'dominant narrative' of ancient texts in order to 'see also the marginal perspectives that are otherwise suppressed'.[104] Drawing on Fricker and de Sousa Santos, Padilla Peralta employs ideas of 'epistemic injustice' and 'epistemicide', in particular, to explore how ancient Indigenous knowledge and culture was appropriated, disrupted, fragmented and deliberately destroyed by various Roman colonisation projects. In contending that 'Roman imperialism was responsible for the extermination of contingent, context-dependent and multigenerational ways of knowing that were tied directly and inalienably to the people and places responsible for their transmission and evolution', Padilla Peralta suggests a new way of seeing Romanisation, not as a benign melting pot of cultural difference but as a kaleidoscope of oppressions rife with episodic epistemic violences.[105]

---

[100] Mills 2007: 21 and 2015. See also Tanesini 2020.
[101] Medina 2013. For epistemic vice, see also Tanesini 2018 and 2020.
[102] Medina 2013: 27–55.
[103] Chae 2018 and Umachandran 2022.
[104] Witzke 2022.
[105] Padilla Peralta 2020.

This volume addresses many different varieties of epistemic injustice that arise in ancient sources and their reception. Some of these contributions also make use of closely related theories in the epistemology of rape, epistemologies of ignorance and epistemic resistance. **McHardy (Chapter 4)** identifies various epistemic injustices perpetrated against a metic woman named Zobia in Demosthenes' *Against Aristogeiton* (25.56–8). She draws an analogy between Zobia's decision to speak out about the epistemic violence she has suffered, which places her at considerable risk, and the epistemic significance of the #MeToo movement. McHardy further locates in Zobia's account a powerful form of epistemic resistance, akin to the philosopher Alison Bailey's 'knowing resistant anger',[106] by which she is able, through unofficial channels outside the Athenian justice system, especially gossip and public opinion, to find 'a voice that effectively pushes back against the weight of imposed silences'. **Kim (Chapter 6)** addresses the monumental presence of Cynisca, a dynastic woman who sponsored athletic events, within the context of Hellenistic dynastic exceptionalism, which, Kim argues, obscures her historical achievements and raises questions about the epistemological gaps facing archival and archaeological work. Kim also compares Cynisca's monuments to the ways in which women are excluded/included in contemporary statuary and identifies in these *comparanda* epistemic injustices, like epistemicide, related to the nature of the construction of evidence. **Witzke (Chapter 7)** explores the testimonial injustice and epistemic silencing that citizen, non-citizen free, and enslaved women face regarding rapes and pregnancies in Plautus's *Truculentus* and Terence's *Hecyra*. Furthermore, Witzke employs Pohlhaus Jr's concept of wilful hermeneutic injustice to argue that the citizen men of Roman comedy deliberately misinterpret the actions and language of non-citizen sex labourers. **Milnor (Chapter 8)** addresses evidentiary injustice in the 'incidental' women depicted in the letters of Cicero. In particular, Milnor argues that these women are part of 'a deeper anti-history, which Cicero both represents and resists in his correspondence'. Milnor further makes use of epistemologies of ignorance to consider why Cicero's letters contain only the information that they do, thereby illuminating the dynamics of history and historiography within his correspondence. **Haley (Chapter 9)** uses the concept of racialised gender to examine the hermeneutical structures that enabled the portrayal of a Black woman as demonic in the *Acts of Peter*. She locates the roots of these hermeneutical structures in the racialised gender of Vergil's Dido and Livy's Sophoniba. Moreover, in her interpretation of these characters, Haley engages with notions of epistemic injustice, especially epistemic silencing and epistemic violence. **Bowen (Chapter 10)** analyses differing accounts of Leucothoe's rape in Ovid's *Metamorphoses* to reveal the hermeneutical resources that rendered rape intelligible/unintelligible in ancient Rome. Bowen addresses how Roman law and false cultural narratives about rape

---

[106] Bailey 2018.

would have reinforced and perpetuated rape myths at the time and argues that Ovid's narrative draws attention, though not unproblematically, to this site of epistemic injustice. In this way, Bowen demonstrates how epistemic injustices frequently play into epistemologies of rape and sexual violence. In a similar vein, **Freas (Chapter 11)** argues that Eumolpus, the narrator of the *Pergamene Boy* in Petronius's *Satyrica*, commits contributory injustice by casting his sexual relationship with the boy in terms of Athenian pederasty and thereby concealing how his actions fit the Roman legal definition of *stuprum*. **Hines (Chapter 13)** explores the ways that medieval literature and theology constructed ignorance of queer sex and desire. By examining several medieval receptions of the Iphis myth, she argues that in some cases this led to a silencing of queer women's desire as *amor impossibilis* and in others a queer resistance to that silence. **Strong (Chapter 15)** analyses popular movies and television shows depicting the rape of enslaved persons by Roman elites. She addresses how the hermeneutical structures that governed sexual violence in the ancient world often differ radically from their portrayal in the mass media and further highlights a variety of undiagnosed epistemic injustice perpetuated against enslaved victims on screen. Obscuring that these acts are rapes – a common theme in the contemporary epistemology of rape – is part of the rose-coloured fantasy surrounding Roman sexual violence against enslaved persons.

METHODOLOGICAL NOTES

As mentioned at the outset, as a volume primarily interested in exploring the relevance of a broad theoretical spectrum to an entire field, this book is not intended to be comprehensive. It should be read, instead, as a series of case studies that apply different feminist epistemological theories to particular ancient texts (literary or material) in order to elucidate both how ancient epistemic systems exclude and pathologise the experiences of ancient women and other marginalised groups and how the institutional biases of modern epistemic systems have resulted in contemporary distortions in the way scholars approach ancient Greece and Rome.

The book is organised chronologically and, as such, retains some of the old disciplinary binaries of Greek vs Roman, prose vs poetry and literary vs material. Even so, we have attempted to demonstrate the broad interpretative possibilities of the feminist epistemological toolkit by including chapters on a breadth of topics including poetry, oratory, drama, philosophy, law, material culture and various receptions.[107] Although considerations of space require that some genres and

---

[107] The book was originally planned to include a broader treatment of Roman prose authors, but in large part because of the exigent demands of the coronavirus pandemic on women in particular, certain planned contributions were not able to be completed in time for publication.

subdisciplines are not fully represented in the volume, and its scope is geographically limited to sources from Greece and Rome, each contribution illustrates the ways in which feminist epistemic theory illuminates systems of dominance in the ancient world, its reception and the disciplinary formation of classics. Furthermore, as a volume that recognises and seeks to highlight the value of authorial positionality to knowledge systems, we feel that a number of important identities are un- or under-represented. The volume does not treat certain marginalised identities at all (for example, it does not treat disability); others are only mentioned cursorily (as is the case with age). In addition, we do not engage thoroughly with non-English-language receptions or with scholarship outside the Euro-Anglo-American academic tradition. The vast majority of our contributors teach at North American colleges and universities. These are major shortcomings of a volume which focuses on, among other things, epistemic injustice, as these exclusions are likely to perpetuate value judgements about who and what matters in the field of classical studies. This volume, by participating in academic discourse in 'standard' ways, by limiting its topics, geographic scope and authorship, among other editorial choices, participates in and reinforces many of the hierarchies that feminist epistemologies intend to disrupt.[108]

A thorny methodological question, importantly related to the disruption of unjust epistemic hierarchies, deserves mention here. Scholars addressing Greek and Roman sexuality, and pederasty in particular, must sometimes contend with whether to cite prominent scholarship by authors who have been convicted of crimes against minors.[109] This is a discipline-specific version of a larger ethical dilemma about whether to cite scholarship by authors who have committed grave injustices. While this volume does not address this larger question, its commitment to disrupting unjust knowledge production systems strongly supports the following methodology: because citation practices are a cornerstone of scholarly knowledge production, some contributions in this volume either omit authors whose morally impermissible behaviours are intellectually entwined with their scholarship or else discuss this entwinement.

A final methodological note concerns authorial intention and anachronism. Some readers may find the use of such a markedly contemporary theoretical apparatus in the interpretation of classical sources worrisome. In anticipation of this, it is first worth pointing out that none of our contributions attribute feminist epistemological motives *to* ancient authors (though **Gilbert [Chapter 3]** and **Nally [Chapter 5]** consider such motives within the realm of possibility and **Bowden [Chapter 12]** considers but ultimately rejects such an interpretation). Instead,

---

[108] Many of these shortcomings are reminiscent of Audre Lorde's 1984 observations in her now famous essay 'The Master's Tools Will Never Dismantle the Master's House'.
[109] Johnson 2016; Scullin 2016; and Yarrow 2020 discuss some of the authors in question.

the vast majority deploy feminist epistemological theories as a critical apparatus for analysing and problematising ancient texts. Furthermore, it may be worth pointing readers towards the classicist Alison Sharrock's helpful discussion of the different possible aims of feminist interpretations.[110] First, a reading can be either *resisting* or *releasing*. A *resisting* reading 'identifies the chauvinist, sexist, or other ideology of the text but refuses to play along with it'. A *releasing* reading, on the other hand, 'opens up possibilities for women's [or other marginalised groups'] voices which exist in the text, but which have traditionally been downplayed or ignored by the critical establishment'. A reading can also be *optimistic* or *pessimistic* about authorial intention. A reading is *optimistic* when the author is regarded as 'sympathetic to women [or other marginalised groups]', and/or shown to be exposing fluidity of gender [or other identities] against the rigidity of . . . norms, in a way that looks remarkably modern'. A *pessimistic* reading, on the other hand, finds the author 'more compromised to his chauvinist social milieu'.[111] These different aims (especially the possibility of a releasing albeit pessimistic reading) create space for interpretations that, while being firmly grounded in textual evidence, also have little or nothing to do with what an author intended. They make space for the analysis of texts from positions radically different from the (largely) male elite authors who wrote them. As **Milnor (Chapter 8)** notices, historical texts often contain a great deal of 'incidental' information about women and other marginalised groups from which we can construct anti-histories. We wager that this is possible with most classical sources, both those that depict marginalised groups and those that do not; from the fringes and the recesses, from an author's choices of whom and what to include, a great deal can be reconstructed. These methods license interpreters to make observations, ask questions and deploy theoretical apparatuses like ours that an ancient author would not have thought (or, in some cases, would have thought repulsive) to make, ask or deploy. Finally, we think it worth pointing out that worries about authorial intention and anachronism can themselves be tools of the patriarchy. Yes, interpreters should be careful when making authorial attributions. However, requiring of an interpretation that it make only authorially sanctioned claims, requiring interpreters to think solely in terms of what was *intended* by elite men who routinely excluded women, found the lives of enslaved persons beneath report, and maintained sys-

---

[110] Sharrock 2020: 35.
[111] Sharrock's taxonomy is related to but somewhat different from Richlin's 1993: 743 'optimistic and pessimistic attitudes'. Richlin, whose topic is something like what feminists and other progressives can learn from the past, writes: 'Optimists see, in the past, or in other cultures, good things to be emulated; pessimists see bad things that determine or elucidate our own ills'. As such, Richlin's optimism/pessimism appears closer to the releasing/resisting dimensions of Sharrock's taxonomy.

tems of mass ignorance by and about most, if not all, non-dominant groups, is an edict that perpetuates and replicates such exclusions. We have at our disposal conceptual resources, resources like feminist epistemology, with which to read well beyond what ancient authors intended, well beyond what they had the conceptual resources to imagine. To reject such resources as legitimate tools for scholarship is, therefore, to claim for ourselves the limited hermeneutical resources of deeply oppressive societies. Surely, we must do better.

CONCLUSIONS

As is fitting for a broad collection of scholars and topics, this volume reaches no overarching conclusion. Nevertheless, the book as a whole has at least three unifying themes. First, it makes a sustained case for the usefulness of the feminist epistemological critical lens, a method that treats epistemic concepts – what is known, believed, thought true, understood, heard, considered evidence and so forth – as reflective of the biases, injustices and power relations of the society in which they are constructed.

Second, the volume as a whole advances our consideration of non-dominant standpoints in ancient texts and in the discipline of classics itself. On the one hand, feminist epistemological theorising lends itself handily to projects that look to authors, texts and evidence that have been underappreciated. It encourages us to look for marginalised resources, to care about the epistemic contributions of non-dominant groups, and to mine dominant sources for anti-narratives. But the feminist epistemological lens is not only useful for examining underappreciated evidence, or what is *there* albeit at the fringes. Feminist epistemological theories can also reveal what is *not there* (or less clearly there), so to speak, by shedding light on issues of sex, gender, race, ethnicity, sexual identities, religion, ability, age, class, familial status and citizenship that would remain invisible otherwise.[112] As Witzke has observed (elsewhere), feminist epistemologies have the power to transform just about any text, author or source, literary or material, into fertile ground for conversations about epistemic dominance/oppression.[113] Understood in this way, this volume makes the case for what is sometimes referred to as 'reading otherwise', a practice by which readers reimagine textual interpretation as an act of epistemological resistance, a practice for not only revealing the misshapen values of dominant narratives but for expanding what is worthy of our consideration to include more than what has been handed down to us. In a time where many scholars are rightly reconsidering how to treat and teach deeply chauvinistic, sexist, racist

---

[112] See Richlin 1993a on the 'optimistic attitude'.
[113] Witzke 2022.

and otherwise oppressive texts (and the institutions built in their image), reading otherwise is a powerful tool for reorienting the future of classical scholarship.

Third, and finally, this volume as a whole exposes a variety of long-standing and complicated forms of epistemic injustice. As such, it lays the groundwork for a richer, more dialectic conversation between modernity and ancient Greece and Rome. In antiquity we find many of the traditional epistemic frameworks that continue to shape knowledge networks today, but also a variety of less appreciated epistemic norms, whose identification may have the power to disrupt and check epistemic injustices that continue to silence and injure in our contemporary world. Readers faced with the intricate, and sometimes strange or foreign, forms of epistemic injustice described herein will be forced to reckon with an uncomfortable fact: for most, the epistemic realm is (and has always been) far from a place of intellectual refuge, a bastion of unfairness, suppression and contempt. If knowledge is possible, then, it will require, perhaps above all else, attention to the ways that one's own worldview has been distorted by injustice.

CHAPTER 2

'For you know how we cared for you': Sappho and Queer Epistemology

Erika L. Weiberg

Feminist scholarship on Sappho in the 1980s and 1990s contributed some of the earliest applications of feminist epistemology to ancient Greek and Roman texts. Although not in direct dialogue with the field of feminist epistemology in philosophy that emerged around the same time, these interventions addressed two central concerns of feminist epistemology.[1] First, they illustrated how an androcentric and misogynistic tradition had warped ancient and modern understandings of Sappho's identity and her poetry, and second, they argued that Sappho's poetry constructed categories of knowledge and strategies of meaning-making distinct from and even resistant to those found in poetry composed by men. To use the language of feminist epistemology, the first claim delineates the 'epistemic injustice' and even 'epistemic violence' of a tradition that obscures and silences Sappho's perspective as a woman poet,[2] whereas the second explores how

---

I am grateful to the editors, Megan E. Bowen, Mary H. Gilbert, and Edith G. Nally, as well as the anonymous reviewer, for their helpful feedback on earlier versions of this essay.

[1] For foundational texts of feminist epistemology, see Collins 1990; Alcoff and Potter 1993; Harding 2004.

[2] For a definition of 'epistemic injustice', see Kidd, Pohlhaus Jr and Medina 2017, as given in the Introduction to this volume. For 'epistemic violence', see Spivak 1988: 282–3 and Dotson 2011. Others in this volume who discuss forms of epistemic silencing and epistemic violence include Gilbert (Chapter 3), McHardy (Chapter 4), Kim (Chapter 6), Witzke (Chapter 7), Milnor (Chapter 8), Haley (Chapter 9) and Strong (Chapter 15).

Sappho's poems pose a kind of 'epistemic resistance' to the hegemonic, masculine order of knowledge and power.[3]

This chapter builds on these foundational analyses by exploring the articulation of desire and embodiment in Sappho's poems from the perspective of queer epistemology. Queer theory challenges assumptions about gender and sexuality as fixed and stable markers of identity, both across different cultures and time periods, and within a single person's life.[4] Thinking queerly about epistemic injustice and epistemic resistance in Sappho's poems and the scholarly tradition yields insights into these fragments' articulation of knowledge, desire and embodiment. By reading the fragments through this lens, this chapter argues that Sappho's poetry can be understood as queer not merely in the sense that many of her poems express desire by women for women. Her poems can also be claimed as queer because they reveal that binary assumptions about gender and sexuality are insufficient for understanding the multifaceted experience of desire that her poetry articulates.[5] The compulsion to interpret her poems within binary frameworks is itself a form of epistemic injustice that suppresses a more expansive understanding of gender and desire expressed through her poetry.[6]

Rather than constructing binary and hierarchical frameworks, Sappho's poems resist these hegemonic simplifications and instead give voice to knowledge

---

[3] Both of these concepts are covered in more detail in the Introduction to this volume. On 'epistemic resistance', see Medina 2013: 48–50. As Medina 2013: 29–30 points out, both privileged and oppressed subjects can adopt stances of 'epistemic resistance'; in the former group, the resistance is to knowledge itself and often results in social injustice, whereas in the latter group, the resistance is to ignorance and oppression. Others in this volume who discuss forms of epistemic resistance include Gilbert (Chapter 3), McHardy (Chapter 4), Kim (Chapter 6), Witzke (Chapter 7) and Haley (Chapter 9).

[4] See, for instance, Foucault 1990; Sedgwick 1990; Butler 1993; McWhorter 1999; Hall 2017.

[5] For a queer reading of Sappho's fragments that resists identity-based arguments, see Haselswerdt 2016, who writes, 'When I first read Sappho (and as I read her even now) the thrill of recognition was not that of encountering the writing of someone who claims the same identity markers as I do. Instead, it is in the expression of an embodied desire that is free from the gendered hierarchies that saturate both of our societies'. See also Haselswerdt 2020; Lesser 2021; Mueller 2021.

[6] See Hall 2017: 159: 'A queer epistemological approach to testimonial injustice attends not only to the silencing of those deemed deviant but also the epistemic violence perpetuated by the compulsion to occupy an identity category, to understand oneself as a certain kind of person because of one's desires and actions'. In pointing this out, I am by no means suggesting that the efforts of LGBTQ+ people to claim Sappho as a queer ancestor constitute epistemic violence. I am instead arguing that scholars resist importing binary assumptions of gender and sexuality into the fragments of Sappho's poems, an epistemological stance that supports the aims of many LGBTQ+ activists.

rooted in sensual and aesthetic experience. Building on the insights of queer theorists of colour Gloria Anzaldúa and Audre Lorde, I argue that Sappho's poetry gives voice to the power of 'knowing otherwise' that locates care and understanding in the erotic, in a sensory, embodied experience that defies binary and static expressions of identity.[7] To lay the groundwork for the perspective that queer epistemology brings to this conversation, it will be helpful to survey first how feminist scholars have positioned Sappho as a resistant knower.

SAPPHO, EPISTEMIC INJUSTICE AND EPISTEMIC RESISTANCE

Many feminist classical scholars have explored how Sappho's poetry encodes knowledge, values and feelings that differ from those expressed by male archaic poets. Eva Stehle argues, for instance, that Sappho's poetry is fundamentally different from that of her male peers because she was faced with the problem of articulating what a woman might desire and offer in an erotic relationship.[8] According to Stehle, before Sappho the Greek poetic tradition had offered scripts for articulating and understanding only what men desire and contribute to erotic relationships. In contrast with male poets, Sappho imagines a relationship between equals that does not conform to the male pattern of 'prostration, domination, and release'.[9] Sappho's knowledge of the erotic diverges from the dominant male pattern, which establishes a strict hierarchy between lover and beloved.

Stehle's reading represents Sappho's poetry as distinct from male articulations of desire. In an influential essay, John J. Winkler reads Sappho's poetry as not simply distinct from but negotiating between masculine and feminine worlds and knowledge systems. He argues that Sappho's poetry demonstrates a 'consciousness both of her "private", woman-centred world and the other, "public" world'.[10] This interpretation is interested in how Sappho's gender situates her as a knower or epistemological subject in relation to a dominant, masculine system of knowledge practices. Because of her marginalised position within society, the argument goes, she has access both to the private world of her social interactions with women, of which men know nothing, and the public world of androcentric poetry and ritual. As Winkler puts it, 'From the point of view of *consciousness* (rather than physical space) we must diagram the circle of women's literature as a larger one which includes men's literature as one phase or compartment of

---

[7] For the phrase 'knowing otherwise', see Shotwell 2011, who frames her theories of implicit understanding through readings of Lorde's essays.
[8] Stehle 1981: 47–8.
[9] Stehle 1981: 52.
[10] Winkler 1981: 166.

women's cultural knowledge' (emphasis in the original).[11] Here Winkler flips the script on an androcentric scholarly tradition that positions women's writing as marginal, a confined subset within the larger realm of literature, which is always assumed to be male. In doing so, he calls attention to the epistemic injustice of this scholarly and literary tradition.[12]

Stehle's and Winkler's interpretations also suggest that Sappho's poetry engages in a kind of 'epistemic resistance' to hegemonic masculine models of erotic relationships and of public/private gender ideologies by asserting alternatives to these hierarchical modes of relation.[13] 'Epistemic resistance' is resistance to oppression on the basis of knowledge (epistemic injustice), and it can take many forms, including the identification and analysis of hierarchical systems and instances of oppression by those who experience them. Without using these terms, feminist interpretations of Sappho's poetry like Stehle's and Winkler's assert that her poems pose a resistant model to masculine epistemic structures, which emphasise hierarchy and domination. Ellen Greene, for instance, has argued that Sappho's poetry 'rejects the conventional roles of a dominant lover and a passive object of desire'.[14] Instead, according to Greene, Sappho describes erotic relationships that are equal and reciprocal.[15] Marilyn Skinner also claims that Sappho's songs provide evidence of a woman-specific social discourse that resists and disrupts masculine systems of knowledge, order and meaning-making.[16] She concludes, 'Whenever her texts trope difference by an appeal to gender, then, the female stance affords a posture of resistance to prevailing male attitudes and practices'.[17] Skinner reads the articulation of gendered difference in Sappho's fragments as a form of 'epistemic resistance' to dominant, masculine systems of knowledge.

---

[11] Winkler 1981: 174.
[12] Winkler (1981: 70–2, 79), however, also commits a form of epistemic injustice by failing to cite the African American scholar W. E. B. Du Bois (1994 [1903]), who had developed the idea of 'double consciousness' that guides Winkler's analysis. In pointing this out, my intent is not to suggest that this omission is evidence of a lack of rigour or dishonesty on Winkler's part, but rather to demonstrate how easy it is for scholars of great rigour and sophistication to reinscribe the epistemic injustices of the societies in which they live.
[13] On 'epistemic resistance', see Collins 1990: 29–30, 32; Hoagland 2001: 140; Medina 2013; and Frost-Arnold 2014: 791.
[14] Greene 2002: 83.
[15] Greene 2002: 84. duBois 1995: 9, however, argues that the 'Hymn to Aphrodite' (f. 1) depicts Sappho's participation in 'the aristocratic drive for domination'. See also Carson 1980.
[16] Skinner 1996: 182–3.
[17] Skinner 1996: 187.

These readings have made important corrections to the epistemic injustices of a scholarly tradition that diminished Sappho's poetic voice by representing her as perverse and sex-crazed or by arguing that her poetry is in some sense inferior.[18] Yet in arguing for Sappho's poetry as a woman-specific discourse distinct from or resistant to the masculine tradition, these essays also sometimes reinforce the binary oppositions that give rise to the hierarchies that they critique. Much scholarship on Sappho, for instance, aligns the feminine with the private and the masculine with the public sphere, since women were ideologically excluded from the public world of men. Yet this formulation is too rigid: in addition to the more familiar erotic songs, Sappho wrote songs critiquing aristocratic women and girls from rival families in Mytilene and advising her brother on political and economic decisions.[19] These songs also fail to conform to male/female and public/private binaries.

Feminist readings of Sappho as a resistant knower also tend to assume a stable or fixed speaking persona, rather than a persona that is constantly reinventing itself. Recent scholarship on Sappho has questioned the idea of a stable Sapphic persona linked to the poet's biography that can be traced across her very fragmentary poetic corpus.[20] Building on these recent challenges to the idea of a stable poetic persona in Sappho's poems, I argue that queer epistemology offers two insights that open up new avenues for reading Sappho's poetry as queer, which I mean not as a marker of identity, but rather as an alternative mode of relation and of knowledge that resists binary frameworks.[21] In my analyses of fragments 16 and 31, I explore the idea that binary conceptions of gender and sexuality oversimplify and mute the complex experiences of desire and embodiment expressed in these poems. Through analysis of appeals to knowledge in her poems, but especially in fragment 94, I argue that these poems explore possibilities for 'knowing otherwise' through sensual, embodied experience rather than a stable identity, persona or standpoint in opposition to masculine ways of knowing.

---

[18] On the ancient reception of Sappho, see Yatromanolakis 2007. On the comic tradition of Sappho as sex-crazed, see Haselswerdt 2016 and Coo 2021. On the erasure or suppression of Sapphic desire in the scholarly tradition, see duBois 1995: 12–13 and Haselswerdt 2016.

[19] See, for instance, fr. 99, 155, 214b. On ethical values such as *aretē*, see fr. 3, 50, 148. On Sappho's public poetry, see Parker 2005: 3–24.

[20] See, for instance, Lardinois 2021. On the first-person speaking persona in Greek lyric, see Slings 1990 and the essays in Bakker 2017.

[21] On sexuality as an epistemic relation, see Foucault 1990; Sedgwick 1990; McWhorter 1999: 40–1; and Hall 2017, among others.

DESIRE AND EMBODIMENT BEYOND BINARIES: SAPPHO 16 AND 31

Influenced by structuralism, scholarship on Greek literature since the 1980s has been shaped by the idea that the Greeks organised knowledge according to strict binary oppositions: divine/human, Greek/foreign, public/private, male/female.[22] These oppositions are used to construct difference and hierarchy in dominant systems of knowledge, to privilege divine over human, Greek over foreign, public over private, and male over female. Whether this binary system of thought is a product of ancient or modern ways of thinking, it constitutes what Gaile Pohlhaus Jr has called 'willful hermeneutic injustice', since it represents a refusal of dominant knowers to be informed by the knowledge of those who are deemed marginal.[23] The construction of binary conceptions of gender and sexuality is a form of 'willful hermeneutic injustice', since these binary schemes fail to describe some queer experiences of desire and embodiment.[24]

Although Sappho's poetry is often characterised as 'feminine' and 'private' against an assumed 'masculine' and 'public', I argue that the speaker in fact eschews binary conceptions such as these, preferring to represent gender, desire and embodiment in more complex and varied ways. Fragment 16 is typical of this queer approach to desire and embodiment. The poem begins with a priamel, a rhetorical technique that introduces a list of alternatives, which serve as foils to a subject or theme revealed in a climax (1–4):

Ο]ἰ μὲν ἰππήων στρότον, οἰ δὲ πέσδων,
οἰ δὲ νάων φαῖσ' ἐπ[ὶ] γᾶν μέλαι[ν]αν
ἔ]μμεναι κάλλιστον, ἔγω δὲ κῆν' ὄττω τις ἔραται.

Some say an army of cavalrymen, others of infantrymen,
and others a fleet of ships is the most beautiful thing
on the black earth, but I say that it is
whatever one loves.[25]

---

[22] For structuralist approaches to Greek myth and literature, see, for instance, Seung 1982: 43–61. See also Zeitlin 1985; Vidal-Naquet 1986; Dean-Jones 1991; Padel 1992: 99; and Loraux 1993. For breaking out of these binary conceptions of the world as a queer epistemological project, see Sedgwick 1990: 14 and Butler 1993: ix.

[23] Pohlhaus Jr 2012: 722. For a more in-depth discussion of ignorance as it contributes to epistemic injustice, see the Introduction to this volume.

[24] See Hall 2017: 159, who writes, 'From a queer epistemological perspective, binary conceptions of gender and sexuality are woefully inadequate for knowing the complex experiences and realities of gender and desire'.

[25] The Greek text I have used is Voigt 1971.

In some poems, the priamel is used to construct hierarchies, as in the beginning of Pindar's *Olympian* 1, which compares the best things in a variety of categories (1–7):

Ἄριστον μὲν ὕδωρ, ὁ δὲ χρυσὸς αἰθόμενον πῦρ
ἅτε διαπρέπει νυκτὶ μεγάνορος ἔξοχα πλούτου·
εἰ δ' ἄεθλα γαρύεν
ἔλδεαι, φίλον ἦτορ,
μηκέτ' ἀελίου σκόπει
ἄλλο θαλπνότερον ἐν ἁμέρᾳ φαεννὸν ἄστρον ἐρήμας δι' αἰθέρος,
μηδ' Ὀλυμπίας ἀγῶνα φέρτερον αὐδάσομεν.

Best is water, while gold, like fire blazing
in the night, shines preeminent amid lordly wealth.
But if you wish to sing
of athletic games, my heart,
look no further than the sun
for another star shining more warmly by day through the empty sky,
nor let us proclaim a contest greater than Olympia.[26]

In this priamel, Pindar introduces his theme – Hieron of Syracuse's victory in the single-horse race at the Olympic games in 476 BCE – by listing a series of 'bests': of elements, water is best, whereas of precious metals, gold is best. Of the stars in the sky, the sun is warmest. And of athletic contests, Olympia is the greatest. This series of superlatives, culminating in Olympia as the best athletic contest, allows Pindar to position Hieron as the winner of the most important event at the most important games. The priamel is used to construct hierarchy, with Hieron and Olympia positioned at the top, through its strategy of foil and climax.

Sappho's priamel in fragment 16 operates differently. She juxtaposes what others have said about what is 'most beautiful' (κάλλιστον, 3) with what the speaker says. Yet rather than elevating the climactic element – what the speaker says – above the foil, her statement is inclusive of what others have said. For she claims that the most beautiful thing is 'whatever one loves' (ὄττω τις ἔραται, 3–4), which could include the martial activities that others described. Many scholars have noted Sappho's relativistic stance in this poem; one scholar has even ascribed a 'beautiful and destructive anarchy' to her statement.[27] Sappho's priamel represents a queer approach to the form that rejects hierarchies in favour of inclusivity.

---

[26] Translation by Race 1997.
[27] See the summary of relativistic interpretations in Race 1989: 17–18. The quotation is from Wills 1967: 441.

In addition, the statement 'whatever one loves' assigns gender neither to subject nor to object. The indefinite pronoun τις is one of the few Greek pronouns that is gender neutral in this way, like the English 'one' or singular 'they'. If her vision is one of 'beautiful and destructive anarchy', it is because she brings a queer sensibility to bear on a form that is traditionally hierarchical and hegemonic, deployed by other poets to affirm social norms of what is 'best', or in this case, 'most beautiful'. Sappho refuses to privilege one vision of what is 'most beautiful' over another, and she does so without resorting to binary thinking about gender or about war and love.

In the strophe that follows, Sappho introduces the example of Helen as evidence that there is no universal standard by which one can judge what is 'most beautiful'. As the speaker explains, Helen left behind her 'most noble' (ἄρ]ιστον, 8) husband and did not think about her parents and child when she sailed for Troy in pursuit of what she found most beautiful. Many scholars understand the exemplum as follows: 'The thought seems to be that Helen, the most beautiful woman on earth, could have had all she wanted, but left the noblest of the Greeks for the man she loved'.[28] Yet this interpretation makes assumptions and fills in gaps with a heteronormative narrative about Helen that falls apart upon inspection. The poem, for instance, does not categorise Helen as the most beautiful woman. Instead, it says that she stands out among all people ([ἀνθ]ρώπων, 7) in her beauty. This summary also assumes that she abandons her husband because of her desire for Paris, whom she considers most beautiful. Yet, as Ella Haselswerdt points out, the poem never mentions Paris (6–11):[29]

ἀ γὰρ πόλυ περσκέθοισα
κάλλος [ἀνθ]ρώπων Ἐλένα [τὸ]ν ἄνδρα
τὸν [ἄρ]ιστον

καλλ[ίποι]σ' ἔβα 'ς Τροΐαν πλέοι[σα
κωὐδ[ὲ πα]ῖδος οὐδὲ φίλων το[κ]ήων   10
πά[μπαν] ἐμνάσθ<η>, ἀλλὰ παράγαγ' αὔταν...

> For Helen, who far surpassed
> mortals in her beauty, left behind
> her most noble husband
>
> and went sailing to Troy
> and she gave no thought at all to her child or her dear parents,
> but [someone/something] led her astray/diverted her course...

[28] Campbell 1982a: 270n7.
[29] Haselswerdt 2020.

The speaker emphasises Helen's decision to leave her family in Sparta and sail to Troy through active verbs and participles, all stacked together in line 9. Although there is a missing line after line 11, the syntax of the final clause suggests that the poem never pivots to describe Helen's desire for Paris.[30] Some scholars suggest that the subject of the verb παράγαγε, usually interpreted as 'led astray', might be Aphrodite or Eros.[31] It is possible to fill in the gap with the narrative that Helen's desire for Paris 'led her astray'. Yet the gap also makes possible a queer reading of this exemplum that resists importing heteronormative assumptions into the story.[32] In a talk that draws on queer theory to reread fragment 16, Ella Haselswerdt argues that it is just as possible that Helen desires instead the act of leaving itself, the possibility of a different life presented by the journey to Troy.[33] By leaving her 'most noble husband', Helen rejects the normative caretaking roles of wife, mother and daughter in favour of an uncertain journey elsewhere. Moreover, I would add that although παράγαγε, translated 'misled' or 'deceived' or 'led astray', is often interpreted as a moral judgement on Helen's decision, it is also possible to read this verb in a more neutral way. Someone or something – what she desired, perhaps – diverted (or queered) her course away from these normative roles and towards a different life elsewhere.

This reading of the Helen exemplum also offers a connection with the personal experience of the speaker, who expresses love not for a normative life, husband or children, but for a woman named Anaktoria (15–16):

..]με νῦν Ἀνακτορί[ας ὀ]νέμναι-
σ' οὐ] παρεοίσας.

> [Someone or something] reminded me now of Anaktoria
>   who is not present.

The verb 'reminded' (ὀνέμναισε, 15) echoes the verb 'gave [no] thought' (ἐμνάσθη, 11), which characterised Helen's decision to leave her family for Troy. Here, however, the speaker claims that she *does* think of Anaktoria, whose sight she prefers over the sight of Lydian chariots and armed infantry in a clear allusion to the opening priamel (17–20). Many scholars have argued that the Helen exemplum

---

[30] Recent papyrological work also confirms this reading. See the additions suggested by Burris, Fish and Obbink 2014 and Obbink 2016: 17–18.
[31] Page 1955: 54n12–13 suggests Κύπρις, but also notes that 'the variety of the attempts at reconstruction [. . .] proves that the extant letters do not suggest, let alone demand, any particular line of approach'. See also Campbell 1982a: 270n12–13.
[32] On 'compulsory heterosexuality', see Rich 1980.
[33] Haselswerdt 2020.

is used to 'elevate' the speaker's desire for Anaktoria over epic, masculine, military concerns.[34] Yet the speaker explicitly rejects the hierarchies implied by this language of elevation. Instead, she claims that she personally would prefer the sight of Anaktoria, but she recognises that others might prefer the sight of Lydian chariots and foot-soldiers marching in armour. One is not better than the other; rather, each is an expression of an unfulfilled desire. Throughout this poem, Sappho resists binary expressions of gender and desire, focusing attention instead on the pursuit of love and beauty that escapes established norms.

Fragment 31 also resists binary expressions of gender and desire by representing the speaker's internal emotions as she watches a man interact with a woman she desires. This poem is preserved by the author of the literary treatise *On the Sublime*, who calls attention to how Sappho selects and combines seemingly contradictory elements: 'Where does she display her excellence? In that she is skilled at both selecting and combining into each other extremes that have been stretched to their limit' ([Long.] *De subl.* 10.1–3). In the poem, the speaker compares the appearance of the god-like man sitting nearby and listening to the woman with her body's reactions to the sound of her voice and her laughter. Her reactions are sensory, vivid and often contradictory: she cannot speak, her tongue breaks (although she now sings this polished song), she sees nothing, her ears hum, she is on fire and sweat drips down her body, but she also trembles as if cold (7–16). She describes her response in such a precise, controlled way, but also evokes how uncontrolled it was, how extreme the breakdown of her senses and the flush of her emotions.

It is noteworthy that in this precise expression of embodied desire the speaker avoids any kind of gendered contrast between masculine and feminine. Adjectives that modify the speaking 'I' are feminine, but the catalogue of reactions is largely composed of verbs: the tongue 'breaks' (ἔαγε, 9), fire 'creeps' (ὐπαδεδρόμηκεν, 10) under the skin, the ears 'roar' (ἐπιβρόμεισι, 11–12), a cold sweat 'grabs hold' (ἔχει, 13) of her, trembling 'seizes' (ἄγρει, 14) her. Moreover, the poem refuses to establish a clear relationship between the speaker, the woman whose voice prompts these reactions, and the man with whom she began the poem. Instead, the poem is startlingly internal, grounded in the individual sensory perceptions of the speaker, as the ring composition of 'he seems to me' (φαίνεταί μοι, 1)

---

[34] See, for instance, Matlock 2020: 46: '"Helen" becomes for Sappho the name of an event in whose image she can negate the epic, masculine valuation of "Lydian chariots and foot-soldiers marching in armor" and, instead, elevate "the step and radiant sparkle" of Anaktoria'. See also Race 1989: 19: '[The example] provides a justification of her passion for Anaktoria on aesthetic grounds that place her private predilection above military displays and, given the exemplum of Helen, above commitments to the family and polis'.

and 'I seem to myself' (φαίνομ' ἔμ' αὔτ[αι, 16) suggests – the emphasis is on the speaker's perceptions.

Despite the poem's silence on this issue, many scholars have attempted to pin down the relationships involved, importing heteronormative assumptions into Sapphic lacunae. Wilamowitz, for instance, claimed that the man was the woman's husband and that the speaker was her teacher, jealous of the husband sitting near her, although there is little evidence in the poem that would allow anyone to define their precise relationships.[35] Wilamowitz's reading marries off the woman and establishes a kind of gendered hierarchy and rivalry between weak speaker and strong husband that has haunted many interpretations of the poem.[36] Even some feminist readings of the poem contrast the feminine, internal voice of the poem with the masculine world of epic: 'It is as if Sappho were saying that what happens in a woman's life also partakes of the significance of the man's world of war'.[37] Yet the poem rejects these gendered hierarchies and binaries (woman's private life/man's public world), giving the listener access only to this individual embodied experience of desire, which, as [Longinus] says, selects and brings together seemingly contradictory extremes.

The insistence on binaries and on heteronormative framing in scholarly responses to these two poems is itself a form of epistemic injustice, since such interpretations silence the more complex experiences of embodied desire that are expressed in these poems, interpreting them instead within simplified frameworks of male/female and war/love. Yet Sappho's poems instead imagine scenarios that upend these frameworks. Fragment 16 uses rhetorical forms like the priamel and the exemplum, which poets often use to establish hierarchy, to express a radically inclusive view of what is 'most beautiful' and to affirm the pursuit of desire that resists established norms. Fragment 31 describes contradictory internal experiences and feelings to express the desire of a single individual who refuses to define her relationship in terms of gender, marriage or rivalry. Binary oppositions fail to describe these expressions of desire. Expanding on this idea, in the next section I draw on the work of queer theorists of colour to analyse how the sensuous aesthetics of Sappho's fragments name an understanding of the world that queers dominant and hierarchical ways of knowing.

'KNOWING OTHERWISE' AND SAPPHO'S SENSUOUS AESTHETICS: SAPPHO 94

From theorists like Monique Wittig to classicists like Ellen Greene and Marilyn Skinner, feminist writers have been keenly interested in Sappho's standpoint as a

---

[35] Wilamowitz 1913: 58. Discussed in Lefkowitz 1996: 29–30.
[36] Most 1995: 29 goes so far as to suggest that it is the man whom the speaker desires.
[37] Lefkowitz 1996: 33.

woman who wrote about desire for women. These critics recognise that knowledge is socially situated and political,[38] and so Sappho's standpoint as a woman who loved women provides a critical angle through which to view and resist dominant (masculine) systems of knowledge, power and aesthetics. Yet Sappho's standpoint is difficult to reconstruct without forging a stable identity for her that reflects modern preoccupations, hierarchies and assumptions about gender and sexuality more than ancient ones. After all, readers today have access to only the smallest sample of Sappho's work, and even this small sample exhibits diverse themes, personas and genres. As a result, readers sometimes rely on biased stories told about her by later authors in antiquity to reconstruct a sense of Sappho's identity and 'circle', or they resort to their own associations with the identities of 'woman' or 'lesbian'.[39] This quest to define Sappho's identity conflicts with the epistemic stance of queer theory, which has shown that the need to claim a singular identity category based upon one's gender or desires in order to be legible to others can itself be a form of epistemic violence.[40]

Queer epistemology provides a different angle through which to analyse dominant epistemic paradigms and the entanglement of knowledge and power that feminist standpoint theory identifies. Queer theory written by queer people of colour in particular outlines strategies for critically negotiating identity and knowledge rather than uncritically claiming or rejecting it.[41] In her writing about the queer epistemic space of mestiza consciousness, for instance, Gloria Anzaldúa describes the borderland as 'created by the *emotional residue* of an unnatural boundary' (emphasis in the original).[42] In Anzaldúa's account, queer knowing is about feeling an 'emotional residue' that results from the experience of constantly shifting between worlds and across 'unnatural' boundaries.[43] Similarly, Audre Lorde describes knowledge of 'the erotic' as 'firmly rooted in the power of our unexpressed or unrecognised feeling'.[44] These affective ways of knowing

---

[38] For the idea that knowledge is socially situated and political, a central tenet of feminist standpoint theory, see Collins 1990 and Harding 2004, among many others (covered in detail in the Introduction to this volume).

[39] For a critical stance towards autobiographical readings of the poetry, see Lardinois 2021.

[40] See, for instance, Hall 2017: 159: 'A queer epistemological approach to testimonial injustice attends not only to the silencing of those deemed deviant but also the epistemic violence perpetuated by the compulsion to occupy an identity category, to understand oneself as a certain kind of person because of one's desires and actions'.

[41] See, for instance, Lorde 1984; Anzaldúa 1987 and 2015; Muñoz 1999: 11–12; and Hall 2017: 162–4.

[42] Anzaldúa 1987: 3.

[43] On queer affect in Sappho's poems, see also Mueller 2021.

[44] Lorde 1984: 53.

articulated by Anzaldúa and Lorde do not rely upon the certainty of identity for their articulation of queer knowledge. Instead, this 'unexpressed or unrecognised feeling' or 'emotional residue' between and across boundaries and binaries locates knowledge in embodied experiences of the world that cannot be named or expressed through dominant systems of knowledge or meaning-making.

Building upon Lorde's synthetic account of poetry and the erotic as generators of queer knowledge, Alexis Shotwell calls this affective, embodied form of understanding 'knowing otherwise': 'The form of understanding bodied forth through aesthetic experience is epistemic – we know the world otherwise through this sensuous knowledge, and that knowing is beyond, beneath, and other than rational, cognitive, propositional knowledge'.[45] By 'propositional knowledge', Shotwell means knowledge that makes a claim that can be evaluated as true or false.[46] For instance, if I say 'I know that Sappho was a poet from Lesbos', I am making a propositional claim to knowledge that can be evaluated as true or false. Shotwell characterises other types of knowledge as 'implicit understanding', especially aesthetic, embodied and emotional knowledge, which cannot be evaluated as true or false and sometimes cannot even be articulated or made intelligible through ordinary language. This type of knowledge often works in the background, and sometimes remains unrecognised and unarticulated, but it provides the framework for propositional claims like the one that I made above.

In what follows, I explore Sappho's sensuous 'knowing otherwise' as expressed in a handful of fragments, but especially fragment 94, which articulates a potent knowledge of pleasure and joy through embodied, sensual experience that can counteract and transform feelings of suffering. Many of Sappho's fragments appeal to the speaker's or an addressee's knowledge. The verb οἶδα, 'know', appears in several fragments, either in the first person singular or plural (fr. 19, 51) or second person singular (fr. 23, 60, 88, 94). In these examples, the speaker makes direct statements about what she does or doesn't know or invokes her addressees' knowledge in some way. Many of these fragments are too lacunose to judge whether the knowledge described is propositional knowledge. Yet in at least two of these fragments (fr. 51, 94), and perhaps more (fr. 88), this knowledge is explicitly not propositional knowledge, but rather a form of implicit knowledge that arises from embodied experience and feeling, from memory of sensual experience. In fragment 51, for instance, the speaker claims, 'I do not know what I should assume/make/do; I have two minds' (οὐκ οἶδ' ὄττι θέω· δύο μοι τὰ νοήμ⟨μ⟩ατα). In this fragment, which otherwise lacks context, the speaker rejects any claim to propositional knowledge, preferring a stance of radical uncertainty. The

---

[45] Shotwell 2011: 49.
[46] On propositional knowledge and implicit understanding, see Shotwell 2011: 1–28.

line suggests that there is not one true or false claim that the speaker could make about their knowledge.

In other examples attributed to Sappho, references to knowledge are often paired with verbs of remembering or forgetting, of emotion and of descriptions of sense perception, even if the very fragmentary nature of most of these poems makes it difficult to determine what exact connection the speaker is making. Fragment 88 is a good example of the predominance of these connections when the speaker addresses her or her addressees' knowledge. Although so fragmentary as to defy interpretation, it pairs invocations of her addressee's knowledge ('you yourself know', 10; 'know this', 22), sense perceptions ('sweeter', 9; 'bitter', 20), declarations of feeling ('I shall love', 14–15, 24) and references to something forgotten or not ('has forgotten', 11). The knowledge invoked in this fragment seems to be the knowledge generated by memory, feeling and embodied, sensual experience.

We can compare these examples with the use of the verb οἶδα to make propositional claims in two fragmentary poems attributed to Alcaeus, another lyric poet from Lesbos and Sappho's contemporary. In fragment 117b, the speaker attempts to persuade his addressees not to have sex with sex workers because, he claims, 'what one gives to a prostitute might as well be thrown into the waves of the grey sea' (26–7). The speaker then says that '[if someone] does not know this' (τοῦτ' οὐκ οἶδεν, 28), he must persuade him,[47] and he continues the argument by listing the bad things that befall people who have sex with sex workers, including disgrace and misery and tears. This is a clear example of a propositional knowledge claim. The speaker claims that it is bad to give money to sex workers and gives his reasons for thinking this is the case. He wants to persuade his addressees of the truth of this knowledge, which can be evaluated as either true or false. Similarly, in fragment 344, the speaker claims that he 'knows for certain' (οἶδ' ἦ μάν) that a man who attempts to move gravel that is not safely workable will hurt his head. In both instances, the speaker makes a claim to propositional knowledge and not to the kind of implicit understanding that characterises Sappho's use of the word. Although Alcaeus's surviving corpus, like Sappho's, is too fragmentary to determine whether this is the primary way that he appeals to knowledge in his poems, the speaker's claims in these two fragments represent a rhetorical tradition in lyric that aims to convince its addressees of the truth of some wisdom that the speaker shares. It is noteworthy that the surviving fragments of Sappho's poems do not invoke propositional knowledge in this way, but rather appeal to a different way of knowing.

---

[47] Fr. 117b is also fragmentary, but the overall sense of this section is fairly clear (26–9): πόρναι δ' ὅ κέ τις δίδ[ωι / ἴ]σα κἀ[ς] πολίας κῦμ' ἄλ[ο]ς ἐσβ[ά]λην. / .']πε[..]ε.ις τοῦτ' οὐκ οἶδεν, ἐ.οι π[.]θην /]σπ[. . .]αισιν ὁμίλλει, τάδε γίνε[τ]α[ι. (Campbell 1982b).

Uses of the verb οἶδα, however, do not exhaust the range of knowledge claims expressed in these poems.[48] For this reason, and before turning to fragment 94, I want to consider some of the nouns referring to organs of cognition and emotion that also frequently appear in Sappho's fragments.[49] The noun *phrēn* (φρήν) occurs most frequently and refers to an organ of cognition, emotion and volition, usually described as residing in the torso or chest.[50] As a result, many translators interpret *phrēn* as the heart.[51] Yet in English the heart is not often associated with cognition, although it is associated with emotion, especially love and desire, and sometimes volition. This is a major difference between English and Greek that affects how English-speaking readers interpret these poems and their presentation of knowledge and embodiment. In fragment 47, for instance, the speaker says that 'Eros shook my *phrenas* like a wind falling on oaks on a mountain'. As in fragment 31, desire has a disruptive and forceful effect on her cognition and emotion (which can't be separated). Similarly, fragment 48 describes the effects of desire on the speaker's *phrēn*: 'You came, and I was seeking you, and you cooled my *phrena*, which was burning with desire'. As in fragment 47, desire torments the speaker's *phrēn*, but the arrival of the addressee assuages her desire and cools her *phrēn*. These passages demonstrate that embodied knowledge, represented by cognitive organs like the *phrēn*, are important for Sappho's articulation of *eros*. This sensual knowledge, moreover, constructs the affective bonds that the speaker of the poems describes between herself and her addressees. The importance of knowledge for these bonds is represented by the speaker's frequent command to her addressees to 'know' and to 'remember'.

Fragment 94 provides one of the best examples of Sappho's appeal to 'knowing otherwise'. In this fragment, the speaker (who is named 'Sappho', 5) reports a conversation with a woman who says that she wishes she were dead (1) and that she is leaving Sappho 'unwillingly' (ἀέκοισα, 5).[52] Although the beginning of the poem has been lost and the reader does not know why this woman must

---

[48] As the anonymous reader for the volume points out, fr. 2 also presents an example of 'knowing otherwise', affective, embodied knowledge expressed through sensory language, even though it does not contain a verb of knowing.

[49] See νόος (fr. 57, 96), νόημμα (fr. 3, 16, 41, 51, 60) and φρήν, discussed at length below.

[50] See fr. 3, 43, 47, 48, 96, 120. On *phrēn* as organ of cognition, emotion and volition, see Darcus 1979.

[51] See, for instance, Campbell 1982b, who translates *phrēn* in fragments 47 and 48 as 'heart'. Miller 1996 translates the word in fr. 47 as 'mind', but in fr. 48 as 'heart'. Carson 2002 translates the word in both fragments as 'mind'. Rayor 2014 translates the word as 'senses' in both fragments.

[52] Since the speaker is named 'Sappho' in this poem, I will refer to her as Sappho throughout my discussion of fr. 94. However, I do not wish to suggest that the speaking persona and the poet share a stable identity.

leave Sappho, the remaining fragment juxtaposes two responses to a situation that is outside of either person's control. Whereas the woman who must leave focuses on what she and Sappho have suffered (ὤιμ' ὠς δεῖνα πεπ[όνθ]αμεν, 4), Sappho reminds her of the beautiful things they have experienced together (κάλ' ἐπάσχομεν, 11). The close connection between knowledge, sensual, embodied experience, and memory is clear from the beginning of Sappho's reported response: she tells her to go 'rejoicing' (χαίροισα, 7) and locates this potential for joy in her interlocutor's memory (μέμναισα, 8) and knowledge (οἶσθα, 8) of how Sappho cared for her. The speaker of the poem thus suggests that her knowledge of mutual care and her memories of erotic pleasure can make this woman feel joy (χαίροισα, 7) despite or within her grief and separation from Sappho. She puts forward a view of knowledge and memory of the erotic and of aesthetic experience that can liberate those who know it from what they find oppressive, from suffering, pain, and what is unwanted.

The rest of the poem is a display of 'knowing otherwise', of sensuous knowledge 'beyond, beneath, and other than rational, cognitive, propositional knowledge'.[53] Sappho tells her addressee that if she doesn't know how she cared for her, she wishes to remind her of the beautiful things they experienced together (9–10). She lists wreaths of flowers that her addressee wore around her neck and perfumed oil with which she anointed her body (12–20). The senses of sight and touch and smell are foregrounded in this description of luxurious bodily care and adornment: her neck is 'soft' (ἀπάλαι, 16), the flower wreaths and oil abundant (πόλ[λοις, 12; πόλλαις, 15; π[όλλωι, 18) and expensive (βρενθείωι, 19). The addressee is the subject of each verb (π<ε>ρεθήκα<ο>, 14; ἐξαλ<ε>ίψαο, 20), performing these actions upon herself, but beside Sappho (πὰρ ἔμοι, 14). The climax of the list is Sappho's reminder that she 'kept satisfying' (ἐξίης, 23) her desire on soft beds. Unlike the earlier second person singular verbs, which were in the aorist tense, the imperfect tense of this verb is marked: Sappho emphasises the repeated satisfaction of her desire within this luxurious setting. The implication is that her knowledge (οἶσθα, 8) of care stems from memories of these 'beautiful things' (κάλα, 11), these sensual, aesthetic, erotic experiences that she repeatedly enjoyed with Sappho.

Why does Sappho appeal to her addressee's knowledge of these embodied, aesthetic experiences? In her essay 'Uses of the Erotic: The Erotic as Power', Audre Lorde writes about the unrecognised liberatory potential of the erotic:

> The erotic is a measure between the beginnings of our sense of self and the chaos of our strongest feelings. It is an internal sense of satisfaction to which, once we have experienced it, we know we can aspire. For having

---

[53] Shotwell 2011: 49.

experienced the fullness of this depth of feeling and recognizing its power, in honor and self-respect we can require no less of ourselves.[54]

It is this internal sense of satisfaction to which the speaker Sappho appeals in this poem, a depth of feeling that she hopes to awaken so that her addressee can rediscover the honour and self-respect that she had when she was wreathing her body with flowers, anointing herself with oil, and satisfying her desires alongside Sappho. The knowledge to which Sappho appeals is not propositional, claim-making knowledge, but an implicit understanding, an embodied feeling of the importance of her pleasure that the addressee can know even when separated from Sappho unwillingly. As Lorde says, there is power in this kind of knowledge that is distinct from the power of propositional knowledge but just as vital. To forget it is to forget what one lives for.

Both the speaker of Sappho's poems and her addressees are sometimes in danger of forgetting the implicit, embodied 'knowing otherwise' that sustains them despite the oppressive forces in their lives. These oppressive forces are not named directly, but they often result in unwilling separations as in fragment 94, perhaps because of marriage or exile. These unwilling separations induce despair, a longing for death. In fragment 95, a speaker declares, 'I get no pleasure from being above the earth and a certain longing grips me to die' (10–11). Against this despair, Sappho prescribes memory of the erotic as 'a measure between the beginnings of our sense of self and the chaos of our strongest feelings', to quote Lorde.[55] She makes this unnamed, embodied knowledge known through the sensual pleasure of her poetry.

So far, my discussion has assumed a kind of false binary between propositional and non-propositional knowledge. I do not mean to suggest, however, that one could not express care and love propositionally. Rather, Sappho's poetry combines these ways of knowing in descriptions of erotic desire. One might even say that the non-propositional ways of knowing the erotic that Sappho expresses set the stage for her addressee's recognition of the truth of the claim that Sappho loved or cared for her. Lorde argues for poetry as a site for the joining of these kinds of knowledge: 'Poetry is the way we help give name to the nameless so it can be thought'.[56] Yet if readers recognise only propositional knowledge as important or meaningful, they miss out on the other ways of knowing, the nameless, queer feelings and sensations, that Sappho invokes.

Even in their fragmentary state, Sappho's poems provoke their readers and listeners to know queerly, to know otherwise. They denaturalise the binaries that archaic Greek and contemporary Anglo-American society have used to create

---

[54] Lorde 1984: 54.
[55] Lorde 1984: 54.
[56] Lorde 1984: 37.

hierarchies and maintain unequal power relations. And they draw on the erotic not merely as theme or subject matter, but as an alternative way of knowing outside of or beyond these binaries and their concomitant hierarchies and hegemonies. Her poems remind their addressees that they know what it feels like to be cared for and to care for themselves. The speaker of Sappho's poems urges her listeners to use that knowledge to counter the despair that arises from epistemic injustice and from other forms of oppression.

CONCLUSION

Feminist classical scholars have illuminated the epistemic injustice of the popular and scholarly reception of Sappho's poems, both in antiquity and today. They have also traced a stance of epistemic resistance in her poems that challenges dominant frameworks of knowledge and meaning-making. A queer epistemological approach to the fragments contributes two insights to this reframing of Sappho's poems and their reception: first, it demonstrates that Sappho's poetry rejects the gender/sexuality binaries and insistence on a stable identity or standpoint that have been used to frame her poems' epistemic resistance to the dominant tradition of poetry and knowledge; and second, it recognises and celebrates the implicit understanding and embodied knowledge of sensual pleasures that she articulates in her poems. Implicit understanding like that articulated in fragment 94 and by Gloria Anzaldúa and Audre Lorde reaches 'beyond, beneath, and other than' propositional knowledge to find transformative potential in memories of care, pleasure and the erotic.[57] Sappho's fragments remind their addressees of their power to 'know otherwise' in a hostile world and they embrace the idea that this knowledge is always in progress, always revisable, always changing. Finally, the fragmentary nature of Sappho's poems requires their modern interpreters to adopt a queer epistemological approach, to embrace the unknowable and the unrepresentable, and to make meaning without requiring a 'stable, unproblematically unifying ground from which to know'.[58] In short, Sappho's fragments remind their readers of the pleasures of queer knowledge.

---

[57] Shotwell 2011: 49.
[58] Hall 2017: 165.

CHAPTER 3

En-gendering Knowledge with the Oceanids in *Prometheus Bound*

Mary H. Gilbert

*P*rometheus Bound, composed by Aeschylus or a near contemporary,[1] has long been considered an extended meditation on the limits of knowledge and power,[2] but the way gender intersects with, complicates and shapes this discourse has attracted less scholarly attention. Although a group of inquisitive women who want to know all about what Prometheus has experienced is on stage guiding the discussion for most of the play, the Oceanids' combination of curiosity, kindness and restraint is often read as little more than girlish naïveté with little bearing on the plot of the play.[3] This chapter argues, on the contrary, that the chorus's eager, engaged listening works to carve out a welcoming space in which Prometheus can explore his thinking about humans, tyranny and authoritarianism. The Oceanids are not merely passive onlookers; rather, they play an essential role as witnesses of Prometheus's suffering and actively shape the contest of epistemic authority the tragedy stages.

A central tenet of feminist epistemology claims that marginalised groups are socially situated in ways that can render them well attuned to issues of knowledge construction and authority. Moreover, marginalised individuals might cooperate

---

[1] The contested authorship of the play is not particularly relevant to my analysis, but I am in general agreement with Griffith 1977 and 1984, who argues that the play was not written by Aeschylus. See Sommerstein 2010 and Bassi 2010 for recent bibliographies.
[2] For example, Griffith 1983: 10.
[3] Griffith 1983: 10–11 characterises the chorus as 'a suitably ignorant and inquisitive audience' that is 'not much involved with the main action of the play', an analysis that undervalues the potentially transformative power of listening. See also Vandvik 1943 and Winnington-Ingram 1983: 176, who describes the chorus as 'shallow' and 'naïve'.

with others to form bonds of epistemic resistance to defy, thwart or challenge established cultural narratives. There are three concepts that offer useful tools for analysing the dynamics of knowledge construction in the play: (1) feminist standpoint theory, an approach that argues marginalised groups are socially situated in ways that can render them particularly adept at knowledge construction;[4] (2) epistemic resistance, defined as the use of epistemic resources by marginalised knowers to defy, thwart or challenge established authority;[5] and (3) epistemic vice, defined as the acquisition of character traits that systematically impair an individual's ability to learn and teach.[6] By using these frameworks to structure close readings of key passages in the tragedy, I aim to reclaim the Oceanids' participation in the stories told by Prometheus and Io as an important mode of knowledge production and to highlight the pivotal role they play in facilitating the exchange of ideas between Prometheus, themselves and, later, Io. By foregrounding the Oceanids' encouragement of Prometheus and their tact in navigating the dualism of the Zeus–Prometheus power dynamic, the *Prometheus Bound* poet stages a series of encounters that foreground the value of enquiry, communication, sympathy and epistemic humility.

QUESTIONING THE GOD OF KNOWLEDGE

When the Oceanids come on stage, they reveal that they are so eager to meet Prometheus that in their hurry they have left behind their shoes (ἀπέδιλος, 135) and 'grave-faced modesty' (θεμερῶπιν αἰδῶ, 134). The combination of the sartorial detail and countercultural mindset underscores their rejection of the gendered expectation that they will be safe waiting at home until the conflict between Prometheus and Zeus is resolved.[7] They express immediate sympathy, substantiated by a mist of tears (ὁμίχλα ... δακρύων, 145–6). They look directly at Prometheus, refusing to turn away from his tortured body ('I see, Prometheus', λεύσσω, Προμηθεῦ, 144). Then, they begin posing excited questions about his predicament (τίς ... τίς, 160–2), but

---

[4] Standpoint theory got its beginnings in the 1970s and '80s in the field of sociology, before being taken up by philosophers in the early '90s. Famous studies include Smith 1974 and 1990; Collins 1986; Code 1991; Harding 1993 and 1995; Alcoff 2006; Fricker 2017 and many others. For a survey of the main views and a recent bibliography, see Anderson 2020 and the Introduction to this volume.
[5] The branch of feminist epistemology known as epistemic resistance developed out of standpoint theory. Some seminal studies that developed the concept include Hurtado 1996 and 2003; Mignolo 2010; and Medina 2013.
[6] Medina 2013; Kidd 2020; Tanesini 2021.
[7] Fineberg 1986: 95–8 characterises the Oceanids' swift and shoeless arrival as a pointed expression of their agency and autonomy. Translations are my own unless noted otherwise.

they also temper their enthusiasm by acknowledging that physical pain may render speech difficult, or, perhaps, that in speaking Prometheus may put himself at greater risk ('teach us, unless speaking hurts you in some way', δίδαξον ἡμᾶς, εἴ τι μὴ βλάπτει λόγῳ, 196). By laying the groundwork for a considerate, compassionate discussion early on, the Oceanids demonstrate their interest not only in the situation at hand but also in Prometheus's wellbeing.

The Oceanids' interest in Prometheus's story combined with their sensitivity to his plight stands in contrast to the hostility of Prometheus's male interlocutors.[8] In opposition to his daughters' empathetic mode, Ocean wastes no time on pleasantries when he arrives on stage. He immediately starts proffering his unsolicited advice ('I want to give you some advice – the best advice', 307–8), a tactic that results in a breakdown of communication between the two gods. After Prometheus insists that he does not require his father-in-law's 'help', Ocean leaves in a hurry, relieved to be freed from this minor inconvenience ('You've said the word and I'm off', 393).[9] By juxtaposing the conversation between Prometheus and the Oceanids with the conversation between Prometheus and their father, Ocean, a standoffish interlocutor, more interested in ensuring his own good standing with Zeus than communicating with the prisoner, the *Prometheus Bound* playwright highlights the way sympathetic enquiry can shape knowledge production by producing rich dialogue, and conversely, how condescension can smother it.

The Oceanids' acknowledgement of the potential for speech to cause pain (196) is a response to Prometheus's incessant verbal abuse of Zeus (186–92), a mode of expression that the Oceanids do not appreciate (as evidenced by their criticism at 178–85 and later at 932). But, instead of engaging Prometheus's invective, the Oceanids respond by reaffirming their interest in his story (193) and then by asking specific questions, carefully steering Prometheus back to their initial question, the reason for his imprisonment (194–5). Here is the passage (193–6):

[8] Hephaistos and Ocean, while uncomfortable with the physical abuse, essentially agree with Zeus and the other Olympians that Prometheus was wrong to give fire to humans. Kratos and Hermes are actively hostile to Prometheus and his intellectual pursuits. Not one of these male characters is willing to listen to Prometheus's side of the story. Kratos and Hephaistos never even address him directly. Ocean offers advice and obtains Prometheus's permission not to intervene, and Hermes does little more than taunt and mock.

[9] The interchange with Ocean is so unproductive that it has been suggested that Ocean does not come to Prometheus to speak with him so much as to locate his wayward daughters and bring them home. Oddly, the daughters of Ocean do not speak directly to their father or even mention his visit after he leaves. I am not totally opposed to the interpretation, which has them travelling from the sky down to the stage in order to elude their father and his gendered ideology that would have them safe at home, but I think there may be more to their silence, as I suggest in the next section. Hurtado 1996 discusses silence as a tool for epistemic resistance, and something like that may be at play here.

Reveal everything and tell us the story!
On what charge did Zeus arrest you
to torture and humiliate you relentlessly?
Teach us, unless speaking hurts you in some way.

πάντ' ἐκκάλυψον καὶ γέγων' ἡμῖν λόγον,
ποίῳ λαβών σε Ζεὺς ἐπ' αἰτιάματι
οὕτως ἀτίμως καὶ πικρῶς ἀκίζεται·
δίδαξον ἡμᾶς, εἴ τι μὴ βλάπτει λόγῳ.

Here, the chorus neither denies nor affirms Prometheus's criticism of Zeus's justice (the adverbs ἀτίμως and πικρῶς do not necessarily imply that they believe Zeus was wrong to punish Prometheus). Instead of weighing in on that issue, they guide Prometheus back to the crux of their enquiry – the cause of his detention, bracketing their question with assurances of their commitment to hearing the story from Prometheus himself (193, 196). They value his perspective and appear to recognise that to discuss Zeus now risks triggering Prometheus's defensiveness in a way that could interfere with their exchange of ideas. Moreover, while they temper the intensity of their interrogation with a genuine eagerness to learn (δίδαξον ἡμᾶς, 196), their pointed follow-up question (ποίῳ . . . ἐπ' αἰτιάματι, 194) suggests that their questioning is intentional, that it comes from a place of informed opinion. Like a good educator, the chorus interrupts and redirects Prometheus's self-centred, one-track thought pattern in order to guide him back to what they consider the crux of the matter – the reason Zeus is angry at him. If the daughters of Ocean seem to repeat the same condolences and ask the same questions again and again, it is in no small part due to the evasions and inconsistencies in Prometheus's replies. Their repetition is characteristic of a teacher's patience and persistence, not of puerile credulity.

Philosopher José Medina claims that a knower's past experiences can result in 'epistemic distortions' that impair their ability to learn and teach, especially if those past experiences involve a combination of privilege and trauma.[10] As a god widely recognised for his intelligence and made to suffer for doing what he thinks is right, Prometheus fits Medina's description of a character prone to such distortions. In the language of Medina, Prometheus's initial reluctance to speak (he is silent for the first scene of the play) suggests that the injustices he has endured and the physical pain he is experiencing have eroded his 'epistemic trust', rendering him defensive and guarded. Read in this light, the Oceanids, by listening closely to Prometheus and responding sympathetically, but also honestly (sc. critically), create for Prometheus a supportive dialogic 'safe space' that frees him to explore

---

[10] Medina 2013, esp. 27–39.

his feelings and ideas. Their gendered cognitive style, which approaches what some feminist educators have termed 'listening with serious intent', works to negotiate a more comprehensive depiction of Prometheus's actions and thoughts by encouraging Prometheus to think through his opinions and put them into words.[11]

To the Oceanids' request, Prometheus responds at length, but even here he stops short of actually answering their question (ποίῳ ... ἐπ' αἰτιάματι, 194). Instead, he lingers on his support of Zeus in the war against the Titans, and then on his deliverance of humanity from destruction (197–241). His answer conveniently glosses over a key bit of the story, his theft of fire from the gods. Once again, the Oceanids' follow-up questions redirect him back there, underscoring the fact that they are looking to have a particular conversation, that their fascination with him stems from prior familiarity with the situation. They recognise the political, potentially revolutionary issues at stake and understand that the conflict between Prometheus and Zeus has the potential to disrupt the entire cosmos. Like their father, the Oceanids have already formed opinions about the conflict, but even so, they want to hear Prometheus's side of the story. To that end, their questions continue (247–58):

> Chorus: You did not go further than that, did you?
> Prometheus: Yes, I did; I stopped humans from seeing their fate beforehand.
> Chorus: What medicine did you find for that disease?
> Prometheus: I planted in them blind hopes.
> Chorus: This is a great boon you have bestowed on humans.
> Prometheus: But after that I gave them fire.
> Chorus: And now the short-lived beings possess brilliant fire?
> Prometheus: Yes, and they will learn many skills from it.
> Chorus: Then it is for these charges that Zeus . . .
> Prometheus: Is torturing me and not relaxing my suffering at all.
> Chorus: No end of your torture has been established?
> Prometheus: Nothing except for whatever seems right to him.

---

[11] Zeitlin 1985: 79–82, however, defines the genre of tragedy and the very concept of mimesis as feminine. While I don't doubt the general conclusions of her influential essay, I do think that the Oceanids are marked out by their especially feminine cognitive style with respect to the other characters within the play. For the concept of 'listening with serious intent', see Stetz 2001. Rooney 1991 demonstrates that cognitive styles are often understood through the lens of gender. Deductive, analytic and quantitative cognitive styles get marked as masculine; whereas intuitive and qualitative cognitive styles get gendered feminine. This can result in the devaluing of epistemic contributions associated with feminine cognitive styles. See also Keller 1985.

ΧΟ: μή πού τι προύβης τῶνδε καὶ περαιτέρω;
ΠΡ: θνητούς γ' ἔπαυσα μὴ προδέρκεσθαι μόρον.
ΧΟ: τὸ ποῖον εὑρὼν τῆσδε φάρμακον νόσου;
ΠΡ: τυφλὰς ἐν αὐτοῖς ἐλπίδας κατῴκισα.
ΧΟ: μέγ' ὠφέλημα τοῦτ' ἐδωρήσω βροτοῖς.
ΠΡ: πρὸς τοῖσδε μέντοι πῦρ ἐγώ σφιν ὤπασα.
ΧΟ: καὶ νῦν φλογωπὸν πῦρ ἔχουσ' ἐφήμεροι;
ΠΡ: ἀφ' οὗ γε πολλὰς ἐκμαθήσονται τέχνας.
ΧΟ: τοιοῖσδε δή σε Ζεὺς ἐπ' αἰτιάμασιν—
ΠΡ: αἰκίζεταί γε, κοὐδαμῇ χαλᾷ κακῶν.
ΧΟ: οὐδ' ἐστὶν ἄθλου τέρμα σοι προκείμενον.
ΠΡ: οὐκ ἄλλο γ' οὐδέν, πλὴν ὅταν κείνῳ δοκῇ.

With their follow-up question in line 247, the Oceanids indicate they know there is more to the story than Prometheus's vague claims of salvation. Still, Prometheus hesitates to admit that he has given humans fire.[12] Instead, in convoluted syntax, he highlights the implications of his famed gift: new skills and improved standards of living (254). He also claims that he gave humans 'blind hopes' (τυφλὰς ἐλπίδας), a cryptic benefit that will have further resonance with the arrival of Io (discussed further below). The chorus's willingness to accept that Prometheus did well by offering mankind this gift of ignorance, even as they are pressing him for the fire story, underscores their epistemic agency. For, as classicist Richard Rader has also argued, this interchange reveals that the chorus disagrees (initially, at least) with Prometheus's decision to give fire to mortals, even if their tone is controlled throughout.[13] Their subsequent displeasure at Prometheus's admission of the gift of fire (259–62) suggests that, at this point in the play, they agree with Hephaestus and Ocean that Prometheus was wrong to give humans fire, an opinion that renders their gentle approach all the more remarkable.

It is unsurprising that the Oceanids, situated within the patriarchal culture of Zeus's Olympus, are apprehensive of Prometheus's actions from the beginning. After all, their father's political proximity to Zeus, whose own metaphorical fatherhood underwrites his epistemic authority throughout the play, is established early on.[14] Their recognition of Zeus's supremacy makes their interest in

---

[12] That all the other gods agree with Zeus that Prometheus wronged them by giving humans fire seems clear enough from the responses of Hephaestus and Ocean, both of whom are sympathetic to Prometheus's plight, but do not agree that he was right to give fire to humans.

[13] Rader 2013: 170–2.

[14] Throughout the play, characters refer to Zeus as 'father'. Richard Rader notes that while Zeus was known from Homer onwards as the 'father of gods and men', the appellations in the play are significant because they link his knowledge authority to

Prometheus's story all the more surprising and bold, especially when compared to the disinterest of Prometheus's male interlocutors. Prometheus seems to expect the Oceanids' position and to work to avoid their direct criticism. Just as they are on the brink of piecing his fragmented responses into an answer to their question, Prometheus interrupts to complain that even if he has done something wrong, Zeus's indefinite torture of him is excessive (255–6). Prometheus's evasiveness here seems to be yet another symptom of his 'epistemic vice', that is, distortions that can impair a knower's ability to engage in knowledge producing practices like conversation.[15] Still, even though Prometheus refuses at this point to engage directly with the chorus's question, his interjection does manage to raise a point on which both parties can agree – Zeus's eternal punishment of Prometheus is excessive.

When Prometheus fails (again) to acknowledge their tacit criticism of him, the Oceanids finally insist (259–60): 'Do you not see that you have made a mistake (ἥμαρτες)?' They follow up this directness with a quick apology for causing him pain (260–1), and then suggest that they move quickly to find a solution (261–2): 'Well, let's drop it (μεθῶμεν) and look for some escape from your struggle'. Although they are eager to hear Prometheus's story and willing to reconsider their assessment of the situation, their ready follow-up questions suggest the possibility that the Oceanids visit their brother-in-law with a specific agenda: to guide him towards a recognition of his mistake and thereby facilitate a reconciliation between Prometheus and the new king of the gods. Consider too that in Hesiod, their older sister Styx effects an alliance between Ocean and Zeus and devises oath as a check on divine power (Hes. *Theog.* 767–806). Given the *Prometheus Bound* poet's close engagement with Hesiod,[16] it is reasonable to explore the possibility that the Oceanids would attempt a similar détente between Prometheus and Zeus. In the first scene of the play, then, the Oceanids encourage open, constructive conversation with Prometheus and try to understand his thought process, potentially in order to convince him he is wrong to continue his fight against Zeus. That they eventually change their mind about the viability of compromise is as much a testament to their willingness to engage critically with new evidence as to Prometheus's persuasive capabilities.

---

his paternity (Rader 2013: 164). Recall, also, that in Hesiod, Ocean encouraged his eldest daughter Styx to give her children Kratos and Bia to Zeus on the eve of the Titanomachy (*Th.* 389–96). If we extend that father–daughter characterisation to the *Prometheus Bound*, we can imagine that Ocean has already spoken to his daughters about how to compromise with father Zeus.

[15] Medina 2013: 27–39. See also Kidd 2020 and Tanesini 2021.
[16] Griffith 1983 and Stamatopoulou 2017: 122–59.

KNOWLEDGE AND POSITIONALITY

As we have established, the Oceanids, who barely manage to obtain their father's permission to leave the house (130–1), want to acquire knowledge despite patriarchal forces that are either indifferent or hostile to their epistemic needs. As minor female deities the Oceanids are particularly susceptible to sexual abuse, a vulnerability of which they are well aware as evidenced by the fact that they self-identify with victims of rape (895–907). Their apprehension of Zeus (895) and the male gaze more generally (ἄφυκτον ὄμμα, 903) recalls the many mythological stories of nymphs who are raped and tortured for their supposed promiscuity. This nymph identity that situates them between goddess and woman may render them initially eager to separate themselves from humans (for example, their dismissive reference to humans as 'short-lived', 253 and 547, discussed further below) but, as I argue in this section, it also makes them sympathetic listeners of Io's story of sexual violence; she is, after all, their niece. Like the Oceanids' nymph-hood, Io's girlhood shapes the questions she poses and the opinions she holds. Their respective nymph and human positionalities, while rendering them particularly vulnerable to patriarchal violence, also provide experiences and insights that shape their interpretations of big issues like theology, politics and philanthropy. In this section I argue that the Oceanids' decentred standpoint with respect to the politics of Mount Olympus facilitates their deepening connection with Prometheus and activates their sympathy for Io and early humans.

Feminist standpoint theory explores the importance of status, both physical and metaphorical, to knowledge authority. As philosopher Lorraine Code describes it, 'Knowers are always somewhere – and at once limited and enabled by the specificities of their locations'.[17] Knowledge, as Code describes it, is not detached from lived experience; it is, rather, the product of intellectual endeavours firmly rooted in and informed by a knower's time, place and identity. As sociologist Patricia Hill Collins's concept of 'the outsider within' has shown in a particularly convincing iteration of the theory, inhabiting a peripheral space can be an asset to knowledge building despite the real barriers an outsider may face in gaining access to epistemic authority.[18] She argues that Black women intellectuals make creative use of their 'outsider within' status vis-à-vis white culture to produce new ways of thinking about race, class and gender.[19] Black feminist thought, then, is uniquely important within contemporary American society in part because of its periphery standpoint. With respect to the Greek pantheon,

---

[17] Code 1993: 39.
[18] Collins 1990: 221–38 coins the term 'matrix of domination' to explore the relationship of race, class and gender as interlocking systems of oppression. See Crenshaw 1989 and 1991 and Haley's chapter in this volume.
[19] Collins 1986: S15.

nymphs share some similarities to Collins's description of African American women. As female deities, they are granted some access to divine spaces, but only as secondary characters. They are the caretakers of divine and human children, the dancers and musicians at some other god's celebration, the hated girlfriends (willing or otherwise) of male Olympians and the companions of more powerful goddesses.

As water nymphs, the Oceanids possess some privileges due to their divinity (or semi-divinity) and some disadvantages due to their gender and semi-mortality. The fact that Prometheus (a god) is married to their sister, Hesione (560), while their brother Iapetus is the father of Io (a human, 634) underscores their in-between status – they may be able to fly through the air, but their husbands and/or children could well be mortal.[20] It has been speculated that nymphs are actually mortal themselves – they just live for a very long time before succumbing to death.[21] This interpretation would add weight to the Oceanids' rather contemptuous naming of humans as 'short-lived' (ἐφήμεροι, 253 and 547), a term used in the play by only one other character, Hermes, who is also dismissive of humankind (945).[22] Perhaps the Oceanids emphasise the short lives of humans as compared to their own long (but terminal) lives. More substantively, the last choral ode the Oceanids sing before Io enters the stage exemplifies their less-than-divine status (527–38). In it they vow to make lavish sacrifices (529–31) and to not offend with words (532), positioning themselves more closely with humans who honour gods than with gods who require devotion. At this point they claim to have 'learned' from Prometheus the importance of submission, not his lessons in philanthropy, suggesting that Prometheus's verbal arguments are not as persuasive as his tortured body: 'I have learned these things from seeing your horrible fortunes, Prometheus' (ἔμαθον τάδε σὰς προσιδοῦσ' ὀλοὰς τύχας, Προμηθεῦ, 552). For the Oceanids, at least at this point in the play, the threat of pain counts for more than the prospect of justice.

At a physical level, Prometheus draws our attention to the Oceanids' lofty position in the sky when he chides the chorus for offering advice from their privileged position of safety (263–5): 'It is easy for someone who stands outside of misery to admonish and rebuke the one faring badly. Descend to the ground to hear about my

---

[20] There is no mention of Io's mother in this play, but traditionally her mother is Melia, another daughter of Ocean. See Gantz 1993: 198.

[21] See *Hymn to Aphrodite* 260–3 on the finite lifespans of nymphs. Larson 2001: 12 also argues that nymphs are not necessarily immortal like the gods; they simply have extremely long lifespans. See Clay 2003 for her theory that the Melian nymphs are the first race of humans.

[22] While ἐφήμεροι is commonly used as an epithet for humans in Homeric epic, the phrase seems to take on a more intentional and derogatory sense in this play.

future fortunes, to learn the whole story ... commiserate (συμπονήσατε) with the one now in pain'. The Oceanids, in turn, agree to exchange the 'pure sky' (αἰθέρα θ' ἁγνόν, 280) for 'this rugged ground' (ὀκριοέσσῃ χθονὶ τῇδε, 281) and come down to the orchestra, as though they recognise the importance of physical proximity to good conversation. They position their bodies close to his – a stance that encourages a greater degree of sympathy with Prometheus.

The first lines the Oceanids speak from Earth (after Prometheus's conversation with Ocean) renew their compassion for the prisoner's pitiable fortune and demonstrate a newfound empathy with humankind (399–410):

> I groan for you, Prometheus, and your ruinous misfortunes; from tender eyes I shed a tear-soaked flow and drench my cheek with wet streams. For Zeus, governing in this unrestrained way[23] with his own laws demonstrates to the gods of old an arrogant spearpoint. The whole earth has already cried out a groaning cry and they groan for [the loss of] your time-honoured privileges and those of your siblings.

> στένω σε τᾶς οὐλομένας τύχας, Προμηθεῦ·
> δακρυσίστακτον ἀπ' ὄσσων
> ῥαδινῶν λειβομένα ῥέος παρειὰν
> νοτίοις ἔτεγξα παγαῖς.
> ἀμέγαρτα γὰρ τάδε Ζεὺς
> ἰδίοις νόμοις κρατύνων
> ὑπερήφανον θεοῖς τοῖς
> πάρος ἐνδείκνυσιν αἰχμάν.
> πρόπασα δ' ἤδη στονόεν λέλακε χώρα,
> μεγαλοσχήμονά τ' ἀρχαι-
> οπρεπῆ <– ⏑ ⏑ –> στένουσι τὰν σὰν
> ξυνομαιμόνων τε τιμάν·

The Oceanids echo Prometheus's sentiment about the excessive harshness of Zeus's punishment and criticise Zeus's arrogance in ruling. Furthermore, they become aware of the widespread lamentations of humans and the natural world, a detail that underscores the fact that their new location on the ground imparts them with a different perspective. Their rivers of tears are followed by a catalogue of the human tribes bemoaning Prometheus's fate (406–24), and finally a description of how the Earth itself is groaning in sympathy for Prometheus (431–5).

Between their decision to change places and this sympathetic choral ode, they fall silent. That they do not speak for the entirety of the conversation between

---

[23] For ἀμέγαρτα γὰρ τάδε Ζεὺς ... κρατύνων, see Griffith 1983: *ad loc*.

Ocean and Prometheus has perplexed scholars of the play.[24] Why does the father not address his daughters, or they him? Do the Oceanids even realise their father is present? Are they intentionally trying to hide from him? I suggest, on the basis of the choral ode, that during the conversation between Prometheus and Ocean, the Oceanids' gaze is intensely focused on human scenes on Earth. Their proximity to the theatrical audience, with whom they are now on the same level, could facilitate a staging of their dawning comprehension and silent horror of life on Earth.[25] In this reading of the scene, the Oceanids withdraw from the conversation between Ocean and Prometheus because their attention is absorbed by the human beings with whom they now share space. Ocean, on the other hand, could easily be staged as too focused on making a quick getaway to notice their presence. Afterall, his daughters are no longer in the sky. That Ocean does not notice his daughters' presence underscores the way the gods in the sky fail to notice happenings on the ground, and as such, reinforces the importance of the Oceanids' change of place. This new physical positionality paves the way for their change of tone towards humankind in their next choral ode (398–435).

By the midpoint of the play, the chorus's dialogic interventions that prefer question to monologue and honesty to defensiveness have produced a much clearer explanation of what Prometheus has accomplished and why than he could manage alone. Even so, after the Oceanids acclimate to the rugged terrain of Earth, they restate their original position about Zeus, asserting that obedience and submission is still the best (and only) approach to authoritarian rule (472–5, 545–51). They advise Prometheus again to leave humankind alone: 'Do not help mortals beyond the proper measure (καιροῦ πέρα) if it means being careless about yourself when you are in trouble' (507–8). The vantage point from Earth may have helped the chorus understand why Prometheus feels sympathy for humans, but it has not yet convinced them that he was right to disobey Zeus. Still, it is worth noting that the Oceanids remain on the ground for the rest of the play. As such, when Io arrives, they are well positioned to hear her story and consider further the hardships early humans, especially women, are forced to endure (as I discuss further below).

When Io enters, her language closely resembles the Oceanids'. Like them, she is keen to learn, both about Prometheus's situation and her own. A persistent desire for acquiring knowledge cuts through the relentless bouts of hallucinatory madness and psychological trauma that characterise her time on stage (593–608).[26] Even before Io is made aware of the identity of the prisoner, she

---

[24] Griffith 1983: *ad loc.*
[25] For this sort of metatheatricality and the self-referentiality in Aeschylean drama, see Bierl 2017: 166–9.
[26] See especially Anhalt 2015: 248, who highlights Io's productive questioning and argues that 'Io exemplifies a connection between experience and knowledge'.

launches into a barrage of questions that echo the pronouns of the Oceanids' original interrogations (τίς ... τί ... τίνα, 561). Moreover, Io's willingness to press the prisoner for further insights echoes the string of imperatives in the chorus's initial requests (193–6, quoted above): 'reveal, if you know, speak, tell the miserable, wandering girl' (δεῖξον εἴπερ οἶσθα / θρόει, φράζε τᾷ δυσπλάνῳ παρθένῳ, 607–8). By highlighting the similarity of their syntax, the *Prometheus Bound* poet suggests that there is overlap in the positionality of Io and the Oceanids; like her divine aunts, Io enters the stage eager to learn and know. That Io starts asking questions even before she realises she is speaking to Prometheus reinforces her desperation for knowledge; her search for answers is central to her (human and female) identity.[27]

AMPLIFYING MARGINALISED VOICES

When Io learns the name of the prisoner, she recognises Prometheus as humanity's saviour and bolsters his claim that the gift of fire was necessary to the survival of humans. In this opinion, of course, she differs from the Oceanids. But then she immediately asks Prometheus what crimes he has committed, echoing the chorus's repeated question from above ('For what mistakes are you being punished?' ποινὰς δὲ ποίων ἀμπλακημάτων τίνεις, 620). As he did earlier with the Oceanids, Prometheus responds with characteristic evasion (621). Both the Oceanids and Io acknowledge Prometheus's intellectual prowess and want to profit from it, but his inconsistencies and vagaries require them to rely on their own epistemic abilities to get substantive answers out of him.

In a rare moment of solidarity between ancient women,[28] the chorus of Oceanids express their desire to hear about Io's experiences in her own words (αὐτῆς λεγούσης, 633) before hearing Prometheus's interpretation of her life. Just as Prometheus is about to launch into an extended statement about Io, the Oceanids interrupt (631–4): 'Not yet! Give a share of the pleasure to me. Let's first ask her about her illness and have her tell us about her horrifying misfortunes. Then she

---

[27] See also Swanson 1994–5.
[28] Any passage in Greco-Roman literature that depicts female characters working together against patriarchal systems is special and deserving of attention. Beyond the story of Procne and Philomela, whose sisterhood and comradery underwrite their rape-revenge story (see Marder 1992) and perhaps Euripides' *Medea*, where the Corinthian women agree to guard Medea's secrets, there are not many moments in mythology that depict women collaborating with other women in ways that have the potential to threaten patriarchal norms. This moment between Io and the Oceanids in *Prometheus Bound* is exceptional for how it depicts women making space for another woman to tell her story of sexual trauma.

can learn from you the future of her struggles'. This move, as I argue in this section, underscores the value the chorus places on Io's (mythologically) lived experience as a woman. It also compels Prometheus to take Io seriously. For, after their interjection, Prometheus changes course. He drops the condescension and joins the Oceanids in encouraging Io to share her side of the story. This epistemic solidarity between Io and the chorus comes to resemble what feminist philosophers have termed epistemic resistance, a concept that Gaile Pohlhaus defines as moments when 'marginally situated knowers actively resist epistemic domination through interaction with other resistant knowers'.[29] By listening to Io, even though her language is marked by bouts of obfuscating madness, and by making space for her personal account of Zeus's abuse, the chorus of Oceanids demonstrates the value they place on marginalised voices and lived experience. It is no small thing that the tragic hero of the play, a god whose name means knowledge, is willing to listen to and learn from a marginalised knower like Io, even though she is a fellow victim of Zeus's authoritarianism.

In the beginning of her scene, Io reveals that she disagrees that ignorance of the future is good for humans, an opinion held by both the chorus and Prometheus (248–9).[30] After Prometheus denies Io's initial requests to hear more about his predicament (563–4, 614), Io changes course and begins to ask about herself. When Prometheus evades those questions too, on the grounds that he does not want to cause undue anxiety by telling her the truth, Io insists that he reconsider his patronising attitude (624–30):

Prometheus: To not learn these things is better than to learn them.
Io: Don't hide from me what I will suffer!
Prometheus: I don't begrudge you this gift.
Io: Why, then, are you waiting to tell me everything?
Prometheus: There is no ill will, but I hesitate to trouble your mind.
Io: Don't take more care of me than I want (ὡς ἐμοὶ γλυκύ).
Prometheus: Since you desire it, I must speak – listen, then.

ΠΡ: τὸ μὴ μαθεῖν σοι κρεῖσσον ἢ μαθεῖν τάδε.
ΙΩ: μήτοι με κρύψῃς τοῦθ' ὅπερ μέλλω παθεῖν.
ΠΡ: ἀλλ' οὐ μεγαίρω τοῦδε τοῦ δωρήματος.
ΙΩ: τί δῆτα μέλλεις μὴ οὐ γεγωνίσκειν τὸ πᾶν;
ΠΡ: φθόνος μὲν οὐδείς, σὰς δ' ὀκνῶ θρᾶξαι φρένας.
ΙΩ: μή μου προκήδου μᾶσσον ὡς ἐμοὶ γλυκύ.
ΠΡ: ἐπεὶ προθυμῇ, χρὴ λέγειν· ἄκουε δή.

---

[29] Pohlhaus Jr 2012.
[30] See my discussion of this above.

This back and forth between god and human is noteworthy because Prometheus, whose traditional obstinacy is on full display in his conversations with other gods, actually listens to Io and revises, at least in this particular case, his policy on human ignorance. It is a rare moment in Greek mythology when a god accepts constructive criticism from a human, rarer still from a woman. Prometheus's reticence to answer Io's questions seems to stem from his opinion that humans cannot handle reality. But Io compels him to recognise that even if it can be painful to communicate in 'plain speech' (ἁπλῷ λόγῳ, 610), 'it is right to open your mouth to friends' (δίκαιον πρὸς φίλους οἴγειν στόμα, 611). His willingness to change his mind demonstrates the healing effect the Oceanids have had on Prometheus's epistemic distortions. Prometheus allows himself to be convinced by Io and prepares to tell of her future. It is at this point that the Oceanids step in to ask Io to speak first.

Io agrees to speak, and what follows is an account of her relationship with Zeus from her own perspective: recurring dreams, oracular abandonment, a traumatic illness, and a continued cycle of torture and abuse. Nevertheless, she ends her tale with a plea for more truth (683–6):

> You hear what I have suffered. But if you are able to say what hardships remain, reveal them. Do not pity me and cheer me up with false stories. For I say that fictional tales are the most shameful diseases.
>
> κλύεις τὰ πραχθέντ': εἰ δ' ἔχεις εἰπεῖν ὅ τι
> λοιπὸν πόνων, σήμαινε: μηδέ μ' οἰκτίσας
> ξύνθαλπε μύθοις ψευδέσιν: νόσημα γὰρ
> αἴσχιστον εἶναί φημι συνθέτους λόγους.

In this passage, Io, whose tortured illness is on full display in the staging of her movements and panicked cries, claims that the most shameful νόσημα is actually falsehood. She remains committed to the truth, no matter how painful reality can be. She rejects pity and unfounded optimism as a false kindness. She has shared her own story and demands Prometheus's honesty in return. The Oceanids chime in on Io's behalf, reversing their earlier views in favour of human ignorance. They agree with Io that it is better to know about additional pains than to be surprised by them: 'Speak, teach us thoroughly; for the sick it is sweet to know a painful future well in advance' (λέγ', ἐκδίδασκε: τοῖς νοσοῦσί τοι γλυκὺ / τὸ λοιπὸν ἄλγος προυξεπίστασθαι τορῶς, 698–9). They echo Io's language of disease and pluralise the participle (τοῖς νοσοῦσί) to generalise Io's trauma. In so doing, they suggest that her story of patriarchal abuse is not unique – it is the lived experience of an entire group of beings, mostly women. While the Oceanids don't actually begin swapping #MeToo stories with the newly arrived human, they do appear to draw connections between Io and other victims. With the punning on Prometheus's name (προυξεπίστασθαι, to know in advance), they hint that Prometheus himself, as another victim of divine violence, might also be considered among the τοῖς νοσοῦσί. They suggest that if Prometheus has found some sweetness in knowing that his pain will eventually find an end, Io could also benefit from that knowledge. This is not the last time the Oceanids and Io work together in an epistemically significant way. Later in the dialogue, when Prometheus agrees to tell Io either more about her own future or about his eventual release, the chorus steps in again on Io's behalf and succeeds in convincing Prometheus to tell both stories (782–5). Prometheus continues to manifest a complex relation to divulging knowledge, in part, perhaps, because his understanding of the future is his best chance of getting freed from his chains, but his willingness to revise his ideas about human ignorance and the relevance of lived experience, at least in this particular instance, demonstrates his own renowned intellectual freedom.

At the end of Prometheus's speech, Io becomes overcome by her madness – her metre shifts from trimeter to anapestic, her eyes roll back in her head, her speech gets excited and confused, and she runs wildly off stage. One might read her response as justifying Prometheus's original opinion that humans are better off ignorant of their future, but the chorus's response to her untimely exit suggests that her madness now (like when she enters the stage) is due to the trauma she endured as victim of divine abuse, not to Prometheus's honesty. The Oceanids, in turn, pray that they will avoid Io's grim fate (894–906):

> Never, o Fates, may you never see me as a companion of Zeus's bed; and may I never draw near any of the heavenly gods (τινὶ τῶν ἐξ οὐρανοῦ) as a spouse. For I shudder when I see Io, an unmarried girl, undone by Hera's ill-wandering roamings of trouble.[31] For me, when marriage is between equals (ὁμαλὸς ὁ γάμος), it is not scary. But I am afraid that the eye of a more powerful god, a gaze from which there is no escape, will look on me with desire. An unwinnable war, an inescapable bind, I would not be able to exist at all. For, I do not see how I could get free of the craft of Zeus.

> μήποτε μήποτέ μ', ὦ
> Μοῖραι <˘ – – –>, λεχέων Διὸς εὐ-
> νάτειραν ἴδοισθε πέλουσαν,
> μήτε πλαθείην γαμέτᾳ τινὶ τῶν ἐξ οὐρανοῦ·
> ταρβῶ γὰρ ἀστεργάνορα παρθενίαν
> εἰσορῶσ' Ἰοῦς ἀμαλαπτομέναν
> δυσπλάνοις Ἥρας ἀλατείαις πόνων.
> ἐπῳδ. ἐμοὶ δ' ὅτε μὲν ὁμαλὸς ὁ γάμος,
> ἄφοβος ἔφυ· δέδια δὲ μὴ

---

[31] Here I adopt, with slight adaptation, Griffith's translation of this awkward phrase (1983: *ad loc.*).

> κρεισσόνων θεῶν ἔρῳ μ'
> ἄφυκτον ὄμμα προσδράκοι.
> ἀπόλεμος ὅδε γ' ὁ πόλεμος, ἄπορα πόριμος· οὐδ'
> ἔχω τί ἂν γενοίμαν·
> τὰν Διὸς γὰρ οὐχ ὁρῶ
> μῆτιν ὅπᾳ φύγοιμ' ἄν.

The Oceanids' uneasy reaction to Io's story stems from the realisation that they are vulnerable in similar ways. If Zeus should decide to assault one of them, they would likely suffer a fate similar to this girl. When they deem a marriage between equals as not scary (901), the Oceanids appear to be saying that they would prefer human husbands to divine ones (μήτε πλαθείην γαμέτᾳ τινὶ τῶν ἐξ οὐρανοῦ, 897). Considering the mythological trope of the gods' disgust at old age and death, the suggestion that the Oceanids now rate mortality as a lesser evil than Zeus's predatory advances is a spectacular reversal of expectations. This ode represents a monumental shift in their thinking. Earlier in the poem they positioned themselves as part of the pantheon, far above humans in status, but now they suggest that an alliance with humanity may be a better option if it can shield them from abusive divine husbands. They now see themselves as similarly bound by a 'helpless, dreamlike fragility' (ἐδέρχθης / ὀλιγοδρανίαν ἄκικυν, 547–8), and so they have revised their original prejudices against humankind.

That Io is not able to take full advantage of the amicable atmosphere she has helped create should not undermine its worth, especially considering the effect her story has had on her interlocutors – both Prometheus and the Oceanids. Io's story about Zeus's violence not only reshapes the chorus's perspective concerning the worth of human life and happiness, but also encourages them, in a particularly impressive display of female agency, to take a stand against tyranny, even if it means risking the life of calm they had imagined for themselves earlier (536–9). By staging the Oceanids' support of Io's eager but vulnerable drive to know and by dramatising their reaction to her suffering, the *Prometheus Bound* poet establishes female experience as an important source of human knowledge, and thereby sets the scene for a final bold act of disobedience that flies in the face of patriarchal authority. Because of their positioning, metaphorical as well as physical, the Oceanids gain new insight into human suffering first through observing it and then by empathising with Io. Consequently, they are able to guide Prometheus into reframing his disobedience as a just act.

FRATERNAL SOLIDARITY

In the final lines of the play, after Hermes orders the chorus to move out of the way of Zeus's wrath, the Oceanids refuse to leave Prometheus's side (1063–70).

They cite as deciding factors both Hermes' insufficient logic and their newfound solidarity with victims of Zeus's patriarchal violence:

> Say something else and speak in a way that will persuade me, because that speech that you just swept by me is insufferable. Why would you urge me to practice cowardice? I am willing to suffer what I must alongside him; for I have learned to hate traitors and there is no disease that disgusts me more than that.

> ἄλλο τι φώνει καὶ παραμυθοῦ μ'
> ὅ τι καὶ πείσεις· οὐ γὰρ δήπου
> τοῦτό γε τλητὸν παρέσυρας ἔπος.
> πῶς με κελεύεις κακότητ' ἀσκεῖν;
> μετὰ τοῦδ' ὅ τι χρὴ πάσχειν ἐθέλω·
> τοὺς προδότας γὰρ μισεῖν ἔμαθον,
> κοὐκ ἔστι νόσος
> τῆσδ' ἥντιν' ἀπέπτυσα μᾶλλον.

The Oceanids are insulted by the patriarchal tone Hermes takes with them and his inability to discuss the matter with them. They bristle at his insinuation that they will desert their friends in need. They mark their movement in favour of humanity by echoing Io's language of disease (νόσος, 1069) as a metaphor. Up until this encounter they had hoped to broker a peace between Prometheus and Zeus, as evidenced by their late criticism of Prometheus's vituperative tone (1036–9), but they have been slowly moving closer to Prometheus and Io throughout the course of the play. And so, when the time comes to make a stand, they do not hesitate.

The Oceanids' expression of loyalty to Prometheus at the end of the play comes as a shock. A tragic chorus who willingly risks bodily harm is unconventional and surprising in and of itself.[32] But the ending is not as unexpected as some scholars have suggested.[33] Their final move is noteworthy less because there

---

[32] Although deForest 1998 suggests that female tragic choruses are always more radical than their male counterparts.

[33] Griffith 1983: *ad loc.* suggests that their solidarity simply underlines the playwright's support of Prometheus: 'This sudden and quite unexpected display of courage and defiance . . . serves to align the audience's sympathies all the more strongly with Prometheus – at the cost, perhaps, of some consistency in characterization'. Moreover, although there is no evidence for it in the text, he would prefer to remove them from the stage before Prometheus experiences Zeus's wrath: 'their readiness to suffer with P. is never put into action, not really put to the test at all: the earthquake and whirlwind sweep him away before they can move to join or abandon him' (n1067). Sommerstein 2009 follows Griffith, as he has the chorus flee at 1090, before Prometheus speaks his

is doubt about where the Oceanids stand, but rather because they are under no illusion as to which god (Prometheus or Zeus) is the more powerful. Before Hermes arrives, when Prometheus prophesies an eventual end to Zeus's supremacy (908–27), they accuse him, with characteristic honesty, of saying things he just wants to be true (σύ θην ἃ χρῄζεις, ταῦτ' ἐπιγλωσσᾷ Διός, 928). Prometheus does not take kindly to their late criticism and accuses them of paying homage to whomever is currently in power (937–8), a cowardice that he later genders as feminine (1002–6).[34] Their displeasure at this may be gleaned from their silence. During the ensuing scene with Hermes, the Oceanids remain quiet until the end, except for a brief request that Prometheus take Hermes' threats seriously, that he reconsider working towards a peaceful compromise with Zeus (1036–9). They know that Prometheus has no chance of defeating Zeus, and they find his patronising arrogance disappointing. They are under no illusions that Prometheus is a perfect leader, but they value his willingness to listen to others and change his mind. In the end, they choose to stand with a brother (in-law) and a friend who has treated them as epistemically relevant. The fact that they know Prometheus cannot win, but nevertheless choose, when necessity requires it, to stand in solidarity with him, provides a strong counterpoint to the cynicism of the 'might makes right' political stance that colours the first scene of the play and that dominates Athenian political discourse in the fifth century.[35]

That they are not totally in agreement with Prometheus, even at the end, does not diminish their impressive display of courage. They choose to stand with him even though he is not a perfect knower or actor. Aída Hurtado has expressed the importance of decisive, even if imperfect, action to the intersectional feminist project, claiming that the 'eternal deconstruction [of knowledge] ... leads to maintaining the status quo' and noting that 'feminists of colour choose to deconstruct by constructing rather than by only rejecting or by taking a nihilist position of fragmentation and inaction'.[36] The Oceanids understand that Pro-

---

final lines. But Scott 1987: 96 argues contra Griffith and anticipates part of my reading. He understands the Oceanids' shift towards Prometheus as the development of their characterisation throughout the play: 'The chorus is a character in the *Prometheus Bound*. It is continually called upon to shift its responses, its judgments, its evaluations, and its perspective. In the course of witnessing the major characters as they come and go, the Oceanids participate in one scene with a character who significantly alters the balance of their belief even though they only acknowledge this effect in terms typical to their timid characterisation. Yet while the characterisation remains constant, the shift in their attitude, which results in their surprisingly powerful words of defiance, is so complete that it must be termed a conversion'.

[34] Even so, Prometheus's characterisation of himself as a stubborn wave at line 1001 reads like a subtle acknowledgement of the Oceanids' strengths.

[35] For example, Pl. *Resp.* 1, Thuc. 5.84–116, Eur. *Tro.* and many others.

[36] Hurtado 2003: 219.

metheus is flawed, but they also recognise that those located at the periphery of epistemic authority rarely have the luxury of a perfect leader. In the end, when the opportunity for peaceful negotiation is taken away, they stand with the god they find more just. The self-sacrificial bravery of their final decision to remain by Prometheus's side, even in the face of imminent disaster, cannot be overstated.

Richard Hutchins names Prometheus a 'poet of witness', claiming that through suffering Prometheus 'becomes a symbol of democratic resistance – and a kind of poet of witness – as he uses his lengthy speeches and tortured body as evidence against Zeus's authoritarianism'.[37] I would add to this formulation that the Oceanids ought to be recognised together with Prometheus for the role they play in bearing witness to Zeus's mistreatment of gods and humans. To witness means to decide to engage in someone else's story, to participate and to stand alongside another as a guarantee that their words will carry weight. For the Oceanids, to witness is not only to amplify suppressed narratives but also to take an active part in the conflict at hand. They establish their epistemic agency by boldly and knowingly rejecting their father's position and choosing Prometheus, Io and humanity over Zeus's reign of terror. By the end of the play, the Oceanids do not have all the answers, or even many of them, but they have reached the conclusion that Zeus is an exploitative leader who does violence to gods and humans. They refuse to cooperate with him in silent obedience.

Throughout the play, the Oceanids' resolute quest for answers is contrasted with the less analytical perspectives of Prometheus's male interlocutors, who range from patronisingly dismissive to actively hostile. Whereas Prometheus's dialogue with Ocean, and later Hermes, reveals very little about the prisoner's aims and motivations, his conversations with the Oceanids produce new insights into his actions and thought processes that substantially reframe the conventional narrative, recounted most fully in the poems of Hesiod, of the conflict between Zeus and Prometheus. As Mark Griffith and Zoe Stamatopoulou have demonstrated, the *Prometheus Bound* poet knows Hesiod's text well and is consciously reframing Hesiod's tale for an Athenian audience.[38] To conclude, I suggest that while the male characters in the play respond to Prometheus with a traditional, Hesiodic pro-Zeus dismissiveness, the novel facets of the Prometheus story that the Oceanids bring to light help situate the myth for an Athenian audience grappling with issues like authoritarianism and civil disobedience.[39] In dialectic collabora-

---

[37] Hutchins 2020. Forché 1993 coins the term 'poetry of witness' to describe poetry that bears witness to extreme violence, war, torture, slavery, sexual violence and other atrocities. See also Forché and Wu 2014.

[38] Griffith 1983 and Stamatopoulou 2017: 122–59.

[39] The inclusion of the Oceanids and Io in the Prometheus story is an innovation of the playwright; Io's inclusion in the play is commented on by Griffith 1983: 6 and Stamatopoulou 2017: 154–5.

tion with the Oceanids, Prometheus, whose refusal to speak in the first scene of the play corresponds to his guise's silence in Hesiod, discovers a voice with which to reframe his divine disobedience as a moral act. Furthermore, the Oceanids' careful enquiry into Io's human and female positionality facilitates Prometheus's reconsideration of the value of human ignorance and also their own ultimate decision to reject their father's epistemic authority and stand in solidarity with Prometheus and humanity. In the course of the play, they move from determined critics to loyal supporters of Prometheus's radical, revolutionary vision.

CHAPTER 4

Women's Complaints about Violence at Athens: Zobia and Aristogeiton

Fiona McHardy

This chapter contributes to the growing scholarly literature on violence against women in classical Athens[1] by considering the case of Zobia, a metic woman who experienced violence at the hands of a man named Aristogeiton according to Demosthenes' *Against Aristogeiton* (25.56–8). The idea of intersectional oppression as developed by Kimberlé Crenshaw underpins this research in that it highlights the particular plight of women of metic status in ancient Athens – a group especially exposed to intersectional oppression based on their gender, non-citizenship and social status.[2] My focus is on the way that Zobia uses public complaints regarding Aristogeiton's violent behaviour, and it is inspired by consideration of women's public vocalisation of their experiences of sexual violence and harassment through the #MeToo movement in recent years.[3] This study is informed by scholarship in feminist epistemology, in particular Alison Bailey's exploration of anger and epistemic injustice, and Karyn Freedman's discussion of the epistemic significance of

---

[1] See esp. Llewellyn-Jones 2011, 2020, and Omitowoju 2016. See also Deacy and McHardy 2013 on instances involving the killing of pregnant wives and intimate partners in Greek myth and history; Synodinou 1987 and Schaps 2006 on Homeric epic; and Scourfield 2003 on domestic violence in Chariton.
[2] Crenshaw 1991.
[3] See https://metoomvmt.org/. The movement was founded by activist Tarana Burke in 2006 and went viral as #MeToo in 2017.

the #MeToo movement.[4] As I go on to discuss, Zobia's decision to speak out about the violence she has suffered places her at considerable risk of retaliation by a powerful man,[5] and there is no evidence that speaking openly about offences against them yielded direct results for women at Athens. Yet, Zobia's ability to gain justice for herself was otherwise limited, and as Alison Bailey argues, employing a 'knowing resistant anger' can be a powerful tool for the marginalised to oppose epistemic injustices.[6] Bailey explains: 'Silence is a condition of oppression, and part of resisting oppression is finding a voice that effectively pushes back against the weight of imposed silences'.[7] By voicing her complaints openly as she does, Zobia resists the systematic silencing and her gossip enters the public sphere where it has the potential to influence people's perceptions of this man and his suitability for public office.

While public speech was a defining feature of maleness at Athens, and the ability to speak publicly in legal and political settings was tied to concepts of manliness,[8] in contrast women's voices, be they citizen, metic or enslaved, were muted in Athenian public spaces.[9] Although women were thought to hold authoritative knowledge on certain key issues, such as childbirth and legitimacy, and they could be asked to swear evidentiary oaths on these topics to serve as evidence that men could refer to in their legal cases,[10] their knowledge and ability to contribute to society was generally devalued in comparison to that of men. Women could not debate or vote in the assembly or present legal cases themselves,[11] nor could they serve as witnesses in court.[12] Instead, they were reliant on men, usually male relatives, to speak publicly

---

[4] Bailey 2018 and Freedman 2020. On epistemic injustice, see esp. Fricker 2007. On links between #MeToo and classics, see Beard 2017.

[5] Freedman 2020: 18. See also Beard 2017: 8.

[6] Bailey 2018: 95. See Allen 2000: 50–9 on the significance of anger in Athenian legal processes. See the Introduction to this volume for a discussion of epistemic resistance. Others in this volume who discuss forms of epistemic resistance include Weiberg (Chapter 2), Gilbert (Chapter 3), Kim (Chapter 6), Witzke (Chapter 7) and Haley (Chapter 9).

[7] Bailey 2018: 96.

[8] Roisman 2005.

[9] Beard 2017 notes the continuing impact of these ancient gendered concepts of public speech.

[10] On evidentiary oaths see, for example, Just 1989: 38 and Todd 1993: 208. See McHardy 2021 on mothers as experts on issues of paternity, and Dean-Jones 1995 on Hippocratic acknowledgement of women's knowledge about gynaecology. See Beard 2017: 9, 24–5 on women's voices being restricted to sectional issues.

[11] See, for example, Just 1989: 26 and Todd 1993: 201, 208.

[12] Todd 1990 is persuasive on this issue. See his n12 for the long history of scholarly debate on the topic. See also Gagarin 1998: 39.

for them.[13] This marginalisation of women in Athenian society and legal silencing of their voices, even in spheres where they were traditionally authoritative,[14] indicates the vulnerability of women to acts of domestic violence. Unable to speak out themselves in a legal setting against violent abusers from their own households, women would have needed to find support elsewhere, but surviving legal speeches make clear that Athenian men were not motivated to bring cases unrelated to their own interests. While this state of affairs was problematic enough for citizen women, who could potentially find support from their kin,[15] the evidence from oratory suggests that the situation was particularly acute for metic women, especially those lacking family at Athens.

An intriguing example highlighting some of these issues is embedded in Demosthenes 47 *Against Evergus and Mnesibulus*, a case regarding false testimony.[16] The speaker explains that at one point in his protracted dispute with the accused,[17] they entered his house in order to seize goods owed from a previous legal judgement (47.52–3). The speaker himself was absent, but his wife and children were there together with his former nurse, an enslaved woman who had been freed by the speaker's father and had married, but had returned to live with the family after the death of her husband (47.55). She is characterised as old and lacking other people to care for her (47.55–6). The speaker describes the violent assault these men inflicted on the old nurse in order to snatch a cup she was hiding in her bosom (47.59) and explains that she subsequently died of her wounds (47.67). Although this woman was living with the family, the speaker is advised against prosecuting for homicide in this case, since this woman is not related to him nor is she his slave (47.70).[18] The speaker is also advised that in the absence of male witnesses, and since he was not present himself, but only his wife and children were there, that the names of the murderers should not be publicly proclaimed as was traditional when the killer was known (47.69). This case indicates some of the problems for non-citizen women at Athens, whose vulnerability to acts of violence was exacerbated by issues associated with lack of legal recourse.[19] At the

---

[13] Just 1989: 29.

[14] See McHardy 2006 on legislation banning women's influence over wills and restricting their voices at funerals. See also Holst-Warhaft 1992.

[15] Hipparete, wife of Alcibiades, allegedly went to live with her powerful and wealthy brother Callias, although the sources suggest that he was either unwilling or unable to protect her from Alcibiades' subsequent violence towards her and that he was himself threatened by Alcibiades (Andoc. 4.15; Plut. *Alc.* 8).

[16] See Scafuro 2011: 290–328 on this case.

[17] See McHardy 2008: 77–8 for discussion of the alternately legal and violent parts of this dispute.

[18] See MacDowell 1963: 13–19 for discussion of the legal issues.

[19] See Kamen 2013, Chapter 4, for discussion of status differences for freeborn metics and freed slaves.

same time, despite the presence of the speaker's wife, who is characterised in this speech as knowledgeable about the dispute in which her husband is involved and who apparently remonstrated with the attackers about it (47.57), the legal and social customs of the time marginalise her knowledge to the extent that no case of homicide is brought when an old woman is violently attacked in front of her in her own house.[20] Rather this story is only told at all because it has been usurped by a male speaker in order to paint a negative picture of his long-standing legal opponents in a case related to his own interests.

In this example, the marginalised position of women in Athenian society and the consequent epistemic injustice they suffer is made all too clear.[21] As Freedman states in her exploration of the epistemic significance of #MeToo, 'part of what it means to be marginalised is to lack the power and influence to tell one's own story, to be denied a voice and a platform to use it, and to risk serious threats to one's health, safety, livelihood, and community when one does'.[22] The social and legal constraints of the classical period subordinate the concerns of women, and in this case, especially an aged, non-citizen woman, even when she has suffered significant violence. Acting in defence of your loved ones and speaking out are not without risk, as this example hints, since male attackers hold significant power over women, while women of both citizen and non-citizen status are relegated to inferior positions where they are not only susceptible to physical violence, but are also inflicted with 'epistemic violence' because they are unable to achieve legal justice for themselves.[23] Significantly, the issue is not straightforwardly one of credibility, in that the speaker articulates the words of his wife to support his own arguments in a setting where she cannot speak herself, suggesting that her articulation of the facts of the case, spoken by him in court, would have lent some credibility to his arguments against his opponents in the eyes of the jurors.[24] Rather in this example and others, Athenian men co-opted the speech and knowledge of women to achieve their own ends.[25] This usurpation of women's knowledge for men's purposes has been termed 'epistemic objectification' by Miranda Fricker

---

[20] Others in this volume who discuss the epistemological frameworks that underlie sexual and physical violence include Witzke (Chapter 7), Haley (Chapter 9), Bowen (Chapter 10), Freas (Chapter 11) and Strong (Chapter 15).

[21] On epistemic injustice, see Fricker 2007 and many others covered in the Introduction to this volume.

[22] Freedman 2020: 3. See also Beard 2017: 8.

[23] See Spivak 1998: 282–3 on epistemic violence. See also Dotson 2011: 236. Others in this volume who discuss forms of epistemic silencing and epistemic violence include Weiberg (Chapter 2), Gilbert (Chapter 3), Kim (Chapter 6), Witzke (Chapter 7), Milnor (Chapter 8), Haley (Chapter 9) and Strong (Chapter 15).

[24] See Gagarin 2001.

[25] See Omitowoju 2016.

in her work on epistemic injustice.[26] Yet, armed with knowledge of the way that opponents used evidence based on gossip in court to try to win their cases, otherwise powerless people, including women and enslaved people, could employ the power of their mouths,[27] as I have argued elsewhere, to achieve justice for themselves indirectly.[28]

The oration at the centre of my discussion in this chapter also details violence against metic women at Athens: Aristogeiton's mother, sister, and Zobia herself, who was seemingly at one point his intimate partner. As in Demosthenes 47, the case is not about these acts of violence against women, rather, the violence appears only to build a negative picture of the character of the accused in an unrelated case. The women similarly appear vulnerable with little to protect them from the aggressive behaviour of a man in their household.[29] Nevertheless, in Demosthenes 25, the description of Zobia's response to Aristogeiton's initial violent attack provides a tantalising glimpse of the way women might be expected to react when suffering from violence, threats and abuse. This oration is a valuable additional source to be considered alongside examples discussed previously by scholars working on the subject of domestic violence at Athens.[30] Building on this work, I argue that a close reading of Demosthenes 25 sheds the tiniest amount of light on the absent women's perspectives[31] and hints at the way in which women could be agents in response to acts of violence against them.

Demosthenes 25 *Against Aristogeiton* purports to be an oration delivered by Demosthenes, acting as a *synegorus* of Lycurgus,[32] for an *endeixis* against Aristogeiton in 325/4 BCE.[33] The charge is that Aristogeiton was illegally bringing

---

[26] Fricker 2007: 133. See also Bailey 2018: 95.

[27] See Aeschylus *Cho.* 720–1 for the chorus's reference to the power of their mouths (στομάτων ... ἰσχὺν). They also comment on the ability of their words to achieve justice (διὰ δίκας πᾶν ἔπος / ἔλακον, 787–8). See McHardy 2018: 166–7 for further discussion of this play.

[28] McHardy 2018. See also Beard 2017: 37.

[29] On the particular vulnerability to violence of metic women at Athens, see Kennedy 2014, Chapter 4, esp. 117.

[30] Llewellyn-Jones 2011 and 2020, following on from Fisher's brief note 1998: 77 on the subject of violence against women at Athens, focuses specifically on wife-beating and consequently omits examples involving metics. Omitowoju 2016 discusses a range of instances from Attic oratory of physical and sexual domestic violence against women of different status, but does not discuss Demosthenes 25.

[31] On the lack of women's perspectives in Attic oratory, see Johnstone 1998. Llewellyn-Jones 2020: 396 notes that it is unsurprising that male-authored texts do not include women speaking out against physical chastisement by their husbands.

[32] Lycurgus had a number of co-prosecutors (Dem. 25.1). Rubinstein 2000: 30.

[33] See Dem. 25.14, 49, 69, 71, 26.1, 17, Dinarchus 2.13. See Sealey 1960.

lawsuits at a time when he was a state debtor and therefore disqualified from participating in legal cases. The prosecution was likely motivated by political rivalries, and the aim was to banish Aristogeiton from the city.[34] Commentators on this speech have not dwelt upon it as a possible source for attitudes towards violence against women in ancient Athens, rather, the main focus of debate regarding this oration has been its authenticity. Discussion about the authorship of the speech began in antiquity when Dionysius of Halicarnassus claimed that it was not Demosthenic on the grounds of style (*Dem.* 57).[35] Further disputes involve whether the speech was composed in the fourth century BCE or was written later as a rhetorical exercise and never delivered.[36] For my purposes, it is not significant whether the oration was composed by Demosthenes or another contemporary orator.[37] Even if the speech is a later imitation, 'nearly every trope, image, and argument in it can be attested in other 4th-century forensic orations, and its rhetorical strategies are all typical of the genre'.[38] Significantly, the style and type of abuse used in the speech can be found in other orations of the period, including speeches delivered by Demosthenes.[39] Further, there are similarities in the depiction of values and of virtuous and problematic characteristics in this oration and in Demosthenes 21 *Against Meidias*.[40]

Commentators who delve beyond the issues of style and authenticity have mainly focused on the portrayal of Aristogeiton. As is typical in oratory,

---

[34] Wohl 2010: 51. Lape 2010: 72 notes that the Athenians did not always prosecute state debtors in these circumstances, but tended to turn a blind eye.

[35] Rubinstein 2000: 30n16 points out the circular argument of Dionysius: Demosthenes does not use vulgar language, so any speech using vulgar language cannot be by Demosthenes. See Choustoulaki 2019 for a detailed account of the long history of debate over authenticity. She notes that other ancient sources that discuss the speech do not question its authenticity (2019: 4). See Plin. *Epis.* 9.26; [Long.] *De subl.* 27.3 and Plut. *Dem.* 15.3.

[36] See most recently Harris 2018, who argues that the oration is a later imitation. See also Lipsius 1883; Schaefer 1887; and Sealey 1967. Choustoulaki 2019 argues against this position. See also Weil 1887; Mathieu 1947; Hansen 1976; Christ 1998: 56; MacDowell 2009; and Apostolakis 2014: 205–8. Blass 1893: 408–17 suggests the speech was a written exercise by Demosthenes.

[37] See Rubinstein 2000: 30–2 on the possibility that the speech was composed by a contemporary of Demosthenes, possibly one of the other co-prosecutors (30n15). See also Treves 1936: 252–8.

[38] Wohl 2010: 51. See also Choustoulaki 2019: 16. Sealey 1967: 254 argues for a later writer who made use of other fourth-century speeches when composing the oration.

[39] Worman 2008: 230–2. See also Wohl 2010: 51 and Apostolakis 2014: 206–7.

[40] Christ 2013: 214 notes that the orations attributed to Apollodorus that appear in the Demosthenic corpus do not share the portrayal of *philanthropia* that he detects in this speech and elsewhere in Demosthenes' work.

Aristogeiton's characterisation forms part of the story told by the prosecutors in their bid to persuade the jurors of their arguments, and the picture painted is not only one-sided, but is also created in an attempt to persuade rather than be completely accurate.[41] The speech is replete with a rich use of imagery and language associated with the vilification of opponents in oratory, and includes evocative themes and terminology inspired by familiar literary motifs and story patterns.[42] It is common for orators to malign the opposing speakers and their families in court cases, making extensive use of insults and information derived from malicious gossip to build a negative picture in the mind of the jurors.[43] This use of insults and stereotypes is intended to generate alienation of the speaker's opponent from the Athenians of the jury and hence allow him to win the case.[44] To this end, Aristogeiton is characterised like a villain from old comedy: he is argumentative and coarse, as well as abusive and threatening (25.36). He is a guard dog who eats the sheep himself rather than protecting them from wolves (25.40), just as Aristophanes depicts Cleon consuming the city rather than guarding it.[45] Like the scoundrel of old comedy who is driven out to the satisfaction of the audience, Aristogeiton, who is characterised as a *poneros* through the depiction of his aggressive, antisocial behaviour, should be removed from the city by the jurors who are encouraged to unite against him and expel him like a scapegoat.[46]

At the same time, Aristogeiton is portrayed as someone who is 'antithetical to democracy' and his acts of aggression are detailed, alongside the use of animal imagery, as a way of demonstrating his bestial savagery and form an argument that the jurors should not feel or act in a tolerant way towards him as he does not deserve their sympathy (25.76).[47] The Athenian men of the jury are imagined by the speaker as quasi family members who are tolerant towards one another to facilitate civic harmony.[48] However, contradicting the expected norms, and therefore being unworthy of the jurors' tolerance, Aristogeiton is shown as not only antisocial with his fellow citizens (25.51, 58, 63), and lacking in friends except his disreputable twin brother (25.79), but also as hostile and straightforwardly aggressive towards members of his own family.

---

[41] See Gagarin 2003 on the use of storytelling in Athenian legal cases and on the different ways each side might tell their stories (esp. 200–1 on Antiphon 3). See also Johnstone 1998.

[42] Gagarin 2003: 206 comments on the reliance on motifs from myth and literature in legal speeches. See also Porter 1997 and McHardy 2018 on Lysias 1.

[43] Hunter 1990.

[44] Worman 2008, Chapter 5. See also Kamen 2020, Chapter 3.

[45] Worman 2008: 231. See Ar. *Eq.* 259–63, 691–701, 1014–34; *Vesp.* 672–7, 970–2.

[46] Rosenbloom 2003.

[47] Christ 2013. See Lape 2010: 72–3 on the political context and the use of bestial imagery.

[48] Christ 2013: 217.

The details of Aristogeiton's behaviour towards his father are somewhat confused, though the gist is clear. It is alleged that when his father died, Aristogeiton refused to bury him and he would not pay those who buried him either (25.54).[49] This lack of respect towards his father indicates that Aristogeiton is at odds with social norms and expectations as far as his relationship with his family is concerned, but the account goes further in claiming that Aristogeiton acted violently towards the female members of his family. The speaker alleges:

> Not content with offering violence to his mother (πρὸς δὲ τῷ τῆς μητρὸς μὴ ἀπεσχῆσθαι τὼ χεῖρε), as you have just heard from witnesses, he actually sold his own sister – not indeed a sister by the same father, but his mother's daughter, whatever her parentage (for I pass that by) – yes, sold his sister for export, as is stated in the indictment of the action which was brought against him on these grounds by his good brother here, who in the present action will help to defend him. (25.55 trans. Murray)

The description of violence done to Aristogeiton's mother in this passage is not graphic and coheres to the principle that violence done to the bodies of women is not depicted in full detail in law court speeches, whereas the details of bodily injuries suffered by men can be fully articulated.[50] The speaker does not dwell on the experience or feelings of Aristogeiton's mother, but mentions her fleetingly only to throw a bad light on Aristogeiton's behaviour.[51] Aristogeiton's behaviour towards his parents goes not only against the laws of the city,[52] but also against the laws of nature (25.65).[53] Violence done to parents is never condoned,[54] and respect towards parents was a fundamental part of being an Athenian citizen, since having citizen parents was part of a man's claims to share in civic privileges.[55] Conversely, maltreating parents was a strong sign that a man was not deserving of having a share in these privileges, hinting as it did at the man's illegitimacy – the ideology of strong family relations between son and parents suggests that a man

---

[49] See also Dinarchus 2.8, 11 on Aristogeiton's treatment of his father, Cydimachus. See Worthington et al. 2001: 47n5.

[50] Omitowoju 2016. See also Cirillo 2009 on the graphic descriptions of the injuries sustained by the speaker of Demosthenes 54.

[51] See Johnstone 1998. As Gagarin 2003: 204 notes, women are present 'primarily as characters in stories told by men'.

[52] On laws regarding neglect of parents, see *Ath. Pol.* 56.6; Dem. 24.103–7; Is. 1.39 and 8.32; Todd 1993: 107–8. Roisman 2005: 42 notes that allegations of beating a mother are much rarer than allegations of a man's maltreatment of his father.

[53] Wohl 2010: 56.

[54] Llewellyn-Jones 2020: 392.

[55] Lape 2010: 74.

who is disrespectful to his parents or abusive towards them cannot truly be their son. At the same time as conjuring an image of the parents of Aristogeiton – two people who are themselves not worthy of Athenian citizenship (his father had wronged the state and been executed, his mother was apparently a metic),[56] and implying that Aristogeiton is not worthy of citizenship because he has inherited their flaws,[57] the speaker also plays on social expectations about good family relations to further damn his opponent and suggest that his behaviour towards his parents anyway means his citizenship is in doubt. A man who acts violently towards his own mother and mistreats his own father (albeit a criminal) cannot be expected to serve the city well. Similarly, Aristogeiton's behaviour towards his half-sister is intended to be shocking – a further indication that he cannot be trusted because of the way he defies social norms and lacks typical Athenian values. In selling his sister he treats her as a commodity rather than a family member and is opposed even by his own brother, currently his ally in this case.[58]

Two further instances of Aristogeiton's aggressive and antisocial behaviour are given in greater detail. In one example, Aristogeiton is said to have been shunned even within prison by his fellow inmates following his vicious attack on a man from Tanagra. The speaker alleges that he stole from this man and when challenged, went to strike him. In the ensuing fight it is claimed that Aristogeiton bit off the nose of his opponent (25.60–1). This episode demonstrates how far he is outside of the community when he is shunned even by prisoners.[59] His attacks are depicted as unjust (in that he had stolen from his fellow inmate then attacked him), antisocial, bloodthirsty and inhuman.[60]

The second episode recounts his treatment of Zobia, a woman who helped him in his hour of need, but whom he repaid with threats, violence and a foiled attempt to sell her into slavery. This episode is characterised as terrible (*deinos*) by the speaker indicating the way in which the jurors are to receive the tale:

> All this is bad enough, Heaven knows; but you shall hear another dreadful performance (πρὸς δὲ τούτοις τοιούτοις οὖσιν ἕτερον δεινόν, ὦ γῆ καὶ θεοί,

---

[56] See Kennedy 2014: 99–100 on the metic status of Aristogeiton's mother and sister.
[57] Rosenbloom 2003: 100. Lape 2010 has pointed out the issues with this argument, as Aristogeiton's alienation from his father shows that they do not share the same views.
[58] Rosenbloom 2003: 109. Schaps 1998: 168 comments that the passage is so overblown we cannot know the truth of the situation.
[59] Rosenbloom 2003: 113 and Wohl 2010: 56. See also Din. 2.9–10. Sealey 1967: 254 notes that Dinarchus mentions only the theft and not the vicious attack, and concludes that this part is probably fictional.
[60] 'He is a beast (*therion*, 8, 31, 58, 95; see Din. 2.10), a serpent or scorpion (52), a rabid watchdog who devours the flocks he claims to protect (40), a snake and a spider (96)'. Wohl 2010: 57. See also Worman 2008: 231.

πρᾶγμ' ἀκούσεσθε). On the occasion when he broke prison and ran away, he visited a certain woman named Zobia, with whom he had probably cohabited at one time. She kept him in safe hiding during the first few days, when the police were searching and advertising for him, and then she gave him eight drachmas journey-money and a tunic and a cloak and packed him off to Megara. When this same woman, who had been such a benefactress, complained to him, seeing that he was giving himself airs and making a great show here among you, and when she reminded him of her services and claimed some recompense, on the first occasion he cuffed her and threatened her and turned her out of his house (ῥαπίσας καὶ ἀπειλήσας ἀπέπεμψεν ἀπὸ τῆς οἰκίας). But when she persisted and, woman-like, went about among her acquaintance with complaints of his conduct (γυναίου πρᾶγμ' ἐποίει καὶ πρὸς τοὺς γνωρίμους προσιοῦσ' ἐνεκάλει), he seized her with his own hands and dragged her off to the auction-room at the aliens' registry, and if her tax had not happened to be duly paid, she would have been put up for sale, thanks to this man who owed his safety to her. (25.56–7 trans. Murray)

The main intention of this episode within the speech is to demonstrate Aristogeiton's unjust nature in that he repays a woman who has helped him and given him money by physically attacking her, threatening her, throwing her out of the house and attempting to sell her into slavery.[61] Aristogeiton goes against the social expectation of helping friends and harming enemies by harming the woman who has been a friend to him and helped him in his moment of need. As in the case of his violence against family members, his violence against someone who helped him demonstrates that he is also incapable of reciprocity to the city and the jurors should not be lenient towards him as he has shown no leniency towards others (25.81–4). This episode serves as 'a cautionary tale to the jurors: if he brutalises the woman who saved his life and tries to sell her into slavery, he can and will betray the jurors who save him'.[62]

The vocabulary used to depict the act of violence is highly suggestive of Aristogeiton's attitude towards Zobia. His initial attack on her is described using the verb *rapizo*, which is one of fifty-six words in this oration that do not occur elsewhere in Athenian forensic oratory.[63] The word does occur in other texts, though, notably in Herodotus's *Histories*, where it is used of Xerxes' lashing of

---

[61] Wohl 2010: 56. Kennedy 2014: 99 notes this episode indicates the bad character of Aristogeiton.
[62] Rosenbloom 2003: 109–10.
[63] Harris 2018: 216. See Choustoulaki 2019 for a refutation of Harris's argument about vocabulary.

the sea, to punish the sea for wronging him by breaking his bridges over the Hellespont (7.35.2) and of his armies' treatment of the sea's soldiers, driving them forward by lashing them with whips (7.223.3).[64] In the first instance, the violence is inflicted following the challenge of the sea to Xerxes' authority. His response is to chastise the sea as if it were human, and symbolically enslave it to himself by throwing fetters into it and lashing it. Similarly, in the second instance, the lashing of the armies of Xerxes indicates their servile nature compared to the free Greeks.[65] Based on these instances, this choice of word to describe violence indicates Aristogeiton's demeanour towards Zobia, whom he treats not just like a woman, but like an enslaved person, even going so far as to drag her through the streets like a war captive in an attempt to sell her into slavery.[66] Again here, his lack of appropriate reciprocity is made clear in that rather than repaying his debt, he sets out to make more money out of Zobia by selling her. The image conjured matches the other accounts of his greed, in which he takes things that do not belong to him and attempts to profit from them.[67]

The trigger for the violence is said to be Zobia's complaints when she remonstrates with Aristogeiton as he has not repaid the money she gave him when he made his escape from Athens while being sought by the Eleven for breaking out of prison. This complaint made by a woman is taken as a challenge to his authority by Aristogeiton and leads to a violent response aimed at preventing a further challenge.[68] The text refers both to Aristogeiton's threats and to actual physical violence demonstrating a similar arsenal to that which appears in the examples from Homeric epic (for example, where Zeus threatens Hera with violence and talks of a previous time when he acted upon his threats physically *Il.* 15.12–23).[69] In Aristophanes' *Lysistrata*, the protagonist also mentions the way in which her husband threatened her with violence because of perceived challenges to his

---

[64] It also appears at Hdt. 8.59 (see Plut. *Them.* 11), where those who start before the signal at the games are said to be punished. The term is used in Aristotle *Eud. Eth.* 2.1222b to refer to suitable levels of anger when a man is struck, and in the New Testament (Matt. 5.39) when Jesus exhorts his followers to turn the other cheek when struck, among other instances.

[65] On whipping as a punishment used against enslaved people, see Dem. 21.180. See Fisher 1998: 78; Schaps 1998: 169–70; and Roisman 2005: 72–3.

[66] See [Dem.] 59 on Phrynion's violent and abusive treatment of Neaera as if she were still enslaved after she has been freed. See Kennedy 2014: 104–6; Omitowoju 2016.

[67] On the depiction of Aristogeiton as a sycophant bringing lawsuits for his own financial gain, see Christ 1998: 56–8.

[68] See Llewellyn-Jones (2011 and 2020) on challenges to the authority of a husband as triggers for violence.

[69] Synodinou 1987: 15 notes that Zeus's threat has potency because of his previous acts of violence. See also Schaps 2006 on this example.

authority and her attempts to move away from the work of women into the political arena of men (Ar. *Lys.* 506–20). Notably, in both these examples the wife is cowed by the threat initially but ultimately continues with her challenges towards her husband and incursion into the male world of military decisions. In the oration, Zobia's response to Aristogeiton's violence is to persist with her challenge by seeking support from acquaintances, causing Aristogeiton to launch a second attack on her person by seizing her, dragging her off and attempting to sell her into slavery. In deciding to voice her complaints and persisting in challenging this man publicly because of his behaviour towards her, Zobia runs a considerable risk. As Freedman has set out, speaking out about the violence of someone both physically stronger than you and more powerful within society entails risks,[70] and in this case, the risk is to Zobia's freedom.

Even though the speaker makes clear that Aristogeiton has wronged her, Zobia's options are limited. Aristogeiton feels in a position of strength in maltreating Zobia because she is a woman and a metic and, therefore, unable to prosecute him herself through official channels, either to reclaim her money or to claim restitution for the assault.[71] Nor is there any indication that anyone brought legal proceedings on her behalf.[72] Nevertheless, Zobia has a sense of righteous anger resulting from Aristogeiton's violence and lack of reciprocity towards her, like male litigants at Athens.[73] By employing this righteous indignation to avoid the silence inflicted on her by the contemporary legal institutions and by levelling her own informal complaint (the verb ἐνεκάλει is resonant of a formal legal complaint), she makes use of unofficial channels to complain to her acquaintances about Aristogeiton's brutality and faithlessness. In this instance it is possible to see how Zobia's 'resistant anger pushes back against the normalizing abuse of silencing practices', as Bailey phrases it.[74]

Despite her gender and lowly status, the woman's use of gossip to complain about how she was treated means that the alleged ill-treatment becomes widely known, not just among low-status women, but also, apparently, among the male elite, including the speaker and, ultimately, the members of the jury. The example demonstrates that once shared broadly in public, this woman's complaint could affect how both men and women, of high and low status, viewed Aristogeiton,

---

[70] Freedman 2020: 18. See also Beard 2017.
[71] Kennedy 2014: 99–103. Neaera ([Dem.] 59) has little choice but to run away from Phrynion to get away from his abusive behaviour (Omitowoju 2016: 128).
[72] Kamen 2013: 47.
[73] Allen 2000: 50–72 connects the concepts of anger, reciprocity, status and honour with the legitimate male punisher who sought justice through the courts at Athens. Women were excluded from accessing this legal punishment.
[74] Bailey 2018: 103.

and Zobia's words could be used in an official channel to attack the man who had violently beaten her.[75]

Significantly, the speaker of this oration stresses that Zobia's reaction is not unique, but 'womanlike' (γυναίου). Women's ability to spread complaints about men is highlighted also by Aristotle (*Politics* 1313b), who associates this phenomenon with democratic societies.[76] In part, these characterisations capture women's lack of ability – they are unable to bring their own prosecutions or speak for themselves in court, so their use of gossip is 'womanlike' in that it is a response that occurs outside of the legal structures used by the socially and legally privileged (mainly elite men). Yet, gossip was significant still within legal contexts because of the use of character-based storytelling within them. As we have seen in discussing this oration, Athenians employed gossip in rhetoric to cast aspersions on their opponents in the law courts. As Aristotle (*Rhet.* 2.6.20) makes clear, people were inclined to employ gossip when they had been wronged, and gossip was open to women as much as to men of all social strata.[77] The presence in legal cases of women's gossip, including gossip spread by low-status members of society, demonstrates that the Athenians did not discriminate about the source, but took advantage of all kinds of gossip in their attempts to defeat their opponents. Through calculated use of gossip, women, non-citizens or enslaved people with no access to official legal channels wielded a potent weapon in their attempts to attain revenge against those who wronged them.[78] Seen in this light, a woman's ability to gossip could be a useful tool for her in attacking an enemy because gossip could move readily throughout the community, as Aeschines details: 'Attaching itself to men's life and conduct, talk travels unerringly and spontaneously throughout the city, like a messenger proclaiming to the public at large details of men's private behaviour' (1.127).[79] Moreover, this case makes clear through its use of the generalising reference to the complaints of Zobia as typical of women ('γυναίου πρᾶγμ' ἐποίει', 25.57) that this approach should be seen as representative rather than an exceptional example.

My reading of Demosthenes 25 *Against Aristogeiton* has centred on the violence committed against Zobia as well as the women in Aristogeiton's family, and

---

[75] McHardy 2018: 162.
[76] See McClure 1999: 29 on the potential for gossip to be 'subversive of social hierarchy'.
[77] For examples that depict a 'network' of male gossipers, see Hunter 1990: 302. On women's networks, see Wolpert 2000–1: 415–17. On enslaved people and prostitutes as conduits for gossip, see Dem. 50.48; Plut. *On Curiosity* 9 with Ober 1989: 149 and McClure 1999: 58.
[78] See above on Bailey's 2018 concept of knowing resistant anger.
[79] Hunter 1990: 302 claims: 'The deme, in other words, was no different from other small communities in being abuzz with gossip, which began with one's immediate neighbours, from whom nothing could be kept secret (Lys. 17.8)'.

demonstrated that this violence formed part of a picture painted by opponents of Aristogeiton showing him to be greedy, unjust and aggressive towards those closest to him, and by extension greedy, unjust and aggressive towards the city of Athens and its people. The actions of Aristogeiton are held up as wrong, for the most part because he is an opponent in a legal case (and indeed not a successful legal case), although it is also likely that these types of attacks are highlighted exactly because they would have been viewed as excessive and unwarranted. His violence demonstrates that he is a man without self-restraint, someone who inflicts his anger and control issues on those close to him and who consequently cannot be trusted with the care of the city. The example adds an extra dimension to the arguments put forward by scholars on violence against women in ancient Athens. The suffering of women is mentioned not to benefit or vindicate the women, but to provide colour in a depiction of the character of a man, and the descriptions of violence serve more as metaphors. Consideration of these points through the lens of feminist epistemology clarifies the way in which women are systematically silenced through the normative practices of restricting speech in legal cases to men and rarely focusing on issues affecting women. The accounts of women of low status are shared and used where they suit the purposes of the men who hear them and how they suit the purposes of the men who hear them, indicating their epistemic objectification. Yet, while Omitowoju is right to say that women are unable to seek legal recourse and that violence against them is not at the centre of legal disputes, nevertheless this example shows that women's unofficial reactions to abuse, using their 'knowing resistant anger' as Bailey expresses it, can make an impact against their abusers in that their complaints shape the public image of a person. Moreover, following the arguments of Karyn Freedman, Zobia's telling of her story serves to increase what she terms 'epistemic value', benefiting Zobia herself when those who listened to her story believed her and spread her version of events to others, as well as readers of this story who benefit from an increase in truth, knowledge and understanding of the lives of metic women at Athens as a consequence of Zobia's decision to speak out.[80]

---

[80] Freedman 2020: 2.

CHAPTER 5

Bodies of Knowledge: Diotima's Reproductive Expertise in the *Symposium*

Edith G. Nally

It is widely recognised that Plato holds radical views about women's intellectual abilities.[1] For example, *Republic* V declares that men and women have the same natures (455d5–6) and that the best women are therefore capable of ruling alongside the best men (456a5).[2] Other works from roughly the same period cast women as inferior and impose ultra-restrictive norms prohibiting their participation in the public sphere.[3] This paper investigates another of Plato's views that has received less attention as a potential protofeminist account: he sometimes draws an analogy between philosophy and childbirth. In the *Theaetetus*, for instance, Socrates compares the midwives' *techne* in birthing physical offspring to his philosophical *techne* in birthing psychic offspring (151c1–2). The *Symposium*

I would like to thank my fellow editors, Megan Bowen and Mary Gilbert, for their constant vision, guidance and friendship, in addition to the organisers and audiences at the 2021 Society for Classical Studies: Believing Ancient Women panel and the 2022 Ancient Philosophy Society for their helpful comments on prior drafts. Thanks also to Benjamin Jasnow for always lending me his expertise, for the untold hours spent discussing and improving my work, and for his extraordinary devotion to caring for our children.

[1] See, for example, Annas 1976; Okin 1979; Tuana 1994.
[2] Spellman 1982 argues that Plato persistently degrades women's capacities and demeanour elsewhere (see *Apol.* 35b; *Phd.* 60a, 112d; *Resp.* 395d–e, 557c, 605c–d; *Tht.* 171c; *Ti.* 42b–c, 76e, 91a; *Leg.* 944e).
[3] See Xen. *Oec.*, Ar. *Eccl.* and Ar. *Lys.*

claims that all humans are pregnant (κυοῦσιν, 206c1) in body or soul and that philosophical activity is a form of psychic reproduction arising from the desire to beget beautiful ideas (209a2–212c2). This paper asks how we ought to interpret these reproduction metaphors. What does Plato find valuable about women's expertise with gestation, childbirth and childrearing? Is their expertise a potential source of epistemic insight? And, if so, to what extent is this a radical or proto-feminist view?

Perhaps the strongest reason to doubt that Plato imbues women's reproductive expertise with epistemic importance lies in the fact that reproduction is a deeply bodily act.[4] Plato is well known for his 'psychophilia' and 'somatophobia'.[5] These tendencies are pronounced in the *Theaetetus*, where Socrates' *techne* is superior to that of the midwives because his concerns 'delivering men, not women, and in tending to the begetting of their souls, not their bodies' (150b8–9).[6] The midwife analogy does narrowly endorse the midwives' *techne*. However, since their proficiency is with bodily birth, it is supposedly less valuable than Socrates' philosophical skill. This is hardly a ringing endorsement of the epistemic weightiness of women's procreative expertise. Instead, it appears to be a canonical example of how the devaluation of bodily experience (in favour of objective, abstract, atomistic knowers) – beginning with the ancient Greeks and continuing through the European enlightenment – negatively impacts the appraisal of 'women's issues' as unworthy of serious intellectual study.[7]

The impetus for this paper, however, is that the *Symposium* treats childbirth differently. To begin with, the view in question is put forth by Diotima, the sole conversant woman in the dialogues, voiced by Socrates himself in the

---

[4] I use the contemporary English terms 'female', 'woman', 'feminine'/'male', 'men', 'masculine' to denote the two sex and gender roles in reproduction as viewed by many Ancient Greeks (see Hes. *Op.* 582–8; *Ti.* 91b–d; Arist. *Part an.* 727b–728a; Sor. *Gyn.* 1.8. 33, 1.10. 37). This terminology should not be taken to perpetuate a rigid, essentialist or binary view of sex, gender or reproduction. It does not assume that there are only two sexes or genders, nor that the Greeks thought so. It does not assume that the experience of conception, gestation, childbirth or childrearing belongs essentially to any sex or gender. It assumes only that in the ancient Greek literary and cultural sources addressed in this chapter, those sexed as females and gendered as women were those with the primary experience of childbirth and early childrearing.

[5] These terms are coined by Spellman 1982.

[6] The translation of Pl. *Theaet.* follows Burnyeat 1990.

[7] See the 'atomistic view of knowledge' in the Introduction to this volume and, especially, Bordo 1987. Others in this volume who discuss sensual, experiential, individual, personal, identity-laden ways of knowing in contrast to conceptions of the atomistic knower include Weiberg (Chapter 2), Gilbert (Chapter 3), Haley (Chapter 9), Bowden (Chapter 12) and Zimmermann Damer (Chapter 14).

midst of a hyper-masculine setting (where even the female flute player is dismissed [176e5]).[8] The best explanation of the appearance of a woman in this setting is that she addresses love's role in procreation; she has a certain amount of authority as a woman versed in birth and childrearing. Even so, Diotima appears to be far more than a woman planted to speak about women's issues. Her view is arguably the philosophical jewel in the crown of the dialogue, so much so that many think she is a proxy for Plato himself.[9] Furthermore, Socrates unironically endorses Diotima's teachings (201d1–6, 212b1–c2); Plato gives her pride of place among the other speakers (198a–199c[10]); and it is she who describes the 'ladder of love' which culminates in a familiar Platonic description of the form of beauty (210e–211d). Diotima has knowledge of the forms and is, therefore, epistemically successful by Plato's own lights.

This paper argues that Diotima's epistemic advantage derives, at least partially, from her gendered insight into erotic reproduction. We see this in the fact that the full meaning of the ladder of love, and her ensuing ethical conclusions, are inextricably linked to her theorising about gestation, birth and childrearing. The ladder of love treats philosophy itself as a form of birth resulting from the love of knowledge (210d1–6). Similarly, the central claim of Diotima's short but potent ethics is that the lover who is the closest to immortal is one 'who has begotten true virtue and nourished it' (τεκόντι δὲ ἀρετὴν ἀληθῆ καὶ θρεψαμένῳ, 212a4–5).[11] As a result, it appears that Plato imbues her epistemic standpoint – that of a woman versed in reproduction – with genuine philosophical authority. Unlike the *Theaetetus*'s narrow endorsement of the midwives' *techne*, the *Symposium* casts a woman's reproductive expertise as a potential source of philosophical insight.

In what follows, I call this the 'standpoint reading', after feminist standpoint theory. Feminist standpoint theory refers to a cluster of views that hold that oppressed groups sometimes have an epistemic advantage over their dominant counterparts, especially with respect to finding lacunae in dominant narratives.[12] A classic example from Marxist feminism holds that women, because they have historically cared for dependents, are in a better epistemic position to see how a capitalist patriarchy fails to meet people's needs.[13] Those who have been excluded from dominant power

---

[8] Pl. *Menex.* 235e8–236c6 attributes the funeral oration to Aspasia.
[9] Bury 1932: xxxix; Dover 1980: 137; Prior 2006: 148; Sheffield 2006: 66–74, esp. n33.
[10] Bury 1932 argues persuasively that Socrates' criticism sets his account apart from the speech of Agathon and the earlier speeches.
[11] The translation follows Nehamas and Woodruff 1989, with alterations noted.
[12] Hartsock 1983a; Collins 1990; Harding 1987 and 1993; Fricker 2007; Intemann 2016.
[13] Hartsock 1983a. For another discussion of the 'caregiver' standpoint, see Zimmerann Damer (Chapter 14, this volume). Others in this volume who give standpoint readings or use standpoint theory as an interpretative lens include Weiberg (Chapter 2), Gilbert (Chapter 3), Witzke (Chapter 7), Haley (Chapter 9) and Bowden (Chapter 12).

structures are in a better position to understand what is wrong with them. The standpoint reading of the *Symposium* views Diotima as knowing something about *erōs* that the dominant group, the other symposiasts (elite Athenian pederasts), do not.[14] Diotima's unique standpoint – her identity as a woman versed in reproduction – exposes a lacuna in their narratives about love. What she adds to the discussion, I shall argue, is that having *erōs* for something does not merely inspire one to pursue or possess it; by attending to reproducing women, we see that *erōs* also manifests as a desire to reproduce what is beloved and care for it. Diotima's standpoint is epistemically revelatory, then, because it exposes that love is a creative and laborious act.[15] In addition, her standpoint is ethically revelatory because it establishes that *erōs* is valuable not merely for making us pursue beauty, but because it causes lovers to intimately foster and nourish virtue in others. Understood in this way, Diotima is espousing something like a protofeminist ethics of care.

Most, however, have not read Plato's treatment of Diotima or the birth metaphor so favourably.[16] As such, after a brief synopsis of the passages supporting the

---

[14] This sort of privileged access is generally thought to be (1) earned via reflection, (2) by an oppressed/outsider individual or group; see, for example, Poole 2021 (cited in the Introduction). One might wonder if Diotima fits these criteria. With respect to (1), it is difficult to establish that her standpoint is earned since her history (whether she is fictional or historical) is excluded from the text. It is nevertheless noteworthy that Diotima is not merely passively reporting facts about her experience; instead, she is theorising about reproduction. This intimates a great deal of reflection on her part. With respect to (2), Diotima is clearly represented as an oppressed person/outsider by the text: her account is presented by Socrates in the symposiastic space, a setting in which women would have been largely excluded save as enslaved servants and entertainers, and have, on this occasion, been sent away altogether. In this setting, Diotima's gender and her gendered topic intimate her outsider status; it is almost as if Socrates sneaks a woman, who would not have been welcome otherwise, into the party.

[15] Nowhere do I mean to insinuate that Diotima is herself a mother. Whether Diotima is likely to have borne children is entirely up for debate. See Hobbs 2007: n40, who cites Halperin 1990 on the chastity/childbearing practices of priestesses and seers at the time.

[16] Though I sometimes write in ways that suggest clear authorial intention, this is inessential to my conclusions. The standpoint reading is viable whether or not Plato intended it: if we are 'optimistic' about Plato's intentions (see Sharrock 2020 in the Introduction to this volume), then this paper gives good evidence for thinking that he views women as having philosophically valuable experiences ignored by elite men. But if we are 'pessimistic', this paper shows that the text of the *Symposium* nevertheless supports the standpoint reading. This would be a 'releasing' interpretation, calling attention to something that made its way into a text without or despite authorial intention. Though we shall see evidence for taking an optimistic view – especially insofar as feminine birth imagery is inextricable from Diotima's most philosophically important conclusions – a more pessimistic reading would not be fatal to the viability of this interpretation.

standpoint reading, the majority of this chapter argues for its plausibility against various objections. Scholars have alleged (i) that the birth metaphor is, in fact, written largely from the perspective of the reproducing male, (ii) that the birth metaphor takes the perspective of the reproducing female but is purely appropriative, playing into masculine pregnancy imagery in the ancient Greek literary tradition and implying nothing positive about women's knowledge or abilities, and/or (iii) that, pace the *Theaetetus*, the ladder of love is so psychophilic and somatophobic that the *Symposium* ultimately advocates for completely non-embodied, and therefore genderless, philosophical practice. This essay reaches a very different conclusion: Diotimian erotic philosophising does rise above the bodily realm, yet, on her account, women's reproductive experiences hold key insights about the proper route to epistemic and ethical transcendence.

CHILDBIRTH ON DIOTIMA'S VIEW

Diotima's view is notoriously complicated, addressing love, beauty, goodness, immortality, the forms and virtue in the span of a few pages.[17] This section attempts to briefly draw out the significance of her reproductive theorising to her epistemic and ethical conclusions.

At the start of the speech, the young Socrates has misidentified the *telos* of Eros/*erōs*.[18] He initially thinks that love aims at the possession of beautiful things (204d8). This is wrong on two counts. First, beauty is not the sole aim of *erōs*; instead, it aims at whatever one finds good or valuable (204d9–206a5). Second, whereas Socrates thinks that possessing beautiful things satisfies love, Diotima argues that the true *telos* of love 'is giving birth (τόκος) in beauty whether in body or in soul' (206b5–6). This is because 'all humans are pregnant (κυοῦσιν) both in body and in soul, and when we reach a certain age our nature desires to reproduce (τίκτειν)' (c1–3).[19] So, Diotima concludes, 'what Love wants is not beauty, as you think it is' (206e3); instead, what Eros really wants is 'reproduction and birth in beauty' (τῆς γεννήσεως καὶ τοῦ τόκου ἐν τῷ καλῷ, 206e6). The birth metaphor is initially part of her attempt to combat a misunderstanding about what satisfies *erōs*. Socrates thinks that pursuing and possessing something beautiful will sate love, but what lovers really want is to reproduce and perpetuate what they value.

The reason that this is love's true *telos*, she continues, is that mortals desire immortality (207d3). Mortals attempt to reproduce different beautiful/good/valuable objects, in order to leave something behind when they die. There are two

---

[17] For a full reconstruction, see Sheffield 2006.
[18] Diotima herself seems to slip between Eros the god and *erōs* the drive, and to draw conclusions germane to both.
[19] The translation is my own.

ways to do this. The first is for those that are 'pregnant in body' and reproduce physical offspring (208e3–6). This is apparently an approximation of immortality on both the part of wild animals and humans, since in physical offspring something of what is beloved lives on (207a5–d4). Physical pregnancies are less successful in reaching love's *telos*, however, since what they produce is itself mortal (209d1–2). Better off are those who are 'pregnant in soul' with 'wisdom and the rest of virtue' (209a1–4). Psychic pregnancies produce offspring by implanting values or ideas in the souls of others (209b1–d1). Heroes like Achilles, poets like Homer and Hesiod, and lawmakers like Lycurgus and Solon are all lovers of the psychic sort (d1–e5), since each reproduced something (such as reputation, poetry, laws and so on) that has long survived his death. They are better off because their psychic offspring are longer lasting; ideas and values can last many generations. Of course, Diotima ultimately thinks that there is an even better way to reproduce. This brings us to the highest rites of love (210a3).

Most read the ladder of love as an ascent by which a lover climbs the 'rungs' or stages of erotic development.[20] For our purposes, it is notable that each rung describes (1) an object that the lover appreciates as beautiful/good/valuable and (2) a corresponding activity by which the lover attempts to reproduce/perpetuate that value. For example, the first-rung lover 'should love one body and beget beautiful [*logoi*] there' (210a8). The object of the first-rung lover's *erōs* is (1) a single body, and his reproductive activity concerns (2) perpetuating that individual's self-presentation. The second-rung lover realises that (1) 'the beauty of all bodies is one and the same' (210b3). Though it is not explicitly stated, it follows that he (2) begets beautiful *logoi* in all the people he encounters. The third-rung lover has the further realisation that (1) souls are more beautiful than bodies, and therefore (2) 'will seek to give birth to (τίκτειν) such ideas as make young men better' (210c2–3). The fourth-rung lover comes to appreciate (1) the beauty of laws and customs (210c4). This makes sense given that these are the avenues by which a society shapes its citizens' characters. The (2) associated reproductive activity is again left unstated, but it seems clear that the lover would aim to beget beautiful laws and customs.

At the fifth rung, Diotima describes philosophy itself as a reproductive activity (210d1–6):

After customs he must move on to various kinds of knowledge. The result is that he will see the beauty of knowledge and be looking mainly not at beauty in a single example – as a servant would who favoured the beauty of a little boy or a man or a single custom (being a slave, of course, he's low and small-minded) – but the lover is turned to the great sea of beauty, and, gazing upon this, he gives birth to (τίκτῃ) many gloriously beautiful ideas and theories, in unstinting love of wisdom (φιλοσοφία) . . .

---

[20] Price 2017: 184–5 gives an excellent overview.

Nussbaum suggests that the fifth-rung lover's beloved object is (1) the beauty of ideas as expressed in different disciplines, for example, the beauty of a mathematical proof, the beauty of a sonata or the beauty of an astronomical trajectory.[21] And, because he has a vast appreciation of beauty in many instantiations (d5), this enables a new reproductive activity: he now (2) 'gives birth to' many ideas by doing philosophy (d6). Thus understood, philosophy is the reproductive activity that accompanies valuing the beauty of ideas.

On the sixth rung, Diotima famously claims that the lover, by properly ascending the ladder, comes to love a final object, namely (1) beauty itself (211a–d). By having addressed the nature of beauty/value across many different instantiations – in bodies, souls, institutions and knowledge itself – the lover finally learns what beauty/value itself is (211a1–d1).[22] And, as was the case at every other rung, the lover then engages in a new reproductive activity. The final-rung lover seeks (2) 'to give birth not to images of virtue (because he is in touch with no images), but to true virtue (because he is in touch with true Beauty)' (τίκτειν οὐκ εἴδωλα ἀρετῆς, ἅτε οὐκ εἰδώλου ἐφαπτομένῳ, ἀλλὰ ἀληθῆ, ἅτε τοῦ ἀληθοῦς ἐφαπτομένῳ, 212a5–7). The final-rung lover understands what is truly beautiful/valuable and is therefore uniquely capable of becoming one 'who has given birth to true virtue and nourished it' (τεκόντι δὲ ἀρετὴν ἀληθῆ καὶ θρεψαμένῳ, 212a8). This sort of lover, Diotima claims, is most honoured by the gods and comes closest to achieving immortality (212a7–b1).

Though the full meaning of these conclusions will become clearer below, this short synopsis provides some initial support for the standpoint reading by showing the extent to which Diotima's insights about childbirth suffuse her view. Childbirth imagery appears in her redefinition of love's *telos*, the discussion of the different sorts of lovers, the ladder of love, and in the final lines of the account, where the lover who has 'birthed' and 'nourished' virtue is the closest to immortal. This is important since these parts of her speech are often thought to express Plato's mature ideas about epistemic and ethical transcendence. What this means, then, is that taking Diotima's standpoint into account – viewing her gendered expertise as philosophically meaningful – is crucial for understanding the full significance of the *Symposium*'s epistemic and ethical conclusions.

From the male standpoint

The first obstacle to the standpoint reading comes from a debate about how the *Symposium*'s reproduction imagery is sexed/gendered. Some think it is unclear from the language of the speech whether Diotima's focus is on the reproducing

---

[21] Nussbaum 1986: 180.
[22] My understanding is that the *kalon* is beauty/value itself. 'Value' is perhaps the better term, given the 'axiomatic role of the *kalon* in Plato's scheme of value' (Sheffield 2017: 217).

female. This is because she uses many sex- and gender-neutral terms, for instance, that humans being are pregnant (κυοῦσιν) or that they desire to beget (τίκτειν) (206c1–3). These and other terms (for example, γεννάω, 209b3) have English translations (for example, to 'conceive', 'bear' or 'birth') that seem to clearly connote what are considered 'female' or 'womanly' reproductive activities. However, in ancient Greek these terms can equally refer to what are considered male/masculine reproductive activities (to 'impregnate', 'beget' or 'bring into existence').[23] As a result, Diotima's reproduction imagery does not necessarily take the perspective of the reproducing female. Rather, she could be speaking primarily of the male role in reproduction. But if Diotima is not focused on female reproduction it is hard to make the case that her unique standpoint, her gendered expertise with childbirth, is philosophically revelatory.

A further reason to think her focus is on reproducing males is that much of the dialogue takes male pederastic relationships as the paradigm erotic relationships.[24] On this paradigm, evident in the other symposiast's speeches, *erōs* between a man and a woman is often considered base or anomalous. For example, the youthful Phaedrus gives Alcestis as an example of the bravery of lovers, noting that this is the case 'even if she is a woman' (179b5). Pausanias, who is perhaps emblematic of the *erastēs*,[25] includes women only in the basest form of erotic relationship. For him, it is 'the Eros of Aphrodite Pandemos'[26] who 'strikes whenever he gets a chance' and is therefore the sort of vulgar *erōs* felt by men attracted to women. These lovers don't mind less intelligent partners because they are attracted to bodies more than souls (181b1–5). By contrast 'the Eros of Aphrodite Ourania' strikes males who find pleasure in 'what is by nature stronger and more intelligent' (181c6–7).

---

[23] For discussion, see Dover 1980: 147 and Halperin 1990: 117. Evans 2006: 14–15 gives an efficient summary of the issue: '*[K]ueo* can mean conceive in the sense that a woman conceives a child and becomes is [sic.] pregnant; but with a male subject, it has a causal meaning, something like impregnate. *Tikto* works the same way. In the most abstract sense, it means bring into the world, engender; used with a female subject, it means bear, and with a male subject, beget. *Gennao* is used mostly with male subjects, but also with female.... In English, beget and conceive are thought to be conceptually different, one used solely of the male, the other solely of the female; but in Greek, each single verb covers the role that both genders play in procreation. Verbs like *kueo* and *tikto* are, in a sense, gender neutral...'.

[24] Edmonds 2000: 263 agrees.

[25] NB: Pausanias himself pushes the bounds of the pederastic paradigm beyond its limits, arguing that the older the beloved, the better (181d3–a5). In addition, his own life-long relationship with Agathon is referenced in Aristophanes' speech (193c2). This evidence reinforces viewing him as an extremist, a proponent of perpetual or lifelong pederastic practices.

[26] I have amended the translation here and below for clarity.

Pausanias views women as deeply bodily and therefore incapable of the sort of spiritual relationship fostered between men. Similarly, Aristophanes thinks that the strongest and manliest men will be drawn to pederastic relationships (192a5–b1) and states his conclusion in terms of the pederastic paradigm (193c5–9). Since women would likely have been cast as base, bodily and/or unintelligent in this milieu, it seems somewhat unlikely that Plato follows these views by imbuing a woman's account of erotic desire with genuine authority.

Hobbs appends to this an even stronger objection: the pederastic paradigm is not limited to the earlier speeches.[27] In fact, Diotima's own psychic lovers are described in *male* terms (209a–211d). This suggests that 'whatever else Diotima may be doing, she is certainly inviting us to see the older male *erastês* as "pregnant"; and whatever else he may be doing, Plato is both placing his discussion of *erōs* at least partly within the Athenian upper-class convention of pederasty'.[28] If this is correct, then, Diotima's childbirth imagery is not about females at all, but about male arousal and orgasm, which Diotima casts as pregnancy and birth.[29] Moreover, Hobbs adds, *Timaeus* 73b–c and 86c grant the common medical view that male semen contains all the parts of the animal within it, such that females are merely the receptacle for male seed.[30] This view is blind to female gametes and thereby reduces the female reproductive contribution to that of a nutriative womb. Aristotle famously holds a similar view, arguing that males possess seminal fluid which provides all of the child's formative qualities. Males are therefore the efficient cause of offspring.[31] Females, by contrast, have no seminal fluid and are solely the material cause, supplying matter in the form of nutrients, like blood, to grow the foetus.[32] Because Plato espouses this view, it is unclear whether Diotima's reproduction imagery should be thought to imply anything about female reproduction beyond the female body being the site of physical insemination by a male.

---

[27] Hobbs 2007: 254.

[28] Ibid. p. 254 notices: '[T]he superior spiritually pregnant lovers of 209a–211d are mainly spoken of as male: *ek neou* 209a–b; *ton andra* 209c; *tous neous* 210c; *tous kalous paidas te kai neaniskous* 211d. Indeed, at 211b they are explicitly said to be engaged in the "correct method of boy-loving" (*to orthôs paiderastein*)'.

[29] Hobbs is here summarising the views of Morrison 1964: 42–55; Dover 1980: 147; Stokes 1986; and Pender 1992: 72–86. To this list we might add Edmonds 2000: 267–8 and Price 2017: 181–2. See also Plass 1978: 47–55.

[30] See Galen *de Semine* 11.3.5–7. Although Galen himself argues against this view in 11.3.8–9.

[31] See Aristotle *Gen. an.* 727b–728a, where he famously devalues the female contribution even further, going so far as to label the female an 'infertile male'. See also Hippoc. *Genit.* 1.1–3.

[32] Ibid. 728a19.

These are serious objections. As a matter of response, let us first get clear on what is not up for debate: Greek medical texts *do* radically underestimate the role of females in procreation. The birth metaphor *does* use some sex- and gender-ambiguous terms. And, many of Diotima's conclusions are stated so as to apply to the male–male homoerotic paradigm.[33] It seems pretty clear, therefore, that the *Symposium* is weighing in on male erotic practices for a male audience. But none of this evidence precludes thinking that a woman's standpoint could be philosophically revelatory in arriving at these conclusions. Furthermore, this evidence is compatible with the stronger conclusion that Plato may be, in keeping with the *Republic*, including women among his ideal psychic lovers. After all, as we shall see in greater detail below, Socrates is engaged in a successful psychic relationship with Diotima in which she is the reproductive progenitor, implanting and rearing the proper values in Socrates' soul. We must be careful, then, not to let the *Symposium*'s misogynistic milieu or its focus on male erotic relationships occlude the fact that Diotima's feminine standpoint may nevertheless be philosophically meaningful.

A stronger response is available. Both the sex- and gender-neutral and the masculine reading of Diotima's reproduction imagery crumble upon closer inspection. In fact, one would have to ignore a litany of evidence to find Diotima's account sex/genderless or masculine.

First, while terms like κυοῦσιν, τίκτειν, τόκος and γεννάω apply to both male and female reproductive activities, these terms take on a decidedly feminine resonance in proximity to Diotima's claim that Beauty (ἡ Καλλονή) presides over childbirth as Moira or Eileithyia (206d3–4). These goddesses are significant in that the Moirai and Eileithyia are worshipped by women in association with pregnancy and childbirth. Thus, even if Diotima (Plato) bends the invocation of these figures to suggest that it is not they but Beauty (ἡ Καλλονή) who presides, this is nevertheless a recognisably feminine deity.

Second, Diotima uses a slew of terms that are not plausibly sex/genderless or male/masculine. Consider, for example, that the lover who is 'pregnant' and thus 'ripe' or 'swollen' (τῷ κυοῦντί τε καὶ ἤδη σπαργῶντι, 206d9) is released from 'labour pains' (ὠδῖνος, 206e1) by beauty. While Diotima may apply these terms to a male lover, their *literal* meanings concern female reproductive experience. σπαργάω is typically used of nursing mothers.[34] ὠδῖνος refers to labour pains during childbirth.[35] The account of how *erōs* affects wild animals also seems to be

---

[33] Of course, this is not to say that Plato, here or elsewhere, condones intercourse within these relationships. *Leg.* 636c–e famously reproaches same-sex intercourse.
[34] *LSJ* σπαργάω A.I.
[35] *LSJ* ὠδίς A.I.; see *Theaetetus* 148e5–6, where *Theaetetus* is having 'labour pains' (ὠδίνω). What this entails is that he is not empty (κενός) but pregnant (ἐγκύμων). Though again applied to a male pregnancy, this is clearly an image of female childbirth.

largely from the female perspective: animals are sick with erotic desire first about procreation and 'then, about the nourishment of the new-born' (ἔπειτα περὶ τὴν τροφὴν τοῦ γενομένου, 207b2–3).[36] In addition, she mentions that animals go to great lengths to nurture (ἐκτρέφω, 207b5) their young, both by protecting them and, when necessary, forgoing food to feed them. There is good evidence to suggest that the nourishment, protection and nurturing of infants would have generally fallen to women in the ancient Greek household.[37]

Third, the so-called 'ladder of love' employs an image tightly linked to Athenian female fertility rites.[38] The exact text from which the passage takes its name claims that to love correctly one must 'ascend' (ἐπανιέναι) from loving the beauty of one body to loving the beauty of many bodies, and so on, 'as if on the rungs [of a ladder]' (ὥσπερ ἐπαναβασμοῖς, 211c4).[39] Remarkably, ladder imagery frequently appears in connection with both the Adonia, as a symbol of the route to the ritual's location on the rooftop, and in Athenian nuptial rituals, as a symbol of female fertility and life transitions.[40] In the context of the Adonia, ladders are especially indicative of Aphrodite Ourania, since she in particular was the consort of Adonis.[41] Ladders also appear more generally in scenes depicting women entering marriage and were left as votive offerings at the shrine of Nymphe on the Acropolis, likely as a utilitarian image of access to women's quarters and/or bridal chambers.[42] The ladder is, therefore, an important Athenian image, associated with the feminine transition to marriage and fertility. Furthermore, Diotima's choice of this widely recognisable image, one associated with Aphrodite Ourania, no less, subtly undermines Pausanias's claim – arguably the dialogue's chief pederast's claim – that heavenly *erōs* is purely male. The image of the ladder is a potentially potent reminder to Plato's audience, therefore, that Aphrodite Ourania also has important connections to female life transitions.

---

[36] The translation is my own.
[37] See Xen. *Oec.* 7.17–29, which argues that, like the 'queen bee', the woman in the household would be in charge of the shelter, nourishment and protection of young children. This is because men are, by nature, more suited to activities outside the house (7.23).
[38] For discussion of Diotima and the Elusinian rites celebrating fertility, see Evans 2006: 22. Edmonds 2017: 196–7 argues persuasively that the text makes use of language and imagery familiar from other mystery rites, including the rites of the Corybantes, the Orphica and Dionysis.
[39] *LSJ* -βασμός v. -βαθμός A.2.
[40] Rosenzweig 2004: 63–8. The *Adonia* were a yearly, city-wide fertility ritual that took hold in the middle of the fifth century, in which women climbed to rooftop gardens and mimicked Aphrodite mourning her consort Adonis.
[41] Ibid. p. 65.
[42] Ibid. p. 66–7. Larson 2012: Section 8 notes that, although marriages were primarily undertaken for reasons apart from love, 'the erotic aspects of marriage were not ignored, especially in the rituals surrounding marriages'.

Fourth, and most importantly, in the conclusion of the ladder of love, the ideal lover ultimately uses his understanding of beauty to beget (τίκτειν, 212a3) true virtue. As we have seen, τίκτειν is plausibly sex- and gender-ambiguous. But Diotima further claims that the lover 'who has given birth to true virtue and nourished it' (τεκόντι δὲ ἀρετὴν ἀληθῆ καὶ θρεψαμένῳ, 212a4–5) will be most honoured by the gods. θρεψαμένῳ is noteworthy, as it often denotes the care of a young child by a mother or nurse. For instance, 'a boy was called τρεφόμενος only so long as he remained in the charge of the women, that is until his fifth year'.[43] It also shares a root with τὴν τροφὴν at 207b2–3, which we saw has connotations with ancient Greek women's household roles as those who nourish infants. Once again these terms are literally about women's reproductive experiences. Diotima is clearly evoking images of ancient Greek mothers and caregivers.

It should now be clear, however, that this also affects the passage's non-literal or metaphorical meaning. The ladder of love is effectively claiming that the psychic lover must – like a young woman who climbs the ladder to marriage, sexual union and motherhood, where she bears and nurtures offspring – undergo a similar transition. The psychic lover must climb the psychic ladder to union with the forms, before bearing and nurturing virtue in others. Diotima's gesture to motherhood would have a certain cultural resonance: what it would mean for an ancient Greek woman to birth and nourish her offspring would be to take an intimate, laborious, and time-consuming role in the life of another person. It turns out, then, that the psychic lover should act as mother and caregiver to the virtue he begets in others, an intimate nurturer and caregiver to the soul.[44] This stands in stark contrast to the common pederastic view that a lover is like a father or progenitor to virtue.[45] On this reading, Diotima is arguing that the Athenian pederastic paradigm fails to account for what love fully is. It fails to account for what *erōs* does to women – it makes them want to reproduce and rear their offspring. As a result, psychic lovers cannot merely inseminate their beloveds with value; they must gestate, birth and nurture their virtue as well. Viewing the birth metaphor purely from the perspective of the reproducing male risks further obscuring this key facet of her ethical worldview: inculcating true virtue in another person will require a motherly, intimate and laborious commitment to that person.

There is so much evidence that the birth metaphor is presented from the perspective of reproducing females/women – from the perspective of an intimate

---

[43] *LSJ* τρέφω A.II.
[44] Nightingale 2017: 159 sees the lover as a 'mother' of discourse. She usefully compares this to the seed metaphor at *Phdr.* 278a–b, where the lover is more clearly a 'father' of discourse.
[45] Note the frequent connections of pederasty and parentage, in particular the *erastēs* in the role of a father/disciplinary figure. See Ar. *Nub.* 988–1000; Xen. *Symp.* 8.16–22, 9.1. For more on this phenomenon, see Skinner 2013: 76–7 and Price 2017: 182.

caregiver, no less – that we should ask why so many have attempted to prove otherwise. Perhaps the value of Diotima's gendered standpoint has been hard to see because Plato is so misogynistic elsewhere. Perhaps her gendered views have been obscured by the fact that her conclusions are applied to male lovers. Perhaps. Yet feminist epistemologists have long supposed that when one finds a persistent and engrained refusal to acknowledge the value of a woman's standpoint, it is worth asking who the devaluation serves. It is worth asking, then, who is served by the long list of Platonists who have thought Diotima's birth metaphor is either sex/genderless or takes the perspective of the reproducing male.

Appropriating the feminine?

The previous section established that Diotima's reproduction imagery is often decidedly feminine. Moreover, the full meaning of her conclusions are obscured when read from a sex/genderless or male perspective. However, it also showed that her psychically pregnant lovers, those whom the text bids us to emulate, are the familiar male lovers of the pederastic tradition (209a–211d). This gives rise to a second challenge to the standpoint reading. Scholars like duBois think that the birth metaphor is, therefore, appropriative. Plato takes insights from female birth and childrearing practices and applies them to male psychic lovers. As duBois puts it, 'the male philosopher becomes the site of metaphorical reproduction, the subject of philosophical generation'.[46] If so, however, then the birth metaphor likely does not support thinking that Plato values Diotima's gendered standpoint, or women's reproductive expertise, more generally. Instead, Plato could simply be, like others in the Greek literary tradition before him (see *Theog.* 885–929), attributing women's procreative abilities to men both to assert masculine domination over creation and/or as an image of men's intellectual paternity.[47]

A closely related objection takes Plato to be using Diotima's gendered standpoint for any number of cultural or literary effects without finding her expertise epistemically valuable. Plato might, for example, be casting Diotima as a foreign woman (she is from Dorian Mantinea [201d2]) with divine foresight (201d5) and familiarity with the mysteries (210a–212c) in order to exoticise her. The rest of the dialogue arguably caricatures different Athenian personalities (the youthful *eromenos*, persistent *erastes*, the natural philosopher, comedian, and tragedian); perhaps, then, Diotima is another stock character, the mystagogue.[48] But this would likely have the effect of devaluing her epistemic standing. If Diotima is divinely inspired, then her views do not result from her own epistemic doing. She

---

[46] duBois 1988: 182–3.
[47] Zeitlin 1985: 88 and Hong 2016 defend the former claim; Leitao 2012 the latter.
[48] Evans 2006 and Edmonds 2017 add fuel to this possibility.

merely gets epistemically lucky by being selected by the gods. Similarly, Belfiore charges that the birth metaphor may be largely comic or insulting, since Plato is thereby casting the psychic *eromenos* in 'the disgraceful, passive, feminine role in intercourse'.[49] Maybe, then, Plato is having an elaborate laugh. These objections amount to the same charge as the appropriation challenge: Plato may recognise Diotima's gendered standpoint for some reason apart from thinking it gives her genuine philosophical insight.

There are a number of avenues by which to reply.[50] Perhaps the most direct is to recall that the text repeatedly suggests that Diotima is an epistemic and moral authority. First, consider her introduction. Socrates says that he learned from her in his youth about the nature of love, claiming that she is wise about love and many other things (201d2–3). Diotima has wisdom, then, not merely *techne* as the midwives of the *Theaetetus*.[51] She also supposedly 'put off the plague for ten years by telling the Athenians what sacrifices to make' (201d3–4). This detail locates her in the Athenian social-historical timeline; she is older than Socrates and directly responsible for postponing one of the more tumultuous events in recent memory, an event that utterly disrupted the laws and social norms of the time.[52] This detail highlights her practical insight. While she may be an older

---

[49] Belfiore 2005 (unpublished abstract) surmises that: 'there are good reasons for believing that Socrates' audience would have found the idea of male pregnancy absurd and even offensive. In Euripides' *Bacchae* (286–97), Teiresias asks Pentheus if he laughs at the story of the "double birth" of Dionysus, to whom Zeus gave birth after sewing the foetus into his thigh. Moreover, to suggest that a man in a homosexual relationship was pregnant was a serious insult, attributing to him the disgraceful, passive, feminine role in intercourse. According to Plut. *Am. narr.* 768F, the tyrant Periander was killed by his beloved after Periander asked him, "Are you pregnant yet?" Diotima's idea that it is the *erastes* who is pregnant is even more offensive, for it casts in a ridiculous and humiliating light the active partner in the relationship that is idealised by all of the symposiasts and by Diotima herself'.

[50] One promising avenue, which this paper does not have the space to pursue, is Diotima's resemblance to Pythagorean women. The Pythagorean women were mostly Dorian, were known for subscribing to rules governing everyday life (including sex), and observed mystery rites (see Pomeroy 2013: 1, 7). Plato's characterisation of Diotima, as a foreign woman with knowledge of reproduction and the mysteries, may therefore serve to cast her as a Pre-Socratic, Pythagorean woman. If this is the case, then her exoticisation would be less a mark of her epistemic devaluation than a mark of her philosophical lineage.

[51] Moreover, her wisdom is about *many other things*. Wisdom is elsewhere differentiated from other, lesser claims to know in precisely this way; see *Ap.* 22c. Thus understood, Plato seems to be making a sincere endorsement of Diotima's epistemic stance: she is a wise woman *in many respects*.

[52] Thuc. 2.53.

woman and an outsider, Diotima's teachings once saved the Athenians, if only for a time. What she has to say is worth hearing. Second, the text insinuates a tutelage between the young Socrates and the older Diotima (207a4–5, c4–6). In the ladder of love, she teases him in a familiar way (210a1–2) before scolding him for failing to pay attention at a critical moment (210e3). They have something like a mentor–mentee relationship in which Diotima is the clear authority figure.

Third, as has already been mentioned, Diotima has epistemic success by Plato's own standards. She knows that the form of beauty is entirely beautiful, unchanging, simple, unified and exists apart from the material world (211a2–b5).[53] She also describes the participation relation, since particular beautiful objects participate in the form without affecting its reality (211b4–5). These are the same metaphysical details Plato emphasises elsewhere in descriptions of the forms.[54] So, it is from her mouth and by considering her unique point of view that one of his own most characteristic doctrines is revealed to the reader. More remarkable still is that, while the forms are arguably a Platonic invention, Diotima's account gives them an imagined pre-Socratic provenance.[55] The text effectively credits Diotima with passing the theory of forms to Socrates, who, we assume, passes them to Plato. One cannot help but see traces of Diotima's views about psychic reproduction in this (imagined) genealogy. She reproduces ideas in Socrates. Socrates reproduces them in Plato. Plato is reproducing them in the reader. Each therefore does what the most successful psychic lovers do; each appreciates what is truly valuable and nourishes that same understanding in another (211d–212c). Diotima would appear to be something like Socrates' psychic progenitor (or better yet his psychic mother). That means she is also Plato's psychic grandmother and the matriarch of one of the most successful philosophical lines in all of history. Diotima, Socrates, Plato (and future generations of Platonists) are thereby made out to be just the sorts of lovers who reach love's true *telos*. They are immortalised by having reproduced their understanding, passing it on through the generations of a lengthy philosophical family tree.

Fourth, Socrates non-ironically endorses Diotima's view in the concluding frame. Socrates, who questions everything, who notoriously chooses death over abandoning the elenctic life, wholly accepts Diotima's view of love (212b2–c3):

> This, Phaedrus and the rest of you, was what Diotima told me. I was persuaded. And once persuaded, I try to persuade others too that human nature can find no better workmate for acquiring this than Love. That's why I say that every man must honour Love, why I honour the rites of Love

---

[53] Blondell 2007: 156 notices this.
[54] *Phd.* 65d–66a, 100c; *Resp.* 476a–e; and *Phdr.* 250b.
[55] Pomeroy 2013: 7 draws a connection between Diotima's Mantinean provenance and the Pythagorean women.

myself and practice them with special diligence, and why I commend them to others. Now and always I praise the power and courage of Love so far as I am able. Consider this speech, then, Phaedrus, if you wish, a speech in praise of Love. Or if not, call it whatever and however you please to call it.

In a rare moment, Socrates claims to be persuaded (πέπεισμαι, b2) by Diotima. Of course, this acceptance is not uncritical; he appears to have changed his mind through questioning and over a number of meetings. Diotima is not merely the mother of Socrates' views on love, then, she is also at least partly responsible for his own philosophical method, a method by which he, in turn, has attempted to nourish virtue in the souls of others. The elder Socrates confirms this influence. It is owing to Diotima that he practises these highest rites of love, giving birth to virtue in others through philosophical understanding. In the closing lines of the speech, Plato is, therefore, encouraging readers to understand Socrates' characteristic method, perhaps even his gadfly-ery, as an act of reproductive love. Following Diotima's advice and example, he has attempted to properly rear the Athenians by generating and nurturing in them a proper understanding of what is valuable.

Given the reverence Socrates shows Diotima and the seriousness with which he regards her views, it looks rather unlikely that Plato is using her feminine standpoint purely to some exoticising or humorous effect. The appropriation challenge is also considerably weakened. While Plato does use male pregnancy imagery, in keeping with a longer tradition of appropriating women's experience, it should now be clear that the male philosopher is not, as duBois surmises, the sole locus of philosophical reproduction. After all, the *Symposium* shows Diotima nurturing in Socrates the very sort of understanding that a psychic lover nurtures in a beloved. Moreover, this understanding arises from her uniquely feminine view to *erōs* – a view that has been left out of the male-centric Athenian pederastic paradigm. Diotimian *erōs*, which Diotima practises with Socrates and Socrates has gone on to practise with others, aims at the perpetuation of value through the same sort of laborious commitment to the soul that a caregiver provides to her offspring. Thus, the *Symposium* suggests that women like Diotima can and should engage in the very sort of psychic relationship often thought to elude women and disqualify them from participating in pederastic educational practices.

Transcending gender?

A final challenge to the standpoint reading arises from Diotima's psychophilic and somatophobic tendencies, especially by devaluing physical reproduction in favour of psychic reproduction. As is the case elsewhere in the dialogues, she seems to view embodiment as inessential for knowing and looks down on material notions of love (210d3–4).[56] Hobbs argues on this basis that Diotima's view entails that gender itself is irrelevant to Diotimian enlightenment:

> Diotima bids us to transcend, as far as possible, not just our gender but, ultimately, even our humanity itself, in an attempt to have intercourse with and perhaps emulate, as far as we can, the non-human and non-gendered Forms. Biological sex and cultural gender and all permutations of their relation are part of the corporeal world of becoming and impermanence: the final goal is the incorporeal, eternal realm of being manifest in the Forms. This is the ultimate context in which Plato's use of female imagery should be viewed. . . . I submit, therefore, that Plato is chiefly concerned not with 'appropriating the feminine' but with liberating men and women alike from inessential bodily and cultural constraints.[57]

On this account, Diotima (Plato) would ultimately reject the importance of gender altogether.[58] Of all the challenges thus far this may be the most attractive, since it aligns the *Symposium* with the rationalist view of gender in *Republic* V, where women are as capable of ruling alongside the best men if they have the same intellectual capacities. There Plato seems so interested in the soul, so exceedingly psychophilic, that he finds a person's gender largely if not entirely inconsequential. These tendencies present an entirely different sort of challenge to the standpoint reading. If Hobbs is correct, then nothing about our embodied identity, gendered standpoint included, has any special bearing on the psychic/philosophical world. This is because corporeality is inconsequential for understanding the incorporeal world of the forms.[59]

There are, however, three key reasons to reject this view. The first is simple: we have already seen that the language of Diotima's speech is, at times, uniquely feminine. Plato is, therefore, simultaneously highlighting Diotima's gender and imbuing her with epistemic authority. If Plato ultimately thinks that her gender has no bearing whatsoever on matters of philosophical importance, one might wonder why he chooses to highlight it.

The second reason to reject Hobbs's reading is that it assumes that because Diotima is a psychophile and somatophobe – because she thinks the highest form of love is not for particular embodied individuals but for incorporeal forms – she

---

[56] See *Phd.* 64c–67b.
[57] Hobbs 2007: 271.
[58] Evans 2006: 15 reaches a similar view on the basis of the gender-ambiguous language of the birth metaphor.
[59] This is an atomistic reading. See the Introduction to this volume for 'atomism'.

would ultimately conclude that gender itself is inconsequential in the psychic realm. But this rests on the wrongheaded assumption that gendered experiences are just bodily experiences. Surely, however, what Diotima's account suggests is that differently gendered people have different psychic profiles. Gender roles may be (historically) assigned largely due to bodily characteristics; for example, nursing a child in the ancient world falls to those with mammary glands. Yet this is not to say that all aspects of these roles are bodily. Surely, after all, nursing a child has psychic ramifications beyond being a physical or bodily act. Surely, one could gain some psychic insight by having stood in such a relationship (or carefully studied such relationships) to another individual. Diotimian love might be psychophilic, then, but this is not a good reason to think that her gendered experiences cannot illuminate the psychic realm.

Third, Hobbs's charge also assumes a common, albeit wrongheaded, view about the impersonality of Diotimian *erōs*. Vlastos famously comments on the moral strangeness of her account: her highest form of *erōs* aims at union with the form of beauty itself, something completely inhuman and impersonal (210d1–4).[60] If she values immaterial forms more than living, breathing persons, Hobbs surmises, then this further supports thinking that Diotima's worldview transcends gender altogether. Yet the standpoint reading has begun to expose a reason to doubt the impersonality of Diotimian love. In particular, we have seen that the ideal lover not only pursues communion with (1) beauty itself but also goes on to (2) give birth to and nourish virtue (212a4–5). Scholars writing about the moral strangeness of her view have tended to focus heavily on (1) the object of Diotimian *erōs*, thinking it odd that the lover has erotic desire for a form. But this is, at best, a partial reading, since the lover also (2) gives birth to and nourishes virtue. Furthermore, it is worth asking in whom this birthing and nourishing takes place. One interpretation is that the lover is engaged purely in his own moral upbringing.[61] Yet it is hard to see how this would be analogous to a form of reproduction. If this were so, there would be no offspring left behind – no approximation of immortality since nothing would outlast the self – as is the case in all other types of physical and psychic reproduction (207d4–5, 209d4). Another interpretation is that this birth and nourishment happens in another person. This makes better sense of the reproduction image, since on this view there is an offspring (an understanding of what is valuable, sown and grown in another person) which outlasts the progenitor.[62] And, if so, if the ideal lover births and nourishes virtue in someone else, then Diotima's account is far less impersonal than it may at first have seemed. Bodily longing may be unimportant

---

[60] Vlastos 1973.
[61] Edmonds 2000: 266 sees the entire reproductive process taking place within the lover himself.
[62] See 209d4.

to her vision of love, but the proper sort of lover will not leave behind or devalue personal/social relationships altogether. Whereas readers like Vlastos and Hobbs think that the highest form of Diotimian love consists in psychic communion between abstract, atomistic knowers and the forms, this is simply *not* the most convincing reading of her ideas about virtue. Instead, it seems that by analogy to human reproduction, the ultimate expression of love is the perpetuation and nourishment of the proper understanding of value in another living, breathing person.

In fact, Diotima might be thought of as expressing something like a protofeminist 'ethics of care'. 'Care ethics' refers to a group of contemporary views, arising out of the women's movement of the 1970s, which take the primary subject matter of ethics to be our relationships with others. Care ethicists think gender is revelatory in ethical reasoning, since the male-dominated theories of the recent past miss out on key ethical insights that are easily gleaned from women's experiences as caregivers.[63] In contrast to the absolutist/universalist traditions of utilitarianism (Mill) and deontology (Kant), both of which focus on moral principles and abstract, genderless ethical reasoners, care ethicists argue that moral understanding and instruction should focus on examining a particular agent's web of relationships, dependencies, needs, commitments and so forth. Diotima seems to be espousing an ethics of care based on her understanding of how *erōs* functions in women's lives: she argues from this standpoint to the conclusion that the best sort of life requires us not only to enlighten ourselves, pursuing understanding of what is truly valuable, but also to intimately foster and nourish that understanding in others. On her account, love is choice-worthy for human beings, then, not merely because it makes us desire personal enlightenment, but because it causes us to turn our focus to caring for the epistemic and moral agency of others.

CONCLUSION

Perhaps the strongest reason to favour the standpoint reading is that it is philosophically more revelatory than a sex/genderless or masculine one. We have already seen a number of arguments to this effect. We have seen that, by analogy to physical reproduction, Diotima establishes that the ideal form of love is procreative. Just as mothers seek sexual union, give birth to children and nourish them, so too must the psychically pregnant lover seek union with the forms before birthing and nourishing true virtue in their protégés. This conclusion would remain

---

[63] Most care ethicists do not essentialise these experiences. The claim is not that women are more naturally caring. Instead the claim seems to be that women have these experiences, historically, in virtue of social norms dictating gender roles. These experiences are nevertheless ethically valuable, giving women key ethical insights that are easily missed by male theorists without similar experiences.

obscured if we attempted to understand it from a sex/genderless or masculine perspective. What is obscured is that nourishing virtue in another person is an act of intimate care. A lover must commit to fostering, with the commitment by which a caregiver nourishes a child, the proper understanding of value in another person.

By failing to consider the uniquely feminine aspects of Diotima's standpoint – that for ancient Greek women the effect of *erōs* is to sustain an interest beyond their own – many interpreters have failed to see the nuance of her ethics. In fact, it is this failure that has led so many to think her account of love is impersonal. But her ethics are anything but impersonal. It turns out that, for her, moral enlightenment is only half about perfecting one's individualistic understanding of value, climbing the ladder of love in pursuit of union with beauty itself (something commentators have focused on in spades); it is equally about deploying that understanding to intimately care for the moral development of another. This conclusion has been largely misunderstood because it is expressed by a woman drawing on shared cultural understandings about conception, birth and childrearing. Recognising that the text highlights and imbues this uniquely feminine standpoint with epistemic authority promises, therefore, to more fully illuminate Diotima's revolutionary ethics.

CHAPTER 6

Monumental Presence and Absence: Approaching the Material Traces of Historical Women in the Classical World

Patricia Eunji Kim

Σπάρτας μὲν [βασιλῆες ἐμοὶ] πατέρες καὶ ἀδελφοί,
ἅ[ρματι δ' ὠκυπόδων ἵππων] νικῶσα Κυνίσκα
εἰκόνα τάνδ' ἔστασε· μόν[αν] δ' ἐμέ φαμι γυναικῶν
Ἑλλάδος ἐκ πάσας τό[ν]- δε λαβὲν στέφανον.
Ἀπελλέας Καλλικλέος ἐπόησε.

Kings of Sparta are my fathers and brothers
And I, Cynisca, winning the race with my chariot
Of swift-footed horses, erected this statue. I assert
That I am the only woman in all Greece who won this crown.[1]
Apelleas son of Callicles made it.

Etched onto the surface of a limestone base, this epigram, written in the voice of Cynisca, marks her triumph as the first woman to have winning horses at an Olympic chariot-racing event in both 396 and 392 BCE.[2] Found just north of the Prytaneum, the fragmentary base was once a pedestal for a monumental

---

[1] *IvO* 160.
[2] Museum of the History of the Olympic Games of antiquity, inv. No. Λ 529. The fragmentary base measures approximately 49 cm in length and 34.2 cm in height.

installation that would have stood amongst heroes, gods and kings within the sacred Altis at Olympia. Writing of these monumental honours almost five centuries later, the traveller and historian Pausanias offers more clues about what the bronze sculptural installation may have looked like. Pausanias tells us that Cynisca's victory monument stood next to the statue of the triumphant Olympic equestrian athlete Troilus and nearby the Temple of Hera (where other votives to Spartan kings and heroes could be found); archaeologically, Hera's temple was located near the Prytaneum, where the base was recovered. The monument was crafted by the sculptor Apelleas and included a portrait statue of Cynisca, a horse jockey and four horses dragging a chariot (*quadriga*).[3] As Pausanias continues to describe his tour of the Altis, he mentions another sculptural monument of bronze horses that was dedicated by Cynisca as a token of her Olympic victory within the Temple of Zeus;[4] some scholars think that a small base that was also inscribed with Apelleas's name and excavated from the *pronaos* of Zeus's sanctuary may have been this very dedication.[5] Cynisca and her accomplishments were made visible throughout the sacred and monumental Altis, while the above inscription takes the voice of the Spartan dynastic daughter to emphasise that she was the agent of her own victory and public representation.

At home in Sparta, Cynisca also received honours across the city's monument landscape. Again, Pausanias tells us a hero-shrine or *heroon* for Cynisca was set up at the Platanistas or Plane-Tree Grove, which comprised an artificial island surrounded by water, and was the site of many youth contests.[6] Further on, Pausanias describes that her *heroon* was built nearby or alongside other shrines for mytho-historical and heroic Spartan men. In addition to textual descriptions of her hero-shrine among the plane trees, a Doric capital inscribed with the name 'CYNISCA' was found at the Menelaion, on a bluff overlooking the Eurotas.[7] The textual and archaeological evidence, though fragmentary, both speak to the monumental presence of Cynisca, who was, evidently, materially embedded within Sparta's landscape that appealed to the collective memory of heroes and victors.

The memory of Cynisca was intentionally crafted throughout the ritualised monument landscapes of both Olympia and Sparta. Yet writers and thinkers, both in antiquity and long afterwards, have seriously debated the nature of Cynisca's triumph, specifically her role and agency in securing these athletic victories. In this essay, I review the status of Cynisca and her monumental presences within history

---

[3] Paus. 6.1.6.
[4] Paus. 5.12.5.
[5] Hodkinson 2004: 321; *IvO* 634.
[6] Paus. 3.15.1. For work on the topography of Pausanias's Sparta and the proposed location of the Platanistas near the Mousga stream, see Sanders 2009.
[7] *IV* V.1.235.

and collective memory, both past and present. I am interested in what the various interpretations of her recorded victories suggest about the epistemological gaps within archival and archaeological work, as well as within the practice of making monuments to commemorate individual historical women more broadly. Specifically, I turn my focus to the problem of excavating 'women's achievements' by situating the evidence for Cynisca within the context of monuments to dynastic women throughout the Hellenistic period. Such difficulties raise into further relief the possible epistemological failures that emerge from the promise of exceptionality; that is, I shall explore the ways in which notions of dynastic exceptionality obscure the historical memory of women more broadly across monument landscapes, both in classical antiquity and our very present moment. To build on this particular line of discussion, I turn to monumental presences and absences across the modern and contemporary United States, with a focus on Sharon Hayes's 2017 temporary art installation *If They Should Ask*. By bringing together fragmentary monuments to, for and by women from ancient and contemporary contexts, I aim to explore the question of epistemic exclusion in visual culture and in public spaces – as well as through the thorny processes of their recovery.[8]

HISTORICAL MEMORIES OF A MONUMENTAL WOMAN

Cynisca in history

The daughter of the Eurypontid king Archidamus and sister of kings Agis II and Agesilaus, Cynisca first participated in the Olympic games when she was about fifty years old by supporting chariot races in 396 and again in 392 BCE.[9] As Sarah Pomeroy has argued, the dynastic daughter may have been an experienced expert in equestrianism and horse-breeding herself, and was thus well positioned for pan-Hellenic glory.[10] While Cynisca followed the examples of other wealthy donors and patrons who employed jockeys and charioteers to drive their horses, her monumental voice echoes the content of extant Greek victory inscriptions on behalf of triumphant athletes.[11] In particular, her claim as 'the only woman' to win a chariot race is emphasised as an exceptional feat. For instance, her monumental inscription elevates her status through the use of *emoi* or 'my', thus highlighting her personal connections, as well as her singular participation

---

[8] See the Introduction to this volume for a discussion of 'evidentiary injustice' and Milnor (Chapter 8, this volume) for a related treatment of gaps in the historical record.
[9] Pomeroy 2002: 21 based on the analysis by Moretti 1953: 41–3.
[10] Pomeroy 2002.
[11] See Tod 1949; Kurke 1993; and Young 1996 for a discussion of Greek record-keeping inscriptions. See Hodkinson 1999 for a discussion of Spartan agonistic culture, as contextualised within the broader Greek world.

(*monan*) in games for which she likely was not physically present; only bodies that were born as male could attend the pan-Hellenic games (with the exception of the Heraean games) as both athletes and spectators.[12]

Historical accounts written by Xenophon (fourth century BCE) and much later by Plutarch (second century CE) explain Cynisca's victories as a result of her personal wealth rather than a sign of any 'manly virtue' (*andragathia*), thus pithily reaffirming the cultural and sociopolitical implications of physical competition as innately masculine – that is, a domain in which men and boys were the only participants.[13] Centring their focus on debates about gender and agency, some modern historians have come to understand Cynisca's victory to be politically compelling precisely because she was a woman. David Young's work on record-setting athletes in the Greek world is important, arguing that Cynisca's inscription 'states a gender record: the only woman to win the Olympic chariot contest'.[14] Whereas the victory inscriptions of men emphasise their exceptionalism in physical sport and athleticism, Cynisca's gender became a site for record-setting in athletic competition. The epigram thus reinforces Cynisca's gender identity as a woman as a significant analytical category and as an immutable matter of fact.

Both ancient writers and modern historians have also explained Cynisca's spectacular triumph and exceptional patronage as inextricably tied to dynastic politics. For example, Xenophon and Plutarch's discussions of Cynisca's victory are situated within biographies written about her brother, Agesilaus, and explained in terms of his own political ambitions as well as the contingencies of broader agonistic geopolitics in the early fourth century.[15] In doing so, Cynisca's claims to exceptionality and Olympic triumph are recast as a dynastic victory on behalf of her brother's kingship (and a testament to his skills of persuasion,

---

[12] Pomeroy 2002: 141–2 argues that Cynisca's inscription preserves her singular 'voice', especially given the use of the first-person singular possessive pronoun.

[13] This is despite the Heraean games, in which women were the prime participants in athletic competition. See Golden 1998.

[14] Young 1996: 181. See also Tod 1949: 110–11 on the use of exclusionary language like *eis, monos, protos* in athletic inscriptions.

[15] Kyle 2003 is concerned with dispelling any ideas that Cynisca's victories might lead us to believe that she was some 'symbol' for women's success in the ancient Olympics; Golden 1998 thinks about the ways that this evidence enforces women's sociocultural and political inferiority to men; Lämmer 1981 doubts the mark that Cynisca made on sports more generally; Scanlon 2002 likewise seems to think about Cynisca's victory as entirely Agesilaus's doing; Hodkinson 2000: 327 sees Agesilaus's sponsorship of Cynisca as a way to create a new ethic of kingship. Though Pomeroy 2002 gives Cynisca more intentional agency, she does contextualise historically and politically. Cartledge 1987: 29 also suggests that Agesilaus influenced Cynisca to participate in Olympic chariot-racing on behalf of the family.

according to Xenophon and Plutarch). These analyses demonstrate the various cultural and political roles that women could play on behalf of the consolidation and exaltation of their dynastic families.[16] Indeed, Cynisca's gender was made meaningful because of its implications for dynastic exceptionality.

Such historical analyses of Cynisca's Olympic victories, however, fail to fully account for her epigram, for her archaeological record and for her monumental presence, which should include a consideration of how viewers may have experienced and engaged with her honours in public. Cynisca's monumental traces constitute only one example of how dynastic women played significant roles in public art and spectacle on behalf of their powerful families throughout politically and culturally significant spaces. During the long fourth century, dynastic women throughout the Mediterranean and western Asia appeared publicly as subjects of representation in royal monuments (for example, the Mausoleum of Halicarnassus, the Philippeion at Olympia) and sometimes as patrons of dynastic art. Thus, approaching the evidence for Cynisca as visual and material culture might yield important insights about her honours specifically, and about the relationship between dynastic women and monuments more broadly.

Cynisca in monuments

As Marcus Tod and David Young have already examined, Cynisca's epigram roughly follows the formula for 'record-breaking' declarations that are found in honours for heroic athletes. Take, for instance, the fifth-century epigram preserved on a statue base from Delphi for the athlete Theogenes of Thasos:

> Θευγένης Τιμοξένου Θάσιος ἐνίκησεν τάδε
> οὐ γάρ τις Ὀλυμπίαι ἐστεφανώθη ωὑ[τὸς ἀνὴ]ρ πυγμῆι παγκρατίωι τε κρατ[έων].
>   οὐδὲ καὶ ἐμ Πυθῶνι τριῶν στεφάνων ἀκονιτὶ ἐς τόδε θνητὸς ἀνήρ οὗτις ἔρεξε ἕτερος.

You, son of Timoxenos [. . .]
  For never at Olympia has the same man been crowned for victory in boxing and in pankration.
  But you, of your three victories in the Pythian Games, won one unopposed, a feat which no other mortal man has accomplished.[17]

---

[16] In contrast to this line of thought, historical work by Elizabeth Carney and Gillian Ramsey on various Hellenistic-era kingdoms has demonstrated the important roles of dynastic women in dynastic politics.
[17] *SIG* 36 A; Moretti #21. Other inscriptions listing Theogenes' exceptional victories have been found at Thasos and Olympia, in addition to Delphi.

Theogenes' epigram continues further with a long list of accomplishments at various athletic competitions emphasising that his abilities exceed those of other mortal men. Yet even this excerpt alone presents what Young calls 'a model for the vocabulary of Greek record-breaking', in particular for the ways in which each line uses the language of exclusivity to showcase Theogenes' exceptionality, and as David Lunt argues, his divine and heroic status.[18] Leslie Kurke has argued for the 'symbolic economy of *kudos*' whereby the victory crown becomes 'the bearer of *kudos* and its dedication the means of sharing that power with the city', revealing the cultural strategies by which divinely bestowed power can be collectively distributed.[19] Like the epigram for Theogenes, Cynisca's inscription first introduces her family lineage, describes her Olympic victory, and then explains why her accomplishments were exceptional. In contrast, however, Cynisca's epigram is written in her own voice, emphasising both her victory and her singular role in constructing her own monument near Hera's temple at Olympia. Regardless of her actual gendered position among other members of the Eurypontid court, the monument was constructed to portray Cynisca as a heroic figure who could publicly declare *herself* as an exceptional patron who shared her triumph with her fathers and brothers, Spartan kings.[20]

Pausanias's description is also worth revisiting, especially since his is the only extant viewer testimony of Cynisca's monument. In it, he describes a portrait of Cynisca and multiple inscriptions related to her, set up alongside a multi-sculptural installation of a charioteer driving a *quadriga*. Although it is unclear how Cynisca was represented and in what way her portrait was positioned in relation to the charioteer and horses, extant evidence suggests that her portrait statue was set up separately from the charioteer. The now fragmentary, rounded stone base from Olympia measures approximately 49 cm in length and 34.2 cm in height, indicating that the pedestal was just large enough for an over-human-size statue, which was likely the bronze portrait of Cynisca.[21] As for the other elements of Cynisca's installation, two earlier extant monuments dating to the 470s BCE offer a tantalising

---

[18] Young 1996: 183. See also Lunt 2009: 383–4. Scholars have questioned the accuracy of such claims on Theogenes' behalf (Finley and Pleket 1976: 68). See also Fantuzzi 2005: 254 for a discussion of Cynisca mimicking the 'common expression in the record-boasts by the agonistic winners of the Hellenistic age', as well as Kurke 1993.

[19] Kurke 1993: 241.

[20] Kyle 2003: 185 believes that Cynisca's 'voice' cannot be heard through this particular inscription, because the author of the epigram would have likely been a man, contrasting with Pomeroy's theory (2002: 141–2). Here, I have no interest in debating this claim around Cynisca's 'voice' – it matters that the text claims to be written by Cynisca, regardless of gender.

[21] I have not been able to study the base in person, and all of my observations have been made via documentary photographs.

sense of what Cynisca's charioteer may have looked like: first is the bronze charioteer of Delphi, made by Pythagorus, celebrating the victory of the tyrant Polyzalus of Gela in Sicily and his chariot at the Pythian Games, and second is the so-called Mozia Charioteer, a marble statue of a charioteer from Sicily that may have commemorated another pan-Hellenic victory.[22] Perhaps the multiple inscriptions that Pausanias describes accompanied the charioteer installation, naming Cynisca for viewers to identify the Olympic victor. Together, Pausanias's description and the fragmentary base demonstrate that the monument was perceived by viewers as a visually cohesive whole that highlighted Cynisca alongside the winning horses. The monument visualised Cynisca's bodily presence to creatively evoke a sense that she was physically 'there' at the Olympic games, even though she certainly was not.

In addition to making her own dedications at Olympia, Cynisca also received monuments and memorials at Sparta, thus achieving heroic and historical status in her hometown. Her name was elevated on colossal public architecture, while, according to Pausanias, a hero-shrine was built in her honour at the Platanistas, where youths would participate in athletic contests.[23] Other shrines to Spartan men – Alcimus, Enaraephorus, Dorceus and Sebrus, all sons of the mythological Spartan king Hippocoon – were built next to the Platanistas, near sanctuaries to Helen and Heracles and the tomb of the lyric poet Alcman. Cynisca's shrine was thus placed in strategic topographical proximity to other important landmark features that commemorated exceptional figures who were either dynastic, divine or culturally significant. Moreover, such monumental features continued to serve as the physical and cultural backdrop for ephebic contests and battles that, as G. D. R. Sanders suggests, may have served as reenactments of important mytho-historical events that were discussed by Alcman in his *Partheneion*.[24] Jean Ducat and later Stephen Hodkinson have argued that Cynisca's hero-shrine would have been particularly meaningful to other Spartan women and girls, who would have trained as athletes at the nearby *dromos* and honoured her memory there.[25] According to their analyses, the physical site of her hero-shrine encouraged Spartan women and girls to collectively activate her memory because of their shared gender identity, an interpretation to which I return (and provide additional nuance) in the next section. Embedded within collective Spartan

---

[22] Charioteer of Delphi, bronze with silver, glass and copper inlay, 1.8m in height. Delphi Archaeological Museum; Mozia or Motya Charioteer, marble, 181cm × 40cm. Museo Giuseppe Whitaker inv. no. 4310. Jenifer Neils 2012 discusses Athenian vase paintings that depict Spartan female charioteers driving *triga*, or three-horse chariots.

[23] Paus. 3.15.1.

[24] Sanders 2009: 203.

[25] Ducat 1998: 168–9 and Hodkinson 2004: 112. See also Kron 1996: 181–2 for a discussion of royal and dynastic women as models for non-royal and non-dynastic women.

memory, Cynisca's material presence linked her with the divine and the mythohistorical, while her shrine signified her exemplary status as on par with other heroes throughout Sparta's storied topography.

Cynisca's monuments in context

Commemorative and triumphal monuments by and for women were relatively rare in the early fourth century BCE. As Sheila Dillon's landmark book on the 'female portrait statue' demonstrates, women of elite and high-ranking status received public honours from their cities and other men in celebration of their roles as good mothers, wives and daughters, as well as pious priestesses.[26] These women could also dedicate their own monuments, mobilising formulas that were already established by cities and men. Royal and dynastic women like Cynisca sometimes made public dedications and monumental honours in important places as well.[27] For example, archaeological evidence from the Argead capital city of Vergina/Aigai indicates that Eurydice (c. 370–340 BCE) either built, expanded, renovated and/or refurbished the Temple of Eucleia, the goddess of Good Fame.[28] There, a heavily draped statue and a portrait head for insertion were excavated, as well as two separate bases with a dedicatory inscription that reads 'Eurydice, daughter of Sirras, dedicated to Eucleia'.[29] Much like the opening line of Cynisca's inscription, Eurydice's dedication claims her descent from her father, the Illyrian king, to highlight her birthright rather than her filial and maternal duties to the kings of Macedon; though it is noteworthy that the names of family members are not explicitly listed. Yet Eurydice's dedications were nevertheless expressions of femininity that aligned with broader notions of women's roles, for she made her name (and perhaps even her own portrait image) within a temple of a goddess, thus presenting herself as a pious woman.

---

[26] Dillon 2010: 12–13, 51–2. See also van Bremen 1996 and Eule 2001, as well as Connelly 2007.

[27] Kron 1996: 155–8, 168 argues that the difference between royal and non-royal women's dedications is the relative 'public character' of the former.

[28] The identity of the patron of the sanctuary itself is unknown, and the specific details of Eurydice's involvement cannot be understood from the evidence. Borza 1990 associates the minor goddess with Artemis Eucleia, whom the Boeotians and Locrians honoured as a goddess of marriage (Plut. *Vit. Arist.* 20.6 on public dedications to Artemis Eucleia by Boeotians and Locrians). Borza 1990: 192–3 has suggested that her dedications reflected Macedon's close connections with Boeotia at that time. See Carney 2019: 89–90 for a full discussion of the Eucleia cult in the Greek world.

[29] Two of the bases and the statuary fragments were found in the vicinity of the sanctuary, while the third base was a spoliated column base for a nearby Byzantine church at Palatitsia. See Saatsoglou-Paliadeli 2000 for the archaeological report and Dillon 2010: 78–9 for a discussion of the statues.

Although Cynisca's victory monument at Olympia is rare compared to the extant corpus of women's monuments, Posidippus's *Hippika*, written in the early third century, consists of epigrams that magnify the role of dynastic women from the Ptolemaic court – an Arsinoe and several Berenices – as triumphant supporters of victorious chariot races at pan-Hellenic games.[30] One of these epigrams (AB 87) is written in the voice of one of Berenice's horses, telling us that the queen was victorious at the Olympic games such that she even took away the ancient *kudos* of Cynisca.[31] Strikingly, Posidippus's epigram evokes and repeats a particular formula for monumental women; indeed, such a reference to Cynisca's 'ancient' triumph (AB 87) clearly demonstrates that Posidippus and the Ptolemies were aware of Cynisca's historical victories, and perhaps even of her monuments at Olympia and Sparta. Another epigram (AB 88), written in the voice of Ptolemy II, follows the general formula of Cynisca's inscription. In it, the king marks the memory of his family's glory in Olympic chariot-racing by celebrating the victories of his father and highlighting those of his mother. Just like Cynisca's declaration, Ptolemy II emphasises the exceptionality of Berenice's victory because of her gender as a woman. These epigrams may or may not describe physical commemorative monuments that were constructed to honour Ptolemaic triumph. Regardless, the epigrams imaginatively evoke dynastic monuments representing multiple generations of dynastic kinsmen and kinswomen in the mind's eye.[32] Verity Platt's work on the provocative relationship between viewing and reading is particularly instructive here: such descriptions seem to encourage the reader (or listener) to imagine the epigram's description – that is, triumphant women and men – as a materially present dynastic image.[33]

Mothers, wives and daughters of dynastic men were sometimes included within dynastic monuments of triumph, beginning in the fourth century and

---

[30] AB refers to Austin and Bastianini 2002, followed by their numerical references. AB 78, 79, 82, 87, 88. Similarly, Callimachus (*SH* 254.1–10) wrote an ode to the queen Berenice II for her victory in quadriga-racing at Nemea.

[31] AB 87. See Fantuzzi 2005: 260–2 for the comparison between Berenice's and Cynisca's *kudoi*, and the ways in which their victories may have afforded them hero-shrines and immortality. Similar to other readings of Cynisca's victory as a *dynastic* one, Fantuzzi 2005: 263 argues that the connections between Berenice and Cynisca would have also drawn important associations between Sparta and the Ptolemaic kingdom with regard to an image of power; in other words, personal *kudos* was dynastic glory.

[32] Clayman 2014: 148–9 sees perhaps a total of seven of these epigrams for the Ptolemies, and also suggests that these epigrams *may* have been written for actual statues. However, Fantuzzi 2005: 267–8 casts doubt on the idea that these epigrams were ever written to describe actual inscriptions on monuments, given the lack of archaeological evidence or literary descriptions (for example, Pausanias) and instead argues for a reading as a literary text.

[33] Platt 2011: 181–2.

throughout the Hellenistic period. Dynasties throughout the Hellenistic world produced monuments and circulated visual and material culture (for example, coins or seals) that included representations of kinswomen in order to emphasise the family unit, sometimes across multiple generations, as a compelling image of power. For instance, the Olympian Altis was later the site of the Argead dynast Philip II's rotunda, in which portrait statues of his parents (Amyntas and Eurydice), one of his wives (Olympias) and his descendant and heir Alexander III were displayed altogether. The Philippeion commemorated the *hegemon*'s victory at the Battle of Chaeronea in 338 by representing select male and female members of the Argead clan, thus claiming dynastic triumph and continuity into the future.[34] Philip's rotunda is an important example to compare with Cynisca's monuments, demonstrating that dynastic women received physical markers and monumental status for their intimate ties to exceptional men. Moreover, these honorific monuments for dynastic hero figures were created in order to reinforce social and political distinctions, asymmetries and hierarchies, just as Theogenes' athletic honours distinguished him as god-like in his singular achievements. By honouring single historical figures who were triumphant in war or sport, monuments crafted heroic narratives that evoked a sense of divine *kudos* in perpetuity. Thus, dynastic victory monuments like Cynisca's sculptural installation at the Altis were aesthetic, material and over-life-sized tools for exerting power in spectacular fashion, and moreover, for evoking a sense of permanence about the very status of those power dynamics.

Altogether, Cynisca's honorific monuments cast her as an exceptional historical figure in two distinct yet closely connected ways. First, the monuments made her gender as a woman a remarkable fact that distinguished her from other Olympic victors, as emphasised by her statue's epigram as well as Pausanias's descriptions of Cynisca's memorial markers at Olympia and Sparta. Second, Cynisca's monuments augmented her gender as a woman in order to reaffirm the excellence and power of the Eurypontid dynasty. For example, her hero-shrine topographically and conceptually positioned her historical memory among other male dynastic heroes of Sparta, while her epigram proclaimed her direct kinship with the kings of Sparta. In other words, the singular 'voice of Cynisca' that emerges from her epigram, her visibility and physical presence evoked *dynastic* triumph across the pan-Hellenic stage. Victory monuments that either honoured or included dynastic women like Cynisca, Olympias and Berenice tell us very little about the achievements and broader histories of women in antiquity, and instead

---

[34] Much later at the Altis, Callicrates, the naval general and priest, commissioned a bicolumnar monument of the royal sibling-spousal couple. Other examples of multigenerational dynastic family portraits include the Mausoleum of Halicarnassus and an extant inscription listing names of the Ptolemies from Thermos in Aetolia, that was once for a sculptural portrait.

illuminate the aesthetic strategies that rulers developed and mobilised throughout the Hellenistic period – including the representation of women's bodies and women's voices – in order to stretch forward a memory of their dynasty's heroism and continuity into the future. With this in mind, I return to Ducat's interpretation that the specific location of Cynisca's *heroon* near the *dromos*, where Spartan women and girls trained, was significant; of course, this does not exclude the possibility that Spartan women and girls did indeed venerate Cynisca's memory. However, Cynisca's hero-shrine made imperative claims about dynastic exceptionality as the 'only woman' who had ever achieved such feats; that is, her monuments construct an image of exclusive femininity instead of a model of exemplary femininity. I elaborate on the material presences and absences of women in the next section, turning to a discussion of the kinds of epistemological ambiguities that emerge from historical monuments and our analyses of them. In this next section, I also turn to the topic of 'women's monuments' in the modern and contemporary United States, and what current discourses around monumental representation might teach us about approaching monuments of the classical past.

ABSENCES AND PRESENCES IN MONUMENTS

> The bigger the material mass, the more easily it entraps us: mass graves and pyramids bring history closer while they make us feel small. A castle, a fort, a battlefield, a church, all these things bigger than we that we infuse with the reality of past lives, seem to speak of an immensity of which we know little except that we are part of it. Too solid to be unmarked, too conspicuous to be canned, they embody the ambiguities of history.... We imagine the lives under the mortar, but how do we recognize the end of a bottomless silence?[35]

In his 1995 opus *Silencing the Past*, Haitian anthropologist Michel-Rolph Trouillot describes the physical and conceptual matter of monuments. With their over-human-size scale and material solidity, monumental structures and statues make particular demands of audiences, asking viewers to remember certain events, heroise specific individuals or groups of people, and assent to power-holders; in this way, Trouillot illuminates the ways in which material things are cast as credible evidence and authoritative narrative devices. Trouillot's careful descriptions of 'material mass' explain how the weightiness of physical markers help powerholders to embed mytho-historical narratives within memory landscapes, and to broadcast those narratives as truth. In other words, the monument

---

[35] Trouillot 1995: 29–30.

is a mode of historical narration that invokes authenticity precisely through the phenomenological and material means by which it engages its witnesses.[36]

And yet, monuments are also significant for what they don't represent, and what they fail to say. Aligned with feminist and postcolonial work on the epistemological violence of silencing, Trouillot grapples with history, whose production comprises material culture and its fragments as well as texts and documents, as 'a particular bundle of silences, the result of a unique process, and the operation required to deconstruct these silences will vary accordingly'.[37] Historical work is central to reaffirming narratives and normalising ways of knowing that undergird power structures, as well as the very process of exercising that power. In other words, the histories authored by victors and the monuments sanctioned by governing bodies necessarily obscure, make absent, and quite literally marginalise the perspectives and lives of certain groups of people – even in cases when they may be physically represented.

Although monuments to women like Cynisca seem to offer at first glance information about the historical achievements and actions of women, as a corpus in context, they make up a 'bundle of silences' that elevate dynastic women's political importance while simultaneously obscuring any trace of their political agency. According to the material and textual evidence for her monuments, Cynisca's singular achievements as 'the only woman' in the agonistic arena were situated within a narrative of heroic dynastic lineage, echoing the traditional formula for honouring exceptional athletes. Indeed, as historian Paul Cartledge writes in *Spartan Reflections*, 'I hope that I may at least have made readers hesitate before seeking to enlist the women of ancient Sparta as allies in the just cause of feminism'.[38] Here, Cartledge is commenting on the stereotypes of Spartan girls and women as wielding much more agency than the women and girls from other cities throughout southern Greece, as well as the broader implications of those stereotypes and the historical methodologies that lead us to such conclusions. Despite the evidence that Spartan women would have wielded more political agency than women of other Greek societies, the broader structural terms by which ideas about gender regulated, organised and controlled female bodies in fact obscure their political presence. This is where thinking about Cynisca's monuments in the context of other dynastic monuments becomes important. Hellenistic-era representations of the mothers, wives and daughters of dynastic

---

[36] Ibid. p. 151.
[37] Trouillot 1995: 27. Others in this volume who discuss forms of epistemic silencing and epistemic violence include Weiberg (Chapter 2), Gilbert (Chapter 3), McHardy (Chapter 4), Witzke (Chapter 7), Milnor (Chapter 8), Haley (Chapter 9) and Strong (Chapter 15).
[38] Cartledge 2003: 126.

men did not mark a historical subversion of gendered roles, and instead presented visual and conceptual formulas that communicated *power* on behalf of a dynasty, along with the expectations for its continuity into the future.[39] Moreover, her epigram mobilises her gender to foreground the Eurypontid dynasty's exceptionality, all while following a particular formula that athletic victors commonly used. Victory monuments reaffirmed political worlds, including the gendered and power dynamics that constituted them; and as Cynisca's monuments reveal, Hellenistic authoritarian politics, much like the Olympic games, were physically and conceptually mapped as spaces of triumphal masculinity.[40]

The archaeological and material traces of Cynisca simultaneously make her present and absent, audible and silent. Such fuzziness around women and 'Other' bodies in histories of art has been the subject of interrogation, especially since the 1970s.[41] Feminist projects in various fields of art-historical enquiry have focused on unpacking the conditions and contingencies of female bodies as subject matter as well as illuminating the achievements of women artists, whose works and perspectives have been omitted from the canon.[42] In the case of classical art history and archaeology, foundational work by scholars like Sheila Dillon, Christine Mitchell Havelock, Ute Kron, Joan Breton Connelly and Mireille Lee, to name only a few, have illuminated the varied conceptualisations of femininity in visual and material culture, especially in exploring female representations across media and women as patrons and viewers of monuments. Nevertheless, the modes of approaching the subject of women in ancient art and artefact is challenging, first, for how we might even formulate our methods for considering gender and 'women' as categories of historical analysis, and second, for the ways in which fragmentary objects and pedestals alongside first- and second-hand descriptions of monuments that no longer exist, make for an incoherent, piecemeal art-historical archive.[43] In other words, as historians of the classical past, we must continue to grapple with the limits

---

[39] Williamson 2015: 191–2 offers a similar argument for the representation of Nefertiti in Amarna-period evidence as 'paradigms that obfuscate', and that rather than 'looking for "power" in the western sense, it is more fruitful to look for "importance"'.

[40] For instance, there is the matter that Hodkinson 1989: 99 raises with regard to Agesilaus urging Cynisca to participate in order 'to emulate male participants precisely in order to discredit the sport'.

[41] Brand 2006.

[42] Foundational feminist art-historical texts include Linda Nochlin's 1971 essay 'Why Have There Been No Great Women Artists?' and the Guerrilla Girls' 2004 *Art Museum Activity Book*.

[43] For more on the historical contingencies of analytically approaching gender and sexuality, see Najmabadi 2006.

and gaps within our archaeological and art-historical archives when excavating the material traces of historical women.

Despite the epistemological challenges that fragmentary evidence presents in recovering the voices, lives and experiences of women in the classical past, fragmentation nevertheless can be a useful aesthetic tool to intervene in the traditional processes by which historical narratives take shape. In this respect, perhaps historians of ancient Greece and Rome might learn from artists like Sharon Hayes (b. 1970), whose critical work includes a reparative revision of Philadelphia's monument landscape, thus offering a vision of what historical narratives *could* be, precisely by putting imaginative pressure on classicising art and archaeology.

If They Should Ask... *and speculative monuments*

In 2017, the multidisciplinary artist Sharon Hayes called out the white patriarchal supremacy of monuments across the city of Philadelphia in *If They Should Ask* (9.5 × 10.3 × 8.7 feet), a temporary installation of cast concrete, steel, and acrylic lettering that was set up in the middle of Rittenhouse Park for Monument Lab's citywide exhibition.[44] *If They Should Ask* mimicked many modern archaeological sites and museums across the Mediterranean world by assembling and displaying together nine emptied classicising architectural features and bases (Figure 6.1). These bases were copies of extant pedestals for monuments to men (like Benjamin Franklin and the Marquis de Lafayette) across the city of Philadelphia, which Hayes cast, reduced in scale and combined into one sculptural installation. Throughout Philadelphia's civic landscape, hundreds of statues to historical men sit atop high pedestals evoking the honorific statuary of classical Greek cities. By appropriating, reinscribing and recontextualising such pedestals, the installation invited audiences to confront the ways that narratives and public monuments reflect a broader system of power in which white men are the dominant producers of historical knowledge and subjects of recognition, especially throughout the United States and its territories.[45]

---

[44] Hayes's work was part of a city-wide exhibition of prototype monuments produced by Monument Lab; see Farber and Lum 2019.

[45] Hayes's understanding of the sanctioned commemorative landscape of the United States aligns with Monument Lab's 2021 *National Monument Audit*, the first data-driven assessment of the nation's monument landscape. It established that the top fifty represented historical figures are overwhelmingly white, wealthy men.

Figure 6.1 Sharon Hayes. *If They Should Ask*. 2017. Cast concrete, steel, and acrylic lettering, 9.5 × 10.3 × 8.7 feet. Rittenhouse Park, Philadelphia, PA. Monument Lab. Photo by Steve Weinick/Mural Arts Philadelphia. Courtesy of Monument Lab.

At the time that Hayes was creating the installation, only two monuments to historical women existed in all of Philadelphia's commemorative landscape: the fifteenth-century French heroine of the Hundred Years' War, Joan of Arc (who had never sailed across the Atlantic to set foot in the Americas), and the colonial-era First Amendment rights advocate and Quaker Mary Dyer. Like the monuments celebrating Cynisca, those commemorating Joan of Arc and Mary Dyer simultaneously depict these women and obscure their perspectives. As Hayes explains, 'Neither of [those women] was from Philadelphia – both were martyred, and both were white [. . .] I'm interested in the obstacles that prevent women from entering the historical record'.[46] Thus, Hayes's installation reckoned with the absences of women, especially those of transwomen and non-white women, in public history and memory in two specific ways.

[46] As quoted from Roach 2017.

First, the emptied pedestals visually called attention to the palpable absences of historical women's bodies within monuments and dominant historical narratives. Second, Hayes inscribed the names and memories of noteworthy Philadelphia women from the mid-seventeenth century to the present day in laser-cut acrylic lettering all across the surfaces of the pedestals (Figure 6.2). The words 'On this site there could be a statue to . . .' were followed by a list of individuals, including Hetty Reckless, Clara Ward and Billie Holiday, whose names were decided upon through a collaborative process with a group of Philadelphia women.[47] During the public exhibition of the installation, Philadelphia residents and visitors were invited to add more names to a digital list, thus calling to the rich potential of collaborative, collective historical work. Additionally, women whose full names are still unknown or lost to us, like 'the transwomen at the 1965 sit-in at Dewey's Café', were included in the roster, demonstrating how our historical archives obscure the recognition and acknowledgement of marginalised groups of people.

Figure 6.2 Sharon Hayes. *If They Should Ask*. 2017. Cast concrete, steel, and acrylic lettering, 9.5 × 10.3 × 8.7 feet. Rittenhouse Park, Philadelphia, PA. Monument Lab. Photo by Steve Weinick/Mural Arts Philadelphia. Courtesy of Monument Lab.

---

[47] A full list of names inscribed, and a place for people to contribute their own names, was once available at iftheyshouldask.com, which has since been deactivated. For a list of advisory-group members, see Roach 2017.

Hayes's work is thus a reparative revision (or an 'unsilencing', to quote Trouillot[48]) that imagines a visual landscape in which speculation – that is, the possibilities of what could or should be – is the primary method of historical work:

> I was interested in working with this kind of conditional, both, I think, on this site, there could be a statue that suggests that in, you know, 1803, in 1890, in 1910 there could have been a statue and there could be one now and there could be one in 2024. It's a wrestle. And so, that they should ask – I think it has all these multiple positions. If they should ask, 'Why are there no statues to women?' If they should ask, 'What do we do about it?' If they should ask, 'What do these women do?' If they should ask, 'Why you want to represent women?' If they should ask.[49]

Here, the artist takes full advantage of the subjunctive's capacities to present a monument that simultaneously engages and reads against dominant historical narratives that operate under the logic of white patriarchy and the rhetorics of triumphalist masculinity. Hayes's project corresponds with the approach of critical fabulation, as coined by Saidiya Hartman in reckoning with palpable, violent absences in the context of the historical archives of Atlantic slavery.[50] This method, like the artistic process and formal aspects of Hayes's installation, takes full advantage of the subjunctive tense in its critical analysis 'with and against the archive', putting forth compelling scenarios for 'what could have been' in order to show precisely what has been lost.[51] Take for instance the installation's emptied neoclassical pedestals: this visual strategy propels the idea that *absence* has its own material substance, thus revealing the corporeal possibilities of what could, should or would be standing on them. Indeed, by taking 'loss as a site for inquiry and reflexivity', artists and historians alike might begin the process of reckoning with what Dan-el Padilla Peralta's incisive work on Roman imperial violence has

---

[48] This might be thought of as similar to (or a kind of) 'epistemic resistance'; see the Introduction to this volume. Others in this volume who discuss forms of epistemic resistance include Weiberg (Chapter 2), Gilbert (Chapter 3), McHardy (Chapter 4), Witzke (Chapter 7) and Haley (Chapter 9).

[49] Hayes, Olivier, and Farber 2020: 277.

[50] See, for instance, Hartman 2008: 13, who writes: 'the *history* of black counter-historical projects is one of failure, precisely because these accounts have never been able to install themselves as history, but rather are insurgent, disruptive narratives that are marginalised and derailed before they ever gain a footing'.

[51] Ibid. p. 11.

understood as epistemicide, or the deliberate obliteration and marginalisation of forms of knowing.⁵²

By drawing out and literally representing monumental historical loss, such speculative work alerts viewers towards multiple possibilities of knowing the past – methods that undo history's status quo while embracing new kinds of collective memories. For instance, it is worth recalling that the names and the individuals that were honoured in *If They Should Ask...* were decided by a group of Philadelphia-based women. The installation's display also included community and public engagement, inviting viewers to add more names to the pedestal through a digital website (Figure 6.3). By envisioning and implementing a memorial practice and process that foregrounds the collective, the installation also casts suspicion on the enduring custom of building honorific monuments to individual hero figures. Furthermore, by appropriating classicising forms that have historically symbolised institutional power, the project's emphasis on *collective action* recontextualised such monumental structures and bases as repudiations of state-sanctioned authority.

Figure 6.3 Philadelphia residents activating Sharon Hayes's sculptural installation, *If They Should Ask*. 2017. Cast concrete, steel, and acrylic lettering, 9.5 × 10.3 × 8.7 feet. Rittenhouse Park, Philadelphia, PA. Monument Lab. Photo by Steve Weinick/Mural Arts Philadelphia. Courtesy of Monument Lab.

⁵² Padilla Peralta 2020.

CONCLUSION: IMAGINING WHAT COULD BE

What do such critical, creative and speculative modes of historical work have to offer classical studies? To classical art histories and archaeologies? The collective force behind contemporary projects like *If They Should Ask* ... mobilises strategies of historical recovery and appropriates classical honorific inscriptions on bases in order to redress the confounding ways in which historical women are simultaneously present and absent. In this way, the sculptural installation operates in polar opposition to the kinds of monumental markers that were built on behalf of Cynisca's memory.

Admittedly, my own writing on the subject of Cynisca and dynastic women's monuments privileges the perspective of authority figures and of dynastic governments. Although the evidence glorifies her victories and even expresses her voice, a closer look at the primary sources for her monuments in their broader art-historical and archaeological context obscure any trace of her political and cultural agency. In other words, approaching Cynisca through her monuments unveils the ways in which the record of her achievements as 'the only woman' mimicked existing formulas for exceptional athletic honours, further situating the processes of dynastic memory-making within a more specific political effort to showcase a heroic lineage on behalf of the Eurypontids of Sparta. Through my art-historical analysis, I have grappled with the fraughtness of our historical and archaeological archives, particularly as they relate to 'women's monuments'. Although individual dynastic women were sometimes represented and honoured in important civic and divine spaces, their monuments are nevertheless ambiguous in their ability to speak to us fully about women's political agency (furthermore, in comparison to monuments to historical men, those to historical women are far fewer). Our records for monuments to exceptional historical women thus make individual women like Cynisca simultaneously absent and present, applying methodological pressure on feminist approaches to ways of knowing that confront art-historical canons. Despite our best efforts to unveil historical information about women in ancient worlds, at the same time, our art-historical and archaeological methods of study illuminate the silences and the gaps within our archives. Perhaps it is only by seeing these gaps that we can begin to fill them with visionary scenarios for what could be.

CHAPTER 7

Plautus's *Truculentus* and Terence's *Hecyra*: Patriarchal Authority and Women's Credibility

Serena S. Witzke

Plautus's *Truculentus* and Terence's *Hecyra* are not often analysed together. The former is an uproarious celebration of a sex labourer's comic *malitia* (badness) at the expense of numerous citizen men, while *Hecyra* is an unfunny showcase of domestic abuse. A survey of the scholarship indicates that *Truculentus*'s triumphant mercenary women are disturbing to modern readers[1] and *Hecyra* (as well as most of Terence's oeuvre) is a real downer.[2] But while their tones are wildly different, the plays' contents are strikingly similar: *Hecyra* is essentially a full-length expansion of the citizen rape subplot in *Truculentus*. In Plautus's play, in the background of the comic shenanigans, a young man has raped and impregnated a citizen woman and broken off his engagement to her to spend more time with his *amica* (girlfriend), the *meretrix* (sex labourer) Phronesium. Through the actions of this *meretrix* and her *familia* (household), the rape and pregnancy are revealed and the young man weds the citizen girl. In *Hecyra* a young man rapes and impregnates a citizen girl, is forced to marry, resents the marriage and lost time with his *amica*, but is eventually reconciled with his wife through the *meretrix*'s revelation that it was his own wife he once raped. In both plays, citizen women are treated abusively and non-citizen *meretrices* and their households are threatened by citizen men.

---

[1] See de Melo 2013. See also Tatum 1983 and Fantham 2000; contra Dessen 1977.
[2] See Anderson 2002. See also McGarrity 1980/81 and Penwill 2004; contra Knorr 2013.

Because *Truculentus* and *Hecyra* share a plot, they are an ideal locus for examining their authors' social commentaries on citizen, masculine power and women's limited ability to voice their truths credibly. Examining the plays side by side reveals their similarities and throws the authors' explorations of gendered epistemology into relief. Both plays ultimately demonstrate that women's credibility is measured only by the service it does for patriarchal authority. This chapter's structure is tripartite: first, I will demonstrate the parallels between the two plays, which seem too numerous to be accidental; next I will apply theories of feminist epistemology and epistemic injustice studies to explore the treatment of women's knowledge; and finally I will illustrate why these women's rape revelations, though deemed credible, are not feminist triumphs.

THE SHARED PLOT

It is difficult to source the provenance of many Roman *palliatae* (comic plays) beyond 'Greek original', though nineteenth-century scholars certainly tried.[3] *Truculentus* has stymied conclusive attribution: Menander, a pupil of Menander, and Diphilus have all been suggested.[4] *Hecyra* is attributed in the *didascalia* to Menander, but Donatus asserts that the author was Apollodorus, a pupil of Menander.[5] It is possible these plays shared a common Greek source, though Plautus made considerable changes to his source material and Terence was both adapting Greek originals (sometimes more than one in a play) and responding to Plautus and the Roman comic tradition as well. Regardless of Greek source, the plays are strikingly similar and unified in their criticisms of elite Roman society.

Truculentus and *Hecyra* share unwanted marriage, a rape, a baby boy in danger of exposure, involvement of citizen women in hiding and disposing of him, angry fathers, and the crucial role of a *meretrix* and her household in the resolution. It is worth a thorough examination of the plots and their parallels to see just how closely they dovetail in content, before exploring how each playwright uses this plot to demonstrate their critiques of the failures of citizen male society and its devaluation of women.

In both plays, an overaged *adulescens* (young man) clings to his *meretrix* after having raped and impregnated a citizen girl. In *Truculentus*, we meet Diniarchus, a resentful young man in a love/hate relationship with his *amica* Phronesium because of what he perceives is a mercurial nature: she loves him when he has money, she rejects him when he doesn't. Presumably his father pressured him to

---

[3] Sharrock 2019: 6–7. See also Lowe 2007 and Witzke 2014 on the Victorian preoccupation with resurrecting Greek originals and tracing source material.
[4] Webster, Enk, Marx, in de Melo 2013: 259.
[5] Barsby 2001: 145n3.

marry at some point, as he became engaged to neighbour Callicles' daughter. After raping her, however, he broke off the engagement and devoted himself once more to Phronesium. She, meanwhile, is involved in the main plot of the story, juggling three men and pretending to have borne a child to one of them. The play begins as Diniarchus returns from a trip abroad to discover these events at home. Pamphilus of *Hecyra* was devoted to the *meretrix* Bacchis but begrudgingly took a wife at the behest of his father. Bacchis rejects her client, now married, and Pamphilus falls out of love because of what he perceives as her mercurial nature. He begins to love the wife imposed upon him by his father but abandons her after learning that she had been raped and has borne a child. The play begins as he returns from a trip abroad to discover this controversy at home.

In both plays, the survivor's mother has worked with her *ancillae* (enslaved housemaids) to hide the pregnancy and birth. In *Truculentus*, the girl is unmarried, so still living at home with her mother. An *ancilla* enlists the help of Phronesium's hairdresser to dispose of the baby boy. The girl's father, Callicles, finds out about the pregnancy and disposal in the aftermath of her labour. In *Hecyra*, Philumena is married to Pamphilus and living in his home, but when Philumena's pregnancy becomes apparent, she flees back home to her mother. Her mother and *ancillae* hide the pregnancy and birth and attempt to dispose of the baby boy, but they are interrupted by Philumena's father Phidippus in the aftermath of her labour.

In both plays, when the angry *senex* (old man) learns of the baby boy, he resolves to enforce reconciliation and marriage. In *Truculentus*, Callicles insists Diniarchus marry his daughter and retrieve the young man's son. In *Hecyra*, Phidippus insists Pamphilus take back his daughter and retrieve the young man's son. Both fathers are infuriated with their wives and daughters for attempting to hide the pregnancy and irritated with the young men for waffling about their duty. The difference here, however, is that in *Truculentus*, Callicles learns that Diniarchus raped his unmarried daughter, while in *Hecyra*, Phidippus's daughter has been raped, but her father is unaware of it, believing the baby boy to be the child of his son-in-law (he will turn out to be right).

In both plays, these patriarchs are faced with a masculine citizen crisis: their households' reputations rest on the legitimacy of their daughters' marriages and children. Callicles must find his daughter's rapist and force a marriage, while Phidippus must discover why his son-in-law hesitates to reconcile with his wife and new son. Despite the ability of the *senes*' (old men's) wives and daughters to resolve these mysteries, they are not approached as credible sources of information: the hiding of the pregnancies and births demonstrates their unreliability to the men. Instead, in both plays, resolution rests with the neighbourhood *meretrices* and their households. Bacchis is menaced by Pamphilus's father outright, while Phronesium's *ancilla* is seized. The *meretrices' ancillae* are either tortured (*Truc.*) or threatened with torture (*Hec.*), as their forced testimony can help resolve the problems of the citizen families. Callicles learns that Diniarchus raped his daughter, and Phidippus and Laches find out . . . nothing really, but they force Bacchis to go inside and speak with Philumena and her mother. Through Bacchis, the women discover the identity of Philumena's rapist. Callicles forces Diniarchus to marry his daughter and legitimate the young man's son, while Phidippus finds his son-in-law now willing to take back his wife and son, though no explanation for Pamphilus's earlier reticence is offered.

Finally, in both plays, there is no staged reconciliation of citizen families (a standard in Greek new comedy),[6] but rather a reconciliation of *adulescens* with *meretrix* in the closing episodes. In *Truculentus*, Phronesium offers her home as a safe harbour for Diniarchus when he wants to avoid troubles at home. They share affectionate speech and Diniarchus entrusts his son to Phronesium's care for a while longer. In *Hecyra*, Pamphilus and Bacchis share a tender moment when he asks her to keep his despicable rape a secret from his father, mother and father-in-law. This secret will be a shared trust between them, and Pamphilus looks forward to meeting and sharing confidences with Bacchis in the future.

FEMINIST EPISTEMOLOGY, PATRIARCHAL AUTHORITY AND WOMEN'S CREDIBILITY

The aspects I want to investigate next are citizen men's prejudices against women and women's testimonies regarding the rapes and pregnancies. Notably, the citizen women are either passed over completely for testimony or are immediately disbelieved by citizen men, while the non-citizen women are consulted to effect resolution. But both plays undermine non-citizen speech from the outset too, with the result that all women's speech is compromised, making justice or vindication of their words almost impossible.

While neither author's biography is known for certain, there are a few details generally accepted by scholars which are relevant to our discussion of epistemological resources.[7] From the scant information of antiquity, Plautus was T. Maccius Plautus,[8] an Umbrian, perhaps from Sarsina. Terence was Publius Terentius Afer, born in Carthage and enslaved to the senator Terentius Lucanus, who manumitted him. Well educated by his former owner, he produced six plays.[9] These loose biographies are important to understanding the social critiques the authors offer: both are non-citizens lacking wealth and privilege. Their perspective, or 'standpoint', as

---

[6] Heap 1998 and Lape 2004.
[7] For a collection of the ancient sources, see Duckworth 1994: 49–51 (Plautus) and 56–9 (Terence).
[8] On Plautus's name and its meaning, see Gratwick 1973: Introduction.
[9] Suetonius *Life of Terence* cited in Donatus's commentary.

outsiders allows them to comment critically on, or show disdain for, the customs, morality and injustices of the citizen elite.[10] Amy Richlin's *Slave Theater*[11] argues that subaltern persons engaged in doublespeak, like that of enslaved persons in the Americas during the period of transatlantic human trafficking, wherein rebellious talk was coded to go unnoticed by the slave-owning elites. Richlin expands on anthropological work on the double fluency of 'muted groups' in the language of both the oppressor and the oppressed and incorporates the evolution of feminist standpoint theory in relation to the master–slave dialectic in Marxism, all the while highlighting types of 'satirical critiques' from Plautus's oeuvre and connecting them to those of historical enslaved persons.[12] My work here draws on Richlin's conclusions and offers further support for her thesis.

The vocabularies and theories of epistemology, particularly studies in epistemic injustice and feminist epistemology as they pertain to marginalised groups and identities, can be applied fruitfully to the study of Roman comedy, given the outsider status of both the playwrights and the large number of subaltern characters in the plays. The myriad ways in which these marginalised characters are disbelieved, undermined and denied agency, as well as their acts of resistance to their marginalisation, can be better understood through these epistemological theories.[13]

Wilful hermeneutical ignorance and citizen men

The epistemic tools of marginalisation work together in a complex web of oppression, but insofar as it is possible to treat them individually, I endeavour to do so

[10] Numerous studies (collected in Hanses 2020: 47–8 and summarised here) have examined how it was possible for state-sponsored theatre (as the comedies were performed at various Ludi throughout the year, financed by the aediles) to criticise the citizen elites footing the bill. First, the conceit of Greek settings and character names divorced the action (superficially) from Rome (see Moore 1998: 50–66). Segal's groundbreaking 1968 study of Roman comedy concluded that the Saturnalian atmosphere of the Ludi offered a liminal space in which subversion of social norms was permissive for the duration of the main action of the play; by play's end, normal order was restored. Finally, McCarthy 2000: 3–34 reminds us that Roman society was so strictly hierarchised that virtually no citizen was invulnerable to the power of another higher up on the social ladder, so all audience members could vicariously appreciate the rebellion of the subaltern figures on stage.

[11] 2017.

[12] Richlin 2017: 311–50, and specifically 313n4–5.

[13] Before moving forward, I encourage the reader to review the Introduction and the following terms: epistemic violence (Spivak 1988), systematic silencing (Smith 1999: 25), feedback loop (Daukas 2006: 116), testimonial and hermeneutic injustice (Fricker 2007), wilful hermeneutical ignorance (Pohlhaus Jr 2012: 716), feminist standpoint theory (Hartsock 1983b) and hermeneutical resistance (Medina 2017: 48–9).

here. First, I explore wilful hermeneutical ignorance as it pertains to the dominant group of elite citizen men. Charles Mills exposed the hypocrisy of the 'social contract' in these terms, highlighting the ways in which a dominant group sets the standards by which marginalised groups are judged, in a way that allows the dominant group to obscure its own privilege and exploit marginalised groups.[14] Regardless of the marginalised group's protests and explanations, as well as the epistemic resources available to the dominant group to understand the marginalised group, the dominant group wilfully chooses, collectively, to misinterpret and misunderstand the marginalised group.[15] We can explore the plays' relations between citizen men and non-citizen sex labourers through this lens of wilful hermeneutical ignorance, specifically in the ways the citizen men and their proxies deliberately misunderstand and misinterpret the women's actions and voices.

Both plays establish in the opening scenes masculine disbelief of women's speech, particularly that of sex labourers. In *Truculentus*, the prologue speaker gives the barest explanation of the plot, noting that Phronesium lives in a house on stage, and that she demands and hauls off (*poscendo atque auferendo*) everything she can from a lover as soon as she discovers she is loved (12–17). The prologue speaker introduces here a recurring verb, *simulat* (pretends). Phronesium *simulat* that she has borne a son to a soldier so that she can profit from him (18–20). So far, we are set up to expect standard comedy fare: *mala* (wicked) *meretrix* bilks a young man for all he is worth with no regard for affection or morality.[16] When the *adulescens* Diniarchus sweeps onstage we see more 'evidence' of bad faith from sex labourers generally: men are tricked (*ludificetur*, 26), women alternate flattering words and angry ones (*blanditiae* ... *iracundiae*, 28), they demand (*poscat*, 51) luxury goods like jewellery, enslaved women, silver and bronze vessels, engraved couches, imported jewellery boxes (50–5). Diniarchus denigrates sex labourers multiple times, calling them *scorta* (whores, 56, 62, 64, 69).[17]

Diniarchus then switches to excoriating the *meretrix* Phronesium specifically: her name, from the Greek φρόνησις, means wisdom (*sapientia*, 78) but she is a bad (*mala*, 83) woman who employs wisdom badly. He asserts with disgust that she pretends (*simulat*, 86, 87) and attempts to conceal (*celare*, 90) her new schemes from him. When Phronesium's *ancilla* comes outside, Diniarchus turns his ire on her, shouting that they are a household of bad women (131–2) who have taken all his stuff (*rem*, 139) and now want nothing to do with him. When Astaphium is unmoved, Diniarchus changes tactics and complains that she doesn't sweet-talk

---

[14] Mills 1997.
[15] Others in this volume who identify hermeneutical gaps in ancient (and medieval) texts include Bowen (Chapter 10), Freas (Chapter 11) and Hines (Chapter 13).
[16] On the *bona/mala meretrix* in scholarship, see Fantham 1975 and 2000; Gilula 1980 and 2004; James 2013a and Knorr 1995.
[17] *Scortum* is a more derogatory term for a sex labourer. See Witzke 2015.

him anymore (162–3) – now he is upset that she refuses to lie to him! He changes yet again a few lines later, complaining that a *meretrix* sweet-talks a man with her honeyed tongue while her heart is steeped in bitterness (*in melle sunt linguae sitae vostrae atque orationes,/facta atque corda in felle sunt sita atque acerbo aceto*, 178–9). He impugns both the voice and the character of such women. In a little over 200 lines, our protagonist has thoroughly soured the (citizen, masculine) audience on the credibility of the women in Phronesium's house, making it easy for the audience to denounce her cynical tricks when we meet her.

In *Hecyra* too, the opening act establishes men's distrust of non-citizen *meretrices*' characters, in a similarly structured exposé: first the bad habits of *meretrices* generally are revealed, then the bad habits of one *meretrix* in particular. Philotis and Syra chat outside of the *meretrix* Bacchis's home. Philotis seems to reverse expectations, complaining that Bacchis's lover Pamphilus has been unfaithful to Bacchis (58–63) and speaking in defence of *meretrices*. But Syra quickly steps into the role of the money-hungry *lena*,[18] urging Philotis to take all a man has (63–5). When Philotis objects that such a thing isn't fair to the good men, Syra argues that men and *meretrices* are enemies (72–5), putting an end to the conversation and entrenching the usual stereotypes.

When Pamphilus's *servus* Parmeno meets Philotis on stage, we move from talk of *meretrices* generally to Bacchis specifically. We learn that Pamphilus was devoted to Bacchis, but his father wanted his son married and procreating. So Pamphilus married, but kept visiting Bacchis. Bacchis, Parmeno says, became unpleasant and even more demanding (*maligna multo et magis procax facta ilicost*, 159) at that point. Because of this, Pamphilus withdrew his affections altogether in favour of his insulted but silent wife (165–70). Bacchis is thus established as the typical comic *meretrix*, demanding and withholding, and our expectations are set to align with those of the citizen men who will confront her later.

Or are they? In both plays the playwrights allow the non-citizen women to make their case to the audience too. Following Diniarchus's nasty opening monologue, Astaphium explains to the audience why these women treat men the way they do: men steal from them (97–8). They come in a group to distract a *meretrix* while the others steal her goods and eat up her food (101–4), and they justify their robbery as a means of recouping *meretrices*' prices (106). Astaphium's next point is that *meretrices* run a business like any other: men must pay for services, or go elsewhere (141–6). Astaphium again addresses the audience, philosophising that nothing in life is certain, Fortune is fickle and circumstances change, so get that money while you can (217–20). Then she argues, men complain that they are treated badly and that *meretrices* are greedy, but how so? All they ask

---

[18] A woman who is a *leno*, pimp. I have yet to find a satisfactory English term for this Latin word.

is payment for services, because there is no security in their line of work. This is Astaphium's third point: *meretrices* can never put away enough for their future safety (237–40). Syra's advice to Philotis bears the same message, if the viewer realigns their perspective away from that of an elite citizen man. Syra says that men are looking to get the most while providing the least; a *meretrix* must understand this and get her money while she can (67–9).

Furthermore, for all the men's assertion that *meretrices* are untrustworthy, these plays offer much evidence of citizen men's reprehensible behaviour and lack of credibility. *Truculentus*'s Diniarchus claims very early that men must swear false oaths (*periurandum est*, 30), ruin the trust others have in them (*periit . . . fides*, 45; *fide perit*, 48; *fidemque . . . perdimus*, 58), and hide (*celamus*, 60) their extravagance from parents. Furthermore, Diniarchus is a callous rapist who violently assaulted his betrothed, then broke off their engagement, which the *adulescens* describes only as *male facta antiqua mea* (my old deeds done badly, 774). After his opening diatribe about sex labourers' lack of fidelity (as Phronesium has not loved him exclusively), he reveals that he has also had *commercium* (paid sexual relations, 94) with her *ancilla* Astaphium. His rival Stratophanes is no better: he quickly contemplates physical violence when annoyed (musing about breaking the ankles of the women inside Phronesium's home, 637–8). When we finally meet Phronesium's third lover, Strabax, he proclaims he will *eradicare* (tear out from the root) his father and his mother (660) because he loves Phronesium more than his own mother (662).[19] *Hecyra*'s Pamphilus turns out even worse than these Plautine lovers. Over the course of the play we learn that he has abused his new wife (165–7), abandoned her when he discovers she was raped (382–404), used his mother as an excuse to divorce his wife (477–81, while making a false oath, 476), has in fact committed the violent rape of his wife (821–31), and has insisted Bacchis keep all of his secrets (866–8), with the result that both his faultless mother and mother-in-law continue to be suspected by their husbands.

Sex labourers defend themselves throughout Plautus's and Terence's plays, while the citizen men persist in making the same arguments.[20] With all of the justifications from the mouths of the *meretrices* themselves that they are not greedy or wicked but simply doing a job for their survival, coupled with the evidence that the men are hypocrites and impugn women's credibility while having none of their own (a point Astaphium herself makes: *qui alterum incusat probri, sumpse enitere oportet*, 160), how can there be such pervasive stereotypes and prejudices

---

[19] Even the titular Truculentus is revealed as a hypocrite: in his first scene he rudely rejects Astaphium and all her kind, then has completely changed his ways by his next scene, when he flatters and hires Astaphium (675–8).

[20] See Witzke 2015: 16 on the *meretrices*' defences. Other plays with citizen men denouncing sex labourers' 'greed' are Plautus's *Bacchides*, *Epidicus*, *Pseudolus*, *Mostellaria* and Terence's *Andria* and *Eunuchus* (among others).

against these women? The failure of citizen men to understand why sex labourers constantly require money for sex and why they flatter men without meaning it may constitute wilful hermeneutical ignorance. These men, despite repeated explanations from the women themselves, despite evidence inside these women's homes, despite proof of their own fickleness and dishonourable behaviour, refuse to hear and understand these women's authoritative assertions of their own truths. The epistemic violence of systematic silencing of the non-citizen Other and the prejudice against the sex labourer's utterance disinclines the men to listen with credulity. Mary McGowan identifies a silencing related to sex and relationships called 'sincerity silencing': systematic silencing becomes sincerity silencing when the hearer fails to recognise a speaker's sincerity because they wilfully do not want to.[21] It is not in citizen men's interest to believe the women's word, because then they would have to acknowledge the mercantile nature of their relationships and see the unpleasant realities of sex labour.[22]

The fictional ancient citizen men are not alone in their wilful hermeneutical ignorance. We must ask ourselves, why does so much scholarship on these plays and others featuring sex labour highlight the swindling, scheming, demanding and lying of the women?[23] Why do scholars classify *meretrices* as *bona* or *mala*, based on their services to the citizen men in the plays?[24] Why does Phronesium not count among the heroes with comic *malitia* (bad[ass]ness)?[25] Why is Bacchis praised because she gives up a significant source of income? Because the tradition of classics (and most literature studies) is established within an elite masculine dominant perspective, one that implicitly aligns with a 'universalizing' masculine protagonist, regardless of the gender of the reader,[26] we are co-opted into the perspective of the elite citizen male of the plays. Because we read from the dominant place of privilege, it is harder to see the flaws in doing so and to hear the voices of the marginalised we are studying. Feminist epistemology argues that we need women's standpoint – that is, the non-dominant perspective of the non-citizen

---

[21] McGowan 2014: 463, building on Hornsby and Langton 1998.
[22] For the elegiac poet (the poetic counterpart to the comic *adulescens*), such an admittance would constitute a complete failure of the genre: one cannot claim their poetry can sway the hearts of women if they are in fact paying for these women's time. James 2003 calls this the 'elegiac impasse': the poet must prove his poetry is good enough to get sex for free, but the *meretrix* cannot afford to give sex away for free because she needs the poet's money to survive.
[23] de Melo's introduction to his Loeb series is particularly egregious.
[24] See note 16.
[25] Anderson 1993: 103–4. See the Introduction of this volume for a discussion of the 'atomistic knower' in addition to Nally (Chapter 5, this volume) and Bowden (Chapter 12) for discussion.
[26] Fetterley 1978 calls this forced masculine perspective in the reader 'immasculation'.

women who are better placed to see the flaws in the politics and privilege of the dominant citizen male group, rather than the dominant group itself, blinded to its own privilege.

Systematic silencing, testimonial injustice and ancient women

Three marginalised groups suffer systematic silencing and testimonial injustice from the masculine citizen elite (dominant society) in these two plays: citizen women, non-citizen free women and enslaved women. Though the unreliability of *meretrices*' speech is the subject of the plays' opening scenes, it is the word of citizen women in both plays that is trusted least by the citizen men. Broadly, systematic silencing refers to the othering and devaluing of a marginalised group outside of the dominant group, but when the dominant group (here Roman citizens) is subdivided, this epistemic violence can be turned inwards to members of the dominant group who do not share the privilege of those in power in that group. Because gender was such a potent legal and cultural marker in Roman society, citizen women also suffer from systematic silencing and testimonial prejudices – perhaps more so, given that there were mechanisms in place to force credibility in non-citizens that were not available to citizen women's testimony (see below).

In *Truculentus*, the citizen women do not speak. It is only late in the play that they are mentioned at all by Callicles and the non-citizen women he interrogates. Through his post-torture interrogation of the enslaved women, we learn that his unnamed daughter gave birth (789–90), that his wife gave the baby to her *ancilla* to give away (796), and that his daughter was raped by her former betrothed, Diniarchus (825). Callicles has clearly not asked his wife and daughter what happened, or if he did, he did not believe them before torturing the enslaved women. Callicles calls the situation a *facinus muliebre* (a woman's crime, 809), implying conspiratorial behaviour from the citizen and non-citizen women, but the details from and experiences of the citizen *mulieres* (women) are clearly unimportant to him. When the rapist is named, Callicles orders Diniarchus to take the daughter and her child, discounts the dowry,[27] and considers the matter sufficiently resolved.

In *Hecyra*, there is onstage questioning and rejection of the testimony of the citizen women. Lines 198–242 contain a screed against citizen women, particularly mothers-in-law, and specifically Sostrata, the wife of Laches and mother of Pamphilus. Laches accuses Sostrata of quarrelling with her daughter-in-law and

---

[27] The dowry is meant to safeguard the wife, so a father's discounting it to punish the groom hurts the bride more.

driving her out of the house. He calls (citizen women) a group of conspirators (198, note the fear of the collusion of women as in *Truculentus*) meddling in their children's marriages. His terminology demonstrates his underlying prejudice that women cannot be trusted, that they work in secret, that they are enemies within. Sostrata claims to have no idea what is wrong (205–7) and calls his accusations *immerito* (unwarranted, 208). Laches refuses to believe her (229), and Sostrata is robbed of any testimonial power.

Philumena's mother, Pamphilus's mother-in-law, is equally disbelieved and discounted by her husband, Phidippus. After seeing that his daughter has given birth, he goes on the offence, accusing Myrrina of making a mockery (*ludibrio*, 526) of him. Phidippus argues that Myrrine never liked Pamphilus and would rather see the baby dead (532) and her daughter miserable (541–56). He refuses to listen to her denials and even sets guards on the baby to prevent his wife from doing it harm (564–5). These accusations reveal the low opinion Phidippus has of his wife. The citizen fathers then share their suspicion of the wives with each other, reinforcing their beliefs of feminine misdeed (629–32). Both women are denied any further speech in the play. We can only guess at their feelings, but some consequences of testimonial injustice are depression, anger and self-doubt.[28] The fact that the women are treated this way, and that the playwright allows the audience to see it, invites criticism of the epistemic injustice perpetrated by the citizen men. Just as the playwrights do not have to let the sex labourers defend their professional activities (but feature it anyway), they do not need to show the damage this psychological abuse has on the citizen family. We are meant to see the cost of citizen patriarchal authority for the rest of the *familia*.

Enslaved persons were routinely dehumanised by both law and practice in Ancient Rome. Without autonomy and not fully human in the eyes of their owners,[29] enslaved persons were subject to quotidian torture, sexual abuse and sometimes fatal overwork.[30] Philosophies were developed to reinforce Daukas's feedback loop – Aristotle's theory of natural slavery (*Politics*), along with Hippocrates' *On Airs, Waters, Places*, asserted that some places produced persons that were naturally more suited to enslavement: indolent, slow-witted, bodies suited to work, these persons were naturally inferior and thus suited to be ruled by the superior minds of free men. The visibility of these persons in the state of slavery reinforced the association of X ethnicity with slavery, a feedback loop that reinforced the assumed inferiority of such persons.

The inferiority and dehumanisation of enslaved persons made their abuse permissible to the citizen body. Plautus's comedies were especially sensitive to

---

[28] Sostrata is convinced of her own fault by Laches, who undermines her memories of interactions with Philumena, a type of manipulation called 'gaslighting'. See Abramson 2014.
[29] I am using here Richlin's 2017 preferred term for a slaveholder.
[30] See Stewart 2012. See also Wiseman 1985 and Witzke 2016.

violence and exploitation suffered by the enslaved.³¹ Unlike ploughshares or livestock, enslaved persons could speak – Varro goes so far as to call the slave an *instrumentum vocale*, a talking tool.³² Because enslaved persons could speak out against the conditions of their enslavement and the abuses they suffered, their voices had to be silenced and thwarted in other ways. One such method was the testimonial injustice of withholding credibility from the enslaved entirely: the only way an enslaved person could offer testimony was under torture.³³ Without violent motivation, an utterance was invalid.³⁴

In *Truculentus*, the enslaved women are ordered to testify after being tortured partially onstage. Callicles has bound and beaten both the *ancilla* of his wife and the *ancilla* belonging to Phronesium (777). After the beating, he marches them outside, still bound, and orders them to repeat their testimony in public under threat of further torture. He reminds them not to have *duplicis linguas* (double tongues, 781), lest they be killed. It is *vis*, force, one woman says, that makes her confess the truth (*verum fateri*, 783). David Sussman highlights the double injustice of torture: first, violence is done to the body of the tortured person, then violence is done to the mind. The torturer makes the tortured person complicit in the violence against them, suggesting that the tortured person has the ability to confess and make the torture stop. If the torture does not stop, it is the fault of the tortured (they are meant to believe), rather than the torturer.³⁵ By compelling a narrative, the citizen man robs the enslaved women of autonomous speech and allows only utterance in service to his own. Plautus twice juxtaposes binding (*lora/vinclis*) and truth (*verum*), reinforcing patriarchal authority's dependence on corporal punishment (783–4). Because a man cannot compel his citizen wife or daughter with violence,³⁶ their testimony cannot be trusted, and indeed, in *Truculentus* it is not even sought. In the end, it is only because Callicles is told what he wants to hear that women's narratives may be believed.

But these women take back the power of utterance and employ epistemic resistance to speak truth to power (which Callicles actually hears, since it is under

---

³¹ Richlin 2017. See also Stewart 2012.
³² Varro *Res Rus.* 1.17, contra Lewis 2011.
³³ Others in this volume who discuss forms of epistemic silencing and epistemic violence include Weiberg (Chapter 2), Gilbert (Chapter 3), McHardy (Chapter 4), Kim (Chapter 6), Milnor (Chapter 8), Haley (Chapter 9) and Strong (Chapter 15).
³⁴ On the practice of torture for testimony, see Bernstein 2012 and sources.
³⁵ Sussman 2005.
³⁶ On violence against wives, Frier and McGinn 2004: 95. See Quint. *Inst.* 7.4.11; *Cod. Iust.* 5.17.8.2; *POxy.* VI 903, L3581 (cited in Fagan 2011). Physical abuse was grounds for divorce (Sen. *De Ira* 3.5.4). On the paterfamilias's power over children, see Saller 1991, who contends that children were not physically harmed, but rather punished monetarily (as with Callicles' cutting the dowry).

the patriarchal legal authority of torture). Their 'oppositional consciousness',[37] their state and standpoint of marginalisation, has opened up resources for them to understand things that citizen men do not, and speak with the authority of that knowledge. When Callicles calls the situation of the pregnancy and exposure of the child a 'woman's crime' (809), the *ancilla* retorts, 'By god, this evil pertains to men more than women: a man, not a woman, made her pregnant!' (810–11). When Callicles blames her for not stopping the man,[38] she reminds him that men are stronger than women, and they take what they want (812–13). Plautus does not have to write this bit of resistance into the mouth of the tortured woman. This scene isn't funny. Staging the *ancilla*'s resistance is part of Plautus's resistance, yet another rejection of the elite male citizen status quo and prerogative in his plays.[39]

When the fathers in *Hecyra* believe Bacchis has turned Pamphilus against his new wife, and thus their own wives against Pamphilus, Laches demands she come outside to speak with him. The audience has been primed by the men's talk to think Bacchis untrustworthy, a money-grubbing *meretrix*. The old men (*senes*) have agreed to threaten her (*minitemur*, 718) if she is intransigent. As she is a free woman, they don't have legal rights over her body, the way Callicles does over his *ancilla*, but Callicles did not own Phronesium's *ancilla* and tortured her anyway. Bacchis cannot be compelled to testify like the enslaved women, and her testimony is suspect, given that it will not come under torture. She nevertheless swears her trustworthiness as best she can, with an oath (750–2).[40] Phidippus is sceptical of an oath from a *meretrix* (772), so Bacchis offers up her enslaved *ancillae* (standing right beside her) for torture and testimony (773). Her offer demonstrates one of the ways citizen men wield their power over non-citizens: friendships, privileges and the desirability of mimicking the dominant group make non-citizens fall in line where threat of force does not. Bacchis does not share affinity with her enslaved women; she is a free woman and identifies with other free people. By her casual offer of the enslaved women we are reminded of the gulf that exists between the free and the unfree and the power of the dominant group over the marginalised.

Because Bacchis tells a story that may reunite the married couple and secure the *senes*' heir, reinforcing their patriarchal authority in the process, the men look no further into it. They are happy to believe their wives have overreacted, Philumena

---

[37] Collins 1989.
[38] By law, enslaved persons were supposed to put their bodies between their owners and dangers, even unto death. See Lenski 2016.
[39] James 2019.
[40] But Bacchis tells a partial truth: she swears she has had nothing to do with Pamphilus since his marriage, but we know from Parmeno's story that she continued to see him for some time after. See Barsby 2001: 225n32.

has been unreasonable and Pamphilus is blameless in the affair. They require no more testimony from Bacchis, and so she is dismissed. But Bacchis knows other information that threatens Pamphilus's reputation and standing: she knows about the rape. And she has told Myrrine and Philumena her truth. But her friendship with the citizen women (promised by Laches, 790) has the effect of further removing Bacchis from her liminal place between citizen and slave. Her status depends on her silence. The citizen *senes* will never question her further, and Pamphilus tells her to keep quiet about what she knows (866–8). Though Bacchis's deductions and revelations have saved his marriage, the masculine status quo has been preserved, and so women's knowledge is no longer necessary.

#MEQUOQUE? WHAT MAKES RAPE CREDIBLE

Women's credibility on rape has been a concern from antiquity to today. #MeToo was created by Tarana Burke in 2006 on the social media platform MySpace as a tool to help identify and unify women and children survivors of sexual assault, particularly those of colour, to begin 'radical community healing'.[41] She wanted to start a larger conversation about the prevalence of sexual violence and the toll it takes on survivors' lives. In 2017 the hashtag trended anew on Facebook and Twitter following reporting by Ronan Farrow and others on the sexual abuses perpetrated by Harvey Weinstein.[42] One of the rallying cries the new movement promoted is 'believe women'. The reason for the demand is that women were not and are not often believed when it comes to sexual assault. This lack of belief is one of the most pervasive and damaging forms of testimonial injustice. Women, whose perspectives are often discounted or considered less credible by virtue of their gender, suffer doubly when their word and their assault are simultaneously ignored. Rape myths, like 'he didn't mean it' and 'she was asking for it', are deployed to further alienate women's testimony.[43] RAINN estimates that out of 1,000 rapes in the US, only 230 are reported, and of them only nine go to court, and of them only five perpetrators go to prison.[44] The silencing of women is systemic and institutionalised, but #MeToo gives survivors a voice that, when spoken loudly and often with the force of thousands, cannot be entirely ignored.

In modern America, women and others can, at least, speak about their assaults, whether they are believed or not. Women in the ancient world rarely spoke of sexual assault at all. For one, rape was not a bodily crime against a woman – it

---

[41] Ohlheiser 2017.
[42] Farrow 2017 and 2019.
[43] Chapleau, Oswald and Russell 2007. See also Rollero and Tartaglia 2019.
[44] See https://www.rainn.org/statistics/criminal-justice-system.

was a property crime against the man who owned or had control of her.[45] Sexual abuse of enslaved persons was commonplace.[46] Sexual assault of Roman citizen women was likely rare, but the cultural anxiety over rape (and thus paternity) is evident in the age at which women were betrothed (often as children, who were sent to live in their husbands' homes for safekeeping)[47] and the prevalence of the rape plot in the comic genre.[48] The comedies offered a safe space for citizens to interrogate their fears of rape and illegitimacy in the Roman family, which makes translators' suppression of rape all the more surprising. The assaults are often removed entirely, turned into seductions and consensual acts.[49] The popularity of the #MeToo movement has encouraged scholars to revisit fictionalised rapes of ancient Rome to call them what they are, ask new questions, amplify women's speech and step outside the masculine citizen perspective.[50]

When rape occurs in Roman comedy, it is a problem solved by marriage, as we saw in *Truculentus*. Admitting a rape was risky, as rape ruined marriage prospects when the rapist was not an eligible citizen, as is the fear in Terence's *Eunuchus*.[51] Even if the perpetrator were both unmarried and a citizen, if the survivor did not have a powerful citizen protector, the likelihood of forcing a marriage was tenuous, and the rape best not made known (as in Terence's *Adelphoe*). What may seem surprising is that in *Truculentus* the enslaved women do speak out and are believed, even though the identified rapist is a citizen man with far more power. But their successful accusation is not a feminist triumph. Their story is believed because it fits a narrative that serves masculine citizen authority. Callicles believes the women because he is a powerful citizen *senex* who can leverage his status against Diniarchus, who does not wish to be taken to court by Callicles. Using the women's identification of Diniarchus, Callicles can force a marriage, be free of his daughter and grandson, and save money on the dowry. What the women have told him is convenient, so Callicles believes it. He expresses no concern for the bodily experience of his daughter or the psychological horror she may feel in marrying her rapist.

In *Hecyra*, Laches and Phidippus do not even hear the rape tale, but the audience does. Bacchis, alone on stage, shares the details of the terrible rape of

---

[45] James 2013b.
[46] Witzke 2016: 260–4.
[47] Treggiari 1991.
[48] Smith 1994; Pierce 1997; James 1998; Sommerstein 1998; Marshall 2015; Witzke 2020.
[49] Packman 1993.
[50] See https://www.newyorker.com/books/page-turner/reading-ovid-in-the-age-of-metoo.
[51] Lines 720–4. The *ancilla* Pythias has been telling the household about the violent rape of citizen girl Pamphila, but another *ancilla*, Dorias, tells her to forget about the rape and the perpetrator, which would do the girl a favour (because it would preserve her marriageability).

Philumena: that Pamphilus met her in the street at night, violently knocked her down, raped her and ripped a ring (which he later gave to Bacchis) from her finger in the struggle (816–32). The lack of narrative audience underscores the injustice of the rape act; Bacchis can speak it, but no one will hear it. Terence's choice to share it with the audience, however, highlights the cruelties repeatedly visited on the women by men in this patriarchal landscape. When Bacchis goes inside to speak with Philumena and Myrrine, they recognise the ring. This recognition does not lead to a moment of solidarity, triumph and the voicing of truth among women. It instead leads to triumph for Pamphilus and a silencing of the women: Pamphilus believes Bacchis's story of rape because it conveniently solves his problems, he can take his wife and child back without explanation, and he can manipulate Bacchis into keeping the rape a secret from the *senes* (865–8). She agrees and says Myrrine will keep her silence (869–71). Even when women have the epistemic resources to be believed, their voices do not bring justice. Instead, they are used to reinforce the citizen status quo and the women are silenced once more.

CONCLUSION

By highlighting the hypocrisies of the citizen men and their callous approach to rape, as well as the epistemic injustice towards citizen, non-citizen and enslaved women, both playwrights are able to expose and critique the inequities of Roman society. Plautus, a non-citizen and possible freedperson himself, does not care about Roman citizens and their patriarchal preoccupations. He stages their petty dramas perfunctorily and uses these plots to promote the antics, voices and resistances of subaltern characters. The rape subplot, an unfunny inclusion in an otherwise nonstop celebration of a *meretrix*'s comic *malitia*, exposes the cruelty of masculine citizen society and the physical and psychological damages it inflicts on citizen women and enslaved persons. We see the ambivalence of citizen men in listening to women's voices and realise the futility of women's speech: it is only heeded when it is in service to the masculine citizen status quo.

Terence uses his non-citizen, freedperson standpoint to focus on the dramas of citizen families to highlight the repercussions of unchecked masculine citizen privilege. He exposes the desperation of citizen fathers to rule their families with unquestioned power and the resultant alienation of families, neighbours and friends. While Plautus limits his use of the rape plot and overbearing power of the paterfamilias, Terence explores these moral injustices and cruelties in nearly all of his plays. Unlike Plautus's, Terence's citizen women are allowed to speak, which makes their subsequent dismissal a further testimonial injustice: they have a voice that citizen men actively choose not to hear. Feminist epistemology and studies of epistemic injustice have only recently been applied to the study of ancient culture, society and literature. Further application of these theories may open more avenues for understanding the creation of truth and knowledge in ancient societies and the ways in which subaltern persons use epistemic resources to resist the dominant narratives that seek to oppress them.

CHAPTER 8

Incidental Women in the Letters of Cicero

Kristina Milnor

> Insofar as ignorance is ignorance *of* a knowledge – a knowledge that itself, it goes without saying, may be seen as true or false under some other regime of truth – these ignorances, far from being pieces of the originary dark, are produced by and correspond to particular knowledges and circulate as part of particular regimes of truth.
> —Eve Kosofsky Sedgwick, *Epistemology of the Closet*[1]

The Romans generally did not conceptualise what in the modern day we term 'social history' – that is, a history which prioritises the evolution of societal relations and identities rather than the story of public events. Thus, when historians such as Livy or Tacitus incorporate women or other socially marginalised people into their writings, they do so to the degree their activities are connected to those of the men around them.[2] Sometimes those women's activities are understood as furthering the movement of public history, such as when at the end of *AUC* 1, Lucretia's rape spurs the Roman state to shift from monarchic governance to a republic; sometimes they appear to resist or sidestep male political processes, as when the co-conspirator Plancina in *Annals* 3 is saved from the fate of her husband by the intercession of the empress Livia. To a certain degree, the stories we can tell about ancient women will always be framed by the male-authored sources on which we depend and will therefore always appear in this 'relational' frame. Here, however, I would like to approach the historical role of women from

---

[1] Sedgwick 1990: 8.
[2] For example, the Roman orator Hortensia, who is praised for manifesting the rhetorical skill of the men of her family (Hallet 1989: 66).

a different standpoint, one which prioritises not the ways that women fit into traditional historical narratives but rather moments when they disrupt them. By 'disrupt' here I do not mean moments such as when the Sabine women intercede in the war between their fathers and their husbands and force a truce, although such moments are certainly important for writing women's history. But by focusing on women whom the ancient historians themselves considered important, we are in essence following their lead, agreeing to prioritise the same ideas, ideals, roles and identities.[3] Instead, therefore, below I will consider some women most scholars would call 'minor' or 'incidental' figures,[4] in an effort to uncover the dynamics of incidentality itself, the ways in which the relationship of important to not-important frames the epistemology of history.

It is widely agreed among ancient historians that Cicero's correspondence with his friends and relatives represents one of our best sources for the social and political history of the Late Roman Republic. On the other hand, it is clear that the letters represent a different kind of historical document from, for instance, Sallust's *Bellum Catilinae*, or Velleius Paterculus's *Historia Romana*, or Tacitus's *Annales*. Canonical Roman historians tend to be quite explicit about their teleological goals, as they pursue particular stories and themes which suit their purposes. Livy's statement in the preface to the *Ab Urbe Condita* is typical (pr. 10):

> hoc illud est praecipue in cognitione rerum salubre ac frugiferum, omnis te exempli documenta in inlustri posita monumento intueri: inde tibi tuaequae rei publicae quod imitere capias, inde foedum inceptu, foedum exitu, quod vites.

> In thinking about history, this is particularly helpful and fruitful, that you look upon the evidence of every example as placed upon a conspicuous monument: from there you will take up, for your own benefit and that of your state, what you should imitate, and – due to its bad beginnings and bad results – what you should avoid.

This kind of moralising is commonplace in Roman historians, and most modern retellings resist seeing it as a 'real' aspect of Roman history, due to its clear generic

---

[3] See the Introduction to this volume for a discussion of 'evidentiary injustice' and Kim (Chapter 6, this volume) for a related discussion about epistemological gaps within archival and archaeological work.

[4] Minor characters in fiction have been the subject of some interest – both scholarly and popular – in recent years. For an analysis of their use in contemporary novels, see Rosen 2016. For a broader approach which opens with a discussion of minor figures in the *Iliad*, see Woloch 2003. 'Minor' individual contributions to the histories of disciplines and genres have similarly been discussed in, for example, Crease, Martin and Pesic 2018 and Edmunds 2010. There has been little interest in minor figures' function in history, however.

and ideological investments.⁵ At the same time, though, it is necessary that we acknowledge the ways in which ancient histories were framed by this teleological idea: that the story being told has a clear message which prioritises its advance within a particular frame and towards a particular result.

By contrast, however, because they originated as personal letters written in the thick of dramatic historical events, Cicero's letters have both an immediacy and a breadth which is not found in more traditional histories.⁶ In other words, even though the correspondence was edited later for publication, the corpus still includes a great deal which does not speak to a streamlined or end-driven narrative.⁷ There is much still to be done to understand fully the historiographical implications of this, which are broad and speak directly to the ways in which we understand the process by which the Roman Republic came to its destructive end.⁸ Here, however, I will discuss one aspect of the letters which is brought into focus by feminist and other kinds of contemporary critical epistemologies, namely the ways in which we can use the appearance of particular female figures to (re)write the history told in the correspondence.

The fact that Cicero wrote a great deal both to and about the female members of his family has proven a useful window onto the lives of elite women in the period. Terentia, Cicero's first wife and the addressee of a number of letters, as well as his daughter Tullia, have enjoyed a significant presence in biographies of Cicero and social histories of the Late Republic.⁹ But the fact that we have so much information about the female members of Cicero's family has tended to obscure the appearances of other women in his correspondence, shadowy female figures who appear and disappear as casual supporting players in the drama of the orator's life. Some of these women have names with which we are familiar, like Caerellia, who apparently absconded from Atticus's library with some unauthorised copies of *de Finibus*;¹⁰ some of them do not, like the otherwise unknown

---

⁵ See Balmaceda 2017: 3–11.

⁶ The effect that this has had on our perception of Cicero as an individual cannot be overestimated. See Treggiari 1998.

⁷ It is worth noting that Cicero's books of correspondence do not seem (at least on the surface) to begin or end at particularly significant moments in history, and that there is a notable gap around the time of Caesar's assassination. For readings that emphasise the 'literary' nature of the collection, see Jäger 1986 and Hutchinson 1998.

⁸ For some important considerations in this context, see Beard 2006 and Gunderson 2007.

⁹ Indeed, Treggiari 2007 has produced a biography solely focused on the Ciceronian women. As Noy 2008 observed in a review: 'There is more primary source material about Cicero's first wife Terentia and their daughter Tullia than about any other Roman women'.

¹⁰ See McCutcheon 2016.

Tertia, who objected to the presence of Cicero's brother-in-law at a dinner party and caused the orator to change the guest list (*ad Fam.* 16.22). Little attention has been paid to these women, especially those in the latter category, but it cannot be denied that they represented an important thread in the social fabric of Cicero's daily life.

In this essay, therefore, I will look closely at some of these 'incidental' women, as a way of exploring their role both as historical actors and as communicative signs within the letters. Ultimately, we will see that such women have multiple roles but often speak to a deeper anti-history, which Cicero both represents and resists in his correspondence. While it is arguable that all narratives, especially historical ones, contain their own subversion, it is my contention that the letters are particularly rife with productive contradictions. This is precisely because when they were originally written, the story of the Late Republic was still in development; in a very real sense, Cicero and the other authors genuinely did not know what was important or even true. There was surely a selection bias in play in the editorial process,[11] but it seems likely that much of what was originally in individual letters remained there, so that they accurately represent both what actually happened and the biases of those reporting it.[12]

There is often a tension in writing progressive history between wanting to excavate stories which have not been told and acknowledging that certain information is simply not there. Both kinds of absence are true at least in part because of injustice, both at the time the history happened and when we are trying to write about it. That is, what is considered important enough to talk about has not changed as much as we might believe or like it to. But this sometimes leads to a kind of historiographical despair: if we cannot know the lives of the female, the poor, the enslaved in the ancient world, what is left to talk about? Can we only tell the stories of those with the power to frame the historical record around themselves? Does the history of women eventually have to devolve to the history of misogyny, the history of disability to the history of ableism, and so on? The power of approaches which foreground epistemology, however – especially epistemology which resists traditional ideas about expertise, authority and normative identities – is that they can attack both of these problems at once, by asking both what we have been allowed to know and why we have only been allowed to know those things. Moreover, it can mobilise the power of ignorance, as articulated by Eve Kosofsky Sedgwick in my epigraph above. She advocates not seeing the

---

[11] The evidence that Tiro was the editor for all the letters is scanty, although he was clearly involved with the publication of some of them. For an exhaustive summary of what we know about the relationship between Marcus Cicero and Marcus Tiro, see McDermott 1972.

[12] White 2010: 31–62.

absences in the historical record as something to be filled with some kind of real, unmediated knowledge, but rather to recognise that knowledge and ignorance are equally partial, conditional and framed by regimes of truth. This is why I have chosen here to focus on 'incidental' women, because they exist on the boundary between the known and unknown, important enough to appear in Cicero's letters but not worthy of being fully fleshed and incorporated into his life's narrative. By looking closely at an illustrative sample of these female figures, I aim to see how their presence illuminates the dynamics of both the history and the historiography represented in the correspondence. In this way, I argue that we can simultaneously fill in some important 'facts' about ancient women's lives and consider how not knowing about women is simultaneously a position of power and of vulnerability for the Roman political historian.

THE MOTHER AND THE WINE BOTTLES

I will begin with the appearance of a woman whose name we do – perhaps[13] – know: Helvia, the mother of both Marcus Cicero the orator and his brother Quintus. Marcus himself rather famously has literally nothing to say about his mother, and it is often surmised that she died when he was young. This does not seem to have stopped people from speculating about her both today and in antiquity, as Plutarch reports, 'they say that Helvia, Cicero's mother, was born and lived nobly'.[14] The truth value of information in Plutarch is debatable, but my point is that she was then and is now accepted as a 'historical' actor, a woman whose existence and activities in time are without question. Yet Helvia's only appearance in the correspondence is as part of an extremely odd letter from Quintus to Tiro, Marcus's freedman and long-time secretary. Only four letters by Quintus appear in the collection, and all four have some connection to Tiro: three are actually addressed to him, and the fourth was written to Marcus Cicero to congratulate him on manumitting his assistant.[15] It is in one of these that Helvia makes her sole appearance: Quintus opens the letter complaining about Tiro's lack of communication, an offence (*culpa*) for

---

[13] Most people take Plutarch's word that she was named Helvia, but Enos 2005 offers some epigraphic evidence to the contrary.
[14] Κικέρωνος δὲ τὴν μὲν μητέρα λέγουσιν Ἑλβίαν καὶ γεγονέναι καλῶς καὶ βεβιωκέναι (Plut. *Vit. Cic.* 1.1).
[15] Given this, it might be warranted to hypothesise some special connection between Quintus and Tiro, which is borne out by the former's rather hyperbolic tone. Thus, for instance, he suggests he will 'thoroughly kiss' (*dissuaviabor*) his brother's assistant the next time they meet, 'even if I see you in the Forum as I am walking in' (*etiamsi te veniens in medio foro videro*, 16.27.2). See Gunderson 2007 for the sexual overtones of the Cicerones' relationship to Tiro.

which he says he has 'beaten' his brother's freedman 'with the silent criticism of thought' (*verberavi te cogitationis tacito . . . convicio*, 16.6.1). The humour, if it is such, comes across as rather ham-fisted: although Tiro had been freed more than a decade earlier, it appears tactless to threaten him even in jest with the quintessential punishment meted out to the enslaved. Moreover, Quintus continues the theme into the next section, in which he warns Tiro not to appear to be 'stealing' from his patron (*ad Fam.* 16.6):

> Plane te rogo, sicut olim matrem nostram facere memini, quae lagenas etiam inanes obsignabat, ne dicerentur inanes aliquae fuisse, quae furtim essent exsiccatae, sic tu, etiamsi, quod scribas, non habebis, scribito tamen, ne furtum cessationis quaesivisse videaris.
>
> Just as I remember once upon a time my mother used to seal up empty wine jars, lest any be said to have been emptied by stealth, in the same way I simply ask you: even if you do not have anything to write, write anyway, lest you appear to have attempted to steal idleness.

Rather than speaking to him as a freedman with at least a certain amount of autonomy and control over his own time, Quintus suggests that any relaxation on Tiro's part is taking something from his patron.[16]

Even apart from its connection to the heavy-handed 'humour' in the letter, the comparison which Quintus draws to his mother's activities is rather opaque. Apparently, she would reseal jars once they had been emptied, in an effort to prevent questions about where their contents had gone. On a practical level, this seems like it would be counterproductive – how would you know which ones were empty, and thus when your stock was running low? The point, though, seems to be twofold: first, a pun on the word *obsignare*, which could be applied equally to sealing wine jars and letters; second, an emphasis on the outside appearance of a thing – the jars 'full' of wine, but actually dry, standing in for letters 'full' of news but actually empty. This is underscored by the passive verbs (*dicerentur, videaris*) used in both halves of the comparison. What is important is not, in fact, what is really there, but what an outside observer might talk about or see. What, though, is the significance of the appearance here of Helvia, the only such appearance in the entire corpus of the correspondence? While it is certainly possible that Quintus simply had a closer relationship to their mother than Marcus, I would argue that she is put to work here with a particular rhetorical and ideological function, one which cannot be divorced from the overall point of the letter itself. Wherever we come down on the question of whether Tiro appreciated Quintus's 'humour' – and whether Quintus himself intended offence or not – the letter is an attempt to

---

[16] Beard 2006 comments on the bizarre usage of the language of enslavement in this letter.

express and exert power, and as such deploys the language of social hierarchy in revealing terms.

The particular image of Helvia here is one which is imbued with traditional domesticity. Her (alleged) thriftiness and care for the household resources is a standard trope in the representations of hardy rustic *matresfamilias* found in Roman literary texts from Cato the Elder to Horace and Juvenal. Indeed, as a young man Marcus Cicero himself had translated into Latin Xenophon's *Oeconomicus*,[17] a text well known and celebrated for its portrayal of the ideal farmer's wife, discussed briefly in the introduction to this volume. The translation as a whole is lost, but we do have part of it in the form of an extended quotation at the beginning of Book 12 of Columella's *de Re Rustica*. Columella's interest in this portion of his work is very much in preservation, as he uses the duties of the *vilica* (the female overseer or 'bailiff's wife') to contain, control and stabilise the agricultural products the preceding books have described.[18] Thus, he quotes Cicero's translation of Xenophon to emphasise the good woman's duties within the house: *nam et fruges ceteraque alimenta terrestria indigebant tecto, et ovium ceterarumque pecudum fetus, atque fructus clauso custodiendi erant* (for corn and other products of the earth require shelter, and the young of sheep and other kinds of livestock, and the harvest need to be preserved in an enclosure, *DRR* 12. pref. 3). The image of Helvia carefully resealing empty bottles, therefore, powerfully evokes this ideal of the good mother and wife whose job it is to guard and maintain the resources of the household.

This image of Quintus's mother performing correct domesticity also certainly redounds to the author's own credit. It cannot be forgotten that this letter was written at a time when women were enjoying a great deal more power and influence than they had previously in Roman public life,[19] something to which Marcus Cicero's letters from the same period abundantly attest. On the other hand, it was also a moment when the display and praise of traditionally virtuous women was being used by men to further their own political ends – as, for example, the proliferation of funerary eulogies for female family members delivered by politicians. Thus, for instance, Julius Caesar in 68 BCE had used his *laudatio* at his aunt's funeral to emphasise his family's connections to the *sanctitas regum . . . et caerimonia deorum* (holiness of kings . . . and the reverence of the gods, Suetonius, *Div. Iul.* 6). Marcus Cicero himself composed a eulogy for Cato's sister Porcia in the mid-40s BCE.[20] Thus, Quintus surely had an investment in representing his mother as a participant in traditional domesticity.

---

[17] For a discussion, see Milnor 2005: 254–65.
[18] Henderson 2002: 124–5.
[19] Cluett 1998.
[20] *ad Att.* 13.48; SB 345.

In addition, however, we might also note the message which the image must have been meant to communicate to the letter's addressee. In the passage quoted above, Quintus uses it to remind Tiro of his responsibilities as a freedman – responsibilities which arose, of course, from his prior role as an enslaved person serving the family. On one level, the image makes the point that, like Quintus's mother, Tiro too has a social function and duties to perform. He, like she, is an integral part of the work of the household. The pun on the word *obsignare* initially leads us to think that the parallel is between Helvia's duty to seal the wine bottles and Tiro's duty to seal a letter to Quintus. By the end of the metaphor, though, there has been a shift: the comparison is not between the tasks themselves, but between the roles and power of those performing them. Quintus warns Tiro that he must avoid the appearance of having performed a 'theft' (*furtum*) by failing to deliver news, which echoes not the sealing of the jars, but the imagined furtive (*furtim*) emptying of them. In other words, Tiro's position is not the same as Helvia's but rather of those people – presumably enslaved or other subordinate members of the household – who might have stolen the wine. Although Quintus begins by implying some sort of equality between Tiro and his mother, he ends by reemphasising Tiro's role as a (previously) enslaved subject under her authority. Like many women who have belonged to the ruling class in a hierarchical society, Helvia is thus implicated in both Quintus's rhetoric and the patriarchal power structures of her time.

Helvia's role in this letter, however, is framed by what I would term her 'incidentality'. That is, on the surface, her historicity is unquestionable: Quintus and Marcus really did have a mother at some point. At the same time, though, the fact that Quintus refers to this female figure as his mother is a red herring, since the information he provides is so generically and ideologically inflected that we cannot discern a real woman behind the image. In this way, then, the appearance of Helvia is an evocation of historicity without substance, a gesture to Quintus's actual historical experience as a child, which is subsequently revealed to be no more than an empty symbol. The appearance of Quintus's and Marcus's mother thus points to the impossibility of finding 'real' women, as distinct from the images used to represent and understand them, in the historical record. At the same time, however, as we might see Helvia as the vanishing point of historical epistemology – a figure who simultaneously offers and withholds knowledge about the past – it is also important to note the ways that knowledge itself is at issue in this letter. As I noted above, on a practical level it would seem to make little sense to reseal empty jars, for how then would anyone know which were empty and which full, and thus where the household's supply stands? The answer is, of course, that the person – the woman – who sealed them would know and could conceal or reveal that knowledge as much as she chose. And, in fact, Tiro too has that power; as much as Quintus may resist the idea, whether Tiro decides to communicate what he knows is actually up to him. Thus, Quintus may have intended to press this image of his mother into service for himself, but ultimately we are left with the idea that those lower down on the male social hierarchy have influence that transcends the strictures on them, with power and knowledge beyond that of the men around them.

The historical figure of 'Helvia' thus dissolves very quickly when subjected to ideological scrutiny, suggesting that historicity itself has limitations when we attempt to apply it to those traditionally marginalised in Roman society. At the same time, though, the letter from Quintus also emphasises how even men high up in the patriarchal social system actually depend on the knowledge of those further down it. Although Quintus tries in the most heavy-handed of ways to assert his authority over Tiro, the image of Helvia's secret wine bottles insists on both her and his ability to conceal what they know. What, however, can we make of incidental women in the letters who do not even pretend to historicity, who are presented as always-already imaginary, even as they are ascribed real social functions? Here we find the reverse, or an expansion, of the Helvia effect, as we see a heavily stylised and symbolic female figure who is placed centrally on the stage of history.

MONEY MATTERS

In 62–61 BCE, Cicero was, as usual, in need of money. He had purchased a mansion on the Palatine Hill that left him so impecunious that he joked to P. Sestius that he was in search of a conspiracy to join so that he could pay it off (*ad Fam.* 5.6.2). According to Aulus Gellius, he had already received a loan of HS 2,000,000 from P. Sulla, whom Cicero had defended against the charge that he had conspired with Catiline. This loan was viewed askance by some, as both law and social custom in Rome at the time militated against an advocate's receiving monetary compensation. The traditions of *amicitia*, however, were such that Cicero could characterise the loan to Atticus as simply using 'the resources of friends' to arrive at 'a certain status' (*homines intellegere coeperunt licere amicorum facultatibus in emendo ad dignitatem aliquam pervenire, ad Att.* 1.13.6). Unfortunately, though, even this infusion of cash did not cover the full price of the house, and the orator was thus forced to seek monetary assistance through different channels. Cicero complains to Atticus at the beginning of January 61 BCE that he may have to resort to an actual money-lender and borrow money at interest due to the sluggishness of a certain 'Teucris', a woman whom scholarly consensus identifies as some kind of financial agent for Cicero's co-consul, Antonius (*ad Att.* 1.12):[21]

---

[21] See Lange 1972 for a full description of this financial episode.

Teucris illa lentum sane negotium, neque Cornelius ad Terentiam postea rediit. opinor ad Considium, Axium, Selicium confugiendum est; nam a Caecilio propinqui minore centesimis nummum movere non possunt. Sed ut ad prima illa redeam, nihil ego illa impudentius, astutius, lentius vidi 'libertum mitto', 'Tito mandavi'. σκήψεις atque ἀναβολαί; sed nescio an ταὐτόματον ἡμῶν. Nam mihi Pompeiani prodromi nuntiant aperte Pompeium acturum Antonio succedi oportere eodemque tempore aget praetor ad populum.

That Teucris is a slow piece of work, and Cornelius has not come again to Terentia. I think I shall have to make my way to Considius, Axius or Selicius; for even his relatives can't get a penny from Caecilius for less than 12 percent. But to go back to those earlier matters, I have never seen anyone more shameless, more cunning and lazier than her. 'I'm sending a freedman', 'I've handed it over to Titus'. *Excuses* and *delays*; but it might be a *blessing in disguise*. For Pompey's representatives tell me that Pompey will move openly that there needs to be a successor appointed for Antony and at the same time the praetor will put it to the people.

A month later, Cicero is still – apparently – waiting for his money, although he asserts that he is hopeful that Teucris will provide the funds (*Teucris illa lentum negotium est, sed tamen est in spe*, *ad Att.* 1.13). Finally, in the middle of February, he writes to Atticus that Teucris has carried out her promises (*Teucris promissa patravit, ad Att.* 1.14.7).

'Teucris' has historically proven somewhat tantalising to scholars, in part because it is not at all clear how and why she might have been acting on Antonius's behalf. Women were formally barred from acting as professional *argentarii*, who were generally responsible in Rome for brokering loans (*Dig.* 2.13.12), but it is not clear what authority a woman would have to represent him informally. It has been supposed in the past that 'Teucris' is a pseudonym for Antonius's wife Cornelia, or possibly an insulting appellation for the man himself. Shackleton Bailey is dubious about both interpretations, however, noting that the way Cicero has her speak of Atticus by his praenomen (*Tito mandavi*) suggests a relationship of more intimacy than existed between Atticus and Antonius[22] – and what was true of Antonius was surely also true of his wife. Finally, when Cicero reports the delivery of the money, it is Teucris to whom he attributes the fulfilment of the promises, not Antonius, using the relatively rare verb *patro*. This is presumably a little bit of a joke, since the word is generated from *pater* and its sense of a male person who has the power to effect things. Joking aside, though, it seems unlikely that he would have used the word if she were simply channelling someone else's money.

---

[22] Bailey 1965 (vol. 1): 297.

Nevertheless, although Teucris ultimately is able to provide Cicero his much-needed loan, the portrait which he draws of her is unflattering, almost a caricature. Indeed, a close examination of it reveals a number of flourishes which seem to be drawn from the world of comedy. First, Teucris's name must be a pseudonym, or at least a nickname: a woman who was on familiar terms with Atticus and with enough money to lend some to Cicero must surely have been at least a freedwoman. 'The woman from Troy' could well have been her enslaved name, then adopted as her cognomen as was common. On the other hand, the letters in which she is so named by Cicero were being sent to a person called 'Atticus' due to his love of Athens. The name 'Teucris' could thus hide a similarly well-born Roman citizen who simply had some personal or ancestral association with the area around Troy. Whatever the source, however, by referring to her by a Greek name which would connect her with a Greek-speaking place, Cicero invokes the world of Hellenistic Magna Graeca which is the setting of much of New Comedy.

Moreover, once he has established her identity as a 'Greekling', Cicero goes on to characterise her with adjectives which recall the comic types of the bad slave and the miser: 'shameless', 'cunning', 'lazy'. He follows this with a brief but notable prosopoeia – a rhetorical device which the orator uses elsewhere for comic effect – in which he has her high-handedly dismiss him (*libertum mitto*) and display a possibly presumptuous familiarity with Atticus (*Tito mandavi*). Additionally, Cicero's description of Teucris as *lentum negotium* ('a slow business', which he uses again of her in *ad Atticum* 1.13) is an unusual comparison of a person to a thing. But it is echoed in Cicero's later description of his enemy Lucius Calpurnius Piso Caesonius in his speech before the Senate after his exile (*post Red.* 14), in a portrait widely recognised as influenced by comic invective: *sine sensu, sine sapore, elinguem, tardum, inhumanum negotium, Cappadocem modo abreptum de grege venalium diceres* (You would say that this piece of work – without sense, without taste, mute, slow, beastly – was a Cappadocian just now taken from the flock of slaves for sale).

Finally, Cicero concludes the brief description of Teucris by switching to Greek and citing a partial line from a lost ancient comedy, perhaps by Menander. Although he only includes 'accident... than us', the full text was likely something along the lines of 'accident provides more cleverly than we do'. As critics have argued, this kind of incomplete quotation depends on the reader's shared knowledge of the source text, so that he can finish the thought and get the joke. Here, I would argue, there is a further effect which builds on the first: once we have recognised Menander, we can also read back through the reference and appreciate the miniature comic portrait which Cicero has just provided, one which is based on a previously unappreciated comic stereotype. But although, as I said before, that type seems to draw some qualities from both the bad slave and the miser, there is also reason to believe that there was an even more apt persona for Cicero to cite. We know that Plautus wrote a play called, in fact, *Faeneratrix* ('The Female

Money-Lender'), and although the play is now lost, the only other instance of the word in extant Latin comes from a context clearly influenced by comedy. In Book 8 of Valerius Maximus's *Memorable Words and Deeds*, under the heading of remarkable private trials, he relates the complicated story of C. Visellius Varro and his mistress Oticilia. The pair came up with a scheme for Oticilia to be able to inherit under Varro's will without disclosing their improper relationship, by having the woman record a fake debt which would then be 'repaid' by Varro's heirs. Unfortunately, Varro did not die speedily and Oticilia got impatient, demanding that the fraudulent loan be returned. Valerius describes this turn of events as *ex amica obsequenti subito destrictam feneratricem agere coepit* (from the attentive girlfriend she suddenly began to play the rigid female money-lender, 8.2.2). Although perhaps not as well known as the *servus callidus*, it would seem that the *faeneratrix* was readily available as a comic stereotype on which Cicero could draw in describing Teucris.

Indeed, it is worth noting that the rest of *ad Att.* 1.12 also seems to allude in various ways to the world of comedy. Cicero moves from his precarious financial situation to complaining about a certain Hilarus, a freedman of Cicero's and a client of Atticus's, who is working with Antonius in Macedonia. Cicero begs his friend to look into Hilarus's activities and *nebulonem illum ... ex istis locis amove*. The word *nebulo* ('shady guy') is most commonly found elsewhere in comedy and satire. Moreover, this letter also represents the first mention of an event which would later take on outsized importance in both Cicero's discourse and his career, namely the Bona Dea scandal involving P. Clodius Pulcher. Considering its later notoriety, Cicero's initial description of it is relatively brief and mild: *P. Clodium Appi f. credo te audisse cum veste muliebri deprehensum domi C. Caesaris cum sacrificium pro populo fieret, eumque per manus servulae servatum et eductum; rem esse insigni infamia*. (I expect you have heard that P. Clodius son of Appius was caught in women's clothes at the house of C. Caesar, while the public sacrifice was happening, and that he was saved and extracted through the help of a slave girl; it's a remarkably disgraceful matter.) Although it is only referred to here in passing, it's clear that the episode contained elements which would later make it comic putty in Cicero's hands: the aristocratic politician dressed up as a woman, sneaking into the respectable chief priest's house; the slave girl (pointedly described with the rare diminutive *servula*) who steps in to rescue and smuggle him out again; even the 'funny' alliteration of *INsigni INfamia* and the combination, as in the theatre, of sight (*insigni*) and sound (*infamia*).

In a certain sense, then, the depiction of Teucris is of a piece with the rest of the letter, which draws on various comic personae and tropes to describe people and events. Teucris, however, stands out, and not just because she is first, but because Cicero seems to go out of his way to pull the female money-lender out of the world of Roman comedy and send her back to (an imaginary) Greece. Indeed, although Plautus's *Faeneratrix* is all but lost, there are signs that it too was interested in highlighting the cross-cultural scramble represented by Roman New Comedy. In one of the two fragments that still remain, the grammarian Festus quotes the play: *Heus tu, in barbaria quod dixisse dicitur / Libertus suae patronae, id ego dico [tibi]: / Libertas salve, vapula Papiria* ('Hey you! What the freedman is said to have said to his patroness in a barbarian land, I say to you: "Hello freedom; get whipped, Papiria!"' (Fest. P. 372 M)). The *libertus* and his *patrona*, not to mention the reference to the old Patrician gens Papiria, firmly situate the setting in a Roman social context. But the speaker also notes that the story originates from *barbaria* ('the uncivilised world'), a humorous description of Rome when placed in the mouth of a Greek, as in *Poenulus* 598. Moreover, the quotation also foregrounds the issue of female property ownership as a cultural phenomenon, as the wealthy, high-born *patrona* is emphatically characterised as originating 'somewhere else'.

In other words, both the role of the title character of *Faeneratrix* and the little that remains of the text seem to suggest – as is true elsewhere in Roman comedy – that the play had more than a passing interest in the conflicted cross-cultural resonances of women's property and the ways they disposed of it. On Plautus's side, there might be various motivations for this, but on Cicero's, the image seems to mark a deliberate attempt to distance himself from the anticipated transaction. After all, when Atticus heard that Cicero had borrowed money from a different woman, Caerellia, he apparently expressed his disapproval: *de Caerellia quid tibi placeret Tiro mihi narravit: debere non esse dignitatis meae* (Tiro has told me what you consider best in regard to Caerellia: [you think] it is not worthy of my station to be in debt, *ad Att.* 12.51). By casting Teucris as a low-status foreigner, Cicero is able to disavow any relationship implied by the loan. Remember that the other half of the money for the mansion had come from Sulla, and was clearly part of the ongoing social and political exchange of favours between the two men. Indeed, Cicero himself invokes the language of *amicitia* (*amicorum facultatibus*) in describing the loan to Atticus. The orator clearly had no intention of establishing a similar intimacy with Teucris; his later representation of his relationship with Caerellia[23] illustrates how ambivalent he was about the obligations entailed by such social and financial dealings with a woman.

---

[23] Caerellia, although we know almost nothing about her outside of her appearance in Cicero's letters, is an interesting figure. Cicero is quite irritated that Atticus gave her access to the preliminary drafts of *de Finibus*, and he speaks rather sneeringly of her 'evident enthusiasm for philosophy' (*ad Att.* 13. 21. 5). He is also later at pains to note that he rejected her petitions about his relations with his second wife (*ad Att.* 14. 19. 4). At the same time, however, we have preserved a letter he wrote on her behalf, asking for some assistance for her from the governor of Asia Minor (*ad Fam.* 13. 72), and his letters to her were friendly enough that later tradition saw the pair as lovers (Dio 46. 18. 4). See Austin 1946.

Like Helvia, then, Teucris is also an incidental woman, one whose historicity is assured, but who is rendered less 'real' by the author's framing of her as a cultural fantasy. While Helvia takes on the role of the good housekeeper, Teucris is the comic *faeneratrix* – a Roman figure placed self-consciously in a fantasised Greek milieu, out of place in the 'historical' Roman world of men, money and social exchange. It is not, perhaps, entirely surprising that it is in the context of money and resources that both Teucris and Helvia appear in the letters. Although the latter's role is more metaphorical than the former's, both are credited (in all senses of the word) with having exclusive access to things required by the men around them. Roman women's participation in economic life, particularly in the context of elite families, was often the subject of some patriarchal anxiety. This was especially true at the time that the letters were originally written, a time of civil conflict, when women were often the ones left behind to manage resources while their male relatives were embroiled in political or actual battle. The idea, therefore, that women should and did fall outside the bounds of history was both true in a real sense – they were not usually politically implicated in the same ways as men – and also aspirational, as they had real and important social functions to perform. Indeed, it seems hardly accidental that the two *laudationes* for women which we have surviving from around this period are quite explicit on this point: that women's virtues are unchanging and thus outside of time, and also that the period of the civil wars represented an unprecedented moment for their public and historical display.[24] The containment of Helvia and Teucris within stereotypes and literary figures is thus one way of mitigating their historical roles, even though some of their 'real' activities nevertheless seep through the letters' descriptions. On the other hand, as Samuel Eliot Morison once observed, 'history is . . . very chancy', and Cicero's correspondence does offer us one more set of female figures worth considering in the context of what and how we know about the ancient past. These figures offer, I will argue, a somewhat more empowered way of thinking about the role of 'incidental' women.

FEMALE FORGERIES

As a last example of what 'incidentality' can tell us about the epistemological role that women play in Cicero's epistolary world, I would like to look at a relationship which they have to the concrete textual medium itself, that is, the physical form of the epistle. There is a certain level of metacognition involved in thinking about letters within a corpus of letters, even as the original epistolary form of those texts was transformed into that of a literary corpus. In this sense,

---

[24] By which I mean the laudatio Murdiae (*CIL* vi. 10230, on which see Milnor 2005: 31–2) and the so-called laudatio Turiae (Wistrand 1976 and Milnor 2005: 215–16).

women's relationship to the letters within the letters can be seen as metonymous for their overall relationship to the Ciceronian story being told. In some ways, these women too – like Helvia and Teucris – are contained by the roles and ideals to which they have been assigned by the letters' authors. At the same time, however, the ways in which the women discussed below actually use letters against factual or 'true' history is instructive and opens up a different space for thinking about the epistemological usage of incidental female figures.

One fairly famous incident in Marcus Cicero's personal life involved letters from his brother Quintus. This was during the extremely fraught period of the civil war between Caesar and Pompey, during which Marcus was pressured by both sides to align himself with them, and he – whether from indecision, cowardice or genuine ambivalence is a matter of opinion – steadfastly refused to do so. Although Quintus, a supporter of Pompey, initially supported his brother's position, he apparently became convinced that Marcus was speaking ill of him to Caesar and wrote a series of letters to friends denouncing his brother. Marcus became aware of the letters' content somewhat by accident, but since they were included in a packet delivered to him and he had not yet delivered all of them, he opened and read the ones which remained. He was naturally distressed by Quintus's words and wrote about it to Atticus, sending along the opened letters so that Atticus himself could judge whether they should still be delivered to their intended addressees. Marcus remarks that, should Atticus decide it would be appropriate simply to pass them on, it could be done without anyone knowing that they had been previously read: *nam quod resignatae sunt, habet, opinor, eius signum Pomponia* (as to the fact that they were opened, I think that Pomponia has his seal, 11.9; SB 220). The implication is that Atticus's sister, married at the time to Quintus but apparently not with him in Sicyon, had the means to return the letters to the state in which they left their author and thus disguise the fact that their contents were known.

There is a great deal that lies behind this brief notation. First, the fact that Pomponia had not joined her husband when he travelled east to support Pompey is not, perhaps, a great surprise – although, as we will see below, other wives and families certainly did so. Indeed, many of the extant letters from Marcus to Terentia deal with his hope and hers that she will join him in his flight from Rome. But Pomponia and Quintus had a tumultuous marriage, such that the very earliest preserved letter from Marcus to Atticus (1.5; SB 1) is much concerned with the pair's unhappiness with one another. So it makes some sense that Pomponia is still resident in Rome, perhaps even living with her brother. In addition, Marcus here seems more than confident that Pomponia will side with her brother and brother-in-law over her husband – so confident, in fact, that he treats it as a given fact. Again, this may be the result of the known hostility between the couple, but her collusion in this scheme against her husband suggests that Quintus has (willingly or not) left her with significant power to harm his interests. By this point in history, many women would have had access to their own seals, in order to conduct their own business,[25] but it also makes sense that wives would have had copies of their husbands', in order to manage affairs in their absence. But this fact would, if true, throw a different light on questions of 'male' authority in the evidentiary record: how much is actually women using, or abusing as in Pomponia's case, the tools of power belonging to the men around them? How much of what we know as the 'true' history of men is actually fabricated for their, and our, consumption?

If this seems like a stretch, I would note that Marcus's letters to Atticus actually provide local and unwitting witness to this process in action. In the early part of the civil conflict between Pompey and Caesar, as the latter marched his troops south from the Rubicon, the former fled to Brundisium and from there took ship to the eastern provinces. The departure was chaotic, especially because the group included not just Pompey and his army, but also the consuls and tribunes who supported him, and many of their households. Marcus, who had left Rome but was not yet willing to throw his lot in fully with Pompey, was on tenterhooks waiting to hear of his departure, in part because he was still hoping there could be a reconciliation between the antagonists. On March 11, Marcus wrote to Atticus that he had just received a letter from an unknown correspondent in Capua who reported that Pompey had departed safely with 30,000 troops and that he had disabled all of the remaining ships in the port, in order (presumably) to prevent pursuit. Cicero quotes the letter he received directly, concluding with the remark, *de hac re litterae L. Metello tribuno pl. Capuam adlatae sunt a Clodia socru quae ipsa transiit* (about this matter a letter was sent to Lucius Metellus the tribune from his mother-in-law Clodia,[26] who herself crossed [sc. with them], 9.6.3; SB 172). The letter received by Marcus was therefore not from Clodia or L. Metellus but some unknown third person. Nevertheless, that person seems to have had sufficient authority and access that Marcus believed them wholeheartedly; he goes on to express his grief and dismay to Atticus that 'Pompey and the consuls have departed from Italy' (*Pompeius et consules ex Italia exierunt*, 9.6.4).

That Marcus believed the information in the letter is significant because almost none of it turned out to be true. Pompey and the consuls were still in Brundisium, although it is possible that they had sent their retinue on ahead. Clodia's troop numbers were, according to a later letter to Atticus, doubled, and the remaining ships, it turned out, not disabled at all. In fact, Pompey would subsequently use those very ships to fight back against Caesar when the latter eventually arrived in

---

[25] See, for example, Becker 2016: 926–7.
[26] It is unclear which Clodia this was, although the connection to L. Metellus gives some pointers. It is possible but unlikely that this is the same Clodia so demonised by Cicero in the pro Caelio. Skinner 2011: 56–7 thinks it was her youngest sister.

Brundisium. Atticus apparently expressed doubt about the letter's veracity in his response to Marcus and on the 17th of March the latter was able to confirm that the information provided had been faulty. He, at any rate, attributes the incorrect troop numbers to Clodia's original letter: *recte non credis de numero militum; ipso dimidio plus scripsit Clodia* (you correctly did not believe the number of troops; Clodia doubled the total, 9.9.2; SB 176). Shackleton Bailey, however, is incredulous that Clodia could have been wrong on so many points, especially the question of whether Pompey and the consuls had actually departed with the flotilla for Greece. He therefore concludes that the fault lies in the transmission of the letter's contents: 'Presumably C.'s unnamed correspondent in Capua had been given a garbled version of Clodia's letter'.[27]

Shackleton Bailey's explanation is, of course, possible, although the specificity of the troop numbers and the errors in all the information conveyed suggests more than merely a 'garbled' transmission. In fact, if we consider the false information as a whole, it becomes clear that all of it could very well have been a plant, intended to mislead Caesar and his advisors. The larger number of troops would make Pompey's position seem less tenuous, and the idea that he had already departed and burned the remaining ships behind him could very well have slowed or even stopped Caesar's advance towards Brundisium. If there was no one there to fight, there was no reason for Caesar to go to the Adriatic port, and indeed, once the battle was over and Pompey actually departed for Greece, his opponent lost no time in turning around and heading back in the direction of Rome. In other words, the intelligence attributed to Clodia here has all the hallmarks of a Pompeian misdirection. In addition, we might also wonder, as Marcus does not, how Clodia would have managed to send a letter about these events so quickly: the supposed departure had taken place on the 4th of March and Marcus's letter to Atticus is dated the 11th. Theoretically, with good weather, favourable winds and fast horses, Clodia could have travelled from Brundisium to Dyrrhacium and then sent a letter back to Capua in about five days, leaving two for the anonymous letter to make its way from Capua to Formiae and Cicero to write to Atticus. But, once again, considering the lack of veracity in the letter's contents, I would suggest that it might also misrepresent the authority of its author – that is, it seems fair to wonder if Clodia had even left Brundisium at all.

Other than emphasising that Marcus Cicero himself was sometimes too credulous, what is the historiographical significance of the letter from Clodia? Given the doubts expressed above, it is possible that the letter had nothing to do with Clodia, that she was chosen as a convenient mask for the purposes of conveying Pompeian misinformation. In a sense, however, it does not matter whether she actually wrote it or was simply imagined to be a believable source for the letter.

---

[27] Bailey 1965 (vol. 6): 364n3.1.

It should be noted that Marcus goes out of his way to name her as its author, a consideration which he does not afford his unnamed Capuan correspondent. It seems likely that he considered her on some level a more reliable source of the information, likely because as a woman rather than an active combatant she might be understood simply to be reporting what she observed. Moreover, her supposed lack of experience in military matters could be used by the Pompeian side as an excuse once the information was found to be false, and her role as the tribune's mother-in-law provided a non-political motive for communicating these details to him. In short, the fact that as a woman she was considered both above and below the problematic actions of the men around her meant that she was an excellent conduit for the propagation of lies. But once again, like Pomponia, we can see the ways in which Clodia adopts and adapts her disempowered position to manipulate not just current events but the history which records them.

For traditional, fact-based historical epistemology, therefore, Clodia represents a problem, one which in some ways is not dissimilar to that presented by Helvia and Teucris as discussed above. Like them, she is a threat, not just to our ability to say what really happened in Brundisium, but to our faith in the historical record itself. What we, and they, believe about Roman women's relationship to and influence on the processes of public history ends up undermining our ability to tell its story. While Helvia and Teucris, however, are almost entirely subsumed by the images which the letters' authors graft onto them, Pomponia and Clodia ultimately have greater purchase on the historical record – in part because they have material access to the actual stuff of history, namely the letters themselves.[28] As I noted above, this has implications for how we imagine the 'truth' of generally presumed male authorship. Yet to take one step further, and inspired by Sedgwick's call for the mobilisation of ignorance, we can also use the doubt incidental women generate as a tool to attack traditional epistemology, which insists on certainty, facts, *knowledge* to fill in gaps in the historical record. After all, as we see above, sometimes ignorance not only serves the interests of the oppressed but is also deliberately generated by them, in a kind of guerrilla action against the supposed stability of epistemology. In this sense, it is necessary to pay attention to the historically disempowered, not just as the known or the unknown, those present in or absent from history, but as themselves the knowers and the ignorant, the generators of historical narratives in their own right.

---

[28] This, of course, opens up the question of class, which, because of the ways in which we consume and transmit most history, is arguably the most important factor in determining who makes an imprint on the historical record. Most people who could read and write in antiquity were members of the elite, although enslaved and formerly enslaved people could also be educated. For a survey of Roman women's participation in education, see Hemelrijk 2015.

CHAPTER 9

Signifying Dido: Constructs of Race and Gender in Augustan Rome

Shelley P. Haley

'What are the words you do not yet have? What do you need to say? What are the tyrannies you swallow day by day and attempt to make your own, until you will sicken and die of them, still in silence?'

—Audre Lorde 1978, 'Transformation of Silence into Language and Action', 41

'Until Lions Have Their Own Historians, the Story of the Hunt Will Always Glorify the Hunter: Africanizing History, Feminizing Knowledge',

—Nwando Achebe 2020, *Female Monarchs and Merchant Queens in Africa*: Preface, 11

As I was preparing a paper for another publication, I came across the following description of a Black woman in the apocryphal *Acts of Peter* 22. In it, Marcellus relays to Peter a dream Marcellus has just had:

For just now as I slept for a little, I saw you sitting on a high place, and before you a great assembly; and a most evil woman, who looked like an Ethiopian (*Aethiopissimam*), not an Egyptian (*Aegyptiam*), but was all black (*nigram*), clothed in filthy rags. She was dancing with an iron collar about her neck and chains on her hands and feet. When you saw her, you said aloud to me, 'Marcellus, . . . take off her head!' But I said to you, Brother Peter, I am a senator of noble family and I have never stained my hands, nor killed even a sparrow at any time'. When you heard this, you began to cry even louder, 'Come, our true sword, Jesus Christ, and do not only cut off the head of this demon (*daemonis*) but cut in pieces all her limbs in the sight of all these whom I have approved in thy service'. And immediately a man who looked like yourself, Peter, with sword in hand, cut her all to pieces, so that I gazed upon you both, both on you and on the one who was cutting up the demon, whose likeness caused me great amazement.[1]

As a Black woman who applies a lens of critical race feminist theory and of Black feminist thought to my research as a classicist, I was astounded. That the *Acts of Peter* is considered apocryphal afforded me no comfort; I see this same anti-Black attitude and misogynoir in every aspect of my life. Always the optimist, I also saw this as another opportunity to put my work in conversation with the concept of racialised gender. Can racialised gender help to reveal the epistemological framework which enabled the crafting of a Black woman as demonic in the *Acts of Peter*? Furthermore, what was the tipping point from noticing race and gender as markers of difference to attaching negative values to Black womanhood in particular? While I will not be able to answer this question within the scope of this paper, it is important to raise it to encourage further exploration. I recently have been exploring the application of racialised gender to the ancient world and particularly to the world of Augustan Rome. I have been wondering whether through racialised gender we can trace the origins of anti-Blackness and misogynoir so patently obvious in the excerpt from the *Acts of Peter* back to the literary tropes of the Augustan age.

To begin, it is important to explain what I understand racialised gender to mean and why I believe it is a valuable analytical tool for interrogating ancient Roman society and culture in the first century BCE.[2] Our understanding of race and gender in the ancient world is situated within the frameworks we employ, knowingly or unknowingly, to analyse these social markers of identity. In recent years, feminist scholars and scholars of race studies have abandoned the approaches of positivism and turned to those of social construction and intersectionality. The term 'intersectionality' was coined by the legal scholar Kimberlé Crenshaw in a 1989 article, and she defined it in a more recent interview as 'a lens through which you can see where power comes and collides, where it interlocks and intersects'.[3] However, as a concept, intersectionality is rooted in the earlier *Combahee River Collective Statement* by Barbara Smith, Beverly Smith and Demita Frazier, which

[1] Quoted in Byron 2002: 17.
[2] My thesis about racialised gender was published in Haley 2021, 'Race and Gender', in Denise E. McCoskey, ed., *Cultural History of Race in Antiquity* (Bloomsbury Academic), 119–36. Much of what follows here is adapted from that chapter.
[3] Crenshaw 1989 and 2017.

articulates very clearly the simultaneity of oppressions which women of African descent endure.[4]

Intersectionality is a critical intervention against the essentialism of critical race theory and is a core concept of critical race feminism (hereafter, CRF). The anti-essentialism of CRF has 'provide[d] a critique of the feminist notion that there is an essential female voice, that is, that all women feel one way on a subject.... CRF highlights the situation of women of color, whose lives may not conform to an essential norm'.[5] Since Crenshaw's articulation, intersectionality has spread as an analytical tool beyond disciplines and borders. Intersectional projects and methods exist in a wide range of fields, expanding from its origins in jurisprudence to sociology, education, history, psychology and even business. For example, Margaret Conkey has explored intersectionality as an analytical tool in her discussion of the intersection between feminist archaeology and Indigenous archaeology.[6] While scholars of the ancient world are finding intersectionality a useful tool for examining ancient societies, they engage with it in a limited way. For instance, often, classicists neglect the core axis of race in their application of the concept.

For some time now, the concept of social construction has also proved fruitful in the efforts to uncover the operation of race and gender in ancient societies. Wing notes that defining race as a social construction helps us realise that 'biological races do not exist, as recent science has clearly shown. There is more genetic difference within so-called races than between them. Instead, races have been socially constructed and the legal system reifies that construction, privileging some races over others'.[7] While both these 'modern' approaches can get us closer to understanding what Tim Whitmarsh has described as 'hybridized ancient Greek and Roman worlds',[8] they still are flawed by the exclusive binaries (that is, 'either/or') inherited by Western epistemological frameworks and arguably first expressed by Aristotle.[9] For race, recasting Whitmarsh's concept of 'hybridisation' as 'creolisation' is a first step in dismantling these binaries. Creolisation is a process of cultural and linguistic blending which creates a new culture. Furthermore, such reframing aids in breaking down the influence of modern social

---

[4] Smith, Smith and Frazier 1977.
[5] Wing 2003: 7.
[6] Conkey 2005.
[7] Wing 2003: 5.
[8] Whitmarsh and Thomson 2013: 4–5.
[9] One flaw of Aristotelian logic is that it relies on exclusive binary opposites for definition and categorisation. So, a woman is defined as not man; the enslaved are defined as not free. See Aristotle's *Politics* and his *Poetics*. Recent scholarship on Artificial Intelligence (AI) points to Aristotelian binary philosophies as the source of bias (implicit and overt) in AI. See, for example, Steele: 2019.

constructs of race and gender which undergird our reception and perception of race and gender in antiquity.

Historically, the Western construct of gender goes back to the nineteenth century, when the rise of eugenics and the 'cult of true womanhood' were the scaffolding upon which the gender construct was based. As Yasmeen Narayan points out, intellectual discourse 'divided "healthy", "normal" bodies into one of two sexes. This sexual binary was used to normalise and elevate European bourgeois patriarchal formations over all other gendered configurations and played a central role in inventions of Englishness and other forms of European nationness'.[10] The concept of racialised gender provides a fruitful way of moving beyond the kinds of Eurocentric assumptions embedded in conceptions of gender that arise from the 'cult of true womanhood'. As Eileen Boris states, 'race and gender exist in tandem to transform profoundly the ways that each works alone. . . . Constructed through gendered representations, race in turn reconstructs gender identities. . . . The concept of racialized gender reflects this interaction'.[11] In addition, racialised gender aids in dismantling the simplistic binary that 'men have race and women have gender'.[12] Up to now, it has been Marxist feminists who have applied the concept to labour movements and labour history where the intersection of race, gender and class has been paramount to the discussion. However, the concept can also shed light on past societies, including those of antiquity.

What did 'race' mean to a Roman of the Augustan era? Here we must tread very carefully and engage in the complex work of shedding our modern constructions of race, which arise from the ideological framework of white supremacy. Physiognomy and somatic traits form the backbone of the construct of race in the United States; it is ahistorical and anachronistic to assume the same is true of the ancient Romans. We know from the literature of the time that the Romans certainly *noticed* somatic traits like skin colour. For example, Lucretius (4.1157–69) discusses how 'love is blind' when it comes to the flaws of one's beloved. One such 'flaw' in the beloved is her very dark-brown skin (*nigra*). In the eyes of her lover the dark-skinned woman is perceived as honey-toned or amber brown (*melichrus*). This demonstrates a negative attitude towards dark skin, particularly in women, but it does not reveal anything about the ancient Roman construct of race. Rather, it throws into stark relief the connection for the Romans between gender, skin colour and standards of beauty.

Given Rome's significant political and, in imperial times, cultural contact with Africa, the issue of whether skin colour had a role in how Romans valued others is a valid question: was there a skin colour 'norm' in Roman society? There was, in fact, a range of skin hues and this is reflected in Latin skin colour

---

[10] Narayan 2019: 1231.
[11] Boris 2003: 10.
[12] Ibid.

terminology. *Albus, ater, candidus, fuscus, niger* are all used by Roman authors to describe the skin colour of peoples with whom they came in contact. However, it is equally important to note that there are many, many contexts where skin colour is not mentioned or described. For example, there is no skin colour given for Aeneas, Dido or Iarbas, the characters under examination in Book 4 of the *Aeneid*. In these contexts, character – or characterisation – was not dependent on skin colour. When the Romans did apply a skin colour descriptor to themselves it generally was *albus*.

What did *albus* mean to a Roman? Nineteenth-century lexicographers render *albus* as 'white' and the related term *candidus* as 'shiny or glistening white'. The opposite of *albus* is *ater*, 'black' ('lustreless black') and opposite to *candidus* is *niger*, 'black' ('shiny or glistening black'). Lloyd Thompson in *Romans and Blacks* persuasively argues against translating *albus* as 'white', which for the modern reader in the United States connotes a Nordic or northern European colouring.[13] If, then the reference point for *albus* is pale brown, not the white of a Nordic consciousness, then it transforms the interpretation and reading of other skin colour terminology. *Ater, candidus, fuscus, niger* become degrees of brownness. However, it cannot be stressed enough that often skin colour is not mentioned, making it clear that it was not the chief component in the construction of racial difference. For the Romans, 'race' consisted of culture, class, citizenship, lineage and even gender. Furthermore, just as today, race was fluid and dynamic, shifting as one travelled from place to place. So, absent any national description like the *Acts of Peter* (*Aethiopissimam*; *Aegyptiam*), Lucretius's dark-skinned beloved is a Roman citizen who falls in the darker range of the skin colour spectrum, distant from the feminine ideal of *candida*, which should be rendered as 'bright pale brown', not 'white'.

Before discussing racialised gender as constructed by the Romans, we need to establish their gender norm. Just as in the United States when we say 'African Americans' we mean Black men and when we say 'Americans' we mean White men, so for the Romans, *Romani* meant Roman men. Roman masculinity (racialised gender in and of itself) was the norm in Roman literature. Roman society was patriarchal and androcentric; the authorship of the texts under examination – being for the most part all male – reflects that. Gender difference is filtered through a male lens and that lens is the framework for gender difference.

In the remainder of this essay, I will examine racialised gender in Rome through two literary case studies: Vergil's Dido and Livy's Sophoniba.[14] To begin, racialised gender was central to the founding of Rome. From whatever

---

[13] Thompson 1989: 10–11.
[14] The Punic form of the name is *Saphanba'al*; the modern English form tends towards *Sophonisba*. The Roman tradition (as given by Livy) is *Sophoniba*, which will be used here.

starting point one takes, whether the legend of Aeneas or that of his descendants Romulus and Remus, the intersection of race and gender form the foundation of Rome's origins. Indeed, the Julio-Claudians, the founding dynasty of the Roman Empire, claimed the ancestry of the god Venus, who herself embodies the concept of racialised gender. Furthermore, the Romans constructed a national identity based upon the Trojan hero, Aeneas; as a son of Venus, he imparted to the Romans a shared ancestry with Venus.

Any discussion of racialised gender as it appears in the literary production of authors such as Vergil and Livy would be remiss without explicit attention paid to Cleopatra VII of Egypt. Indeed, her defeat was the foundation of Augustus's power. The intersection of Cleopatra's race and gender is paramount to the treatment the historical Cleopatra received from prominent Romans such as Cicero and Octavian (later, Augustus) himself. The purpose of this paper is not to untangle the web of reception of Cleopatra's race. Suffice it to say that the Romans viewed Cleopatra as racially other and treated her with suspicion and bias because she was Egyptian and female. The question of her race continues to haunt Cleopatra studies in the twenty-first century, with white supremacist tropes stated as fact.[15] Regardless of how we 'read' her race, Roman male authors never mention her by name but depersonalise her by identifying her through her relationship with Antony, in particular. For instance, Vergil refers to Cleopatra directly in *Aeneid* 8.688 as the 'Egyptian wife' (*Aegyptia coniunx*); Ovid uses the same phrase to describe her in *Metamorphoses* 15.826. Earlier, Cicero mentions her in his letters to Atticus (*ad Att.* 14.8.1 and 15.15.2) simply as 'the queen' (*regina*). The jury is still out as to whether Cicero meant this as a slur, since he knew full well that she was not a consort but a pharaoh. Arguably, then, all roads of exploration into racialised gender during the literary production of the Augustan period lead back to Cleopatra. As we shall see, she haunts the writings of Vergil, particularly the *Aeneid*, and Livy's accounts of the Second Punic War.

Vergil, through his character of Dido, especially in Book 4 of the *Aeneid*, demonstrates that the intersection of gender, culture and geographical location rather than the somatic trait of skin colour is the main component of Dido's 'Otherness'. Dido is a Semitic queen who is founding a new city, Carthage, on the northeastern shores of Africa. By so doing she embodies the racialised gender which pervades all the fears of Roman ruling-class men: a foreign woman with political power in a geopolitical area which, historically, produced Rome's most tenacious and feared rivals, Hannibal (whose coming is prayed for by Dido in *Aen.* 4.625–30) and Cleopatra. Dido through her conflation with Cleopatra likely triggered the most recent racialised gender threat in the memory of Vergil's contemporaries. By

---

[15] See, for example, Tarn and Charlesworth 1965: 45–6; Foss 1998: 82; Schiff 2009; Roller 2010.

having Aeneas abandon Dido, Aeneas demonstrates the moral supremacy of the racialised gender of the Romans, best expressed by *virtus* and *pietas*. In this regard, Aeneas stands in stark contrast to Marc Antony who – according to the propaganda – surrendered to the wiles of a foreign seductress and enmeshed Rome in a messy war, thereby betraying both his race and his gender.

Vergil heightens Dido's racialised gender by first endowing her with the traits of ideal Roman femininity and then stripping them away. When readers first encounter her towards the end of Book 1, Dido is the model *univira* – a one-man woman – having taken a vow of celibacy and fidelity to her dead husband. She sublimates her sexuality and diverts her energy and attention to the founding of a city for her people. In the beginning, she embodies the solid moral and asexual character of a Roman *matrona*. Furthermore, like Livy's Lucretia, she is industrious and works hard for the welfare of those dependent on her. Vergil (*Aen.* 1.430) reinforces the parallel by using a metaphor of bees[16] in June to describe the activity of the city builders. Before Aeneas arrived, Dido had rejected an offer of a marriage/political alliance from a native African prince, Iarbas, showing that she could remain true to her vow to her dead husband.

Clearly, Dido had to change. As she stands at the beginning of the episode, she represents the ideal Roman woman. Within the frame of a misogynistic lens, what destroys the moral fabric of women, even seemingly good women? What is the *essence* of foreign women that makes them especially alien to Romans? The answer, of course, is passion and control of their sexuality. Passion was a cultural stereotype projected upon Africans by Romans and Greeks. In this way, Vergil moves Dido further away from Rome and closer to Africa by implicating her in the flaw of passion. Feminist scholars have noted that in a Roman male mindset the intersection of race and female gender is seen as an imbrication of the categories of female and foreign. Regarding the essentialist category of 'female', Suzanne Dixon states in *Reading Roman Women* that it has been employed as 'a category of discourse, *the other*, against which to define the insider qualities of the normative, hypothetical male'.[17]

It is interesting that much of Octavian's propaganda against Cleopatra centred on her base seduction of Marc Antony, heretofore an exemplar of Roman masculinity. To further discredit their relationship, it is smeared by the innuendo of concubinage and never raised to the level of a legitimate Roman marriage. Vergil replicates the ambiguity and vagueness around whether Cleopatra and Antony were partners in a valid marriage in the relationship with Dido and Aeneas. Arguments abound about whether the 'ceremony' between Dido and

---

[16] This metaphor appears often in ancient European literary production. Recall that bees figure prominently in characterisations of women and women's work in Semonides of Amorgos and Xenophon's *Oeconomicus*.

[17] Dixon 2001: xi.

Aeneas in the cave and duly witnessed by Venus and Juno constituted a legal and binding marriage. Dido clearly thought so; Aeneas, however, was easily dissuaded of this fact. Any marriage between Cleopatra and Antony would not have been acceptable to the Romans, even if they thought Cleopatra was a paragon of virtue. Sheila Ager points out in her article 'Marriage or Mirage? The Phantom Wedding of Cleopatra and Antony' that 'Roman law would not in any case have allowed for a Roman citizen to marry a *peregrina*, a foreigner.... [A]nd since Cleopatra was indisputably a foreigner, her ethnicity would have been a permanent barrier'.[18] The question about the legitimacy of Cleopatra and Dido's marriages to a Roman is a consequence of racialised gender and yet another link between them.

In the genre of historiography, there is one episode in Livy's narration of the Second Carthaginian War which lends itself to analysis via racialised gender and offers insight into the racial ruptures of Roman history. Livy's 'tragedy' of Sophoniba delineates not only the racialised gender of Roman men but also that of men and women of African descent. Further, the character of Sophoniba can be seen as the crucible for the formation of racial and gender identities for the Roman male elite in the age of Augustus. Therefore, Roman racial formation and racialised gender formation are constructed on the bodies of two exotic 'Others': Sophoniba and Masinissa. The result, then, is the social reproduction of 'ideal' Roman masculinity through the transformation of Masinissa's racialised gender from that of a Numidian to that of a Roman. However, none of this is possible without Sophoniba, who undertakes an equally transformative racial and gender performance, moving from a Cleopatra-esque figure to a Lucretia-esque one, that is from African to Roman, mirroring as well as enabling the performances of Masinissa.

It is best, perhaps, to begin with a summary of the story of Sophoniba, since it is not a familiar one and is full of twists and turns. The primary ancient sources for her story are Polybius, who never mentions her by name, and Livy, who gives the most fulsome account. Sophoniba was the daughter of the Carthaginian leader Hasdrubal, the son of Gisgo – to distinguish him from Hasdrubal Barca, the brother of Hannibal. Although Sophoniba had been betrothed to Masinissa, the son of the leader of the Eastern Numidians, to cement a diplomatic alliance between the Eastern Numidians and Carthage, Masinissa began to reconsider his alliance with Carthage after witnessing how Scipio and the Romans successfully drove the Carthaginians out of Spain. When Syphax, the leader of the Western Numidians, was able to conquer Eastern Numidia, Masinissa, now the leader of Eastern Numidia following the death of his father, switched his allegiance to Rome. Needing a new Numidian alliance, Hasdrubal then married Sophoniba to Syphax. When the Romans invaded Africa, under the command

---

[18] Ager 2013: 142.

of Scipio and Laelius, they, with the help of Masinissa, were able eventually to defeat Syphax and Hasdrubal. After Masinissa captured Cirta, Syphax's capital, he met Sophoniba and impulsively married her to prevent her from falling into Roman hands. When Masinissa was persuaded by Scipio that Sophoniba was the property of Rome, Masinissa sent poison to his wife. In heroic fashion she drank it and died.

The story, of course, is much more complex and nuanced than this simplified summary can relate. For instance, each of the two significant ancient sources for the story of Sophoniba relies on racialised gender stereotypes in the characterisation of Sophoniba and Masinissa. Polybius relates that Scipio thought it likely that Syphax had grown tired of his young child-bride, whom he never names, and hence of his alliance with the Carthaginians. The reason Polybius attributes to Scipio for thinking this is what is important here. For Polybius says it was 'because of the **natural fickleness of the Numidians** and their **perfidy** towards the gods and men' (διά τε τὴν **φυσικὴν τῶν Νομάδων αψικορίαν** καὶ διὰ τὴν πρός τε τοὺς θεοὺς καὶ τοὺς ἀνθρώπους **ἀθεσίαν**, 14.1.4) (my emphasis). Later, Polybius does give a hint of Sophoniba's charming and persuasive personality when he depicts Sophoniba begging Syphax not to desert the Carthaginians and he is moved by her entreaties (14.7.6).

Livy is the source who spends the most time on Sophoniba. We learn from him that Sophoniba was a 'maid of marriageable age' (*nubilis erat virgo*, 29.23.4). Livy then describes how Hasdrubal took advantage of her beauty and charm and Syphax's passion to bind the Numidian leader more closely to the Carthaginian cause (29.23.6–10). Livy's portrayal of Sophoniba is taken up again when Masinissa captures his rival Syphax's capital of Cirta (30.11–12). He is spotted by Sophoniba, now named by Livy, who begs the Numidian leader to save her from the Romans (30.12.11–16). In the act of naming her, Livy gives Sophoniba not only agency but accountability. She is no longer the dutiful '*nubilis virgo*' doing her father's bidding. She now has the potential to act in her own name and on her own behalf. Captivated, Masinissa agrees to help her, and impetuously marries her (30.12.18–20). None of this is pleasing to Scipio, who pedantically reminds Masinissa that Sophoniba is the property of Rome and he must turn her over to him (30.14.4–11). Masinissa, like the good student of Roman ideals that he is, goes off to consider the advice and admonition of Scipio and resolves to send Sophoniba a cup of poison, which she bravely accepts (30.15.1–9).

Later sources, Diodorus, Cassius Dio, Zonaras, give notice of her beauty and education, noting that she was well versed in grammar and music. These authors go on to say that Sophoniba was clever, ingratiating and altogether so charming that the mere sight of her or the sound of her voice sufficed to vanquish everyone, even the most indifferent. Through such qualities these later sources, no doubt because of their distance from the events of the Late Roman Republic, make the conflation with Cleopatra more explicit than Livy needs to. There is a strong parallel to Plutarch's description of Cleopatra in his *Life of Antony* at section 27.

Whereas the later sources seem to be retelling a touching romantic story, Livy's agenda is very different: re-establishing the Roman moral fabric of old, one which has become badly frayed. His main vehicle for this is racialised gender. As a result, each of the male characters has his own political and/or moral crisis and each crisis gets resolved by reasserting the normative racialised gender. For instance, earlier in Book 29, Livy describes Scipio's crisis surrounding the subjugated city of Locri in Magna Graecia. There had been a senatorial investigation into the Locrian complaints and Scipio's role in them. Livy recounts the following charges against Scipio, revealed during the Senate's deliberations (29.19.10–13):

> ...[M]uch was also said against the commander-in-chief himself – **his dress and bearing were unRoman, and not even soldierly; he strolled about the gymnasium in a Greek mantle and sandals and wasted his time over books and physical exercise.**... The discipline of the whole army had gone to the dogs, just as at Sucro in Spain and again at Locri, so that it was more of a menace to its friends than its enemies [my emphasis].

While many or even most of these charges were untrue, Scipio does have an image problem and he must reclaim both his moral position as the exemplar of 'ideal' Roman masculinity and his political reputation as a military commander. Masinissa and Sophoniba are the tools to his success in this reclaiming. When Masinissa conquers Cirta and defeats Syphax, he is an ally of Scipio and becomes his proxy in terms not only of military success but also Roman racialised gender. However, Livy makes very clear that Masinissa is racially different from the Romans he is emulating. Sophoniba is the vehicle through which Livy reminds us that our Numidian hero is a non-Roman hero. The beautiful Carthaginian woman will seduce him and cause him to slip back into his 'natural' racialised gender and stereotype of the Numidian.

A quick review of Masinissa's encounter with Sophoniba in Livy supports this interpretation. When Livy first mentions Sophoniba (29.23), it is clear that Hasdrubal is the architect of the scheme to win over Syphax from the Romans; Sophoniba is a pawn in a political move. Hasdrubal is relying on his daughter's beauty and Syphax's *passionate* nature. However, when Sophoniba is an agent of her own destiny and comes out to greet Masinissa, Livy gives her a speech that demonstrates her persuasive power as well as the racial rupture caused by the Roman invasion of Africa (30.12.15):

> If I had been nothing other than the wife of Syphax, I would have preferred to trust the honour **of a Numidian and one born, like me, in the same Africa** than that of an alien and outsider. What a daughter of Carthage,

not to mention a daughter of Hasdrubal must fear from a Roman you do understand. If you are able of nothing else, then I beg and beseech you to save me through death from the Romans' will [my emphasis].

It is worth noting that Sophoniba reflects something of Cleopatra by denying Scipio her participation in his triumph, as Cleopatra did Octavian.[19]

Livy overshadows Sophoniba's appeal to Masinissa's race loyalty by again repeating the racial stereotype of the Numidians as hypersexualised. Following Sophoniba's speech, he describes her as, 'Outstanding in beauty and at a blooming age' (30.12.17). From Livy's perspective, Masinissa heard Sophoniba's speech more as blandishments of a lover rather than entreaties of a supplicant, because he is a Numidian and 'the race of Numidians is inclined (*praeceps*) towards passion' (30.12.18). Consequently, Livy says, 'the victor is captured by the love for the captive' (30.12.18).

The subsequent marriage between Sophoniba and Masinissa also gives Livy the context in which to contrast the 'recklessness' of Masinissa and the 'self-control' of Scipio. Livy focuses on Scipio, showing his controlled handling of Syphax's defection as well as his disappointment and even anger over Masinissa's yielding to his 'baser' instincts (30.14). When responding to why he turned from his alliance with Rome, Syphax places the blame on his having wedded a Carthaginian woman (*Carthaginiensem matronam*, 30.13.11). It was madness bred from passion (30.13.12). More worrisome to Scipio – but consistent with Livy's view that lack of restraint has unfortunate consequences – is Syphax's observation that Masinissa is neither more prudent nor more restrained than he. In fact, he is less cautious because of his youth. Masinissa's hasty, impulsive marriage to Sophoniba supports Syphax's image of Masinissa and provides the most telling evidence to support Scipio's growing anxiety (30.14.1). Scipio clearly sees the possibility that Masinissa, although he had been very loyal up to this point, might now turn to the Carthaginian cause due to the influence of Sophoniba. In addition to his anxiety, Scipio is disgusted because, following *mos maiorum*, he practised self-control and resisted the beautiful female prisoners when he was in Spain (30.14.3).

When Masinissa arrives, he receives him warmly and lavishes public praise on him for his military accomplishments. There follows, however, a private tongue-lashing (30.14.5–8):

But of these virtues for which I would seem to have been sought out by you, I should have been prouder of none as much as my self-control and my resistance to bodily lusts. How I wish that you had added this also to your other outstanding virtues, Masinissa! There is not – absolutely not,

---

[19] I thank Mary H. Gilbert for this suggestion.

believe me, as much danger to men of our age from armed enemies as from the constant presence of sensuality all around us. The man who reins these in and tames them with his own self-control has earned for himself more honour and a greater victory than we have with the conquest of Syphax.

Livy demonstrates that Masinissa, passionate Numidian though he may be, desires the approval of the Romans and shares many of their ancient values. However, Masinissa, like Livy's contemporary Romans, has lost sight of these virtues; Scipio's exhortation to Masinissa not to destroy the many good qualities with the one defect of passion could well be Livy's words to his fellow Romans.

Masinissa fully grasps the logic of Scipio's speech and, like many colonised people, is caught between two worlds. Does he abandon the coloniser and lose all the political advantages that might flow from that alliance? Or does he become a race traitor and turn over the woman he loves to Rome? After privately venting his grief, he hits upon a solution (of sorts) and provides Sophoniba with the opportunity to take her own life. However, he clearly does this without Scipio's permission and he risks Scipio's anger.

When Sophoniba accepts the cup of poison, she reverts to her previous gender performance of the obedient woman. By moving from a passive, silent and obedient daughter to a forthright vocal agent of her own sexual and political destiny, she violates the norm of Roman femininity and becomes the Cleopatra-esque exemplar of the corrupting foreign beauty. When she accepts the poison, she moves back to the obedient (although certainly not passive or silent) wife and restores authority to the Roman male view of gender norms in the time of Livy. While we might see her drinking the poison as an act of resistance and a refusal to join Masinissa in being split between two worlds and so a refusal to be colonised, the speech that Livy gives Sophoniba as she receives the poison places her in the tradition of Lucretia, the noble Roman woman who takes her own life for honour: 'I receive this wedding gift, one not unwelcome, if a husband can offer his wife nothing greater. But tell him this: I would have died a happier death if I had not wed on the day of my funeral' (30.15.7). For this she earns praise from Livy: 'She spoke calmly as she drained fearlessly the received cup, with absolutely no indication of any trepidation' (30.15.8). It is notable that Sophoniba's agency, choice and will to die by suicide and thereby avoid Romanisation – which in 30.12.15 she clearly voices as her own free choice – is undermined by Livy's comparison to Lucretia. This is an aspect of epistemological oppression/epistemological violence: freedom of choice, or how free a choice appears to Livy's audience, is affected by systems of dominance, in this case by the retelling of her story through a Roman racialised gender lens.[20]

---

[20] I thank Edith G. Nally for this suggestion.

Even though Scipio loses a trophy to be paraded in his triumph, he gains so much more because of Sophoniba. His crisis of masculinity is resolved by the assimilation of an African man who becomes a shining example of Roman racialised gender and by the suicide of an African woman whose beauty and intense self-determination might have dismantled the Roman imperial agenda. Nonetheless, Livy's treatment of Sophoniba's choice as an act of obedience rather than a radically free statement of her autonomy/resistance seems like an instance of 'epistemic silencing' or 'epistemic violence' against her.[21]

When we reconsider the excerpt from the *Acts of Peter* with which we started this essay, the application of racialised gender reveals that the author is working within a pre-existing epistemological framework which exoticised foreign women, especially women of African descent. The whole passage can be viewed as an allegory of the tension between Gnosticism, a doctrine of personal spiritual revelation and the emerging Christian church. The passage from the *Acts of Peter* seems to use the woman of African descent as a metaphor for personal spirituality, while valorising violence against her body as a solution to the threat this non-doctrinal approach poses to its institutional legitimacy.[22] Within that framework, the leap from exoticisation to demonisation is not implausible.

However, the question does arise: are there positive, female-authored representations of women of African descent which counter this leap? It is a difficult question to answer, since to paraphrase Nwando Achebe, until recently, Black women have not had their own storytellers. Indeed, the voices of all women have been relayed by men, especially in ancient patriarchal societies. Nevertheless, wittingly or unwittingly, the Roman authors who have handed down the female characters of Dido and Sophoniba have created women figures who tap into our sympathy and empathy.

One approach to grasping the interiority of these characters is the concept of racialised gender. In the end, this brings us closer to understanding the lived experience of historical women in Rome and the Roman Empire. In this way, we can begin to see the Ethiopian woman in the *Acts of Peter* not as a demon but as an abused and oppressed human woman.

---

[21] On epistemic silencing, see Fricker 2007 and Medina 2013. On epistemic violence, see Spivak 1988. Others in this volume who discuss forms of epistemic silencing and epistemic violence include Weiberg (Chapter 2), Gilbert (Chapter 3), McHardy (Chapter 4), Kim (Chapter 6), Witzke (Chapter 7), Milnor (Chapter 8) and Strong (Chapter 15).

[22] I thank Edith G. Nally for this suggestion.

CHAPTER 10

But She Didn't Complain: Ovid's Leucothoe, Rape Myths and Hermeneutical Injustice

Megan E. Bowen

Contemporary studies demonstrate the enormous impact rape myths (that is, false cultural narratives about rape) can have both on a rape victim's own ability to understand their experience(s) of sexual violence[1] and other parties' (including perpetrators') interpretations of sexual encounters.[2] For instance, a prominent 2004 study found that women who accepted the rape myth 'if women don't fight back, it's not rape' were less likely to conceptualise their own experience of sexual violation as rape if they themselves did not fight back.[3] Similarly, a 2020 study determined that respondents who identified as male were less likely to reject rape myths and as a result were less likely to conceptualise their own unwanted sexual experiences as rape. This suggests that the myth that 'only women can be sexually assaulted' can influence the ability of victims who aren't women to understand their unwanted sexual experiences as rape.

---

[1] Jenkins 2017. Mason 2021 develops this idea further in her critique of Fricker's definition of hermeneutical injustice. See also Warshaw 1988; Harned 2005. The difficulty for women to conceptualise their own experience of sexual violence as rape within the context of rape culture also forms the basis of Roxane Gay's collection of essays, *Not That Bad*, though without the theoretical framework and analysis.

[2] For example, Rollero and Tartaglia 2019. See Olson 2022 for a discussion of the persistent influence of these myths even amid a seeming victory for the #MeToo movement, the conviction of Harvey Weinstein. See Tilton 2022 for an analysis of how issues of race, gender and class play a vital role in rape myths that distort epistemic resources.

[3] Peterson and Muehlenhard 2004.

In response to this phenomenon where victims do not apply the term rape to their own experiences, Katherine Jenkins argues that rape myths (and sexual abuse myths) constitute hermeneutical injustices.[4] According to Miranda Fricker's influential definition, hermeneutical injustice is:

> the injustice of having some significant area of one's social experience obscured from collective understanding owing to a structural identity prejudice in the collective hermeneutical resource.[5]

Jenkins argues that 'myths mean that victims hold a problematic operative concept, or working understanding, which prevents them from identifying their experience as one of rape or domestic abuse. Since victims in this situation lack the conceptual resources needed to render their experience sufficiently intelligible, they are suffering a form of hermeneutical injustice'. She adopts Sally Haslanger's terminology of a 'manifest concept' versus an 'operative concept' to explain why these women do not conceptualise their rape or domestic abuse as such, even though their experiences meet the legal definition of rape or domestic abuse. In reference to rape, Jenkins identifies the 'manifest concept' as the legal definition of rape in any particular jurisdiction and differentiates it from the 'operative concept' as 'widely shared informal and implicit working understandings that people have' about rape. While an operative concept may not be entirely unified among a group, often the manifest and operative concepts of rape do not align because the operative concept of rape incorporates 'distorting factors stemming from myths'.[6]

Rebecca Mason further develops this variety of hermeneutical injustice in a critique of Fricker's definitions of the term.[7] In particular, she argues that hermeneutical injustice may result not just from lacking a concept/term (for example, not having the phrase 'sexual harassment') but also from failures in applying a term (for instance, having the word 'rape' but failing to apply it among spouses). This failure, she argues, arises from a distortion of hermeneutical resources: 'subjects possess the requisite concepts but fail to apply them in ways that illuminate the nature and normative significance of their social experiences'.[8] According to these frameworks, then, rape myths distort the collective hermeneutical resources, which in turn may render a victim's experience of rape unintelligible to themselves or others, constituting a hermeneutical injustice.

---

[4] See the Introduction to this volume for more on hermeneutical injustice.
[5] Fricker 2007: 155.
[6] Jenkins 2017: 196.
[7] For Fricker's definitions, see the Introduction to this volume.
[8] Mason 2021: 266.

In a similar vein, this chapter will analyse the episode of Leucothoe's rape in Ovid's *Metamorphoses* through the theoretical lens of hermeneutical injustice.[9] Leucothoe's story is unique in that it presents Leucothoe's own articulation of her rape after the event in direct speech to compare with characterisations of the same event by two other women, Leuconoe (the narrator of the entire episode) and Clytie (an internal character, who desires Leucothoe's rapist).[10] These different understandings about what happened to Leucothoe, along with the narrative of her ultimate fate, provide a site for thinking through factors that render the experience of rape in ancient Rome intelligible (or unintelligible) to various audiences. In particular, this chapter analyses the inset narrative of Leucothoe's rape in the context of Roman law, her own belief, and a cultural ideology distorted by rape myths. Leucothoe's story provides insight into how false cultural narratives and ideas about rape in ancient Rome contribute to hermeneutical injustice, and how Ovid's narrative both problematises and reinforces epistemic injustice.

The god Sol's rape of Leucothoe is narrated by the similar-sounding Leuconoe,[11] one of the daughters of Minyas who deny Bacchus's divinity and refuse to celebrate his rites in favour of staying at home to weave (4.1–4, 32–5). As they are working, one of the Minyads suggests that they tell each other stories (4.37–41), which prompts a series of inset amatory tales. An unnamed Minyad begins by recounting the tale of Pyramus and Thisbe (4.55–166) and her sister Alcithoe ends the sequence with an account of Salamacis and Hermaphroditus (4.274–388). In between, another of the daughters, Leuconoe, relates the so-called 'loves of the Sun' (*amores Solis*, 4.170) (4.169–273), which include both the Homeric tale of the affair between Mars and Venus and Leucothoe's rape by Sol.[12] In typical Ovidian fashion, there is a thin transition linking Leuconoe's two stories. Venus, as punishment for disclosing her affair with Mars to Vulcan, inflicts Sol with a passion for the Persian princess Leucothoe (4.190–203). In his obsession with Leucothoe, he ignores a catalogue of other women (4.204–6), including Clytie,

---

[9] Others in this volume who discuss the epistemological frameworks that underlie sexual and physical violence include McHardy (Chapter 4), Haley (Chapter 9), Freas (Chapter 11) and Strong (Chapter 15).

[10] Leucothoe is one of many women to suffer rape or attempted rape throughout the poem, and her story resembles those of these other women in myriad ways. On rape in the poem, see Parry 1964; Segal 1969; Stirrup 1977; Curran 1978; Richlin 1992; Segal 1998; and James 2016. On erotic motifs and patterns, see Ludwig 1965; Davis 1983; Nagle 1984; Knox 1986; Nagle 1988; Wills 1990; Heath 1992; Myers 1994; Gentilcore 1995; Holzberg 1999; Miller 2009; and Moreno Soldevila 2011: 453–8.

[11] On the resemblance of the two names and their meaning, see Rosati 2007 on 4.167–273. See also Keith 2010: 206–7.

[12] On the relationship of the narrative of the Minyades and their inset tales to the larger Thebaid narrative and the genre of tragedy, see Keith 2010.

who although spurned by Sol, desperately wants Sol's affection (4.206–8). The god decides to pursue his amatory interest by disguising himself as Leucothoe's mother (4.219–25)[13] so that he can isolate the girl without any witnesses (*sine teste*, 4.225). Therefore, while Leucothoe is weaving,[14] he asks the girl's enslaved servants to leave the room, so that mother and daughter can discuss a private matter (*'res' ait 'arcana est: famulae, discedite neve / eripite arbitrium matri secreta loquendi'*, 4.223–4). With everyone else out of the room, Sol reveals his true identity (4.226–8). Leucothoe is terrified by his speech and drops her weaving equipment,[15] before the god resumes his form as the sun and rapes the girl (*vim passa est*, 4.233), who is overwhelmed by his brilliance (*victa nitore*, 4.233). Afterward, the jealous Clytie decides to disclose the incident to Leucothoe's father (4.236–7). He becomes enraged and punishes his daughter by burying her alive as she desperately stretches her hands towards the sun and pleads that she didn't consent (*ille vim tulit invitae*, 4.238–9). Sol is unable to rescue her but eventually scatters fragrant nectar on the ground above her lifeless corpse, which transforms into a frankincense-shrub (4.241–55).[16] Thereafter the sun rejects Clytie, who is so distraught at the rejection that she becomes fixed in her grief and transforms into a plant that always tracks the sun, the heliotrope (4.256–70).

LEUCOTHOE'S RAPE IN THE ROMAN LEGAL CONTEXT AND CRIMINAL CULPABILITY

Scholarship on Leucothoe's story now consistently (and, I think, correctly)[17] classifies the encounter between Sol and Leucothoe as rape.[18] Scholars have

---

[13] On the pattern of cross-dressing as a vehicle for sexual violence in Ovid, see Raval 2002.

[14] On the importance of the setting and its connection to the frame narrative, see Rosati 1999.

[15] On the symbolic meaning of this detail, see Rosati 2007 on 4.229.

[16] On the connection of incense to Bacchus and the frame narrative, see Keith 2010: 208.

[17] See James's discussion on the appropriateness of applying this term to cultures that do not use a single word akin to 'rape', and in particular her analysis of Rozée's work (James 2013: 41–4). While I wholeheartedly agree with James's assertion that 'Athenian women could well have felt themselves raped in ways that are recognizable to contemporary Western perspectives, even if those feelings were unrecognizable to Athenian men', along with her warning against androcentrism as well as ethnocentrism, I believe contemporary terminology is also problematic – not specifically in its application to the ancient world, but in its deficiency to fully capture the range of experiences of sexual violation and how people themselves process those experiences. Thinking through Latin terminology for rape, I believe, reveals not just hermeneutical injustices in ancient Rome, but contemporary hermeneutical injustices as well (see also Phillips 2000: 7; Fricker 2007; Jenkins 2017; Jackson 2019).

[18] For example, Richlin 1992; Janan 1994; Anderson 1997; James 2016.

emphasised that no Latin word contains 'the same semantic field as the modern English word 'rape''.[19] Similarly, in the legal realm, no single Roman crime exactly matches modern definitions of the crime 'rape'.[20] As Nguyen explains, 'For the Romans, the act of rape was covered under a variety of legal terms, but each of those words possessed wider definition fields than the modern word "rape". Thus while charges of seduction, attempted seduction, adultery, abduction, or ravishment all covered rape, there was no legal charge consisting solely of rape itself'.[21] Under Roman law in the Augustan age, four different charges might be applied to a rapist, none of which strictly conform to a modern concept of the crime of rape: *vis*, *iniuria*, *raptus* and *stuprum/adulterium*.[22] Additionally, whether or not any particular action could be considered a crime was deeply dependent on the social status of the victim involved.[23] Charges of *vis* covered physical assault (for various purposes, including sex); *iniuria* covered a wide range of actions (for example, physical or verbal insults, defamation, sexual approaches, seduction and rape)[24] that could be considered damaging and worthy of monetary compensation; *raptus* involved abduction (penetration was not required to have committed *raptus*); and *stuprum/adulterium* involved illicit sexual behaviour with a virgin, widow, boy or married woman (the illegality was not necessarily tied to the victim's lack of consent).[25] Later juristic literature makes a distinction between *adulterium* (illicit sex that specifically involves a married woman) and *stuprum* (which involves a widow, virgin or boy) but notes that the *lex Iulia de adulteriis coercendis* treated the terms as synonyms, as I will suggest Ovid does in the case of Leucothoe.[26] For each of these offences there were a variety of laws and praetorian edicts at the aggrieved party's disposal (either the woman herself, or more likely her father or husband).[27] Additionally, *raptus* and *stuprum/adulterium* were charges concerned not solely with the rapist's guilt, but also the culpability of victims.

---

[19] Harris 1997: 483.
[20] Which are themselves varied and often problematic.
[21] Nguyen 2006: 76.
[22] The grounds for treating *stuprum* and *adulterium* as a single term is explained below.
[23] See Gardner 1986; Fantham 1991; McGinn 1998; Nguyen 2006; Witzke 2015.
[24] Treggiari 1991: 309; Nguyen 2006: 92.
[25] On *struprum*, see especially Fantham 1991; Botta 2004.
[26] *Dig.* 50.16.101 *inter stuprum et adulterium hoc interesse quidam putant, quod adulterium in nupta, stuprum in vidua vel virgine vel puero committitur, sed lex Iulia de adulteriis hoc verbo indifferenter utitur* ['some people think that this is the difference between "disgrace" and "adultery", that adultery is committed against a married woman, disgrace against a widow, virgin, or boy, but the Julian law on adultery uses this language indifferently'].
[27] Gardner 1986; McGinn 1998; Nguyen 2006.

The passage that narrates Leucothoe's story is imbued with legal terminology that encourages thinking about the events in a legal context and invites comparison with the Augustan legal framework.[28] For instance, Leuconoe (the tale's main narrator) reports that Clytie divulged the *adulterium* (4.236). This terminology, especially in combination with the nearby *arbitrium* (4.224), *sine teste* (4.225) and *indicat* (4.237),[29] activates legal associations, in a sense asking the audience(s) to treat the events in the narrative as details for a trial.[30]

There are a number of logical problems with treating this story like an *actual* trial for *adulterium*. For instance, none of the characters are Roman citizens and the events take place in Persia[31] (in a time before the enactment of the *lex Iulia de adulteriis*).[32] Additionally, Sol is a god, and therefore of higher status than Leucothoe – does this mean we should think of their relationship as more akin to that of a citizen man and enslaved woman, rather than of two elite citizens? While these details may present challenges for arguing that the story represents grounds for an actual, formal trial before Roman judges, they do not negate the relevance of a broader Roman legal context for audiences struggling to conceptualise the ethical ramifications of what happened.[33] To take a modern comparison, though the confirmation hearings for Brett Kavanaugh were not in fact a legal trial, different narratives about the event used legal terminology that encouraged viewing the hearings in the context of a legal trial; for instance, the appellation of Dr Christine Blasey Ford as 'Kavanaugh's Accuser' in the transcription and Donald Trump's assertion that Kavanaugh was 'innocent until proven guilty'.[34]

---

[28] On legal language in Ovid, see especially Kenney 1969 and Ziogas 2021. A number of other scholars also consider legal language in Ovid, for example, Coleman 1990; Fantham 2009; Gebhardt 2009; Balsley 2010; Jones 2019.

[29] Clytie's disclosure is also called *indicium* at 4.557. See Brazouski 1998 on the importance of informers and the act of informing after the enactment of Augustan moral legislation.

[30] In combination with this other terminology and context, we may also see *res* in 4.223 as announcing the 'case'.

[31] Janan (1994: 428) describes the Eastern setting of the Minyads' tales as, 'less as geographic reality than as a "feminine" re-imagination of the sisters' familiar Greek hometown'.

[32] Note, however, that Cicero's exile suggests some comfortability with ex post facto law.

[33] Roman rhetorical education may also have encouraged conceptualising the episode according to a legal framework, insofar as it involved arguing fictitious legal cases. By this I do not mean to suggest that this episode bears any resemblance to the rapes of Roman declamation, which as Kaster 2001 (and Corbeill 2007 following him) notes do not describe the rape itself, do not explore motivations or culpability of the rapist, and are always focused on possible damages to a community. For a summary of influential scholarship on Roman rhetoric, see Dugan 2007.

[34] See Gilmore 2019.

Commentators on the *Metamorphoses* note that the use of the term *adulterium* is focalised through the jealous Clytie, who imagines herself as the aggrieved wife of Sol (*stimulata paelicis ira* 4.235), but the term also evokes the specific crime that can be charged in Roman courts. According to later legal jurists, *adulterium* should only apply to married women (*matronae*).[35] Even if Clytie had a valid claim to think of herself as Sol's wife, strictly speaking he would only be capable of adultery if he were to have sex with a woman who was herself married (that is, there is no legal case that either Sol or Leucothoe committed 'adultery'). As noted above, although *adulterium* technically applied only to *matronae*, Augustan legislation used the terms *adulterium* and *stuprum* indiscriminately, and literary sources similarly tend to employ them interchangeably. In addition, the term *adulterium* appears to be preferred to *stuprum* in Latin verse.[36] Consequently, I propose that this episode should be evaluated in terms of the crime of *stuprum* (that is, sex with a *virgo* without her father's permission for marriage).[37]

The charge of *adulterium/stuprum* was considered a *crimen commune*,[38] meaning, in theory, both Sol and Leucothoe might be liable to criminal charges. Yet, statutes in Augustan times were more focused on the rapist's guilt than the victim's; legal procedure for *adulterium* required the *adulter* to be tried and convicted before a case could be brought against the woman.[39] Likewise, Lauren Caldwell notes that as *stuprum* came to be regulated in Augustan legislation, its punishment 'chose not to focus on the girl but on her assailant'.[40] Nonetheless, scholarship has concentrated more on the question of Leucothoe's culpability than Sol's. In part, this emphasis results from the dramatic action taken by Leucothoe's father to bury her alive (4.239–40). Her father's harsh punishment encourages audiences to consider the validity of his judgement and thus questions of Leucothoe's culpability and consent.

Michaela Janan, for instance, notes that Leuconoe's telling 'frames the essence of a rape case by posing the question of whether Leucothoe consented to, or refused, the Sun God's sexual advances, and thus of the exact nature of the crime for which she dies'.[41] In Janan's analysis, the question of consent hinges on the ambiguous description of Leucothoe's rape (4.232–3):

---

[35] McGinn 1998.
[36] Dixon 2013: 134–5.
[37] See Botta 2004.
[38] Ibid.
[39] From this text it is not entirely clear whether the procedure was true also for *stuprum*.
[40] Caldwell 2014: 61.
[41] Janan 1994: 429.

> at virgo, quamvis inopino territa visu,
> victa nitore dei posita vim passa querella est.

> But the maiden, although terrified by the unexpected sight, overcome by his brilliancy, suffered rape, with complaining set aside.

In particular, the phrase *victa nitore* causes interpretative consternation. Because *nitor* can mean both physical attractiveness and brightness, commentators have questioned whether Leucothoe was physically overcome by the sun's blinding rays or 'seduced by his comeliness'.[42] In terms of Sol's guilt in a Roman court, the answer is irrelevant, since a woman's consent is not the primary issue at stake in a charge of *stuprum*.[43] Because the crime of *stuprum* required intentional[44] penetration of a *virgo*,[45] Sol is clearly guilty. The use of a disguise to isolate Leucothoe from witnesses demonstrates intent. The relationship between the phrase *victa nitore* and Leucothoe's perceived culpability, however, proves more complicated. Leucothoe's own words about her experience, spoken as her father buries her, unambiguously express lack of consent: *'ille vim tulit invitae'* ('He forced me unwillingly', 4.238–9). Her testimony, however, is undervalued in comparison with both Clytie's designation of *adulterium* and the narrator's description of events, as I will discuss further below.

Janan's discussion of the passage that describes the rape eventually challenges the idea that Leucothoe is portrayed as a unified subject capable of giving or withholding consent. The assessment of Leucothoe's incoherence centres on the perceived inconsistency in Leuconoe's description of the rape between the concessive phrase *quamvis inopino territa visu* and the rest of the sentence. In reference to lines 4.232–3, Janan states, "'Although [quamvis] she was terrified ... she suffered rape' makes no sense, given that it sees the princess's capitulation as happening despite terror rather than (more logically) because of it'.[46] Presumably, the characterisation as 'capitulation' stems both

---

[42] Janan 1994: 441. Rosati's commentary on these lines (4.231–3) echoes the ambiguity. These lines also encourage a discussion about conflating perceived sexual desire with implied consent (for the same topic among US college students, see Lofgreen et al. 2017).

[43] See Gardner 1986; Fantham 1991; Caldwell 2014. See also Paul *D.* 47.11.1.2.

[44] Ulp. *D.* 48.5.13: *Haec verba legis 'ne quis posthac stuprum adulterium facito sciens dolo malo' et ad eum, qui suasit, et ad eum, qui stuprum vel adulterium intulit, pertinent.*

[45] See Caldwell 2014 on the specific meaning of this term in legal contexts and the importance of the victim's status for considering a crime to be rape. As noted above, the crime could also be committed against widows and boys.

[46] Janan 1994: 141. See also Raval 2002 for a similar discussion and interpretation.

from the ambiguity about the sense of *nitor* (4.231, 233) and the description of *posita querella* (4.233).[47] If, however, we treat the words *posita vim passa querella est* (4.233) closely together (as their interlocking word order encourages), and we take *posita querella* to mean not so much 'having laid aside her complaint', but more 'without expressing complaint', that is, without making a verbal protestation,[48] the concessive *quamvis* makes more sense. The meaning may more closely resemble the English 'although she was terrified . . . she suffered rape without crying out' or 'although she was terrified, . . . she didn't complain and suffered rape'.[49] The interpretation that *querella* here conjures the external, verbal expression of a grievance (rather than the internal feeling of an objection) is strengthened by the subsequent appearance of the same word to refer to the sound the Minyads make upon their transformation into bats (*conataeque loqui minimam et pro corpore vocem / emittunt peraguntque levi stridore **querellas***, 4.412–13). This reading resolves the interpretative problem that the concessive clause only makes sense if it contrasts Leucothoe's fear with her desire (that is, if *victa nitore* means 'seduced by his comeliness') and presents the opportunity to see the passage contrasting Leucothoe's fear with her lack of screaming. This interpretation may not entirely eliminate the ambiguity about *nitor*'s definition, but it does demote the phrase's importance for evaluating the rape.

FALSE CULTURAL NARRATIVES ABOUT RAPE

The above interpretation also acknowledges the culturally operative rape myth that if a woman was *truly* fearful, she would verbally cry out for help.[50] Graziana Brescia (Foggia), for instance, draws attention to the irony that while ideal female behaviour generally consisted of keeping quiet, in *controversiae*, Roman women were expected to verbally cry out for help against unwanted sexual advances. Failure to do so risked implicating the woman herself, since it was assumed that the girl would have been rescued by neighbours if she shouted.[51] This rape myth (that lack of verbal protest during an attack indicates consent) was not codified in law, where a woman's culpability instead depended on whether or not force (*vis*) had

---

[47] Translated by Janan 1994: 440 as 'having laid aside her complaint' (1994: 440).
[48] OLD 1(a): 'An *expression* of grievance, complaint, protest' (emphasis added).
[49] Translating the whole sentence into English in the order it comes in Latin does not necessarily shift the overall sense, for example: 'Although terrified at the sight, having been overcome by his brightness/appearance, she suffered rape without crying out'.
[50] Brescia 2015: 76.
[51] Brescia 2015.

been used.[52] As regards this issue, the text is quite clear. Both the narrator and Leucothoe's direct quote specifically use the word *vis* to describe the rape (*vim passa est*, 4.233; *vim tulit*, 4.239).[53] By this standard, the 'case' seems relatively cut and dry: Sol was guilty of *stuprum/adulterium*, and Leucothoe could not be condemned of *stuprum/adulterium* because she experienced violence (note the verbal parallelism between *vim passa* in Ovid's text and *vim patitur* in the juristic literature).[54]

This idealised application of law does not, however, account for the full range of ways audiences may have interpreted the episode's narrative complexity. While Leucothoe may be 'innocent' according to the manifest concept of rape, Leuconoe's narrative description brings into play an operative concept of rape influenced by ancient Roman rape myths (that is, misunderstandings of rape). Again, the term 'manifest concept' refers to official or legal definitions of an idea, whereas 'operative concept' refers to 'the implicit definition that would be extrapolated from actual usage in a given community'.[55] As in the instances Jenkins discusses, the manifest and operative concepts of rape in ancient Rome did not align, in part because of distortions resulting from false cultural narratives about rape. Such rape myths, ancient and modern, contribute to epistemic injustice;[56] they harm women as knowers, since they cause hearers to question and undervalue women's testimony about their own experience (undervaluing their experiential knowledge in favour of false cultural knowledge).

As regards Leucothoe's story, the author has staged a scene that presents at least three competing female voices: Leuconoe's, Clytie's and Leucothoe's. Of

---

[52] Ulp. *D.* 48.5.14(13).7 *ceterum quae vim patitur, non est in ea causa ut adulterii vel stupri damnetur* [but if a woman experiences violence, there is not a case against her to be condemned of adultery or disgrace]. There was also a praetorian edict that defined the idea of duress, with violence and fear being the constitutive elements (*quod per uim aut metum abstulisset, in Verr.* 2.3.65.152). See also *ad Quint. fratr.* 1.1.7.21; Bauman 1993. The text emphasises Leucothoe's fear, and while the intent may be to eroticise her terror, it also provides grounds to argue her *pudicitia* was stolen under duress (*pavet illa,* **metu**que *et colus et fusus digitis cecidere remissis. / ipse* **timor** *decuit*, 4.228–30; **territa**, 4.231).

[53] Contra Curran 1978.

[54] Quoted above at n52. Ulpian's passage occurs in the middle of a discussion about war captives but has been taken to apply more broadly. The interpretation that Leucothoe would not be legally culpable is opposed to Janan's 1994: 442 conclusion that Leucothoe is guilty in the eyes of the law: 'Language cannot express the complexity of Leucothoe's desire, nor Justice grapple with it – and each incapacity, resting upon an impossible demand for a unified subject, intertwines with the other to represent her as a simple criminal before the Law'.

[55] Jenkins 2017: 195.

[56] See Fricker 2007; Medina 2017; Pohlhaus Jr 2017.

course, at one level, all these 'voices' may be thought of as either Leuconoe's (since she narrates the inset tale) or Ovid's (qua author), but setting this issue aside temporarily allows us to observe some interesting features about the episode's presentation. Each of these women has a different interpretation of 'what happened': Leuconoe's interpretation is represented in the title of her stories and the complex narrative description at lines 4.232–3, discussed above; Clytie's interpretation is not presented in direct speech, but indicates that she envied Leucothoe's experience and promulgated the events as *adulterium* (***invidit** Clytie ... stimulata paelicis ira vulgat **adulterium** diffamatamque parenti / indicat*, 4.235–7); and Leucothoe's interpretation is represented in direct speech expressing that Sol raped her without consent ('*ille vim tulit invitae*', 4.238–9).

Significantly, Leuconoe introduces her narrative as *amores Solis* (4.170). This terminology is consistent with the way other tales of rape or attempted rape in the poem are referred to (programmatically, the story of Daphne and Apollo is introduced as Apollo's *primus amor* [1.452][57]) but is at serious odds with Leucothoe's description of the encounter as *vis*. Setting aside the importance of the generic associations of the word in this poem, labelling Leucothoe's experience of rape as *amor Solis* prioritises the feelings of the sun over the feelings of Leucothoe.

Leuconoe's main description of the rape also specifically includes the detail *posita querella*, which conjures the culturally operative idea that 'real' rape victims make verbal complaints for help, otherwise they are actually willing participants in sex.[58] We can compare Leuconoe's inclusion of this detail, for instance, to a modern news story about a woman who is raped that includes a description of a miniskirt the woman was wearing at the time. In theory, the woman's outfit is irrelevant to understanding events and evaluating whether or not she was raped, but the operative concept of rape excludes women who wear revealing outfits from

[57] For relatively recent work on Apollo's *primus amor*, see Nicoll 1980; Myers 1994: 61–3; Knox 1986: 14–17; Holzberg 1999; Keith 2002; Hardie 2002: 45–50, 128–30; Barchiesi 1999, 2005; Martindale 2005: 203–17; Miller 2009; Battistella 2010; Ziogas 2013: 66–9.

[58] In this viewpoint, the use of force is not the most important factor in determining consent, since it takes for granted the idea given voice in Ovid's *Ars Amatoria* 1.673–4: *vim licet appelles: grata est vis ista puellis;/ quod iuvat, invitae saepe dedisse volunt*. Whatever the intended tone by the author in that specific passage, it represents a culturally salient viewpoint. The view Ovid describes is akin to what Hilkje Hänel 2021 has termed as 'hermeneutical misfire' in the context of contemporary sexual violence. Hänel builds on work about pornography that determines pornographic speech forms the expectation that women mean 'yes' when they say 'no'. She argues that rape myths like this distort dominant hermeneutical resources in ways that cause perpetrators to fail to adequately understand their actions. Importantly, she identifies hermeneutical misfiring with epistemic ignorance that stems from a person's position of power and privilege and thus does not absolve them from accountability.

being victims. Including the detail that Leucothoe didn't complain stages a discrepancy between the operative concept of rape and Leucothoe's own testimony, which maintains that she was unwilling (*invitae*, 4.239). This opens the possibility for hermeneutical injustice.[59] José Medina articulates hermeneutical injustice as:

> the phenomenon that occurs when the intelligibility of communicators is unfairly constrained or undermined, when their meaning-making capacities encounter unfair obstacles.[60]

Leucothoe's intelligibility is unfairly undermined when the narrative introduces the detail that she does not verbally protest because it activates a rape myth found in the operative concept of rape.

Clytie's interpretation of Leucothoe's experience similarly presents and reinforces an operative concept of rape influenced by rape myths. Rather than interpreting Leucothoe's experience as negative for or harmful to Leucothoe, Clytie is envious (*Invidit Clytie*, 4.234). Her jealousy at Leucothoe's experience frames it as pleasurable/desirable, echoing the idea found in *Ars Amatoria* 1.673–4 that women enjoy being able to say they were forced unwillingly.[61] This rape myth creates an operative concept of rape that does not acknowledge unwillingness and undermines Leucothoe's ability to effectively make her experience intelligible, amounting to a case of hermeneutical injustice.[62] Notably, it is unclear how Clytie

---

[59] Although I discuss Leucothoe's testimony, I have chosen here to characterise this as a hermeneutical injustice rather than a testimonial injustice, since the episode deals less directly with Leucothoe's credibility by a hearer (at least internally to the episode) (see Fricker 2007: 9) and more with prejudice in the collective hermeneutical resources that obscures the intelligibility of a significant part of her experience. Within the text, both Leuconoe's description and Clytie's interpretation are provided before Leucothoe's speech, such that designating them as hearers becomes somewhat problematic. In Fricker's initial explanation of hermeneutical injustice, she was primarily concerned with instances in which people were unable to make sense of their own experiences because of insufficiencies in language/resources, but subsequent work emphasises that hermeneutical injustice deals with both expressive and interpretative oppression (Medina 2017: 41). More recent critiques of and additions to Fricker's work reveal that testimonial and hermeneutical injustices are often intertwined and that distinguishing between the two ideas is often difficult (see Maitra 2010; Dotson 2012; Medina 2017: 43–4).

[60] Medina 2017: 41.

[61] See n58 above.

[62] It may also be worth noting that Clytie seems to be portrayed as an insufficient knower; she gravely misunderstands her relationship with Sol, imagining that it is akin to that of Juno and Jupiter and fashioning herself as an angry wife (*stimulata paelicis ira*, 4.235). The portrayal of her unbridled passion (*neque enim moderatus in illa / Solis amor fuerat*, 4.235) as an impediment to her judgement (and eventual madness) (*tabuit ex illo dementer amoribus usa*, 4.259) also appears decidedly gendered.

comes to know about Leucothoe's experience; that is, it is not evident that Clytie directly disbelieves or dismisses Leucothoe's articulation of it. Nonetheless, the narrative itself presents Clytie's understanding of the experience in opposition to Leucothoe's understanding of the experience.

EPISTEMIC INJUSTICE

This presentation dramatises and problematises the multiple ways of viewing and understanding Leucothoe's experience. It presents opposed ways of understanding the rape – through a manifest concept of rape (suggested in legal terminology and Leucothoe's own testimony) and an operative concept of rape (implied in Leuconoe's description of the rape and Clytie's jealousy). The discrepancy between these ways of knowing stages a hermeneutical struggle[63] between Leucothoe's understanding and the dominant culture. Identifying agency for the resultant epistemic injustice is challenging within the complex narrative structure of the *Metamorphoses* in that there are multiple subjects to consider at multiple levels (main narrative, frame narrative and extra-textual). Still, we may not need to identify a single subject responsible for this injustice, since, importantly, epistemic injustice does not necessarily mean a subject or their experience needs to be *disbelieved*. Ishani Maitra draws attention to contexts where the act of suspending judgement (not making a determination of belief) can constitute a sort of epistemic injustice.[64]

At least one agent of epistemic injustice is clearer to define, however, namely Leucothoe's father, who represents a special case. In terms of the hermeneutical resources at Leucothoe's disposal, I argue that she should be treated as having the relevant concepts to understand the experience. While there may be reasonable objections to this view – for example, that her language does not exactly match a manifest concept of rape in Roman law,[65] or that the semantic range of *vis* is too broad[66] – overall her words are capable of accurately communicating her experience;[67] it is clear she is able to process the experience as a rape that she did

---

[63] See Medina 2017: 43.
[64] Maitra 2010: 200–1.
[65] The counterargument being that it is the manifest concept that is lacking in this instance.
[66] The counterargument here being that there is no reason the concept of rape needs to be expressed in a single word as opposed to three.
[67] See Medina 2017: 43: 'Instead of focusing on complete success or failure of understanding, it is important to appreciate that intelligibility is a matter of more or less: doing better or worse in understanding oneself and others is a matter of trying as hard as one can, of paying attention to the emerging expressive and interpretative possibilities, no matter how inchoate or embryonic'.

not consent to (*invitae*). Her father, on the other hand, may be seen as perpetrating what Gaile Pohlhaus Jr has termed 'willful hermeneutical ignorance', that is, 'when dominantly situated knowers refuse to acknowledge epistemic tools developed from the experienced world of those situated marginally'.[68] When Leucothoe's father learns of her experience from Clytie, he immediately begins to bury his daughter alive. Although Leucothoe tries to communicate that she was raped and the experience was non-consensual, there is no indication that her father understands the concept of rape as she experienced it, and instead he piles a mound of heavy sand on top of her (4.236–40). As Janan describes, 'He does not debate the question of rape, substituting her body's seemingly unambiguous physical state for the slipperier task of evaluating testimony as to her mental state – her consent or nonconsent to the Sun's advances'.[69] Leucothoe's attempt to be understood is unfairly constrained as her father (a dominantly situated knower) continues to misunderstand the world. Whether Leucothoe's father blames her for the sexual encounter or believes that her *pudicitia* is more important than her personhood, he is misunderstanding the world in a way that obscures Leucothoe's experience and harms her (both physically and in her capacity as a knower).

At a broad level, the narrative seems to recognise this particular act as an injustice, since it characterises Leucothoe's father as cruel and savage (*ferox inmansuetusque*, 4.237) and Leucothoe's fate as pitiable (*nil dolientius*, 4.245–6).[70] Ovid's framing of this scene invites sympathising with Leucothoe to some extent, as happens elsewhere in the poem to other victims of rape and attempted rape.[71] And at the same time, the broader narrative of the *Metamorphoses* seems to reinforce collective misunderstandings of rape that obscure women's social experience. For instance, the only women capable of preventing an attempted rape in the poem are those who verbally cry out for divine assistance.[72] In these cases women avoid rape through being changed into other forms (for example, a tree, a bird, and so forth). Although their corporeal transformations may encourage sympathy, they nevertheless reinforce the false cultural narrative that rape entails victims shouting for help.[73]

---

[68] Pohlhaus Jr 2012: 716. Others in this volume who discuss wilful hermeneutical ignorance include Weiberg (Chapter 2), Witzke (Chapter 7), Freas (Chapter 11) and Hines (Chapter 13).
[69] Janan 1994: 439–40.
[70] This observation supports what Sharrock 2020 would term an 'optimistic' reading of the text.
[71] See especially Sharrock 2020.
[72] Bowen 2018.
[73] Bowen 2019: 309.

Leucothoe's story also resembles the story of Callisto,[74] whose narrative highlights a similar rape myth, namely that a woman cannot be *truly* unwilling unless she physically fights against her rapist. The narration of Callisto's rape involves the following reference to her struggle (2.434–7):

> illa quidem contra, quantum modo femina posset
> (adspiceres utinam, Saturnia, mitior esses),
> illa quidem pugnat, sed quem superare puella,
> quisve Iovem poterat?

> Indeed she struggled against him, as much as a woman might be able to (If only you'd seen it, Juno, you would have been gentler), but whom has a girl been able to overcome or who has been able to overcome Jove?

This passage seems to acknowledge that physically fighting against a rapist (especially, but not only Jupiter) is pointless and doomed to fail. It also, however, values Callisto's resistance as proof of her unwillingness. Even this, however, does not entirely release Callisto from the possibility of being blamed but merely suggests her punishment might be lighter.[75] The lack of consistency in these ideas about Callisto's consent may destabilise rape culture but does not unambiguously condemn it. By giving voice to the rape myth, the text at some level perpetuates it.

Similarly, the different understandings of what Leucothoe experienced simultaneously reinforce and problematise ancient false narratives about rape and existing gendered power structures. On the one hand, the text sets up a scene that labels Leucothoe's experience with different terms (*amor, vis, adulterium*).[76] Ovid's staging of multiple interpretations and viewpoints on what happened to Leucothoe accords with some of the major thematic and poetic concerns that have been identified in the *Metamorphoses*, particularly the poem's ambiguity and attention to the issue of narrative credibility.[77] Throughout the poem, Ovid casts doubt on narrative authority through drawing attention to ambiguities in stories and introducing multiple viewpoints and interpretations of events. In the case of Leucothoe's story, these differing understandings reveal conflicts between the manifest definition of sexual violence and the operative concept in Roman

---

[74] Anderson 2.422–4.
[75] See Sharrock 2020: 40 on the sympathetic treatment of Callisto's eventual metamorphosis.
[76] Different individuals terming the same thing differently appears explicitly in the poem when it is noted that mortals called one of the sons of Sleep 'Phobetor', whereas the gods above call him 'Icelos' (11.640–1).
[77] For example, Graf 1988; Feeney 1991; O'Hara 2007 (with additional bibliography at 113n28); Miller 2009; Feldherr 2010.

culture. This lack of alignment reveals how false cultural ideology about rape distorts the dominant hermeneutical resources in ways that obscure Leucothoe's experience and harm her as a knower. This has a destabilising effect, as it brings into question the actions and beliefs of those at the top of Roman power structures. At the same time, the episode also reinforces a number of rape myths. As noted briefly above, the only women in the narrative who escape an attempted rape are those who verbally cry out to a god for help. Noting that Leucothoe is raped after she 'didn't complain' gives voice to this myth that continues to have uptake today. The scene also reinforces a distorted vision of who is rape-able and who bears responsibility for preventing rape. Leucothoe's attractive physical appearance (4.208–11) and her elite status (4.212–13) are key details in setting the scene for her violation and portraying her as a sympathetic victim. Additionally, the narrative focuses on Sol's need to disguise himself to gain entry to Leucothoe's space; this reinforces the idea that women must be vigilant to keep themselves out of dangerous situations. Though the detail of Sol's deception works to exculpate Leucothoe, it indulges in the idea that it is her responsibility to prevent rape rather than challenging it. While Ovid's work may reveal fractures in the set of knowledge that underpins the operative Roman concept of rape, it does not ultimately dismantle Rome's gendered epistemology.

CHAPTER 11

'Feebly fighting back': *Stuprum* in Eumolpus's *Pergamene Boy*

Debra Freas

In Petronius's *Satyrica*, Eumolpus tells Encolpius the story of the *Pergamene Boy*, which recounts his former sexual relationship with a pupil.[1] This chapter argues that the narrator Eumolpus trivialises and suppresses his victimisation of the boy by strategically ignoring Roman legal and social custom when presenting this sexual relationship through the literary and cultural lens of Athenian pederasty, specifically by parodying Plato's *Symposium*. The framing of the tale through the lens of Athenian rather than Roman social customs is so successful, in fact, that scholarly assessments largely fail to acknowledge that Eumolpus's actions amount to *stuprum*, a legal charge governing unsanctioned sexual relations with Roman boys, women, widows and girls.[2] I argue that Eumolpus commits a type of epistemic injustice – contributory injustice – by utilising prejudiced hermeneutical resources that harm the epistemic agency of the boy and his parents.[3] By applying the concept of contributory injustice to

---

[1] I would like to thank the editors for their insightful comments and suggestions.
[2] Fantham 1991: 269–70 observes that in the early Roman Republic, *stuprum* could reference any public disgrace and only gradually acquired the more specific meaning of unlawful intercourse with citizens. Williams 2010: 103–4 offers the following definition: 'Roman writers often use the term *stuprum* to describe the offense consisting in the violation of the sexual integrity of freeborn Romans of either sex: pederasty was therefore a subset of *stuprum* and for that reason liable to condemnation'. For more about *stuprum* during the Republic and Empire, see Gardner 1986: 121–5; Fantham 1991; Richlin 1993b: 561–6; Nguyen 2006; and Williams 2010: 103–36.
[3] For a discussion of epistemic injustice, hermeneutical injustice and contributory injustice, see the Introduction to this volume.

a literary narrative from ancient Rome, my aim is to show how narration raises epistemological issues related to authority, reliability and privilege that are particularly relevant for the legal and cultural recognition of sexual violence. After identifying the contributory injustice done to the family, I apply the modern concept of child grooming to the story to improve our understanding of the victims' experience that is largely silenced in the abuser's narrative.[4]

In arguing that Eumolpus as interpreter and narrator does epistemic harm to the Pergamene boy and his parents, this chapter builds on Fricker's foundational work on epistemic injustice, which she further breaks into testimonial and hermeneutical categories.[5] Subsequent theorists object to Fricker's notion that hermeneutical injustice is structural and nonagential,[6] and Pohlhaus Jr proposes that hermeneutical injustice also exists in the distinct form of wilful hermeneutical ignorance, 'when dominantly situated knowers refuse to acknowledge epistemic tools developed from the experienced world of those situated marginally'.[7] Dotson, in turn, builds off this notion to propose a third type of epistemic injustice, contributory injustice, which

> is caused by an epistemic agent's situated ignorance, in the form of wilful hermeneutical ignorance, in maintaining and utilizing structurally prejudiced hermeneutical resources that result in epistemic harm to the epistemic agency of a knower. Both the structurally prejudiced or biased hermeneutical resources and the agent's situated ignorance are catalysts for contributory injustice.[8]

Theorists like Fricker and Pohlhaus Jr have turned to literary works to explicate their definitions,[9] and I will expand on this approach to consider how contributory injustice arises in the *Pergamene Boy* when the narrator Eumolpus intentionally conceals his crime by privileging a Greek pederastic framework over a Roman

---

[4] Others in this volume who address hermeneutical injustices in ancient texts or their receptions include Weiberg (Chapter 2), Witzke (Chapter 7), Bowen (Chapter 10) and Hines (Chapter 13).
[5] Fricker 2007.
[6] Fricker 2007: 1, 159, 161, 162; Mason 2011: 295; Pohlhaus Jr 2012: 725; Medina 2012: 216–18 and 2013: 110–13; and Dotson 2012: 31 claim that hermeneutical injustice is agential. In *The Routledge Handbook of Epistemic Injustice*, Fricker 2017: 55 maintains the earlier position in response to these theorists, whereas Medina 2017: 42–5 maintains the critique of Fricker.
[7] Pohlhaus Jr 2012: 715.
[8] Dotson 2012: 31.
[9] Fricker 2007: 23–9 and Pohlhaus Jr 2012: 724–31 clarify their definitions of hermeneutical injustice using the trial of Tom Robinson in Harper Lee's *To Kill a Mockingbird*. See the Introduction for a discussion of this.

social-legal context, a perspective that places the family in an epistemically marginalised position.

Before turning to the *Pergamene Boy*, it is worth acknowledging that feminist epistemology has traditionally been concerned with identifying prejudices that disadvantage the epistemic agency of women and other marginalised groups.[10] It may seem odd, therefore, to include a story told by a man about a boy in a volume titled *Believing Ancient Women*, since these individuals represent to some extent the dominant and privileged epistemic class of ancient Rome. However, the legal charge *stuprum* (*D.* 47.11.1.2; 48.5.6.1; 48.5.35.1) protected boys alongside unmarried women and girls – individuals who were marginalised in Roman society. Moreover, a penetrated male occupied the feminine sexual role in Roman thought and was consequently feminised.[11] Male victims of sexual violence would thus have encountered social and legal obstacles in ancient Rome – just as many still do today – that impeded their willingness to reveal their victimisation or to have it recognised as such.[12] Yet, despite the fact that the Roman law of *stuprum* applied equally to male and female victims, scholarship on the *Pergamene Boy* most often registers Eumolpus's actions as seduction rather than sexual violence,[13]

---

[10] When tracing a historical genealogy for epistemic injustice in the field of feminist epistemology, Tuana 2017: 126 offers the following overview: 'in addition to focusing attention onto knowledge obscured by dominant interests and values, feminist and liberatory epistemologists were attentive to the subject of knowledge through a second lens, namely, attention to what kind of subject one must be in order to be (seen as) a knowing subject. Through this lens, questions about who counted as a knowing subject and who did not led feminist and liberatory epistemologists to examine what qualities were deemed necessary to be a knowing subject and how the social situations of groups impacted who counted as a knowing subject and who did not'.

[11] When discussing Roman notions of masculinity, Masterson 2013: 27 notes that 'the possible victim of rape is derided as smooth and as less of a man'.

[12] Richlin 1993b: 564–6 points out that a male victim of *stuprum* could also be prosecuted if it is alleged that he allowed himself to be penetrated; see also Williams 2010: 133. Quintilian claims that a male victim of *stuprum* faced particular scrutiny: *illic maior aestus, ubi quis pudenda queritur, ut stuprum, praecipue in maribus . . . hoc iniuriae genus verecundius est fateri passis quam ausis* ('There is greater embarrassment when someone complains of shameful things, like *stuprum*, especially committed against males . . . it is more embarrassing that this type of injury be admitted by those having suffered it than by those having dared it', *I.O.* 11.1.84).

[13] While not an exhaustive catalogue, the following use the language of seduction to describe the sexual relationship: Beck 1979: 251; Dimundo 1986: 85; Slater 1990: 94n13; Hunter 1996: 203; McGlathery 1998a: 211; Obermayer 1998: 155; Anderson 1999: 57; Habermehl 2006: 92; and Schmeling 2011: 360. Hubbard's 1986: 209 misleading account of their relationship warrants note: 'Eumolpus himself was once a teacher – in the Pergamene episode – pandering to his student's wishes and desires (85–87)'.

and no other scholars, as far as can be determined, have identified Eumolpus's crime as *stuprum*.[14] For all these reasons, feminist epistemology offers an approach well suited to explicating anew the perspective of Eumolpus's victims, since the boy's experience is construed and understood differently as a result of his gender.

*

Eumolpus enters the extant *Satyrica* in Chapter 83 when he approaches Encolpius in an art gallery. Encolpius visits the pinacotheca to comfort himself after his sixteen-year-old lover Giton leaves him for another man, yet he is drawn to paintings that depict pederastic pairs from myth that only exacerbate his grief. The images of Ganymede, Hylas and Hyacinthus remind Encolpius of Giton's betrayal, and his unhappy reverie is interrupted by the arrival of Eumolpus, who presents himself as a poet and wise interpreter of human nature and the arts. Eumolpus plays a major role in what survives of the novel, stepping in to become Encolpius's travelling companion and fellow conman. He also becomes an internal narrator, composing the longest poems and telling two inset Milesian Tales:[15] the *Pergamene Boy* and the *Widow of Ephesus*. Within moments of meeting Encolpius, Eumolpus tells him the *Pergamene Boy*, although it is not entirely clear why he does so, since a lacuna precedes the story.[16] Whatever his motives may be, Eumolpus rightly discerns that Encolpius shares his sexual proclivities and will enjoy the tale.

To summarise the *Pergamene Boy*, Eumolpus travels with a Roman quaestor to Pergamum, a city in the Roman province of Asia, presumably during the first

---

[14] Dimundo 1983: 263–4 suggests that the *Pergamene Boy* reflects critical Roman attitudes towards pederasty but focuses on the boy's actions rather than Eumolpus's criminal ones. Richardson 1984: 119 observes that Eumolpus's sexual behaviour is predatory. Taylor 1997: 323 writes that the Pergamene boy is 'sexually exploited'. McGlathery 1998b: 4 calls the relationship 'pederastic or pedophilic'. Courtney 2001 notes that Eumolpus 'assaults' the boy (137) and describes this as 'molestation' (139), yet calls it a 'hilarious story' (137). Habermehl 2006: 97 points out that Eumolpus acts contrary to Roman law and cites the *lex Scantinia* rather than *stuprum*. Williams 2010: 103–36 offers a lengthy discussion of *stuprum* yet does not apply the charge to Eumolpus's criminal behaviour when discussing the *Pergamene Boy* (205–6). In a recent article, I state that Eumolpus commits *stuprum* (2021: 631).

[15] Milesian Tales, named after the supposed originator of the genre Aristides of Miletus, are short, erotic, bawdy tales. For more on the elusive genre, see Lefèvre 1997: 8–15; Harrison 1998; Jennson 2004; and Bowie 2013.

[16] Sullivan 1968: 60–1 proposes that Eumolpus tells the *Pergamene Boy* to console Encolpius, who reveals Giton's sexual betrayal, whereas Slater 2009: 25 suggests that Eumolpus attempts to seduce Encolpius with the erotic story.

century. He lives with a local family and becomes a tutor to their teenaged son,[17] and while their citizen status is unclear, Eumolpus calls the father a *paterfamilias*, the boy is freeborn, the parents are concerned about their son's sexual integrity, and the family is involved in Roman politics, circumstances that warrant applying a Roman social-legal understanding to what transpires. Eumolpus lives in the same house as the boy, eats meals with the family, and teaches and escorts his ward to the gymnasium; the parents trust Eumolpus to protect their son from sexual predators, but they have been manipulated into trusting the wrong man. Eumolpus exploits his proximity to the boy and promises him gifts late at night to gain more and more advanced physical contact, moving from kissing, to touching, to sex. After Eumolpus fails to produce an expensive gift he promised, the boy withdraws and threatens to tell his father when pressured to continue the sexual relationship. Eumolpus then forces the boy to have sex, and the latter initiates three more sexual encounters on the same night. Eumolpus refuses the last offer and ends the story by repeating the boy's own threat to tell his father. The narrator jovially recounts this process and his success to Encolpius, treating the encounter as a trivial affair even though he is breaking the law: seducing and having illicit sex with a freeborn boy was *stuprum* and the offender could be sentenced to death.[18]

Eumolpus tells the *Pergamene Boy* to impress and amuse his new acquaintance Encolpius, and the latter's response to the story confirms that the former succeeds: 'aroused by this speech, I began to consult the more knowledgeable man . . .' (*erectus his sermonibus consulere prudentiorem coepi, Sat.* 88.1).[19] Encolpius is titillated, and Schmeling correctly notes that the story earns Encolpius's respect: 'E. will soon consider Eumolpus an authority and interpreter, because by his story of the Pergamene youth he shows how to seduce young boys, a talent E. admires'.[20] Encolpius, like Eumolpus, enjoys having sex with boys and identifies with the storyteller's perspective and willingness to break the law to satisfy his desire.[21] Encolpius takes the older man on as a travelling companion, likely because he is lonely in the wake of Giton's departure and shares Eumolpus's sexual and literary inclinations.[22]

---

[17] Eumolpus variously calls the boy a *puer, ephebus* and an *ephebus plenae maturitatis*, which suggests the age of puberty.

[18] Paulus's entry in the *Digest* (47.11.1.2) lists death as the punishment for penetrative *stuprum*; Williams 2010: 124 and 132, however, suggests that penalties for pederastic *stuprum* were less harsh than adultery and may have typically been a monetary fine rather than death.

[19] I use Müller's text for the *Satyrica*, and all translations are my own unless otherwise indicated.

[20] Schmeling 2011: 353.

[21] Encolpius reveals that he is aware of the charge *stuprum* at *Sat.* 81.4 when he alleges that Ascyltos obtained his freedom through *stuprum* ('*stupro liber, stupro ingenuus*').

[22] Conte 1996: 2 famously calls Encolpius a mythomaniac narrator and *scholasticus* who is the 'victim of his own literary experiences, who naively exalts himself by identifying with heroic roles among the great mythical and literary characters of the past'.

The *Pergamene Boy* is an intricately wrought story that has long been recognised to engage pederastic themes from Plato's *Symposium*.[23] Eumolpus, for example, alludes to the dialogue early in his tale by setting the initial discussion of pederasty at a dinner party, *in convivio* (85.2), and by describing himself as a philosopher, *unum ex philosophis* (85.2). McGlathery thoroughly explores this intertextual relationship and proposes that:

> structural elements and literary allusions in the tale of the Pergamene boy indicate that it enacts a deliberate reversal of the situation in Plato's *Symposium*, in which the youth Alcibiades, enamored of Socrates' love of truth and mastery of his own desires, unsuccessfully attempts to seduce his chaste tutor.[24]

While a full account of this reversal cannot be offered here, McGlathery convincingly establishes that the *Pergamene Boy* 'consciously alludes to the Athenian provenance of the pederastic paradigm' through its close engagement with the *Symposium*.[25]

Eumolpus's parody of the *Symposium* displays his wit and cultural sophistication, yet the storyteller also wilfully ignores Roman sexual conventions by depicting his relationship with the boy as a humorous corruption of an ideal pederastic relationship. According to Courtney, Eumolpus not only reworks Alcibiades' failed seduction of Socrates from the *Symposium* but also exposes 'the distance between the ideal pederastic relationship as envisaged by Plato' and that shown in the *Pergamene Boy*.[26] Habermehl more specifically observes that Eumolpus caricatures Pausanias's idealisation of a heavenly type of pederasty where an *erastes* educates an *eromenos* in socially valued pursuits and participates in an intellectual and erotic relationship based on mutual respect (*Symp.* 182d–185c).[27] Eumolpus presents himself and the boy as lovers who fail to conform to these ideals in the following ways: the tutor is only superficially interested in the boy's education;[28] the older man manipulates the boy into having sex by giving him gifts; and the

---

[23] See Cameron 1969: 369; Dimundo 1983; McGlathery 1998a; and Repath 2010 for more on the story's parodic relationship to Plato's *Symposium*. The following discuss the complex narrative structure of the *Pergamene Boy*: Dimundo 1983 and 1986; Sega 1986; Fedeli and Dimundo 1988; Fraga 1997; Lefèvre 1997; McGlathery 1998a.
[24] McGlathery 1998a: 209.
[25] McGlathery 1998a: 209.
[26] Courtney 2001: 138.
[27] Habermehl 2006: 93.
[28] McGlathery 1998a: 212 claims that Eumolpus and the Pergamene boy 'make it explicit that they desire a sexual union not for moral or philosophical purposes but for sexual and materialistic ones'.

boy is depicted as a greedy and overly eager sexual partner.[29] This privileging of the pederastic model in the story enables Eumolpus to avoid openly acknowledging that the Romans fundamentally diverged from Greek practice by criminalising sexual relationships with freeborn boys.[30] In the end, Eumolpus and his pupil break both Athenian and Roman sexual protocols in the *Pergamene Boy*, yet the humour of the story rests on flouting Greek pederastic norms rather than defying Roman laws governing the sexual integrity of freeborn boys.[31]

Furthermore, Eumolpus's localisation of the story in the province of Asia draws additional attention to his choice to emphasise Greek pederastic standards at the expense of a Roman legal context. Pergamum was in the eastern part of the Roman Empire and, as its gymnasium attests, had strong ties to Hellenistic culture (*Sat.* 85.2). Yet Lefèvre is correct to note that Eumolpus begins his story with Roman technical terms like *quaestor, stipendium, educere* and *hospitium* (*Sat.* 85.1).[32] Eumolpus may include these details to add authenticity to the story and to gesture to his real or imagined importance, yet by including this terminology at the beginning of the tale, the narrator establishes that he is living and working in a Roman environment.[33] This admission implicates him in committing contributory injustice, since according to Dotson's definition, 'the agent plays a role in contributory injustice by willfully refusing to recognise or acquire requisite alternative hermeneutical resources'.[34] Eumolpus almost certainly knows of the Roman prohibition on *stuprum* but carefully evades acknowledging it openly in his story.[35] For example, he uses the term *paterfamilias* – the figure charged

---

[29] McGlathery 1998a: 212–13 observes that the boy's materialism and excessive sexual enjoyment do not conform to Greek standards of homoerotic behaviour.

[30] Roman men faced no legal obstacles to having sex with male prostitutes and enslaved men, but as Lear 2013: 214 observes: 'pederastic relations of the kind idealized by the Greeks, involving a mentoring relationship between males of similar social levels, had no place in Roman sexual-social ethics'.

[31] Laes 2019: 124 rightly observes that 'it is only with the specific context of pederasty and Greek philosophers in mind that the reader can understand some of the humor that lurks in the Milesian Tale on the boy from Pergamum'.

[32] Lefèvre 1997: 9–10.

[33] Eumolpus's ethnic and social status are unclear, but as Panayotakis 2019: 184 notes, he is familiar with Roman customs: 'Despite the ambiguity of the extant text, then, I am inclined to conclude that certainly Eumolpus, in all likelihood Encolpius and Giton, and probably also Ascyltus are freeborn men who are circulating in the gutter of Roman society and are well read, or scheming enough to pass off as well read, in order to exploit whomever they encounter'.

[34] Dotson 2012: 32.

[35] Schmeling 2011: 363 points out that 'from 109.2 we learn that Eumolpus knows enough about the law to draw up a complicated document with specific limiting clauses'.

with maintaining the sexual reputation and integrity of his children'[36] – when he vaguely explains that he must conceal his criminal intentions from the boy's father: *excogitavi rationem, qua non essem patri familiae suspectus* ('I developed a plan so that I would not be suspected by the *paterfamilias*', *Sat.* 85.1). The directness of the Roman legal term *paterfamilias* contrasts notably with what amounts to only an implicit admission that he intends to break the law. As the story progresses into the pederastic courtship phase, moreover, Eumolpus's use of Roman terminology becomes less obtrusive.

Eumolpus continues to distance his sexual encounter with the boy from *stuprum* through cultural and linguistic substitutions that ignore Roman law and custom, an action that is further elucidated by Dotson's definition of contributory injustice. He, for instance, disregards the parents' concern for their son's *pudicitia* by euphemistically translating language from the Greek vocabulary of pederasty into Latin (*Sat.* 85.2):[37]

> quotiescumque enim in convivio de usu formosorum mentio facta est, tam vehementer excandui, tam severa tristitia violari aures meas obsceno sermone nolui, ut me mater praecipue tamquam unum ex philosophis intueretur. iam ego coeperam ephebum in gymnasium deducere, ego studia eius ordinare, ego docere ac praecipere, ne quis praedator corporis admitteretur in domum.

> For whenever mention was made at dinner about the sexual use of beautiful boys, I grew so vehemently hot, I wished with such stern severity that my ears not be violated by obscene conversation, that the mother especially came to view me as, so to speak, one of the philosophers. And now I began to lead the ephebe to the gymnasium, I began to direct his studies, to teach and instruct, in order that some predator of the body not be admitted into the house.

Eumolpus relates that the boy's parents voiced their concern about *de usu formosorum* on multiple occasions, but it is unlikely that the parents used this language, since the phrase, as McGlathery notes, 'refers explicitly to the χρῆσις ἀφροδισίων,

---

[36] Saller 1999: 191 notes that at Cic. *Catil.* 4.12 and Petr. 85, the term *paterfamilias* uniquely means 'the head of household with responsibility to protect his wife and children'. Fantham (1991: 272) more fully explains that the *paterfamilias* was a sexual guardian for his dependents: '*pudicitia* was originally the concern of the family and above all the *paterfamilias* whose honour was affected by the behaviour of his children of either sex'.

[37] Richlin 1993b: 545 remarks that the Romans in general were so invested in differentiating sexually off-limits freeborn boys from enslaved ones that the former wore a *toga praetexta* and *bulla* to signal their citizen status.

which was a privileged topic of philosophical discourse in Greek philosophical texts' about appropriate pederastic activity.[38] It is more likely, in fact, that the parents used language akin to '*praedator corporis*' to describe the crime, a designation that Eumolpus carefully distances from his own actions.[39] He uses other terms associated with pederasty as well, such as *ephebus* and *gymnasium* (85.3),[40] to characterise the relationship as a pederastic one. McGlathery is quite right, therefore, to draw attention to – if only briefly – the consequences of this relationship from a Roman perspective:

> clearly, the physical enjoyment of a passive sexual role would be disgraceful for a boy such as Eumolpus's *mignon*, destined as he is by virtue of his pedigree to become the head of a household and a leading participant in public affairs.[41]

Public discovery of this sexual relationship, however, could negatively impact the family from a social and legal standpoint irrespective of the boy's 'enjoyment',[42] a Roman concern Eumolpus never acknowledges.[43]

After Eumolpus convinces the parents of his integrity, they grant him unrestricted access to the boy, and the story continues to relate the first days of

---

[38] McGlathery 1998a: 209n23.

[39] Eumolpus also manipulatively dissociates his actions from *stuprum* and sexual violence – what the parents worry about – by pretending that his ears are assaulted, *violari* (Petr. 85.2), by this topic of conversation.

[40] Williams 1995: 524 notes that Roman authors associate the gymnasium and ephebes with the Greek custom of pederasty.

[41] McGlathery 1998a: 214.

[42] As Strong 2021: 182 rightly points out, the ancient Romans recognised the risk of divulging sexual victimisation: 'Quintilian warns that male Roman rape victims may lose more than they gain from public testimony. Although they may be able to find vindication in denouncing their assaulters, these survivors also risked being labeled as sexually passive and losing their status as virtuous male citizens'. Richlin 1993b: 566 raises the possibility that a boy could be prosecuted for allowing himself to be penetrated: 'there is also a group of sources that indicate that a voluntary act of passive homosexuality by a free man of any age was in itself liable to be punished'. According to the jurist Paulus (*Pauli Sententiae* 2.26.12–13), moreover, a freeborn man found guilty of consenting to *stuprum* faced steep penalties: he lost half his property and the right to testate the other half.

[43] Richlin 1993b: 563 notes the social scrutiny Roman women and boys faced when it came to maintaining a family's standing: 'even the act of accosting or following a boy or woman might affect the victim's reputation because of the implication that there might be a reason to think the accoster would succeed, and of course such an affront also affected any adult male responsible for the boy or woman'.

their sexual relationship. Eumolpus depicts the boy as a greedy *eromenos*, who exchanges sexual favours for gifts and lacks sexual restraint.[44] A very different picture emerges, however, if we apply a Roman legal framework to these events, which highlights the criminality of Eumolpus's actions. Paulus, for example, provides the following definition of *stuprum* in the *Digest* (*D*. 47.11.1.2):[45]

> Qui puero stuprum abducto ab eo uel corrupto comite persuaserit aut mulierem puellamue interpellauerit quidue impudicitiae gratia fecerit, donum praebuerit pretiumue, quo is persuadeat, dederit: perfecto flagitio punitur capite, inperfecto in insulam deportatur: corrupti comites summo supplicio adficiuntur.

> One who persuades a boy, abducted by himself or by a corrupt attendant, into indecency or who solicits a woman or girl or does anything for the purpose of impurity or who offers a gift or a reward whereby to induce indecency will, if the offense be complete, suffer capital punishment; if it be not fully effected, he is deported to an island. Corrupt attendants undergo the supreme penalty. (trans. Watson 1985: 784)

According to this jurist's opinion, Eumolpus is guilty of *stuprum* on multiple counts. Eumolpus's narrative, however, obscures this and raises the epistemological concern that what we, the readers, believe is influenced by whom we believe. If we accept Eumolpus's parodic narrative at face value by applying the same Athenian pederastic standards to his relationship with the boy as he does as storyteller, then the boy appears to us as a humorously debauched figure, not as the victim of *stuprum*.

As critical readers, we are therefore compelled to bracket Eumolpus's own efforts as narrator to frame his story as parody, and thereby elide his complicity as an actor within his story, by attending more closely to the details of his narrative

---

[44] McGlathery 1998a: 205 describes their relationship thus: 'Although their courtship, with its careful sequence of meeting places, trysts and exchanges of gifts, retains the elaborate stylization of Platonic or conventional homoerotic love and even a veneer of philosophical earnestness, the motives of the lovers in our tale are much baser than those advocated in Greek philosophy'. Schmeling 2011: 361, furthermore, describes the boy's response to Eumolpus's first sexual advance in the following manner: 'the speed and greed with which the youth complies are unseemly – so also for example, at Tibullus 1.4.58 and 1.9.11, but directly counter to the old standards of Pausanias in Plat. *Sym*. 184a'.

[45] Discussions of *stuprum* from jurists like Paulus are historically later than Petronius, but Williams 2010: 108–9 observes that these categories of sexually off-limits individuals remain the same for over four hundred years, from Plaut. *Cur*. 33–8 to the third century CE, and thus the *Digest* provides suitable historical context for the *Satyrica*.

which resist his parodic framing. Such a counter-reading of the *Pergamene Boy* offers the opportunity to consider the boy's experience, which exists counter to Eumolpus's narrative.[46] Eumolpus, after all, construes the boy's actions in ways that support his pederastic narrative. On the first night, for example, Eumolpus suggests that the boy acquiesces to his sexual proposition for material gain: '*domina . . . Venus, si ego hunc puerum basiavero ita ut ille non sentiat, cras illi par columbarum donabo*'. *audito voluptatis pretio puer stertere coepit* ('Mistress Venus, if I shall have kissed this boy, so that he not feel it, I will give him a pair of doves tomorrow'. After hearing the reward for my pleasure, the boy began to snore, *Sat.* 85.5–6). Eumolpus manipulatively encourages the boy not to respond verbally or react physically to being kissed,[47] and he implies that the absence of explicit physical or verbal resistance is complicity. It is certainly possible, after all, that the child pretends to fall asleep to avoid responding out of fear, shame and uncertainty when faced with a sexual proposition from his teacher, yet the narrator offers one interpretation that lays the groundwork for depicting him as a greedy *eromenos*.[48]

There are other instances in the story where Eumolpus construes events to depict the boy in an unflattering light. When he offers roosters in exchange for touching on the second night, for instance, he insinuates that the boy is venal and sexually eager:[49] *ad hoc votum ephebus ultro se admovit et, puto, vereri coepit ne ego obdormissem* (To this prayer, the ephebe moved himself on his own and, I think, began to fear that I might fall asleep, *Sat.* 86.2). His biased perspective is nonetheless revealed by the limiting verb *puto*, 'I think',[50] and Eumolpus soon admits, moreover, that his motives and exchanges with the boy are driven by his licentiousness (*ad licentiam redii*, 87.1), swollen libido (*libido distenta*, 87.1)

---

[46] As Dotson 2012: 31 notes: 'We do not all depend on the same hermeneutical resources. Such an assumption fails to take into account alternative epistemologies, countermythologies, and hidden transcripts that exist in hermeneutically marginalized communities *among themselves*. It also fails to curtail the role power plays in hindering the hermeneutical resources of the marginalization'.

[47] Eumolpus also references the Greek idealising notion that *eromenoi* should not enjoy being penetrated by introducing the caveat '*ut ille non sentiat*' (see McGlathery 1998a: 214). For more on this idealising notion in Greek pederasty, see Dover 1978: 103; Foucault 1985: 223; and Veyne 1985: 25–35.

[48] Habermehl 2006: 104 observes that the boy acts contrary to Pausanias's recommendation that an *eromenos* must not be easily won over with gifts (Plat. *Symp.* 184a).

[49] Eumolpus offers the boy animals, customary gifts *erastai* give their *eromenoi* in Greek vase paintings and literary accounts (McGlathery 1998a: 211n29).

[50] Sega 1986: 78 notes that Eumolpus's '*puto*' indicates a present interpretation of a past event. Goldman 2007: 6 more generally observes that Eumolpus occasionally uses limiting words like '*puto*' and '*credo*' which indicate that 'Eumolpus does not simply narrate the events, he responds and analyses them subjectively'.

and dishonesty (*improbitas*, 87.3), indications that he hardly makes for a reliable narrator.

Eumolpus's most explicit attempt to trivialise the boy's victimisation coincides with the latter resisting the former verbally and physically. After the tutor offers a stallion in exchange for sex on the third night, the boy discovers that he has been deceived and attempts to refuse Eumolpus sexually: *at ille plane iratus nihil aliud dicebat nisi hoc: 'aut dormi, aut ego iam dicam patri'* (But the boy was clearly angry and kept saying nothing else except this, 'Either sleep, or I will tell my father'. *Sat.* 87.2). Eumolpus responds with violence yet attempts to neutralise it by presenting the boy as a willing sexual partner: *dum dicit: 'patrem excitabo', irrepsi tamen et male repugnanti gaudium extorsi* (While he was saying 'I will wake up my father', I nonetheless crept up on the boy and forcefully obtained my joy from him feebly fighting back. *Sat.* 87.3). I have followed Slater and Ruden and used 'feebly' to translate '*male*' since this can connote lack of strength or lack of conviction; Eumolpus implies the latter meaning.[51] Richlin rightly recognises, however, that the adverb does not negate Eumolpus's violence: 'on the final night Eumolpus at first forces the boy, who is described as *male repugnanti*, "hardly fighting back" (§87.3)'.[52] The verb *extorsi* and other language used throughout the episode,[53] moreover, strongly suggest that this should be considered rape.[54] Eumolpus, however, perpetuates the Roman rape myth – defined by Bowen (Chapter 10) as a 'false narrative about rape' – that a victim 'cannot be truly unwilling unless she physically fights against her rapist' by implying that the boy only feigns physical resistance.[55]

---

[51] Slater 1990: 93 and Ruden 2000: 67.
[52] Richlin 2009: 88.
[53] McGlathery 1998a: 9 notes that Eumolpus uses military vocabulary like '*aggressus*' and '*invasi*' (85.6) which 'seems to allude specifically to the dynamics of a homoerotic relationship in which the active "lover" (*erastes*) is perceived as in some sense violating the passive "beloved" (*eromenos*) by penetrating him'.
[54] Obermayer 1998: 158n72 considers the possibility that Eumolpus commits rape based on the following criteria: he disregards the boy's feelings; the boy defends himself '*male repugnanti*'; and the verb *irrepsi* (87.3) connotes aggressive penetration. Obermayer concludes, however, that this is not rape since the story develops to show that the use of physical force in *pedicatio* is one of the sexual practices accepted by both sides ('Die weitere Entwicklung der Geschichte zeigt, daß die Anwendung körperlicher Gewalt bei der Pedicatio zu den von beiden Seiten akzeptierten Sexualpraktiken gehört'). The suggestion that the continuance of the sexual relationship somehow neutralises the violence in this encounter, however, is problematic.
[55] Others in this volume who discuss the epistemological frameworks that underlie sexual and physical violence include McHardy (Chapter 4), Witzke (Chapter 7), Haley (Chapter 9) and Strong (Chapter 15).

Eumolpus continues to make light of the sexual assault by claiming that the boy enjoyed being forced: *at ille non indelectatus nequitia mea* (But the boy was not displeased by my wickedness, *Sat.* 87.4). This sentiment is disturbingly reminiscent of Ovid's (*Ars. am.* 1.659–78) declaration that women who fight back like to be raped and suggests, in fact, that Eumolpus eroticises the boy's resistance in the same way that the *Ars Amatoria* eroticises women's resistance to sexual violence.[56] Eumolpus thus propagates another rape myth that reinforces biased cultural beliefs at the expense of the boy's victimisation.[57] In the end, the sincerity of the boy's resistance is immaterial for assessing Eumolpus's guilt, since the child's freeborn status, his age and parents' desire to protect him leave no doubt that the tutor is committing a criminal act, but the narrator's perpetuation of rape myths distorts what survives of the boy's agency in the story.

The boy initiates the next sexual encounter on the same night, a development which points to the complexity of understanding his agency, since he appears to become a willing participant in his victimisation. Several scholars comment, in fact, that the two switch roles at the end of the story:[58] 'The boy seeks sexual contact three times, as Eumolpus has earlier, indicating the extent to which their roles have switched. Indeed, at this point the boy plays the aggressive role of Alcibiades and Eumolpus that of the "besieged" Socrates'.[59] This interpretation fits nicely within Eumolpus's pederastic narrative framework, since it exaggerates the boy's aggressiveness and downplays the significance of his recent experience with sexual violence. Eumolpus, after all, is never in danger of being overpowered physically or psychologically by the child,[60] and he even ends the story with a joke by repurposing the boy's earlier words (*voces suas*) to refuse him:[61] *aut dormi, aut ego iam patri dicam.* (Either sleep, or I'll tell your father, *Sat.* 87.10). This appropriative claim diminishes the seriousness of the boy's earlier utterance and brings home Eumolpus's persistent attempts to discredit him within the pederastic framework of the story.

---

[56] Courtney 2001: 137 and Schmeling 2011: 364 point out that Eumolpus echoes Ovid (*Ars am.* 1.665, 676 and *Fast.* 2.331).

[57] See Bowen (Chapter 10, this volume) for a discussion of how rape myths contribute to epistemic injustice.

[58] The following claim that Eumolpus and the boy switch roles at the end of the tale: Dimundo 1983: 257 and 1986: 90; Sega 1986: 75–81; Fedeli and Dimundo 1988: 144; Fraga 1997: 565; Lefèvre 1997: 13–14; and McGlathery 1998a: 215. Dimundo 1983: 257, for example, goes so far as to say that the boy harasses Eumolpus at the end of the tale.

[59] McGlathery 1998a: 215.

[60] Slater 1990: 94 is right to comment that Eumolpus's sexual refusal of the boy affirms his dominance in the relationship.

[61] Beck 1979: 251 and Richlin 2009: 88 note that the story is structured like a joke and ends with this punchline.

Encolpius accepts Eumolpus's story at face value, likely because he enjoys the content and its Platonic pedigree. His response, moreover, affirms Conte's[62] assessment of the ironic interplay between the narrator and hidden author Petronius, since Encolpius once more succumbs to his naïveté and obsession with literary models by uncritically admiring Eumolpus's confession and foolishly befriending a devious man whose base story should have destroyed 'any possible illusion of grandeur provoked by his entrance'. Petronius's implied audience, on the other hand, may have found Eumolpus's brazenness humorous or been disinclined to take the legal implications of the story too seriously given its parodic framework and Eumolpus's insistence that the boy was complicit in the crime.

Thus, despite the legal protection afforded under *stuprum*, the Roman law and ancient viewpoints are insufficient for recognising the complex victimisation suffered by the child in the story, since the Romans did not have a conceptual-legal framework for addressing why a boy might become a willing partner in his own abuse. This is why we, as modern readers, should look beyond the Roman legal context to consider the intricacies of the story. Petronian scholar Nikolai Endres has taken up a similar approach when considering the *Pergamene Boy* from a contemporary pedagogical perspective. For example, Endres insightfully identifies the most challenging aspects of the tale to reconcile when reading it with students: 'then Petronius completely twists the story, with victimiser [Eumolpus] and victim [boy] switching roles'.[63] Endres's proposed solution is to compare this encounter to sexual harassment. While the impulse to find a modern parallel for what is happening to the boy may in principle help us better conceptualise the criminality of Eumolpus's actions, the comparison to sexual harassment proves ultimately to be unhelpful, since it inadequately addresses the physicality of the boy's interactions with Eumolpus, its domestic setting, and the boy's age. Moreover, to say, as Endres does, that the boy becomes the 'victimiser' uncritically takes Eumolpus's implication that the older man is aggressed by the boy's insatiable desire at face value. Finally, Endres's suggestion that we, as modern readers, are too quick to believe the victim, together with the startling assertion that 'a large number of sexual harassment claims is [*sic*] fraudulent', simply recapitulates Eumolpus's efforts to conceal the criminality of his actions and to disregard the boy's victimisation.[64]

Instead of sexual harassment, the events of the story merit consideration through an alternative framework that accounts for the physical and psychological abuse of the boy without implicating him in Eumolpus's criminal action, even though he, at the end of the story, appears to be a willing participant. By way of

---

[62] Conte 1996: 58.
[63] Endres 2014: 217.
[64] Ibid. pp. 217–18.

conclusion, then, I will attempt to offer a counterpoint to Eumolpus's biased perspective and situated ignorance by applying an understanding of child sexual abuse[65] – namely, child grooming, the process of preparing a child for sexual abuse – to the *Pergamene Boy*.[66] As Dotson notes, 'addressing contributory injustice is difficult but not impossible. It requires third-order changes. A third-order change requires perceivers to be aware of a range of differing sets of hermeneutical resources in order to be capable of shifting resources appropriately'.[67] Applying a modern understanding of child grooming to the *Pergamene Boy* may run the risk of anachronism,[68] since the ancient Romans, admittedly, did not have the same notions of uninformed consent that underpin a modern understanding of differentiating abusive from non-abusive sexual acts with children. For other reasons, however, they did criminalise unsanctioned sex with freeborn children, and Roman law specifically protects freeborn boys and girls from those who would try to persuade or bribe them into having sex and pays particular attention to the role of chaperons who have direct access to children.[69] Child grooming similarly involves a trusted adult using persuasion and the giving of gifts to build a relationship with a child in order to sexually abuse them.

Child grooming can be defined as follows: 'A process by which a person prepares a child, significant others, and the environment for the abuse of this child. Specific goals include gaining access to the child, gaining the child's compliance, and maintaining the child's secrecy to avoid disclosure'.[70] The grooming process

---

[65] Desai 2010: 348 offers the following definition: 'The UN has defined child sexual abuse (CSA) as contacts or interactions between a child and an older or more knowledgeable child or adult (a stranger, sibling or person in position of authority, such as a parent or a caretaker), when the child is being used as an object of gratification for the older child's or adult's sexual needs. These contacts or interactions are carried out against the child, using force, trickery, bribes, threats or pressure'.

[66] The modern concept of grooming has been mentioned in reference to the *Satyrica* by Roth 2021: 220, who suggests that Trimalchio grooms his *pueri capillati* (Petr. 27) to prepare them for sexual abuse.

[67] Dotson 2012: 314.

[68] Roth 2021: 211–15 offers a thorough account of the ethical and methodological difficulties of applying the modern concept of child sexual abuse to Petronius's *Cena Trimalchionis*, and persuasively advocates for pursuing this line of enquiry: 'it is not only possible to hear the voice of the abused child in the text under scrutiny but . . . we must listen to that voice in the ancient evidence and resist participating in silencing and marginalizing the abused'.

[69] The Romans were particularly aware of the risk for teachers to commit *stuprum* with their students, for as Laes 2016: 70 points out, 'the ancient discourse on "wicked" and "lecherous" educators who were ready to sexually abuse their pupils' was widespread in Greek and Roman literature.

[70] Craven, Brown and Gilchrist 2006: 297.

involves many steps, including, but not limited to, identifying a victim, gaining access to the child, developing trust with the child often by giving gifts or going on outings, and desensitising the child to touch.[71] McAlinden observes that abusers are most often family members or well known to a family and groom both parents and the child to gain trust and access to the victim.[72] McAlinden additionally notes that in this type of intrafamilial abuse, victims often do not realise that they are being abused:

> the shame and guilt which lie at the heart of the abusive process when combined with the power dynamics between adults and children within intra-familial relationships also help to ensure the child's silence whether or not the offender has specifically warned the child not to disclose.[73]

It is not uncommon for child victims of abuse to passively submit to or willingly participate in sexual activities,[74] and such behaviour can impede social and legal recognition of their victimisation.[75] Victims who are groomed, abused by a close acquaintance or family member, and male, furthermore, rarely disclose their abuse out of feelings of guilt and shame.[76]

This basic understanding of child grooming helps elucidate the experience of the boy and his parents who are Eumolpus's victims. The parents grant Eumolpus access to their son after being groomed into trusting him.[77] The boy develops a close relationship with his tutor and pedagogue, who accompanies him on trips to the gymnasium. The boy receives attention and gifts from Eumolpus, who desensitises him gradually to sexual touching. The boy, lastly, passively submits to and eventually willingly participates in sexual activities and does not disclose the relationship to his father.

---

[71] This summary of the stages of child grooming comes from Winters and Jeglic 2017: 725–7.
[72] McAlinden 2012: 120.
[73] Ibid. p. 129.
[74] Desai 2010: 352 lists the category 'Passive Submission or Willing Participation of the Child' among several common factors experienced by children who are sexually abused.
[75] McAlinden 2014: 186 argues that the actions of some victims compromise the legitimacy of their victimhood: 'in relation to sexual offending, the common depiction of victimhood as being synonymous with innocence and complete blamelessness does not always accord with the realities of lived experience . . . where the victim may themselves have engaged in sexually harmful behaviour or been complicit in facilitating further offending'.
[76] Winters et al. 2020: 589.
[77] Fraga 1997: 561 points out that Eumolpus must first gain the trust of the parents to advance his relationship with the boy.

An understanding of child grooming offers modern critics the opportunity to assess more sensitively the complex reactions of the boy beyond the limited protections offered to children under Roman law and without perpetuating the narrative of the corrupt *eromenos* presented by Eumolpus. Burgess and Hartman, for instance, explain that the term child grooming first came into currency in the 1970s in a law enforcement context in order to:

> explain the impact on victims and, in particular, the compliance of the victim with the offender. This conceptualization in part has come about to help educate the public to the complicated reactions during and post event since most of our knowledge is arrived at after the abuse itself has occurred.[78]

This survivor-centred perspective provides an important modern counterpoint for understanding that the boy's participation offers further evidence for his victimisation rather than undermines it. His willingness – the very detail that may make the boy guilty of *stuprum* from a Roman perspective – poignantly demonstrates the difficulty of making sense of his epistemic agency as both a victim and subject of narration.

This analysis of the *Pergamene Boy* has focused on the epistemic harm Eumolpus as interpreter and narrator causes the boy and his family by wilfully ignoring a Roman understanding of *stuprum* and concealing his crime through the literary, philosophical and cultural framework of Greek pederasty. The *Satyrica* may be a polyphonic text that frequently revels in philhellenism, but this should encourage rather than discourage applying other ancient and modern interpretative frameworks to the *Pergamene Boy* that look beyond the narrative frame provided by Eumolpus, who is complicit in committing sexual violence as a protagonist in his own story. Contributory injustice and child grooming offer conceptual resources for understanding the story in a different light – namely from the child's untold perspective – and for explicating more fully the victimisation of a boy who was recognised by the ancient Romans to be just as vulnerable to sexual violence as women and girls under *stuprum*. While feminist epistemology stands to deepen our understanding of the many forms of oppression faced by women in ancient Greece and Rome, it can also reveal aspects of marginalisation experienced by other non-dominant groups.

---

[78] Burgess and Hartman 2018: 18.

CHAPTER 12

The Viability of Feminist Stoicism: On the Compatibility of Stoic and Feminist Epistemology

Chelsea Bowden

INTRODUCTION

Scholars have noted that the Stoics, like many of the Hellenistic philosophical schools, held nascent or protofeminist views,[1] and that their commitment to such views may even represent the first wave of feminism.[2] Recently, this has prompted scholars to explore whether and to what extent Stoic philosophy is compatible with feminist philosophy and feminist thought more broadly. Consequently, some philosophers have contended that the Stoic philosophical programme is compatible with (or even amenable to) contemporary feminist ethical theories to such an extent that we can posit a 'feminist Stoicism'.[3] Even beyond the confines of academia, Stoicism (and Neo-Stoic philosophy) remains relatively popular, in part because of the philosophy's egalitarian and universalistic positions, especially regarding gender and class.

This paper intends to further explore the compatibility between Stoic and feminist philosophy. Scholars have previously examined this topic by focusing

---

I would like to thank the editors of this volume for inviting me to contribute, Brad Cokelet and Ben Eggleston for their insightful comments and suggestions, and Craig Jendza for reading multiple versions of this paper and his characteristic unwavering support.

[1] Gummere 1954: 72–5; Arnold 1958: 270; Motto 1972; Manning 1973; Hill 2001; Nussbaum 2002; Engel 2003; Aikin and McGill-Rutherford 2014; Hill 2020; McGill 2022.
[2] Hill 2001.
[3] Hill 2001; Aikin and McGill-Rutherford 2014; Hill 2020; McGill 2022.

primarily on Stoic ethics and Stoic political theory. However, the question of whether Stoic and feminist philosophy are compatible in other areas has been given little attention. My aim is to offer a preliminary analysis of how compatible Stoic epistemology is with some prominent and central views within feminist epistemology. While some scholars have been optimistic about a feminist Stoicism, I will argue that some of the fundamental commitments of Stoic epistemological theory pose significant challenges to the viability of a fully satisfactory feminist Stoicism.

A note on methodology: given that neither Stoic nor feminist philosophy represent static philosophical doctrines, with both undergoing revisions and shifts in emphasis over time, my approach in this paper is to concentrate on some of those epistemological commitments that appear to be essential or foundational to each philosophical programme. That is, I examine those commitments without which Stoic and feminist epistemology would cease to be recognisable as themselves. I believe this approach has two benefits. First, by demonstrating that there is philosophical tension in the central tenets of each epistemological theory, we may more clearly see the depth and significance of the incompatibility. Second (and decidedly more hopeful), by making clear where in the epistemological bedrock the two philosophies are in conflict, we may more readily identify exactly where adjustments could be made by those wishing to build a more satisfactory feminist Stoicism. My aim is not to provide a comprehensive overview of *every* aspect of each epistemological conflict, but more modestly, to provide a first foray into exploring the two epistemological programmes.

THE STOIC EPISTEMIC AGENT AND FEMINIST CRITIQUES OF THE ATOMISTIC MODEL OF KNOWERS

A natural starting point when comparing Stoic and feminist epistemology is to explore how each philosophy conceives of human beings in their role as epistemic agents. In trying to understand the Stoics' conception of the epistemic agent, it is important to first draw attention to a notable feature of their philosophical system, namely that they took their philosophical commitments and views to be interdependent. Diogenes Laertius tells us that the Stoics saw the parts of their philosophy as interconnected, likening it to the anatomy of an animal: 'Philosophy, they say, is like an animal, logic corresponding to the bones and sinews, ethics to the fleshy parts, physics to the soul' (DL 7.40).[4] Given that this is the case, many

---

[4] Additional metaphors were also employed to express this interdependence: 'Another simile they use is that of an egg: the shell is logic, next comes the white, ethics, and the yolk in the center, physics. Or again they liken philosophy to an orchard: logic being the surrounding fence, ethics the fruit, physics the soil or the trees' (DL 7.40).

of the conclusions that we draw about the Stoics' conception of the epistemic agent, and indeed their epistemology overall, are (and must be) derived from textual evidence concerning Stoic ethics and physics (of which epistemology is one part). Indeed, their egalitarian commitment, widely considered to be especially progressive, to the belief that all human beings belong to a universal moral community or world state – the *cosmopolis* – permeates all branches of Stoic philosophy.[5] The Stoics believed that in virtue of our common humanity (*humanitas*) and our shared descendance from the gods, we are all members of the cosmopolis. Epictetus claims that 'Zeus is the father of us all' (1.22.82) and Seneca tells us that all individuals 'if traced back to their original source, spring from the gods' (*Ep.* 44.1).[6] The cosmopolis embodies a type of universal moral community to which every individual endowed with reason belongs. However, the distinctly epistemic requirement for inclusion in the cosmopolis – reason – indicates that it is not merely a universal *moral* community (as commonly described in the literature), but also a universal *epistemic* community. In addition to considering all individuals as belonging to the cosmopolis, the Stoics were committed to the idea that all human beings are endowed with the same capacity for reason and virtue. That is, that all human beings have a 'rational soul' which is both our most important and our most essential feature. The rational soul is, in fact, that which distinguishes us *as* human.[7] It is the perfection of this capacity to reason that constitutes virtue and is the distinctive marker of the Stoic sage (*sophos*, 'the wise person'). Attaining virtue is the main aim of the Stoic, and indeed the Stoics are strongly committed to the belief that only virtue, that is, living in accordance with one's rational nature, is actually good, and likewise that only vice, the corruption of reason, is actually bad. The Stoics maintained that virtue (and sagehood) can be attained, at least in principle, by both men and women. Seneca tells Marcia, the daughter of the historian Aulus Cremutius Cordus, that women have capacities for virtue that are on par with men (*Cons. Marc.* 16.1) and elsewhere claims that 'a noble mind is free to all . . . we may all gain distinction' (*Ep.* 44.2); Musonius Rufus holds that both men and women should be educated in philosophy (Lecture 3);[8] Marcus Aurelius states that every human being has a capacity for virtue (*Med.* 4.4); and Cleanthes says that women and men are equal in virtue (DL 7.175). Zeno, in his *Republic*, abolishes any distinctions in dress between men and women (DL 7.33),

---

[5] On the cosmopolis, see Epictetus 2.10.1–6; Cic. *Nat. D.* 2.78–87; Cic. *Fin.* 62–4; Sen. *Ep.* 120; and Plut. *De Alex. fort.*1.6.

[6] Stoic physics identify God as a type of eternal reason (*logos*); our capacity to reason is a fragment of God's as our soul (*pneuma*) is a fragment of God's *pneuma* (Sellars 2006: 91–106). See Sen. *Ben.* 4.7.1 and 4.8.2.

[7] Hill 2001: 17. See DL 7.129; Epictetus 1.6.18–22; Cic. *Fin.* 3.67; and Cic. *Off.* 1.14.

[8] Text of Musonius Rufus from Lutz 1947. Citations are to lecture number, page and line number in Lutz.

and it is generally accepted that this is because he views them as equals in respect to virtue.⁹

There is, however, reason to pause before accepting that the Stoics were complete egalitarians regarding an individual's capacity for virtue and reason. One point of concern is what Aikin and McGill-Rutherford have referred to as 'the limited audience problem', wherein all significant Stoic texts are addressed only to men, rather than women.¹⁰ If the Stoics did indeed believe that women possessed an equal capacity for reason, this lacuna in their philosophical texts is somewhat puzzling.¹¹ Additionally, there are indications that various Stoic philosophers held particularly sexist views towards women. Seneca and Cicero use the feminine adjective *muliebris* to signify moral failings while masculine adjectives such as *virilis* pick out laudatory moral actions or traits.¹² Musonius Rufus claims that women are inferior to men and are naturally meant to be ruled by men (Lecture 4).¹³ Epictetus claims that Epicureanism does not befit even women (3.7.21). Additionally, there are many occasions where Stoic philosophers emphasise that a woman's most important virtue is her chastity and her display of modesty (Epictetus, *Encheiridion* 40), and that women should confine their virtue to the domestic sphere only.¹⁴ Sexist criticisms of women are not limited only to the moral sphere but are present in the epistemic realm as well. For example, Seneca contends that among those practising philosophy, it is the Stoics alone who think like men (*de constantia sapientis* 1.1), and he praises Marcia for being 'as far removed from womanish weakness of mind as from all other vices' (*Cons. Marc.* 1.1).

Given that this textual evidence for Stoic sexism is quite damning, one way to argue that feminist and Stoic epistemology are antithetical is simply to draw attention and give sizeable weight to these (and other) overtly sexist remarks. However, I do not believe this to be the most philosophically fruitful path: first, because the textual evidence for the Stoics' position on this matter portrays irregular and often asymmetrical views on women as epistemic (and moral) agents; second, because the majority of the overtly sexist remarks are confined to the moral rather

---

⁹ Schofield 1991: 43; Grahn-Wilder 2018: 244; Hill 2020: 415.
¹⁰ Aikin and McGill-Rutherford 2014: 12–13. See also Nussbaum 2002: 303.
¹¹ It should be noted that this lacuna exists not only for texts addressed directly to women but also for attestations by later commentators as to the existence of any now lost Stoic texts which may have done so.
¹² Manning 1973: 171.
¹³ Nussbaum 2002: 303 and Engel 2003: 281.
¹⁴ Musonius Rufus Lecture 3; Hierocles in Ramelli 2009: 93. It is hard to pin down Musonius Rufus's actual opinion on this matter given that there are other occasions where he appears to be arguing quite the opposite: 'All human tasks are a common obligation and are common for men and women, and none is necessarily appointed for either one exclusively' (Lecture 4, p. 47, 27–9).

than epistemic sphere;[15] and third, because eliminating Stoicism as potentially compatible with feminist philosophy simply because some of its proponents are sexist or made sexist remarks says nothing about the compatibility of the philosophical view itself. It does not seem to me that any of the core tenets of the Stoic epistemological programme necessarily *must* include a commitment to the idea that women are inferior epistemic agents precisely because they are women, or because they possess 'womanly traits'. In other words, we can excise such sexist remarks and still preserve the principal components of Stoic epistemology. Thus, to show that there is real conflict between Stoic and feminist epistemology we need to demonstrate that there is conflict at the core of the two epistemic theories. To that end, I will assume a very charitable reading of the Stoic position by setting aside such remarks and taking the epistemic theory to be the egalitarian one they often espoused.

Because, on the Stoic view, all human beings are equal in our capacity for reason, and reason is the only essential property of human beings, they considered all other properties of individuals (for example, gender and class) inessential and devoid of any real epistemic or moral value. Seneca states that only those qualities that are innate in and unique to human beings are praiseworthy.[16] For these reasons, the Stoics often expressed reservations about the practice of slavery, believing it to be unnatural and arguing that individuals from different classes should be viewed as fundamentally the same.[17] For the Stoic, when we consider the epistemic agent, we should not consider their gender, social class or circumstances as morally or epistemically relevant. In fact, one should strive to ignore such features. What

---

[15] One might argue that regardless of whether Stoic and feminist epistemology can be reconciled, the viability of a feminist Stoicism is already extinguished by these glaring concerns about sexism in Stoic ethics. Whether such an argument is convincing will depend on whether one believes that *all* areas of the Stoic philosophical programme must cohere with *all* areas of feminist philosophy to have a thoroughgoing feminist Stoicism. Additionally, previous scholars who focused on Stoic ethics and political philosophy have presented multiple arguments as to how these instances of overt sexism may be reconciled with feminist philosophy: Arnold 1958: 270–1 suggests that the sexist remarks are a stylistic convention of the time; Motto 1972: 57 minimises their importance; Manning 1973 contextualises the role of *officia* and *decorum*; Hill 2001 argues that the majority of the conflict is the result of the later Stoa and that (early) Stoicism is 'at heart feminist'; and Aikin and McGill-Rutherford 2014 argue that the 'liberal feminist requirement' can be satisfied by Stoic philosophy through emphasising the ethical role of choice.

[16] Sen. *Ep.* 41.7–9. See Epictetus 3.1.24–7.

[17] Sen. *Ep.* 47.1, 47.10–19; Musonius Rufus 18A, p. 115, 19–22; Epictetus 1.13.1–5. It is important to note that some scholars, such as McCarter 2019, interpret these Stoic passages about slavery as reflecting a more romantic, patronising view of slavery, where the slaver can be recognised as a morally upright person even though he enslaves.

matters is that the agent has the relevant epistemic reasoning capacities: the capacity to receive *impressions* (*phantasiai*) which create a connection between the agent and the external world, and the capacity for *apprehension* (*katalepsis*) of *cognitive impressions* (*kataleptikai phantasiai*). Through these capacities, held in common by all, s/he could, after extensive training and persistent effort, eventually attain knowledge (*episteme*) and wisdom, thus becoming a Stoic sage. As *phantasia* and *katalepsis* are the only significant epistemic features of the agent, all other aspects of the individual should be treated as irrelevant. While the Stoics do not *explicitly* list or discuss what features of an agent are epistemically relevant, their continuous deemphasis of the importance of gender and class, their express assertions that such features are worthless for the purpose of evaluating persons, and the belittling of these as 'accidental' or merely the product of fortune make it reasonable to conjecture that these features were not relevant to epistemic questions such as how and when an agent gains knowledge. The fact that the agent is a woman or an enslaved person does not make any kind of significant epistemic contribution.

The Stoics also emphasised the importance of a particular kind of autonomy (*autarkeia*).[18] In 'Stoics, Rights, and Autonomy', Meyer lays out two ways of understanding autonomy:

> 1) an individual has autonomy if and only if his or her will is not determined by certain uncontrolled urges or impulses; or 2) an individual has autonomy if and only if he or she is not controlled by others.[19]

Meyer refers to these as 'positive autonomy' and 'negative autonomy' respectively. The Stoics maintained that all human beings have the capacity for positive autonomy and should strive for it. As Meyer notes, 'Strikingly, for the Stoics the conception of negative autonomy has no practical or theoretical importance. In fact, for the Stoics it is a mistake to believe that one's relations with others must have any effect whatsoever on individual autonomy'.[20] The way one avoids having one's will determined by urges, desires, impulses and the like is through the capacity of the commanding part of the soul, that is, through the use of reason. This is an *individual* capacity which does not rely on anything or anyone outside the agent for its exercise. Each agent stands as a lone individual who *chooses* whether to exercise reason and maintain autonomy. The fact that the Stoics characterise the pursuit of autonomy through reason as a sole volitive act of the individual

---

[18] Epictetus *Gnomologium Epicteteum (e Stobaei libris 3–4)* 16; see also Sen. *Ep.* 9.
[19] Meyer 1987: 267.
[20] Meyer 1987: 267. In contrast to my characterisation of Stoic *autarkeia* above, McGill 2022 proposes a new interpretation of the Stoic notion of *prohairesis*, which she argues is a form of personal autonomy consistent with contemporary accounts of relational autonomy.

suggests strongly that *epistemic* autonomy was part and parcel of the overall goal of autonomy which the Stoics so intensely sought and valued. Moreover, that the Stoics seem to consider the failure to achieve autonomy an *individual* failure of one's reason demonstrates that they located epistemic responsibility with individual epistemic agents.[21] That epistemic responsibility lies with an individual agent is a compelling indication that the Stoics conceived of good epistemic action as a form of perfected autonomous epistemic agency – a perfected form of reason – and bad epistemic action as reason which is in some way affected, inappropriately, by things extrinsic to it, such as emotions, other individuals, circumstances and so on. Thus, autonomy is not only a goal of Stoic ethics, but also of Stoic epistemology. The Stoic epistemic agent, at least ideally, is wholly autonomous, neither depending on others to attain knowledge and virtue, nor deeply affected by her social and political categories and circumstances. Therefore, the paradigmatic (and idealised) Stoic epistemic agent is essentially individual, autonomous, genderless, classless, raceless, ageless and so on. To the Stoics, when we consider and evaluate epistemic agents, it is epistemically appropriate for us to disregard their gender, class and so on. Although, by the Stoic's lights, most of us are vicious (as only the Stoic sage is virtuous), we are, at least, all the same as regards those epistemic capacities and features of significance.[22]

In many ways the Stoic conception of the epistemic agent parallels the one found in many traditional mainstream epistemological theories. Feminist epistemologists have identified that from Descartes onward, mainstream epistemology has long constructed the archetypal epistemic agent as individual, autonomous and interchangeable.[23] Even in contemporary epistemology the standard formulations of knowledge, often structured as 'S knows that p', assume that it is irrelevant who S is and that S is interchangeable with any other epistemic agent. This conception of the epistemic agent is sometimes referred to as the 'atomistic model of knowers'.[24] In strong opposition to this model, feminist epistemology encom-

---

[21] Self-sufficiency is a clear instance of something which would fall under what Epictetus categorises as 'up to us' or 'within our power' (*Encheiridion* 1.1).

[22] According to Plutarch, the Stoics believed that, 'just as in the sea the man an arm's length from the surface is drowning no less than the one who has sunk five hundred fathoms, so even those who are getting close to virtue are no less in a state of vice than those who are far from it . . . . [t]hose progressing remain foolish and vicious right up to their attainment of virtue' (*Comm. Not.* 1063a).

[23] Code 1991, following Bordo 1987, locates Descartes as the starting point for this. Tanesini 1999: 40 maintains that the individualism in epistemology has a 'distinctive empiricist strand' such that it would not be misguided to locate its inception with Locke. The view of this imagined agent is sometimes referred to as the 'view from nowhere'; see Nagel 1986.

[24] Grasswick 2004 and Grasswick 2018.

passes a wide collection of philosophical views which, though varied, are all committed to the idea that social and political categories to which an agent belongs (for example, gender, class, race, ability status, ethnicity, age and geographical location) are pertinent and often significant to the production of knowledge. A simpler way of understanding this is to say that feminist epistemologists are committed to the notion that, when investigating epistemological questions, *who S is* and *the social context in which S is situated* matter.[25] For this reason, feminist epistemology may (arguably) be characterised as a subset of social epistemology.[26]

Feminist epistemologists have long criticised each component of the atomist model. For example, feminist epistemologists argue that by conceptualising knowers as primarily individual, the atomistic model may overemphasise the kinds of knowledge which are attainable in isolation, such as simple cases of observational, perceptual and propositional knowledge, for example, 'there is an oak tree on the hill'. In doing so, the adoption of the atomist model can result in a failure to consider more complicated forms or instances of knowledge, particularly those that pertain to social concerns, such as injustice, inequality and differential power dynamics.[27]

Similarly, an individualistic and autonomous conception of knowers unduly represents the knowing agent as wholly self-sufficient, drawing attention away from forms of knowledge that are only attained through group interaction or by groups themselves rather than individuals.[28] Some feminist philosophers have argued that we should adopt communities as primary knowers rather than individuals, something that the atomist model is not capable of accommodating. In particular, some feminist epistemologists have focused on how and what kind of knowledge is produced in formal communities such as the scientific, legal or medical community. Not only do many knowers who lack the relevant expertise depend on these communities to produce knowledge, but, given that positions of power and authority within these communities are predominately occupied by men, much of the knowledge produced by them reflects the standpoint and assumptions of men rather than women.[29] Additionally, much of our knowledge more broadly relies on the testimony of others and cannot be attained by a lone

---

[25] For example, Tanesini 1999: 38 argues that 'what characterizes feminist epistemology in its broadest sense is the belief that gender is a category that is relevant to the study of knowledge'.

[26] Anderson has construed feminist epistemology as social: 'the branch of epistemology that investigates the influence of *socially construed conceptions and norms of gender and gender-specific interests and experiences* on the production of knowledge' (1995b: 54, italics in original). See also Tanesini 1999; Fricker 2007; Grasswick 2018.

[27] Tanesini 1999 and Grasswick 2018.

[28] For a recent account of group knowledge, see Lackey 2021.

[29] Addelson 1983 and Grasswick 2018: 18–22.

knower. Not only does the atomist model not fully appreciate this fact, but also, in doing so, it ignores forms of epistemic injustice, such as testimonial injustice that can result from such social phenomena as credibility deficits or hermeneutical marginalisation – forms of injustice that disproportionately affect women and people from marginalised groups.[30]

Likewise, assuming that knowers are interchangeable causes us to overlook the fact that some knowledge or forms of knowing may depend on how a knower is socially situated. Many feminist epistemologists maintain that much (if not all) of our knowledge reflects and is embedded in the specific social, historical and cultural conditions in which it was produced – conditions such as the knower's social and political identity. The concept of 'situated knowledge', first introduced by Donna Haraway in 1988,[31] plays a key role in feminist epistemology and is one to which most feminist epistemologists are committed. Given that this is the case, feminist epistemologists are often concerned with how some knowledge is sex-specific (for example, knowing pain during childbirth), while other knowledge often results from social activities which tend to be sex-specific.[32]

Furthermore, some methods of belief formation are socially acquired and derived from experiences which are highly differential, and thus the social circumstances in which the epistemic agent operates can influence which method that agent comes to use.[33] From the fact that some knowledge may be sex- (or class-) specific, some feminist epistemologists have argued that knowers from marginalised or subordinated social groups, such as women, actually occupy a *privileged epistemic* standpoint and may thus be more reliable than knowers who are not from these groups.[34] So-called standpoint theory argues that individuals from different social groups have different perspectives on society and its social relations and that epistemic reliability covaries with social group membership.[35] Knowers from the dominant patriarchal group have a vested interest in preserving the systems and institutions which benefit them, while those from the subordinated group, who gain little to nothing by preserving the status quo, are better able to see the shortcomings and faults of those same

---

[30] Fricker 2007.

[31] Haraway 1988.

[32] Grasswick 2018: 13. Tanesini 1999: 140–1, drawing upon Hartsock 1983a: 292, states that 'Even in the sphere of the production of goods for subsistence, women's activities differ structurally from men's. Women spend more time in the production of goods in the house, goods which are not sold as commodities'.

[33] Grasswick 2018: 14.

[34] See the Introduction to this volume for more on 'privileged epistemic access'.

[35] Proponents of standpoint theory include Hartsock 1983a; Rose 1983; and Harding 1993. For more on standpoint theory more generally, see the Introduction to this volume.

systems and institutions. As some of these shortcomings and faults may be invisible or difficult to see for those occupying privileged social positions, it is in this way that knowers from subordinated or marginalised social positions have more reliable knowledge of social reality. Thus, some feminist epistemologists argue that there is reason to privilege the epistemic perspective of women who, under the patriarchy, occupy a subordinated position and are thus better positioned to identify inequalities or negative aspects of social reality which go unnoticed by those in the dominant group. While standpoint theory has faced criticism due to some of its underlying assumptions, some of its most essential features, such as the existence of situated knowledge and the close interconnection between epistemic perspective and social location, are still widely accepted by feminist epistemologists.[36]

In considering the Stoic conception of the epistemic agent above, we can see that the atomistic model of knowers arguably predates the early modern period and is quite clearly at work in Stoic epistemological theory. Given that the atomistic model is widely rejected by feminist epistemologists, a deep point of conflict emerges between the two philosophical theories. However, this does not yet indicate that such a conflict cannot be resolved, for one might assume, as with some contemporary epistemological theories, that the core ideas found in feminist epistemology could simply be accepted and incorporated into Stoic epistemological theory. In this way, the possibility of a feminist Stoic epistemology could be preserved. On further examination, however, such a hybridisation does not appear promising. This is because Stoic epistemological theory lacks the flexibility of many contemporary epistemological approaches to discharge the atomistic model. Unlike many contemporary epistemological theories which have simply assumed an atomistic theory of knowers but could dispense with the model if desired, it is *essential* to Stoic epistemology that knowers be atomistic. The Stoic maintains not simply that we are individual, autonomous and interchangeable knowers, but also that that is the kind of knower that we *should* be. While the claim that knowers are individual and autonomous is merely descriptive (and often incidental) for many contemporary epistemological theories, for the Stoics it is robustly normative. The Stoics tell us that we *ought to* aim at being individual and autonomous and, indeed, self-sufficiency is the *goal* of the rational soul and a primary feature of the Stoic sage. As our ability to gain autonomy depends on our capacity to control our reason, and this capacity is ours alone as individuals, it is necessarily built into the Stoic epistemic programme that we undertake our

---

[36] Some key criticisms include (1) the assumption that there is (or that it is possible to identify) a single coherent feminist standpoint, particularly while also wishing to maintain the commitment that knowledge is situated, and (2) that there is a single central power in society; see Bar On 1993.

epistemic endeavour as isolated beings.[37] Additionally, as I have shown, the Stoics' notion of epistemic responsibility as regards autonomy and their estimation of the epistemic agent more generally is inextricably linked to how well s/he fares at this form of individual rational governance.

Furthermore, the Stoics' deemphasis of an agent's gender, class, and so on, in her role as knower is in direct conflict with the feminist commitments to the existence of situated knowledge, as well as with any feminist theorist committed to some form of standpoint theory. The Stoics do not take a knower's gender or class to be of any real epistemic relevance to knowledge acquisition. For the Stoic, gender or other social categories to which a knower belongs, as well as social relations that a knower might have, are aspects of the agent which are accidental and unimportant. In fact, Epictetus suggests an exercise, which Brenk refers to as a 'torturous form of mental gymnastics',[38] through which we might enhance our reason by jettisoning epistemic considerations of our physical attributes and social relations from the epistemic process:

> This is what you ought to practise from morning 'til evening. Begin with the most trifling things, the ones most exposed to injury, like a pot or a cup, and then advance to a tunic, a paltry dog, a mere horse, a bit of land: thence to yourself, your body, and its members, your children, wife, brothers. Look about on every side and cast these things away from you. Purify your judgements for fear lest something of what is not your own may be fastened to them or grown together with them . . . (Epictetus 4.1.111–12)

The social situatedness of the knower is something which, if anything, hinders the Stoic's epistemic goal and does not contribute any epistemic value. The agent's gender and class are in fact of so little value that we should ignore those features in our evaluation of knowers and should ourselves aim to remain unaffected by them in our own epistemic pursuits. Moreover, to the extent that individual Stoic philosophers did think gender was of any epistemic relevance, far from offering any form of epistemic advantage, being a woman was often considered epistemically injurious.

Stoic epistemological theory results in two unacceptable consequences for feminist epistemologists: first, it necessarily overlooks the social situatedness of knowers and the social dimensions of knowledge by firmly maintaining and advocating for an atomistic model of knowers, and second, it undervalues the unique epistemic perspectives afforded by social categories such as gender and class and

---

[37] Nussbaum 2002: 302 has noted that the Stoics also often fail to appreciate the effects that social relations have on us in our role as moral agents.
[38] Brenk 2002–3: 84.

their role in knowledge production. These commitments are at the centre of the Stoic epistemological theory and are indispensable to their overall philosophical view. It is not possible to excise these commitments from their epistemological theory (particularly given the interdependence of the Stoics' broader philosophical system) while still leaving the epistemic theory properly recognisable as Stoic. Given that this is the case, we can see that the Stoic conception of the epistemic agent is incompatible with core commitments regarding epistemic agents in feminist epistemology.

THE ROLE OF EMOTIONS IN STOIC AND FEMINIST EPISTEMOLOGY

Having just examined how the Stoics conceive of epistemic agents, it is now helpful to consider how the Stoics describe the epistemic process for acquiring knowledge. As is the case with most philosophical schools of the Hellenistic period, the Stoics are empiricists and thus believe that knowledge is procured through sense data.[39] How the world appears to us is the product of our *impressions* (*phantasia*, pl. *phantasiai*).[40] The impression serves as the link between the agent and the external world and is so named because the Stoics believed it to leave a physical imprint on the governing part of the soul.[41] When our senses interact with an object in the external world, it causes a change in the governing part of our soul, and as a product of this change, the agent is presented with an impression of that object. The Stoics maintain that for rational animals such as ourselves the *phantasiai* contain propositional content, and in this way we can understand *phantasiai* as thoughts.[42]

When we are presented with a *phantasia*, it is now up to us to make a kind of judgement concerning the impression, more precisely, whether or not to *assent* (*sunkatathesis*) to it; that is, to accept the *phantasia* as true or reject it as false. The Stoics maintained that we should only assent to a specific type of *phantasia*, namely, the apprehensive impression (*kataleptike phantasia*). According to

---

[39] Annas 1990: 185 notes that the Stoics believed that we most certainly can have knowledge of things like mathematical, logical truths despite the fact that these do not strike us as being the product of the senses. Hensley 2020: 139 concurs that the Stoics are empiricists. Nawar 2014: 8 tentatively suggests that it is possible that the Stoics took mathematical, [logical], moral, and theological properties to be natural rather than *queer* non-natural properties. Frede 2008: 321 finds fault with interpreting the Stoics as empiricists, instead asserting that they are rationalists.

[40] Some philosophers translate *phantasia* as *appearance*.

[41] Annas 1990: 186 states that the *phantasia* is therefore both a mental and a physical event.

[42] Graver 2007: 24 and Hensley 2020: 136.

Sextus Empiricus, in order for an impression to qualify as apprehensive, three independently necessary and jointly sufficient conditions must be met – the impression must be one that '(i) arises from what is; (ii) is stamped and impressed exactly in accordance with what is; and (iii) is of such a kind as could not arise from what is not' (*M*. VII.248). While philosophers dispute how exactly to interpret these conditions, one widely accepted reading is as follows:

> (i) seems to specify that the impression should be appropriately caused; (ii) seems to specify that the impression should be true (in virtue of its content being true); and (iii), which may have been a later addition (Cic. *Acad.* 2.77–8; Sext. Emp. *Math.* 7.253), *seems* to specify that the impression should instantiate a certain property ('is of [such] a kind') which it could not instantiate if (i) were not met.[43]

Assenting to an apprehensive impression is a particular form of assent termed *katalepsis*, 'apprehension'. Although this form of assent is in some sense 'getting it right' epistemically, merely assenting to an apprehensive impression is not sufficient for knowledge (*episteme*). Most people can, and frequently do, assent to apprehensive impressions. As I look out the window, I have an impression that there is a cardinal on the tree branch outside, and I may then assent to that impression. Assuming that (i) my impression is caused by an actual cardinal, (ii) the content of my impression that this is so is true, and (iii) my impression has the properties it has in virtue of the fact that it was caused by the real cardinal, my assent counts as apprehension. Real knowledge, however, consists of (a) assenting to all and only apprehensive impressions (never making a mistake by assenting to false impressions)[44] and (b) assenting *strongly* to the apprehensive impressions. Here, 'strongly' means that the agent's assent is not *changeable*; they are *certain* of the truth of the apprehensive impression (Sext. Emp. *Math.* 7.151–2). This form of certainty isn't mere stubbornness but involves the agent's recognition that there are no rational grounds available that either could or should compel her to change her mind. Knowledge requires that the agent be able to firmly maintain her assent to all and only apprehensive impressions in the face of any counterfactual challenges. The only person who is able to achieve this (and gain knowledge) is the Stoic sage. All other agents who have not reached sage status will frequently assent to non-apprehensive impressions, something which Stobaeus characterises as a form of weak assent known as *opinion* (*doxa*) (2.112.3) in contrast to 'the wise man . . . [who] does not assent

---

[43] Translation adapted from Nawar 2014: 2.
[44] An illustrative example from Chrysippus is Orestes' hallucination (*phantastikon*) of the Furies (Aetius *Views of Philosophers* 4.12); see Graver 2007: 112–16. See DL 7.51 and Sext. Emp. *Math.* 7. 244–5.

at all to anything that is non-apprehensive' (2.111.18–19). Thus, the distinguishing feature of the Stoic sage is that her epistemic performances constitute a type of achievement. The sage possesses a skill that allows her to properly discriminate between the impressions presented to her and to assent, strongly, to only those that are apprehensive. The sage can determine when there is reason to reject or withhold assent to an impression. For example, when an impression arises from non-ideal circumstances (for example, the lighting is too dim to reliably identify the bird *as a cardinal*), or when there are deficits in experience (for example, a lack of knowledge concerning species of birds), or when the senses are not functioning well (for example, one's vision is compromised post pupil dilation at the optometrist's office), or when one's mental states are impaired (for example, one's emotions are impairing proper judgement). As a result of this skill the Stoic sage will never assent to anything false.[45] Hensley describes the skill as follows: 'Counterarguments to her beliefs will not cause her to withdraw her assent, unless they can demonstrate that the circumstances, her mental state, or the phenomenology of her impressions were somehow defective'.[46] The Stoics regarded the sage as the epistemic ideal and considered her epistemic actions to be the sort towards which we should all strive. We can see, however, that the path to sagehood is narrow and arduous, requiring that we never fall into epistemic error.[47] This is one of the reasons the Stoics claimed that the sage is 'rare as the Phoenix' while the rest of us remain in the ignorant flock.[48]

Having outlined the mechanics of the epistemic process and identified the workings of the ideal epistemic agent, I would now like to focus on the non-ideal epistemic agent, that is, everyone who is not the sage. One way in which an agent's mental states could be defective such that she is prone to frequently make epistemic errors occurs through her emotions. The Stoics conceived of roughly two categories of emotion. The first, which most people experience and which are detrimental, are the *passions* (*pathe*), the primary examples of which are appetite and fear (and their related counterparts, pleasure and distress). The

---

[45] How exactly we are to understand false impressions is a particularly puzzling feature of Stoic epistemological theory. The Stoics were materialists (more accurately, corporealists) who believed that only corporeal bodies exist and are capable of causation. If impressions must be caused by objects that exist, then how is it that we can have impressions that are false, such as hallucinations? Some argue that such impressions are in some sense caused by a real object but have been altered or inadvertently manipulated in some way by our perception (for example, an oar in water appears to be bent rather than straight, or a blowing sheet on a clothesline appears to be a ghostly figure). Others argue that we have concepts in our mind that we blend together (for example, our concepts of 'horse' and 'horn' produce the impression of a unicorn).

[46] Hensley 2020: 145.

[47] For an interesting challenge to the claim that the Stoic sage is infallible, see Aikin 2022.

[48] Alexander of Aphrodisias *On Fate* 199.14–22.

second are moderate positive emotions (*eupatheiai*) which are permissible (for example, kindness, warmth, generosity) and the only kind which the sage experiences. Because of the ubiquity of *pathe* in human beings, I will occasionally refer to them simply as the emotions.

We will recall that for the Stoic, only virtue (the perfection of one's reason) is actually good, and only vice (the corruption of one's reason) is actually bad. According to the Stoics, all other things which we might typically think of as good or bad are in fact 'indifferents'.[49] When we judge something other than virtue or vice to be good or bad, we fall into epistemic error. Our *pathe* are epistemically damaging because they represent a kind of mistaken judgement about what is good or bad – the mistake of assenting to a false impression. Let us say that through some unjust social or political policy, I am deprived of my freedom, making me angry, fearful, despondent and depressed. When I have these *pathe* concerning this state of affairs, the Stoics take me to be making a *judgement* – specifically, a judgement of value.[50] The judgement I am making is that my loss of freedom is *bad*. But this, according to the Stoics, is a type of epistemic mistake, for only vice is actually bad. My loss of freedom may be a *non-preferred indifferent*, but it is not actually bad. Put another way, I was presented with a false impression, that *I have lost my freedom and that this loss of freedom is bad*, and I then chose to assent to that impression. While it is objectively true that I have lost my freedom, the Stoics would consider this state of affairs value-neutral (although non-preferred). It is *only* the objective and value-neutral part of the impression (*that I have lost my freedom*) that is true. The additional, value-laden part of the impression (*this loss of freedom is bad*) is false (for only the corruption of reason is bad), and thus the impression cannot be apprehensive. The *pathe* essentially disallow the agent from appropriately, that is, objectively and value-neutrally, evaluating impressions. *Pathe*, in other words, entail a loss of objectivity, leading to misinterpretation and resulting in assenting to false impressions. Assent that is the product of *pathe* can never count as apprehension. The passions are harmful precisely because they lead you away from assenting to apprehensive appearances and consequently away from knowledge.

As the sage never assents to that which is non-apprehensive, that which distinguishes the sage as wise and all non-sages as ignorant comes into sharp relief. Most people, even most Stoics, regularly experience *pathe*, and therefore regularly

---

[49] On indifferents, see DL 7.101–3, Stob. 2.5, Sext. Emp. *Math.* XI. 61–7, and Sext. Emp. *Pyr.* 3.168–78.

[50] Diogenes Laertius states: 'They [the Stoics] think that the *pathe* are judgments, as Chrysippus says in his work *On Emotions*. For [he says that] fondness for money is a supposition that money is a fine thing, and similarly, with drunkenness, stubbornness, and so forth' (7.111). See Graver 2007: 38–42.

assent to false impressions. Thus, one crucial aim of the Stoics is to rid oneself of one's passions and become *apathetic* (devoid of one's *pathe*) and their negative effects on one's epistemic activity.[51] The goal of being apathetic can be properly likened to a goal of becoming objective and value-neutral in the epistemic process. Indeed, becoming apathetic was part of the larger Stoic goal of being autonomous, for once an agent frees herself of her *pathe* she is able to be autonomous, no longer ruled by anything other than her reason. Only the apathetic Stoic sage achieves this goal.

What now emerges are three clear commitments by the Stoics regarding emotions: (1) that emotions are epistemically harmful, for they negatively affect the agent's ability to assent to apprehensive impressions, and (2) that *pathe* are epistemically injurious and never count as apprehension because all *pathe* represent the agent's assent to a false impression that something other than virtue is actually good and/or that something other than vice is actually bad, and (3) that the epistemic ideal (sagehood) can never be attained if one experiences *pathe*.

These three Stoic commitments are at odds with how many feminist epistemologists view the role of emotion in the epistemic process. Far from being harmful, feminist epistemologists have argued that emotion can be beneficial in the pursuit of knowledge. As Jaggar has convincingly argued, emotion can play a vital role both in the pursuit and the construction of knowledge, as 'the individual experience of emotion focuses our attention selectively, directing, shaping, and even partially defining our observations'.[52] The emotions may help direct our attention to particular objects of enquiry, but more than that, they may help us to perceive information and evaluate evidence and states of affairs differently than we otherwise would, and in some cases more reliably. For example, perhaps I am one of very few women working in my academic department and I become angry at the fact that I and my female colleagues are being burdened with far more service work than my male counterparts. My anger and subjective experience can cause me to not only investigate the policy that is generating this unfair division of labour (enquiry), but also make me more likely to perceive particular facts about that policy that are unjust (evidence) and come to know that the policy is a bad one (knowledge). If someone who lacked the subjective experiences and emotions I possess reviewed the same policy, it is quite possible that they might not gain knowledge concerning the policy's inequity. My emotions and my lack of objectivity may actually aid me in my epistemic pursuits.

The feminist view that the emotions are useful in the production of knowledge is contrasted with those theories in mainstream epistemology which like the

---

[51] On the goal to rid oneself of passions, see Cic. *Tusc.* 3.23–35, as well as Sellars 2006: 116–18 and Graver 2007.
[52] Jaggar 1989: 160.

Stoics consider knowledge, and particularly scientific knowledge, to be untainted by the knower's values and emotions. The concepts at work in contemporary mainstream theories are noticeably similar to those found in the Stoic system. For example, the Stoic notion of impressions is quite close to the way some contemporary theories in epistemology and philosophy of mind describe mental *representations*. Knowledge, on these theories, is sometimes described in terms of how well an agent represents her environment.[53] An agent can be said to know when, among other criteria, her *representations* accurately reflect the objects or states of affairs in the external world – when the propositional content of her mental representations is *true*. Feminist epistemologists have objected to the implicit assumption made by some of these (and the Stoics') theories, that representations are value-neutral.[54] They also note that these theories fail to see the ways individual and social perspectives figure in representations and knowledge. If one assumes that representations are value-neutral, it is easy to see why some contemporary epistemologists have, like the Stoics, conceived of the agent's emotions and values as problematic. For if the agent is not objective and value-neutral, if her emotions are muddying up the epistemic process, then she will not properly engage with the representations and will not acquire knowledge. Feminist epistemologists, however, have argued that representations are value-laden and imbued with social content. Given that this is the case, the agent's values, emotions and subjective experiences, far from hindering her, can prove a significant boon to evaluating which representations are true and which are not.[55]

If representations and impressions are inherently comprised of social and value-laden content as the feminist epistemologist maintains, then the Stoic is incorrect in believing that all instances of *pathe* involve assent to a false judgement. For the Stoic conceives of *pathe* as assents to the subjective, value-laden and, most importantly, *false* content of an impression. If, as feminist epistemology suggests, that subjective and value-laden content of an impression (representation) is sometimes *true*, then there will be cases where *pathe* count as veridical assent. What follows from this is that at least *some* occurrences of *pathe* will count as apprehension. Moreover, if some occurrences of *pathe* are apprehension, then it will no longer be inappropriate for the Stoic sage to have *pathe*. The epistemic ideal (sagehood) can be attained while preserving one's *pathe*. While

---

[53] Tanesini 1999: 9–11. The representational (or computational) theory of mind underlies many of the standard contemporary accounts of knowledge, in which knowledge is some form of accurate or justified representation.

[54] Tanesini 1999: 11–16 maintains that 'value neutrality can seem appealing only if we conceive of knowledge as a relation between things devoid of meaning and human representations of them' (15).

[55] Tanesini 1999: 15.

becoming a Stoic sage would still be no easy feat, the path to sagehood would widen considerably, and the occurrence of the Stoic sage less of the mythological Phoenix and more of a semi-rare species of bird.

I have demonstrated how the role of emotions for many feminist epistemologists directly conflicts with Stoic commitments (1) through (3) above: (1) Where the Stoics think that the emotions are detrimental in the pursuit of knowledge, and that they hinder our ability to assent to apprehensive impressions, feminist epistemologists argue that emotions can play a valuable and important role both in enquiry and knowledge acquisition. (2) The Stoics' commitment to only virtue being actually good and only vice actually bad, together with their conception of the *phantasia* as value-neutral, lead them to conclude that *pathe* are necessarily assents to false impressions and no *pathe* are apprehensive. In contrast, the feminist epistemologist's view of representations as necessarily value-laden and socially constituted means that there will be some occasions where *pathe* are veridical and count as apprehension. And (3) while the Stoics believe the epistemic ideal of sagehood is unattainable unless one is *apathetic*, feminist epistemology would permit sagehood while preserving one's *pathe*.

One might think that perhaps the Stoics could simply adjust their views on the emotions such that (a) *pathe* are no longer epistemically injurious and (b) *pathe* can sometimes count as apprehension. This adjustment, however, is not possible because of the Stoic's commitments concerning the value of virtue and vice. We recall that *pathe* are partially defined as assents to false impressions, but more specifically to a *particular kind* of false impression, namely, false impressions of what is actually good (virtue) and what is actually bad (vice). In order for the Stoics to alter their theory such that *pathe* are no longer assent to what is false, it would be necessary for them to relinquish their commitment to only virtue being actually good and only vice being actually bad, something which is integral to their philosophical system.

CONCLUSION

What I have demonstrated in this paper is that there are significant points of conflict between Stoic and feminist epistemology. In the first section I argued that the Stoics' deemphasis of an agent's social relations (for example, gender and class) and their dismissal of these categories as epistemically irrelevant is in deep conflict with feminist epistemology's commitment to the importance of situated knowledge and the role an agent's standpoint plays in knowledge acquisition and production. Furthermore, the Stoics' use of the atomistic model of knowers, and their goal of being individual and autonomous epistemic agents, is antithetical to feminist epistemology's commitment to a deeply social conception of knowers and the social dynamics of knowledge. In the second section, I illustrated how the mechanics of the Stoics' epistemic system, specifically their views on the nature of impressions as value-neutral, the requirements for apprehension, and their commitments concerning virtue and vice, lead to a conception of emotion as epistemically harmful. I then argued that this view of emotion stands in stark contrast to the beneficial role many feminist epistemologists attribute to emotion for shaping enquiry, viewing evidence and gaining knowledge. Lastly, I showed how, for the Stoics, the epistemic ideal of sagehood is only attainable by being apathetic, while feminist epistemology would permit, and sometimes encourage, the sage to maintain her *pathe*. I believe that these conflicts, found within the core commitments of each epistemology, indicate that there are significant challenges to the viability of a feminist Stoic epistemology, and consequently a feminist Stoicism. While it is possible to construct some impression of the feminist Stoic sage, that impression seems far from apprehensive.

CHAPTER 13

What Everyone Knows: Hermeneutical Injustice in the Medieval Iphis

Jessica Hines

> Si sorent tuit, grant et menus,
> Qu'Yphis fille est filz devenus.
>
> Everyone, high and low, knew
> that Iphis the daughter had become a son.
> —*Ovide moralisé*[1]
>
> Nature, which doth every wiht
> Upon hire lawe for to muse,
> Constreigneth hem, so that thei use
> Thing which to hem was al unknowe;
>
> Nature, which does every person
> Upon her law cause to muse,
> Constrains them, so that they use
> Thing which to them was all unknown;
> —John Gower, *Confessio Amantis*[2]

---

[1] Quotations are from de Boer 1938; translations are by Griffin, Gutt and McCracken 2019.
[2] Quotations are from Gower 2013; translations are my own.

Ovid's account of Iphis and Ianthe from Book Nine of the *Metamorphoses* tells of miraculous transformation and escape from near death. Iphis, born a girl to a father who considers raising a girl a burden and promises to condemn a girl born to him to death,[3] is only saved by the miraculous intervention of the goddess Isis, who guides Iphis's mother, Telethusa, to raise the child secretly as a boy. The secret is threatened, however, by Iphis's betrothal to the young woman Ianthe. Iphis longs for her but fears the coming marriage and what it will reveal in the private spaces of marital intimacy. It is only when Isis once again intervenes that the story turns. While leaving Isis's temple, where Telethusa has made a final desperate plea, Iphis transforms (9.786–91):

> ... sequitur comes Iphis euntem,
> quam solita est, maiore gradu, nec candor in ore
> permanet, et vires augentur, et acrior ipse est
> vultus, et incomptis brevior mensura capillis,
> plusque vigoris adest, habuit quam femina. nam quae
> femina nuper eras, puer es!

> Iphis followed [her mother] as she left, as she was accustomed to do, with a wider gait than she used to have and no whiteness was left in her complexion. Their strength (*vires*) increased, their features became sharper, their hair shorter in length, and there was more vigour than they had as a woman. You who were recently a woman are a boy![4]

This familiar Ovidian story has a complex medieval reception history shaped by both the larger Ovidian commentary tradition and medieval hermeneutics surrounding homoerotic desire. As I discuss in detail later in this chapter, this medieval commentary tradition repeatedly translated and altered the *Metamorphoses*, wrapping it in dense allegory and exegesis. In the case of Iphis, the commentary tradition offered competing – and, in many cases, contradictory – interpretations of the story's meaning. These exegetical layers constructed a complex hermeneutic puzzle for readers to interpret, particularly around questions of public gender performance and what can be known with absolute certainty about the bodies and desires of others. Alongside this tradition, the discourse around homoerotic desire in the Middle Ages was one of pervasive and (often) deliberate obscurement. This

---

[3] ... *onerosior altera sors est, et vires fortuna negat* (A girl is a heavier burden; misfortune denies strength to them, 9.676–7); quotations are from the Loeb *Metamorphoses*; translations are my own.

[4] In my translation, I've tried to capture Ovid's intentional avoidance of gendered language after the initial *quam solita est*, switching from the feminine pronouns to the more gender-neutral 'their'.

obscurement created gaps in the collective hermeneutic resources for understanding homoerotic desire, what Miranda Fricker has identified as a form of epistemic injustice she calls hermeneutical injustice.[5] Silences and distortions about homoerotic desires and practices arose in the gaps created by this hermeneutical injustice, and these silences in turn shaped what writers said, and did not say, about Iphis.

This chapter builds on recent studies of the cultural work of Iphis in describing gender and homoerotic desire in post-classical reception,[6] in order to consider how the interlocking of the hermeneutic complexities of the commentary tradition and the hermeneutical injustices of medieval homoerotic discourse not only foreclosed but also, critically, opened up important epistemological spaces in late medieval versions of the Iphis story. These spaces were created, I will argue, as medieval authors attempted to navigate the inherent tension between tale itself and the commentary tradition, which not only acknowledges homoerotic desire but potentially rewards it, and the culturally pervasive hermeneutic injustice that worked to silence knowledge of the homoerotic in the Middle Ages.[7] Medieval writers, like the English poet John Gower and the author of the *Ovide moralisé*, the two works that are the focus of this chapter, used this tension to explore key epistemological questions about desire, gender and the body: how can we know how someone's desire is oriented? How can we know for certain that gender performance pairs gender and sex in normative ways?

These medieval writers responded differently to the spaces these narrative tensions opened up. For the author of the *Ovide moralisé*, that space made possible Christian allegorical readings of the text, but it was also socially dangerous. Medieval anti-sodomy discourse sought to impose epistemological certainty about the nature of desire (as inherently heterosexual) and the body (as always aligning biological sex and gender expression). The Iphis legend, with its bodily transformations and homoerotic desires, threatened to destabilise this certainty. The *Moralisé* author thus attempts to delimit the space of the epistemological uncertainty through extended allegorisation. For John Gower in his poem the *Confessio Amantis*, homoerotic desire functions as a generative, if temporary, space. Gower changes critical details of the narrative from his medieval sources, including the *Moralisé*. He uses the tension between homoerotic narrative and cultural silence to show private and unknowing explorations of the homoerotic as a temporarily productive space through which to explore new forms of knowledge related to desire, gender and the body. In reading these versions alongside each other, we can see the ways that homoerotic desire was a productive space for

---

[5] Fricker 2007:147–75, discussed in greater detail in the next section.
[6] Traub, Badir and McCracken 2020.
[7] Others in this volume who address hermeneutical injustices in ancient texts or their receptions include Weiberg (Chapter 2), Witzke (Chapter 7), Bowen (Chapter 10) and Freas (Chapter 11).

medieval texts to consider the nature of desire and the body as a whole and the ways that medieval texts found this space both dangerous and generative.

EPISTEMOLOGY TROUBLE: GLOSSING OVID AND UNDERSTANDING SODOMY

As I suggested at the start of this chapter, understanding why the story of Iphis was such a site of tension in medieval texts relies on both understanding the reception history of the *Metamorphoses* and the status of homoerotic desires and sex acts in the Middle Ages. To the first, medieval Ovidian reception was a robust narrative field that thrived on the construction of hermeneutic uncertainty and deliberately created interpretative challenges. This was partially the result of the manuscript history of the *Metamorphoses*; the earliest manuscript fragments survive from the ninth century and the earliest complete extant witnesses date from the eleventh century.[8] Between the eleventh and the fourteenth centuries an elaborate subculture of commentary on the *Metamorphoses* developed in monastic and cathedral schools in which commentators glossed words, offered allegorical interpretations and developed a rich set of critical apparatuses for approaching the poem.[9] When medieval readers encountered the *Metamorphoses*, then, they did so primarily as part of an elaborate commentary tradition in which it was heavily glossed and allegorised. These allegorisations in turn proliferated a wide range of often contradictory interpretations of the poem, so much so that, as Alastair Minnis has suggested, the poem during this period was 'marked by inherent instability of meaning'.[10]

This commentary tradition itself transformed in the fourteenth century with the arrival of the heavily glossed *Ovide moralisé* (c. 1316–28).[11] Composed by an anonymous Franciscan author, the *Moralisé* translated the *Metamorphoses* into French verse. The anonymous author paired these translations with Christian allegorisations, which sought to explain the underlying theological moral of the text, and euhemerist interpretations, which connected the poem to historical or natural events. The popularity of the *Moralisé* was such that it largely replaced

---

[8] Hexter 2007 and Tarant 1995.
[9] Gillespie 2005. See also Traub 2020: 2–4.
[10] Minnis 2001: 12. Lochrie 2019: 80–1 notes that 'Ovid in mediaeval drag was decked out in so many moral and spiritual exempla, framed by glosses and interpretative apparati that overwhelmed the original stories'.
[11] As Mills 2015: 99–100 argues, this is a misleading name. Typically the *Moralisé* refers to an early fourteenth-century poem likely written for Joan of Burgundy, but it also circulated in two fifteenth-century prose abridgements. The *Moralisé* itself is extant in twenty-three manuscripts, all of which have considerable variations. See also Hexter 2007: 1354.

earlier Latin antecedents,[12] and it became one of the primary ways that medieval people encountered Ovid alongside the prose *Ovidius moralizatus* composed by Pierre Bersuire (c. 1340).[13]

The *Moralisé* preserved from the commentary tradition, however, an interest in developing and encouraging hermeneutic uncertainty. This hermeneutic uncertainty had an epistemological function. One of the aims of the *Moralisé* was that readers approach the *Metamorphoses* as a text to be puzzled through – one that, with enough careful study, might reveal hidden knowledge and universal truths about such diverse topics as the relationship between God and the human soul and the nature of desire.[14] By wading through hermeneutic uncertainty in pursuit of answers to these complex epistemological issues, readers were challenged to engage in the deep work of epistemological investigation. But neither the process of uncovering these universal truths nor the nature of the truths themselves was straightforward; readers of the *Moralisé* were required to navigate hermeneutic complexities to reach epistemic truths about the universe. Through both its translations and the glossed explanations, the *Moralisé* offered multiple interpretations of any given Ovidian story.[15] These interpretations were called to stand alongside each other, often with meanings that contradicted or existed in tension with one another.

The result of the development of the Ovidian commentary tradition from its earliest manifestations in the cathedral schools to the *Moralisé* was that 'surprisingly flexible modes of allegoresis' developed alongside versions and translations of the *Metamorphoses*.[16] Different texts might seek to curtail or exploit those tensions, as we'll see with fourteenth-century versions of the Iphis story, but the sheer proliferation of versions and glosses meant that reading Ovid in the later Middle Ages required living with hermeneutic and epistemological uncertainty.[17] The task of trying to understand what one knew or might come to know about Ovid was one of juggling multiple, shifting interpretations at once.

As I suggested in my introduction, with Iphis this hermeneutic and epistemic challenge was amplified by the culture of hermeneutic injustice that developed around homoerotic desire in the Middle Ages. Hermeneutical injustice, as laid

---

[12] Copeland 2009: 114–17.
[13] On the history of various Ovidian glosses and translations after the *Moralisé*, see Dimmick 2002 and Mills 2015: 99–100.
[14] Scholars have discussed reading this process as a metamorphosis. See Possamaï-Pérez 2006. All of these 'truths' are central to the *Moralisé*'s version of Iphis.
[15] See Copeland 2009: 107–26 and Griffin 2012 on the *Moralisé* and translation and transformation.
[16] Traub 2020: 3. Traub cites her antecedent for this claim as Moss 1982.
[17] As several scholars point out, the commentary tradition, even before the fourteenth century, often adopted a 'playful' nature in response to Ovid's own linguistic and conceptual play. See Minnis 2001; Gillespie 2005; Coulson 2007.

out in the Introduction to this volume, is a form of epistemic injustice described by Miranda Fricker in which 'someone has a significant area of their social experience obscured from understanding owing to prejudicial flaws in shared resources for social interpretation'.[18] In the case of medieval cultural attitudes towards the homoerotic, this hermeneutical injustice resulted in both distortions of homoeroticism – reading it as faulty, sinful or dangerous – and also in deliberately constructed ignorance. Homoerotic sex acts became known as the sin of 'sodomy' and were identified as *crimen nefandum*, the unmentionable vice.[19] As scholars like Mark Jordan and Robert Mills have argued, these distortions and ignorances were the product of theological and social efforts, a sort of precursor to the forms of deliberately harnessed and maintained ignorance described by Eve Sedgwick in modern Western culture.[20] These efforts grew up in the sweeping clerical and episcopal reforms of the twelfth century, and they sought to make sodomitical discourse and practice be read as not only sinful (as many sex acts were) but a particularly dangerous form of sexual sin: one that threatened social stability by upsetting gender hierarchies. Sodomy, this discourse claimed, dangerously invited men to accept passive (that is, penetrative) social positions or encouraged women to take on active sexual and social behaviours.[21]

So dangerous was sodomy that discourse on it was deliberately obscured and silenced above and beyond other sexual sins like adultery or other non-procreative sex acts. When spoken of 'directly' in works like Alain de Lille's *De planctu Naturae*, one of the early leading figures and works in silencing sodomy, sodomitical acts were shrouded in euphemism and cloaked in worries over gender performance: *Praedicat et subjicit* (He becomes both predicate and subject); *Cudit in incude, quae semina nulla monetat* (He strikes on an anvil that admits no seeds).[22]

---

[18] Fricker 2007: 147–75.
[19] On the history of sodomy and its unspeakablity, see Scanlon 1995 and Mills 2015: 3–5. For the long history of sodomy in the Middle Ages, see Goodich 1979; Jordan 1997; and Olsen 2011.
[20] On the development of sodomy in the twelfth-century reforms, see Jordan 1997. For an extension and revision of this argument beyond clerical reform, see Mills 2015. On the constructed and maintained forms of ignorance in twentieth-century America, see Sedgwick 1990: 1–7.
[21] Examples of this include, most famously, the portion of Alain de Lille's twelfth-century *De planctu Naturae*, discussed below for male sodomy, and Étienne de Fougères's description of women sodomites, whom he condemns as jousting without lances in the twelfth-century conduct book *Le livre des manières*. On critiques of sodomy being often critiques of gender performance and challenges to social stability, see Mills 2015: 90–7.
[22] Alain of Lille 1978 807.20–30 (translation my own). As numerous scholars have pointed out, part of what made sodomy so unspeakable was not so much the act itself, but the ways that it upset gendered behaviour, particularly making men passive. On gender and sodomy, see Lochrie 1999; Burgwinkle 2004; Karras 2005; and Mills 2015: 81–132.

Even texts where we might expect to see sodomy explicitly described and condemned, such as penitential manuals that guided priests through the sacrament of confession by identifying particular sins and their remedies, were incredibly circumspect. The concern was fundamentally epistemological. Texts worked to avoid introducing ideas about sodomy to readers who otherwise might not have known about it.[23] The inexpressibility *topos* that developed around same-sex desire, then, became a means of epistemological control, a carefully constructed and continuously maintained ignorance. To never speak of sodomy might mean that no one would ever know of it, never perform it and thus never risk the social instability associated with it.

The problem, of course, as the historical and literary record makes clear, was that people did know or, at least, came to learn, about homoerotic desire and sex acts.[24] This reality that silence around sodomy did not somehow end the practice of sodomy created new sets of epistemological questions for medieval writers immediately relevant to versions of the Iphis story considered in this chapter: how did so-called sodomites come to know unspeakable sins? Could private sodomitical desires and acts be concealed through secrecy? And how could a person find out if someone else experienced homoerotic desire or acted on it?[25]

While medieval theological and ethical texts that concerned sodomy were primarily interested in male homoerotic desire, medieval texts often characterised desire between women as an impossibility, which compounded the silence and distortions around medieval people's conceptual knowledge of women's sodomy. In much of medieval discourse, women's sodomy was understood as that which could be longed for and lamented but, on a bodily level, never accomplished – in Valerie Traub's terms, *amor impossibilis*.[26] This impossibility further complicated the epistemological questions that surrounded sodomy. Love between women not only opened up space for asking how homoerotic desire might be recognised or come to be known, but it also asked what in an impossible love can even be known.

---

[23] As Dinshaw 1999: 9 describes: 'This sin against nature would seem to be something that can be learned, a dangerous knowledge to which some – or maybe all – people are vulnerable'. See also Frantzen 1996 and Tentler 1977.

[24] See, for example, the conundrum for priests who should not mention sodomy but should encourage its confession in John Mirk's *Instructions for Parish Priests*, discussed in Dinshaw 1999: 9–11.

[25] Versions of these types of questions also appear in the thirteenth-century romance *Le Roman de Silence*; John Mirk's fourteenth-century English *Instructions for Parish Priests*; Alain de Lille's *De planctu Naturae*; Étienne de Fougères's *Le Livre des manières* and even the trial records of accused sodomites like John/Eleanor Rykener or Katherina Hetzeldorfer.

[26] Traub 2002 and 2020: 10–11.

It is in this space of multiplying hermeneutical injustices that we find medieval versions of Iphis. The story of Iphis, concerned as it is with bodies known and unknown, desires and how they are learned and expressed, finds rich space for the sort of hermeneutic and epistemic questions that populate medieval explorations of homoerotic desire and the body. In navigating these shifting desires, identities and bodies, in this chapter I will follow the language of the individual medieval stories, calling Iphis 'she' when the texts refers to them as such and 'he' when the text shifts. My intention here is less to express surety about Iphis's gender identity and more to reflect the ways that, on the micro-level within texts, that identity and its relationship to (homoerotic) desire is negotiated and renegotiated.[27] It is in these spaces of shifting textual transformation that we can see these texts navigating the tensions between narrative and silence, and it is in these spaces that we can see a range of shifting and contradicting interpretations of gender identity and homoerotic desire taking shape.

WHAT EVERYONE KNOWS: PUBLIC KNOWLEDGE AND PRIVATE FEARS IN THE *OVIDE MORALISÉ*

The version of Iphis in the *Ovide moralisé* is one transformed both through its translation into French verse and by its two attendant explanations.[28] The first, which follows immediately on the tale itself, connects Yphis to a supposed historical event in which a woman, who seemed to be a man in her clothing and behaviour: *D'abit et de cultivement / Sambloit home* (tries and fails to trick her wife during sex by means of a dildo) (9.3118–19). The second is a Christian allegory that reads Yphis as the lost 'feminine' soul that must be transformed into the pure 'masculine' reformed soul to unite with God.

The translation itself follows that of Ovid's Latin verse with a few critical departures. Yphis's parents, Ligdus and Theletusa, are changed to wealthy nobility and the desire for a male heir is the impetus behind Ligdus's proclamation that any girl children will be murdered (9.2763–98). It has its most critical point

---

[27] My thinking here has been shaped by trans discourses, and, in particular, discourse on trans/trans-/trans* identity as marked by either clear transitions between categories or the deliberate blurring of lines between categories. See Traub's 2020: 20–1 discussion of this. In Iphis and Ianthe, what is transformed depends on the version and, similarly, the boundaries of that transformation are blurred or marked out in ways particular to each version.

[28] It is unclear from what Latin manuscript the *Moralisé* author translated. On this as well as the number of variations from modern versions of Ovid, see McCracken 2019: 45. Hexter notes that this form, translation followed by glosses, belonged to the earliest Ovidian commentaries.

of departure, however, in its navigation of the tensions between the story's subject matter and the culture of hermeneutic injustice surrounding sodomitical narrative.[29] The transformation begins similarly to Ovid's, with its necessity hingeing on worries over what might be revealed in the private spaces of the wedding bed. Yphis decries the complete absurdity of her foolish hope, *fole esperance*, and laments her desire: *Qui si t'embrase et si t'enlace / Et si ne pues en nulle fin / De ta volenté traire à fin* (It inflames and binds you and there is no way that you can bring your desire to fulfilment, IX.2945, 2966–8). Even more than an impossibility, however, Yphis and Theletusa both fear discovery. Shortly before Hyenté and Yphis's wedding, they go to the temple of Isis. Theletusa frames the problem (IX.3066–9):

> Or te pri que sans demorance
> D'ore en avant t'en entremetes
> De la sauveur et cure i metes,
> Quar je n'i puis plus conseil metre,
> Se tu ne t'en veulz entremetre

Now I beg you that you proceed straightaway and without delay to save her and care for her. For I cannot keep the secret any longer if you will not intervene.

These lines, which do not appear in the original, hint at, but do not directly express, a fear of what might be revealed in the private spaces of the marriage bed. Theletusa and Yphis worry that Hyenté will learn that her love is *amor impossibilis* – that she will learn the truth of Yphis's body. The secret will then become known, and Yphis will not be able to be saved.

Isis is merciful and grants their plea. Like Ovid's text, the translation describes changes to Iphis's appearance: the darkening of features, the increased vigour of the body. The *Moralisé* author then writes (IX.3092–112):

> Tout ot son estat et son estre
> Et sa nature femeline
> Chanchiee, et prise masculine:
> Yphis fille est devenus filz.
> De ce soient seürs et fis!
> Ce fu aperte veritze,

---

[29] Begum-Lees 2020 has argued that Ovid's public transformation scene is a moment of changed social gender with no mention of biological sex change. Whatever ambiguities might exist in the Latin text, the *Moralisé* works to eliminate them.

Sans mençonge et sans faussetz!
Offrandes et sacrefices amples
Et dons vait presenter aus temples,
Si sorent tuit, grant et menus,
Qu'Yphis fille est filz devenus.

L'endemain, quant il ajorna,
Yphis li vallès s'atorna
Pour prendre s'espouse Hyenté.
Là ot deduit, là ont chanté.
Li dieu des noces tuit y furent
A tel joie, come estre y durent:
Hymeneüs, Juno, Venus.
N'en y failli nulle ne nulz.
Yphis fu liez et plains de joie.
Hyenté prist come la soie.

Her stature and being, and her feminine nature had completely changed and become masculine. Iphis the daughter had become a son – this was certain and sure! It was the clear truth, without a word of a lie! Telethusa made generous offerings, gifts and sacrifices at the temples. Everyone, high and low, knew that Iphis the daughter had become a son.

When the next day dawned, the boy Iphis left to take Ianthe as his wife. There was great joy, and everyone sang. All the gods of marriage – Hymenaeus, Juno and Venus – attended joyfully, as they should. Nothing and no one was missing from the festivities. Iphis was happy and full of joy. He took Ianthe as his own.

There are two critical changes in this passage. The Latin lines are extended,[30] and the French text emphasises that Yphis's feminine nature has been fundamentally changed. Here that change is twice reiterated and framed as nothing like a deception, the surety ('seürs') and open truth ('aperte veritz') repeated several times within the same lines. The *Moralisé* links that certainty and truth to public knowledge: 'Si sorent tuit, grant et menus, / Qu'Yphis fille est filz devenus'. The importance of this public knowledge is such that it is the means by which the text signals the transformation. The text then again signals the import of public acts by pulling the public into the wedding ceremony itself: 'everyone sang'.

---

[30] [N]am quae femina nuper eras, puer es! date munera templis, nec timida gaudete fide. (Take your gifts to the temple, Iphis: rejoice, with confidence, not fear! You, who were lately a woman, are now a boy) (9. 790–2).

But what is it that everyone knew, and why does the public nature of this knowledge matter? The grammar of the line implies a revelation of the transformation itself (that everyone knew about the transformation), but, of course, the point of Yphis and Theletusa's prayerful supplication at the temple was to make sure that no one knew that any transformation had taken place. The curious nature of the text's framing of public certainty tells us something about how the *Moralisé* understands the work of public spaces in navigating epistemological obscurities around homoerotic desire, gender performance and bodily change. This scene casts into doubt what others thought they knew about Yphis before the transformation. They might have thought they knew that Yphis was a son, but that was not certain. Only in this moment of public revelation is Yphis's identity as son certain and sure [*seürs et fis*], without lies and falsity [*Sans mençonge et sans faussetz*] – the implication being that earlier certainty was the result of lies and false seeming. It is only when outer performance and appearance match private expression and bodies that everyone can know with true certainty. In fact, the public nature of the acknowledgement of what everyone now knows with certainty serves as a correction to an earlier error. Public knowledge of Yphis is corrected and miraculously transformed. The social danger of an epistemological falsehood is corrected, and the public's earlier – unknown and false – assumption of a normative match between gender performance and body is corrected and transformed into surety and open truth.

To get to this conclusion, however, the text still has to navigate a few difficult interpretative realities that result from that tension between the homoerotic nature of the narrative itself and the condition of hermeneutic injustice in medieval sodomy discourse. First, Yphis's homoerotic desires and gender performance are rewarded with miraculous actions from Isis. Second, the tale has skirted the cardinal rule of medieval sodomy – never speak of it. That the *Moralisé* is aware of both of these problems and tries to curtail them is apparent in the two subsequent interpretations. Immediately after the text announces that Yphis took Hyenté as his own (*Hyenté prist come la soie*, 3112), the *Moralisé* moves to suppress any celebration of homoerotic desire through its historical explanation. The *Moralisé* author writes that long ago, a woman lived who *D'abit et de cultivement / Sambloit home* (seemed to be a man in her clothing and behaviour, IX.3118–19). Such was her presentation that everyone who saw her in this clothing, *en tel habit*, believed her to be a man, a belief her mother bore witness to, *tesmoignoit* (IX.3119–22). Eventually a young maiden sees and, truly believing that she was a man, *et crut de voir / Que fust homs*, hungers for love and marriage, knowing nothing of the disguise (IX.3124–7).

The woman in man's clothing agrees to marry, a decision the historical interpretation laments as foolish and impossible to fulfil: *Tout n'eüst elle point de vit / Ne de membre à ce convenable* (she had nothing like a penis or any other member to serve this purpose, IX.3130–2). It is only with the aid of a witch that the woman is able to fulfil her desire by means of a *member apostis*, a false member (IX.3149). This deceit allows the marriage to proceed, but, according to the gloss, it does not last (IX.3150–7):

> Quant la meschine l'aperçut,
> Ne fu la chose plus celee,
> Ains fu en apert revelee,
> Si en tenoit chascuns son conte,
> Et la fole en fu mise à honte,
> Qui bien ot honte desservie.
> De tele oeuvre n'ait nulz envie,
> Quar trop est et dampnable et vis.

> When the maiden realised what was happening, the trick could no longer be concealed, but was fully revealed: everyone talked about it, and the woman was thoroughly shamed, as she so richly deserved. May no one desire to undertake such an act, for it is most damnable and vile.

The public nature of the woman's punishment – a full revelation, a public shaming, everyone talking – mirrors the public nature of her masculine performance. The public nature and the success of that gender performance, however, is never acknowledged to be more than deceit. In the gloss's logic, gender performance cannot overwrite bodily reality and desire. Unlike in the Yphis story, no amount of desire, gender performance or divine intervention can render *amor impossibilis* possible.

With this assurance the interpretations shift again, moving into a Christian allegory. Ligdus becomes God, the spiritual father, Theletusa, Holy Church, and Yphis the soul whose *femeline nature*, feminine nature, has led her astray (9.3202). Through Isis, true repentance, confession and penitence (. . . *voire repentance, / Confession et penitance*, 9.3261–2), granted to the soul through divine mercy, the feminine fallen soul can transform to the masculine reformed soul to whom God will give heavenly glory (9.3331–44).

While the Christian allegorisation is appallingly misogynist, I draw attention to it because it helps to illuminate the cultural anxieties and silencing efforts underpinning the euhemerist gloss. Without the historical interpretation, the story of Yphis and its allegory make space for ambiguity and could even be read as celebrating a certain form of homoerotic desire.[31] While framed as *amor impossibilis*, Yphis's desire for Hyenté and Theletusa's prayers are what propels her transformation. And

---

[31] On this, see McCracken's 2020: 53 discussion of the supplement in the *Moralisé*: 'Derridian logic of the supplement, that is the claim that the supplement exposes incompleteness in the original; the very fact that the original can be supplemented demonstrates an incompleteness that was not earlier apparent. The supplement adds to and replaces, it completes – and in completing, it exposes a prior incompleteness'. McCracken considers not just the glosses that supplement the original tale (and reveal incompleteness and inconsistencies) but the dildo; her antecedents are Wills 1995 and Derrida 1976.

this transformation is not condemned as false or as begun in sodomitical desire, but is instead celebrated as the granting of a rightful wish. It is further given a public acknowledgement and celebration. The Christian allegory, moreover, also suggests that earnest desire for reform and fervent prayer are the methods by which Christian salvation can be achieved. Through them, Divine Mercy will guide the fallen (feminine) soul to be transformed into the reformed (masculine) soul. We see once again a celebration of a desire to move across gender and sex categories as a catalyst for necessary transformation.[32]

It is also striking that neither the Yphis story nor the Christian allegorisation outright condemns Iphis. Valerie Traub has written about how different medieval and early modern versions of the Iphis story participate in trans/trans-/trans* discourse either through marking clear transitions between gender and sex categories or the blurring of lines between these categories.[33] While the *Moralisé*'s euhemerist gloss intends to reinforce firm categorical boundaries, the actual story of Yphis and its Christian allegory reflect movement between categories without any sign of condemnation. In the story itself, Theletusa worries about what the marriage bed will reveal about Yphis's biological sex, but that worry is relieved when their wish is granted and Yphis transforms in a moment of miraculous celebration: a narrative detail that suggests testing or wishing for movement across gender and sex categories is rewarded. Perhaps even more astonishingly, in the theological schema that the Christian allegory establishes, the soul should want to enact, and needs to embody, a supposedly 'masculine' virtue ethics in order to become the masculine soul that can be saved.

This is not to suggest that either the tale or the allegorisation are receptive to homoerotic desire or intend to celebrate Yphis's movement across gender and sex categories. But in teasing out some of the implications of these stories, we can see exactly what interpretations the euhemerist reading was designed to

---

[32] This gender play around the Christian soul and union with the divine is part of a long and complex history in which body politics and erotics become a lens through which to understand the relationship between humanity and divinity. For two influential studies of this intersection, see Bynum 1984 and Newman 2005.

[33] Traub 2020: 20–1. As Traub notes, there are both resemblances and alterities between contemporary categories of sex and gender and medieval and early modern, but she argues for the value of of trans/trans-/trans* discourse: 'It is thus with awareness of both alterity and resemblance across time that we affirm, as theoretical and thematic motivations, the resonance to our project of the contemporary terms trans (a stand-alone category referring to a spectrum of non-normative genders, the disarticulation of sexed bodies from gender as well as gender transition), trans- (the hyphen signifying a prefix connecting trans to a specific set of referents) as well as trans* (the asterisk referring to as-yet-unknown sex and gender possibilities)'. Traub's antecedents for thinking about trans/trans-/trans* discourse are Enke 2012 and Styker and Aizura 2013.

obscure. The historical interpretation reveals an anxiety over the limits of what we can truly know about the bodies of others underneath outward appearance: an echo of the larger cultural fears that sodomy would upset normative gender practice and hierarchies. The woman's masculine performance was so good that everyone knew her to be a man. And, for a time, she successfully led the maiden to know her as a man in marriage.[34] Equally evident is an anxiety over Ianthe and the maiden's unknowing desire for their partners. Returning to the epistemological questions sodomitical desire raises in the Middle Ages, the historical narrative describes the maiden as both being deceived and consequently coming to desire her spouse. The euhemerist gloss then reveals a dangerous problem: might a person have sodomitical desires and not realise it? The *Moralisé* tries to silence these epistemological worries as well as the interpretative uncertainties framed by the Christian allegory and the tale itself; it works to perpetuate a system of hermeneutic injustice, by assuring that the 'truth' will always come out. The maiden will always eventually realise the 'truth' about her spouse; others will always come to know (and punish) movement across categorical boundaries of gender and sex.

WHAT NO ONE KNOWS: PRIVATE KNOWLEDGE AND PUBLIC SILENCE IN THE *CONFESSIO AMANTIS*

The English poet John Gower's version of the Iphis legend offers a significant shift away from public to private spaces as the locus of epistemological revelation and in so doing it also offers the possibility for moving beyond fixed boundaries and silences around gender and sodomitical desire. Gower's Iphis is part of a larger, intricate work called the *Confessio Amantis*, written in the 1380s and revised periodically over the next decade. The *Confessio Amantis* details how Amans, a failing, desperate lover, makes a confession to his priest, Genius. Genius, serving as both priest and counsellor, offers Amans guidance on how to avoid love's sins. He presents much of his advice through recounting stories from Greek and Roman sources, with the *Metamorphoses* being one that he returns to repeatedly.[35]

The story of Iphis takes place in Book IV of the *Confessio Amantis*, which considers the sin of Sloth. Sloth was a medieval sin of inaction, one associated with states of innervation and depression – deeply harmful to standards of pursuing

---

[34] The ambiguity over length of time here is fascinating – how long did it last? What finally revealed the member as 'false'? Billings 2019 notes that even when something is 'certain' or 'sure', the temporality of gender transformation, including the how and when, is fundamentally uncertain in the *Moralisé*.

[35] On Gower and Ovid, see McKinley 2011 and Galloway 2016.

and achieving love.[36] Genius tells the story of Iphis as a positive example of the antithesis of a form of Sloth called *pusillamité*, cowardice. Iphis serves as an example of a person able to achieve their desire because of the fervency of their longing, a contrast to the slothly lover Amans (IV.24–71).

Gower's source for his Iphis legend was, like almost all of his stories from the *Metamorphoses*, drawn from the commentary tradition and primarily from the *Moralisé*.[37] Gower, however, significantly transforms his source material. Following the *Moralisé*, he begins by outlining the birth as well as Iphis's secret (although, notably, it is never clear that Iphis knows that any deception has taken place). Gower begins to diverge from the *Moralisé* when Iphis is betrothed at age ten to Iante, a full three years younger than in either Ovid or the *Moralisé*. During their betrothal '[t]hese children' would often lie together 'sche and sche', since they were of the same age. The result was that, over the years while they waited to become of marriageable age,[38] they became 'pleiefieres', playfellows (IV.482). It is as playfellows that their relationship transitioned and, one night, in a scene unique to Gower's version of Iphis (IV.483–92):[39]

> Liggende abedde upon a nyht,
> Nature, which doth every wiht
> Upon hire lawe for to muse,
> Constreigneth hem, so that thei use
> Thing which to hem was al unknowe;
>
> Lying abed upon a night,
> Nature, which does every person
> Upon her law cause to muse,
> Constrains them, so that they use
> Thing which to them was all unknown;

Exactly what happens Gower leaves intentionally unclear. Gower makes explicit that Iphis and Iante are not simply lying next to each other, but that they are

---

[36] On Sloth's position in the schema of sins in the *Confessio Amantis*, see Peck's discussion in Gower 2006. This dialogue around the pursuit of love, including schemas for pursuing love and the necessary action for diligent lovers, had also been highly influenced by Ovid's *Ars Amatoria* and medieval versions of it, like the twelfth-century *De Amore* by Andreas Capellanus. On Gower's debt to the *Ars Amatoria* tradition, see Irvin 2014.

[37] On Gower's relation to the *Moralisé*, see McKinley 2011 and Galloway 2016.

[38] Twelve for girls, fourteen for boys; see the discussion of age in Gower in Watt 2003: 75, discussed below.

[39] While this scene does not appear in Ovid, analogies can be found in the *Herodites* and Bersuire's *Ovidius Moralizatus*. See Mainzer 1972: 217; Brown 1982: 18; and Watt 2003: 175.

constrained – impelled, possibly even compelled – to make use of a mysterious and unfamiliar 'Thing' to satisfy the whims of nature. Robert Mills argued for reading this as a dildo, and, having read the euhemerist gloss in the *Moralisé*, it is hard not to think of one here.[40] This is especially the case as the subsequent lines make evident that what happens centres on Iante and Iphis's 'grete love' (IV.489).

Gower's vagueness is enormously effective in laying the groundwork for him to trouble the inherent tension between the hermeneutic injustice of medieval sodomy discourse and the homoerotics of the narrative. The 'Thing' is unnamed because to name it (whether it is a sex toy or even a set of practices[41]) would be to break taboos of speaking of sodomy. Even more critically, it underscores Iphis and Iante's lack of understanding. What they use is to them 'al unknowe'. They have not learned about whatever sex acts they perform from another source (no one has spoken of sodomy to them). Consequently, their actions come not from particular knowledge but are driven by natural compulsion.

It is at this moment that Cupid intervenes. Driven by the lovers' unknowing actions, Cupid takes pity and allows them to set love above nature and have their lust excused. Furthermore, because love (IV.493–501):

> ... hateth nothing more
> Than thing which stant agein the lore
> Of that nature in kinde hath sett.
> Forthi Cupide hath so besett
> His grace upon this aventure,
> That he acordant to nature,
> Whan that he syh the time best,
> That ech of hem hath other kest,
> Transformeth Iphe into a man ...

> ... hates nothing more
> Than a thing which stands against the learning
> That nature has set in the essential nature of something.
> Consequently, Cupid has so beset
> His grace upon this occurrence,
> That he accords to nature,
> When he sees the time is best,
> And that each of them has the other kissed,
> He transforms Iphis into a man ...

---

[40] Mills 2015: 108–9.
[41] Lochrie 2020: 85–6, contra Mills 2015, reads 'thing' as deliberately opaque and not a reference to a specific apparatus, which I have followed here.

The logic here is fascinating. Cupid is compelled by their love and the unknowing acting on that love to fix the problem of homoerotic desire that 'stants agein the lore' that nature has set. This happens, not by ending Iphis's desire for Ianthe, but by transforming Iphis into a man. Cupid notably acts when the time is best, during a moment of intimate physical affection – when 'ech of hem hath other kest' – to create an accord between desire and nature. From there, the tale rapidly ends with Iphis winning the love 'Of lusti yonge (lusty young) Iante his wif' and Genius assuring us that then 'thei ladde a merie lif, / Which was to kinde non offence (they led a merry life / Which was to nature no offence)' (IV.503–5).

There is no public wedding, no prayerful appeal to Isis, no anxious worry of discovery. There is, in fact, no evidence that Iphis knows that there is anything to be discovered. Diane Watt has written about the consequences of the early age of betrothal in Gower, arguing that it absolves Iphis of criminal responsibility in the medieval imagination.[42] One of the consequences too is that Gower preserves the space of coming to know something about sex and sexuality as a process of private, experiential, bodily knowledge. Iphis and Iante's unknowing exploration is an extension of their childhood as 'pleiefieres', lying in bed together, and their mutual love recognised by Cupid.

The consequences of these changes are significant. Gower resists making questions of desire and knowledge public acts – or ones that are navigated primarily on public stages, and, in the process, he uses the medieval epistemic space of silence around homoerotic desire to create the foundations for an unknowing, private exploration of sex, gender and the body. It reconstitutes the space in which gender matters, moving the locus to private moments of intimacy, and it challenges visions of lesbianic homoerotic desire as *amor impossibilis*. In the case of the first, the move away from public spaces and the relocation of the transformation to the betrothal bed transforms the anxieties the tale raises about gender. As I discussed earlier, the public nature of the *Moralisé*'s story of Iphis and the euhemerist reading's focus on the epistemological problems of public gender performance, speak to an anxiety over the reality that one can never know fully how someone is embodied or whom they desire. Gower's focus on private spaces resists making desire or knowledge things that must be negotiated in public spaces. It is the private spaces that matter for coming to acknowledge or know anything about one's own body, desires, even the role that one takes in sex and marriage. In Gower this is not a thing to fear – to be pusillanimous, cowardly, about.

In fact, this shift in focus runs concurrent with a celebration of sexual exploration and an embracing of hermeneutic and epistemic uncertainty around the body and desire. Iphis and Iante engage in 'Thing which to hem was al unknowe', an indulgence that the tale celebrates as resisting the forces of *pusillamité*. Their

---

[42] Watt 2005: 75.

willingness to act on desire in their ignorance results in Cupid's approval of the relationship. I am reluctant here to say that Gower celebrates a sort of epistemological uncertainty generated by homoerotic desire, but, as Lochrie frames it, 'by installing the riddle of "the thing that was unknown to them" at the centre of his tale, Gower undoes the epistemological certainty that provokes moral condemnation lodged against the sex between Iphis and Iante and the very need for change in the first place' (93).[43]

In the case of *amor impossibilis*, representations of lesbian desire as impossible rely on perceptions of women's bodies as incapable of completing sex.[44] What the private spaces of Iphis and Iante's bed reveal is that this is not an inherent problem of the body. Some *thing* happens. While Gower resists revealing exactly how that love was accomplished, this opacity is generative rather than obstructionist – an almost apophatic technique that encourages imaginative speculation and proliferation.

Whatever happens, Gower makes clear that it is a product of nature and love, albeit via a complex logic. The couple is constrained by Nature to use the Thing and enjoy their love, and Cupid acts to bring their love in accord with nature's law. How this works is, in Karma Lochrie's terms, riddling – does nature act against nature's own laws when compelling Iphis and Iante in the first place?[45] What is particularly striking, however, is the deliberate way in which Gower stringently avoids gendered pronouns, focusing instead on references to Iphis and Iante's actions as joint. The effect of this is that, at the critical moment that spurs transformation, the tale refuses to commit to particular delineations of gender, body or sexual identity. While the suggestion of homoeroticism ultimately proves temporary, and Cupid must step in to realign nature's law and nature's constraints,[46] this brief moment of ambiguity creates a new epistemological space that moves beyond the silence and distortions constructed by the hermeneutical injustices of medieval sodomy discourse. In that space, desire – regardless of sex, gender or sexuality – is allowed to exist on its own and to move towards some unknown, exploratory knowledge that meets the demands of 'grete love'.

---

[43] On how the intersection of Gower's translation works alongside his Latin notes (which operate often in direct opposition to the complexities of the tale itself), see Lochrie 2020: 86–9.

[44] Traub 2002: 276–325.

[45] On the complex role of nature and 'kinde', particularly focused on the tensions surrounding the 'naturalness' of nature's acts, see White 2008: 192–4; Lochrie 2012: 214–15; and Lochrie 2020: 90–4.

[46] On this realignment and the particular forms of violence it engages in by failing to act in dialogue with Iphis, see Bychowski's 2016 discussion of the medicalisation of gender dysphoria as it intersects with Cupid's actions.

OVIDIAN VARIATIONS AND EPISTEMOLOGICAL UNCERTAINTIES

In a recent edited collection on Iphis in medieval and early modern reception, essays in the collection repeatedly returned to issues of uncertainty and opacity. As Valerie Traub 2020 in her introduction describes it (15):

> ... this tale raises important questions not only of subjectivity, desire and embodiment, but also of temporality (the status of past, present and future), ontology (the origins of gendered being and erotic desire) and epistemology (how embodied, desiring subjects know and are known).... What exactly has been transformed? On what grounds do we know that a transformation has occurred? What is the basis of our certainty? Is her transformation an externalisation of essential, internal character? Is this metamorphosis an example of change-within-continuity or continuity-within-change? Is Iphis always, already, really a man – and what would it mean to assert that she is or isn't? What is at stake – hermeneutically, ethically, politically – in our answers to these questions?

Rather than answer these questions, in this chapter I have worked to pause at the moments of uncertainty and the glimpses of epistemological obscurity we get in two medieval versions of this story. In doing so, my aim was to consider what spaces this uncertainty might open up, to consider why it opens them up, and how these two medieval texts wrestle with the tensions between cultural silences around sodomy and the nature of the Iphis narrative. Doing so speaks to cultural anxieties around epistemological opacity centred on sex and the body. It also offers brief glimpses into what sort of generative spaces that uncertainty might allow.

Gower's version of the Iphis legend is a fascinating one in no small part because we might read it as a revision of a revision, a rewriting not just of the *Moralisé*'s version of Iphis, but of the euhemerist interpretation in particular. That gloss – anxious to suggest that the miraculous nature of the tale itself could never exist in any positive form outside of myth – shows how a woman, acting as Iphis did, sought dangerous knowledge that should remain unspoken and unknown. She pursued that knowledge and put it to intimate use, only to be discovered by her wife and publicly punished. Gower reframes the betrothal bed of Iphis and Iante so that it becomes a space of mutual, unknowing exploration that resolves in private fulfilment of desire without public punishment.

I do not want to oversell what's happening here – Gower is no proto-queer theorist[47] – but in thinking of the ways retellings of the Iphis legend offered

---

[47] I mean that there is no reason to think that Gower is challenging the public valuation of medieval sexual values or heterosexuality, as in Berlant and Warner 1998.

critical spaces for thinking through and around the silence and distortions of medieval sodomy discourse, it is worthwhile to pause to consider the epistemological spaces homoerotic desire opens up in these texts. For the *Moralisé* it is primarily a dangerous space. While the language of homoerotic desire opens up space for the story of the soul's transformation from feminine to masculine, that opening up also threatens the cultural silence around sodomy, destabilising the social structures that the deliberately constructed obscurements and distortions of homoerotic desire were supposed to protect. Iphis's desire, their public gendered performance, speaks to the epistemological uncertainty that is inherent in our understanding of others. How can we know how someone's desire is oriented? How can we know for certain that gender performance pairs gender and sex in normative ways? The euhemerist reading attempts to assure its readers that this uncertainty is temporary. Errors might happen, but they will always be corrected – always be punished.

The tale itself, however, fails to echo that certainty. Telethusa and Iphis both worry that Iphis will be found out when the marriage happens but that threat is never realised due to divine intervention. No one ever realises Iphis's history. And, moreover, both the tale and the Christian allegorisation valorise fervent desire for transformation. Iphis gets what Iphis desires, and the soul is depicted as properly oriented when it does desire transformation. Sitting alongside each other, we can see what the euhemerist gloss would deny. There is no guarantee that any punishment might happen at all, and what we can know about each other's desires, bodies and histories will always exist in some form of obscurity.

For Gower, sodomitical desire is necessarily a temporary but generative space. The possibility of epistemological uncertainty, which sodomitical desire and gender opacity construct by challenging culture norms of deliberate silence and ignorance, creates a space for desire to move into new expressions of desire and types of knowledge. Iphis and Iante, building on their long familiarity and great love for each other, are moved by nature to go beyond nature's law and into something unknown. In this space, Iphis and Iante temporarily are allowed to transcend – to act beyond – what nature should allow. From this beyond space, Cupid is able to see and recognise the strength of their mutual desire and love. Gower does not allow us to see or understand fully exactly what it means to exist in this state of unknowledge, but it exists for a time and allows for a place in which natural love and desire can exist and explore beyond their typical bounds.

There is something shockingly moving in the fact that Gower brands this expression of desire as a cure for cowardice. It frames the willingness to exist in the epistemological uncertainty constructed by sodomitical desire as a type of courage. It suggests that the willingness to move into the unknown spaces of desire and bodily union transforms desire and makes bodily impossibilities possible.

That there is something to be desired and worthy of imitation – something that slothly lovers should learn from – in the dwelling of epistemological obscurity, in the unknown spaces, of sex and desire. It is this sort of daring that does the most work to challenge the structures of hermeneutic injustice shaping medieval sodomy discourse.

CHAPTER 14

Religious Authority and Classical Reception in Baroque Rome: Martha Marchina's *Musa Posthuma* and Feminist Epistemologies of Care

Erika Zimmermann Damer

The difficult question of what women writing Latin looks like is richly answered in early modern Italian states. Where in the classical period we have a profound scarcity of texts, and turn to Perpetua's *passio* and Egeria's *Peregrinatio* in late antiquity to find full books (likely) written by a woman, Martha Marchina's (1600–1646) posthumous book of poetry and correspondence, *Musa Posthuma* (1662), finds surer footing. What is apparent from her contemporaries, from her editor and in her own published correspondence is that Martha Marchina was internationally lauded in her time as an exemplary Latin poet, for her piety and for her status as a working-class educated Roman woman.

 The sixteenth century saw a flourishing of women writing in Italian and Latin, displaying deep humanist learning of classical antiquity. In the past, scholars argued that the seventeenth century, or the period of the Baroque, was much more hostile to women writers and overtly misogynist in the views of Counter-Reformation Catholicism.[1] Virginia Cox has challenged that view, showing that the flourishing of women's writing in Italian continued and even expanded in the Counter-Reformation, while Jane Stevenson's foundational work has demonstrated how many women have written Latin poetry since antiquity.[2] This essay points readers to the poetry of the nearly

---

[1] Stevenson 2005.
[2] Cox 2011.

unknown Martha Marchina and celebrates its elegance and Latinity. I explore her woman-centred Catholic writing, which prioritises embodied experience, critically engages emerging seventeenth-century scientific understandings of the world through the lens of faith, and reinvents patriarchal classical epic and lyric models by advancing woman-centred, caregivers' perspectives focused on Mary or women saints. Throughout, my readings of Martha Marchina's poetics resonate with feminist epistemologies, finding common ground with the insights of Patricia Hill Collins's concept of 'othermothers', of a Black feminist standpoint, intersectionality, and with Sara Ruddick's maternal thinking as a standpoint.[3] These epistemologies centre an ethics of care committed to material, bodily realities and prioritise mutual relations between selves and othermothering that extends beyond biological families. Feminist standpoint theories, particularly those emerging in Black and women of colour feminisms, share the claim that marginalised social positions occupied by the knower – including her gender, race, class, ethnicity, sexuality and ability – can become interlocking sites of epistemic privilege that grant her what Collins has termed 'outsider within' status, a site of radical transformative authority.[4]

It is my hope that this chapter will be one of many exploring the poetry of Martha Marchina. She is remarkable in so many dimensions, but her work is nearly unknown. This chapter begins with a small autobiographical note. During the first year of the pandemic, Skye Shirley, founder of Lupercal, a remarkable researcher, scholar, teacher and activist for women and non-binary Latinists, created the Martha Marchina Challenge. This challenge took wing and morphed into a lasting literary community devoted to reading, enjoying and discussing the entirety of Marchina's work and to weaving a shared, loving, compassionate feminist life together through Zoom and Martha Marchina. The ritual of our gatherings, and the shared conversations that emerged from themes in Marchina's poems, provided me and all of us so much solace, joy and connection in dark pandemic days. Our method was unlike any I've ever encountered: we read together and then we discussed in English or in Latin, diving rarely into thorny syntax or seventeenth-century Latin's challenges, but most often illuminating the text as an act of mindfulness, delighting with Marchina and with each other in the miracles and wonders she invites her audience to contemplate. While most analyses in this

---

[3] Collins 2000 and Ruddick 1989. See also Nally (Chapter 5, this volume) for a similar reading of Plato's *Symposium*. Others in this volume who give standpoint readings or use standpoint theory as an interpretative lens include Weiberg (Chapter 2), Gilbert (Chapter 3), Witzke (Chapter 7), Haley (Chapter 9), Bowden (Chapter 12) and Strong (Chapter 15).

[4] Collins 1986.

chapter are mine, I will make a practice of citing our shared insights as those of the Martha Marchina Group (MMG).[5]

Particularly in Italy, women were able to become members of the *Respublica litterarum* as published poets, members of intellectual life in public spaces, and, later in the seventeenth century, to become members of learned academies. Women gave public orations in Latin, and Italy is the home of the first woman to earn a PhD, Elena Cornaro Piscopia, who was awarded her doctorate in Philosophy after a public, *ex tempore* defence in Latin at the University of Padua in 1678.[6] By the 1580s, Italian women published widely, with writers publishing in 'practically every polite literary genre of the day'.[7] Italy is also exceptional in the number of women publishing printed texts in the sixteenth and seventeenth centuries, and in the number of Latin texts that continued to be produced.[8] Here Latin was not a 'minority interest' in written and published texts as elsewhere, and

---

[5] Our group was an international one that brought together intrepid high school students, graduate students, college professors and many K-12 teachers from around the world, among them Skye Shirley, Mercedes Barletta, Sharon Kazmierski, Rachel Beth Cunning, Elspeth Currie, Noel Grisanti, Lauren Fletchersen, Diane Warne Anderson, Jacqui Bloomberg, Amy Gawtry, Oceáne Puche, Séverine Clément Tarantino, Claire Mieher, Roberta Stewart, Dorota Dutsch, Sophia He and me. The digitised text of *Musa Posthuma*, work shepherded by Mercedes Barletta, Elsbeth Currie, Claire Mieher, Séverine Tarantino and Océane Puche, is available on *Project Nota*, a digital resource for the study of women writing Latin, directed by Sophia He. Rachel Beth Cunning has created a remarkable teacher's guide for Martha Marchina's poetry at bombaxpress.com. I owe deep thanks to Skye Shirley, to all of our group members, and to our Latin reading group that endures.

[6] The tradition of Italian women giving public orations, or being asked to publicly compose Latin poems, precedes Piscopia by several centuries. See Stevenson 2005: 141–76 and 279–323. Anna Maria van Schurman is the first woman to attend a university in Europe, at the University of Utrecht in 1636, where she was required to study behind a screen in a box to separate her from male students.

[7] In 1538, Vittoria Colonna's *Rime* became the first print edition of a collection of poetry by a woman writer, and became an immediate bestseller (Brundin, Crivelli and Sepegno 2016: 4). Most women's published writing of this period is in Italian (Cox 2000: 53).

[8] In sixteenth-century Italy, Cox 2011 records over 200 Italian women writers. France, which saw the second highest group of women writers, saw only thirty (Stevenson 2022: 139). Italian women were also celebrated as artists, actresses, composers and singers. Women's writing remained marginal, but rather than 'exceptional' model minorities who break the mould of social norms and expectations, Cox 2011: xiv argues for an 'established minority presence, increasingly accepted over time'. Martha Marchina will prove, rather, to be an exceptional writer, when examined from an intersectional lens.

30 per cent of printed texts were written in Latin in the seventeenth century.⁹ Latin thus persisted as an important language of letters in the Italian states throughout the period of Marchina's life. While Cox demonstrates the prominence of women writers as an accepted 'minority presence' among published authors, women publishing complete books of Latin poetry in this period are truly exceptional, and Martha Marchina as author is rarer still.¹⁰ Her collection, an entire book of poetry in Latin, places her among only two peers, as far as I know: Lorenza Strozzi and Anna Maria Arduino, both aristocratic women.¹¹

By the sixteenth century, it had become conventional to place a woman writing Latin among her learned sisters in the *Respublica litterarum*, a global network of intellectuals, connected by literary networks of letters across Europe and in the Americas. We find this placement in the opening dedication to the readers by Martha Marchina's editor, Francesco Macedo. Marchina's poetry is found even more remarkable, in his judgement, than the Latin writings of Lorenza Strozzi, Margarita Sarrochi, Tarquinia Molza or Veronica Gambara, because of Marchina's humble family origins.¹² Unlike other women Latinists, however, we lack evidence that Marchina corresponded with other women of the *Respublica mulierum*. This may be because of her social status: she is a Neopolitan émigré to Rome and a member of the working class. Before turning to a close reading of selected poems, I begin with a study of Martha Marchina's biography and career to understand her distinctive social position.

Many of the women whose Latin work survives were members of the aristocracy, such as Elizabeth I of England, or children of humanists or teachers themselves, such as Camille de Morel in Paris. We must celebrate Martha Marchina as a woman writing Latin in the terms her contemporaries used: not only is she a woman who composes flawless classicising Latin poetry, something most women of her period could not have had educational access to, but she is also working-class, pious and an unmarried woman. Thinking about her using our feminist killjoy survival kit,¹³ we must note the intersecting axes of oppression present in Marchina's life: her gender, class, immigration status and her marginal status relative to marriage and religious orders excluded her from normative social power

---

⁹ C. 52 per cent of sixteenth-century Italian publications were in Latin; 30 per cent of seventeenth-century texts were; and the majority of publications (56 per cent) from Padua were Latin (Stevenson 2005: 283–4).

¹⁰ Cox 2011.

¹¹ See Skye Shirley Chapter 2, forthcoming, on Martha Marchina. Arduino's *Rosa Parnassi* (Naples: S. Castaldun, 1687) is now inaccessible outside of Naples; Strozzi's *Hymni* are in the selected bibliography and digitised on Google. On Arduino, see Shirley, forthcoming.

¹² Stevenson 2022: 158–9 describes that these women writers were highly praised Italian Latinists, poets, and of a generation prior to Martha Marchina.

¹³ Ahmed 2017.

in Roman society of the seventeenth century and may have helped articulate the characteristic standpoint of *Musa Posthuma*, with its remarkable claim to female authority in post-Tridentine Christian thought and its woman-centred critique of classical models and contemporary science in favour of an ethics of care.

Martha Marchina's skills in Latin poetry, and a few epigrams, were praised in Rossi's *Pinacotheca Imaginum Illustrium, Doctrinae vel Ingenii Laude* (Cologne, 1648) and anthologised in Carlo di S. Antonio's *De Arte Epigrammatica, sive de Ratione Epigrammatis Rite Conficiendi, Libellus* (Cologne, 1650), published twelve years before *Musa Posthuma*. Rossi also quotes a monumental epigram to her tomb in Santa Maria in Vallicella. Along with the biographical essay at the beginning of *Musa Posthuma*, these are the records of Martha Marchina's literary career from her lifetime.

Martha Marchina (1600–1646) was a contemporary of Gian Lorenzo Bernini (1598–1680) and Artemisia Gentileschi (1593–1653). She was the daughter of a working-class soap maker from Naples, whose family moved to Rome. By the time she was eight her mother had died and Martha was left in charge of the education of her two brothers, who attended the school run by the Oratorian Fathers at Santa Maria in Vallicella, or the Chiesa Nuova. She also had a sister, Magdalena, who died before the age of seven. By asking her brothers daily what they had learned at school, Martha began to learn Latin second-hand. Her father wanted to encourage her studies as well and asked to borrow Latin books from Father Ludovico Santolino. Santolino refused this request, instructing Martha to cultivate feminine skills of clothing making, weaving and needlework instead. Indeed, in her adult life, Martha Marchina was known for her ability to produce cloth woven with gold.

After several years, Santolino wondered how the brothers were such good students. When he learned that thirteen-year-old Martha was tutoring them, he asked her to write a Latin epigram for him. Noting how polished and elegant the poem was, Santolino began to share Latin books with her. Eventually, after she had demonstrated her ability to compose Latin poetry *ex tempore* under the testing of learned Oratorian men, Cardinal Bernardino Spada became Martha's patron.

The course of Martha Marchina's adult life and literary career is remarkable as well. She did not marry or become a nun, but she did have a vibrant intellectual life under the patronage of the Spada family in Rome and at the Oratorio's Vallicelliana library, the first public library in Rome (est. 1581). Marchina lived out her life in a poor working-class neighbourhood in Rome, between the newly built Chiesa Nuova, completed in 1605, and Sant'Agnese in Agone, along the western edge of the Piazza Navona. Her talent was so pronounced that she was offered several academic positions. First, Santolino offered her a teaching position in Santa Sofia, in Emilia-Romagna (*Pinacoteca* III.237). She reluctantly went to take up this position, travelling with her brother Giuseppe, but he became ill and she returned to Rome (781). Macedo says that next a 'Romae Princeps' offered her a chair in Latin at La Sapienza in Rome, an offer she refused out of maidenly shame (Stevenson 2022: 144). Her patrons offered her placement in two different convents, but, after the Council of Trent, she would have been fully confined to the cloisters and likely would have lost access to Latin. Instead she lived in Rome with her father, cared for children in her family, made perfumed soaps and produced gold embroidery for the Chiesa Nuova, perhaps as a means of income from her patrons,[14] while continuing to write anthologised Latin poetry. Her talent as a Latinist and her connections to the Oratorians thus granted her upward social mobility, as her brother also found, who became an Oratorian priest. Marchina's carefully attained educational and economic autonomy, outside of a traditional social position for women in seventeenth-century Rome, reverberates with the ways Collins theorises Black daughters have used work and education to survive the misogynoir of the USA while rejecting and transcending power relations of domination.[15] Marchina's poetry speaks from her marginalised social position as an unmarried, educated woman and caregiver to make her an 'othermother' who 'mothers the minds' of her audiences and creates a shared community of Marchina and her readers.[16]

In 1662, the Spadas published a posthumous collection of Marchina's poetry, *Musa Posthuma Marthae Marchinae Virginis Neapolitanae*, at Rome, edited by Fr Francisco Macedo, a Jesuit priest, scholar and professor who published over 100 books.[17] The volume is dedicated to Queen Kristina of Sweden and opens with an essay naming Marchina the Tenth Muse.[18] It is not clear if Marchina arranged any of the poems, or if her editor did, and the second half of the volume contains a mixture of letters and poetry produced by Marchina, Cardinal Spada

---

[14] Stevenson 2022: 144–7.
[15] Collins 2000: 183–9.
[16] Ibid. pp. 178–94.
[17] This book had a second edition, with some corrections, printed at Naples in 1701. Following *Project Nota*, I print the 1701 edition of poems with Latin spellings standardised, except where the first edition offers a better reading.
[18] The Tenth Muse became a poetic conceit used for learned women writers and poets. In the seventeenth century alone, Sor Juana Inés de la Cruz became known as the Tenth Muse of Mexico, Anna Maria van Schurman became the Tenth Muse in the Netherlands, Macedo called Marchina the Tenth Muse, and Anne Bradstreet called her 1650 book of English poetry *The Tenth Muse, Lately Sprung up in America*. In the *Palatine Anthology* (9.506), Plato asserts that Sappho is the Tenth Muse, καὶ Σαπφὼ Λεσβόθεν ἡ δεκάτη. See Gosetti-Murrayjohn 2006, who demonstrates that the trope of Sappho as the Tenth Muse became standardised and frequent in Hellenistic epigram.

and other members of his patronage circle.[19] It is also likely that the titles for each poem were produced by Macedo, the editor. The editorial hand seems strongest in the deliberate selection of letters from Cardinal Spada to his brother and to Marchina, from Marchina to Cardinal Spada, and from Marchina to her brother Giuseppe. This mixture of correspondence and literary work is typical for collections of women's writing in Latin in early modern contexts.[20] Throughout, these letters testify to Martha Marchina's profound philological gifts as a writer of Latin, to the admiration Spada has for her talents, and to her own faith.

Musa Posthuma publishes a collection of Marchina's correspondence and poems of her patron and her circle, together with more than 210 of her own poems. These letters offer us a rare insight into how Martha Marchina constructed her self-presentation, her learnedness and her continued connections to her early patron Fr Ludovico Santolino, Cardinal Bernardino Spada and her brother. In her correspondence with Cardinal Spada, Marchina acts ashamed of her meagre poetry, declaring her own work virtually worthless, but expresses this in an elaborate cloak of Baroque modesty (*ad Em. Card. Spadam*, p. 133):[21]

> exilia carmina quamvis non exiguo parta labore, tamen, indocta, parumque expolita & mihi etiam invisa, quae maxime detestor ... amissam iterum lucem aspiciunt.

> These feeble poems, though not produced through meagre effort, nevertheless, unskilled, too little polished, and hateful, even to me, which I utterly detest, see the lost light again.

---

[19] Several pages of the volume represent a poetic contest about the plague at Bologna (Latin Felsina), and competing praise for Bologna and Lucania with its famous rose, including a poem composed by Cardinal Spada to his brother Vergilio Spada, a bishop of the Oratorians (pp. 101–4). Another cluster of humorous poems includes some by Marchina, by Alexander Pollinus, and by anonymous poets on the mice who have eaten away the books containing Caesar's Gallic Wars (pp. 104–8). Stevenson 2022: 156 speculates that Bernardino Spada had intended to publish this volume, but died in 1661. He authored the introductory poem, in Latin and again in Italian, to Queen Kristina of Sweden.

[20] Stevenson 2005: 277–408. On women publishing English Baroque poetry, see Wright 2013 and Waller 2020. On women writing Baroque Italian poetry, see Cox 2008 and 2011.

[21] Marchina's claims of modesty are a trope found in women's published correspondence in Italy in the sixteenth and seventeenth centuries, one confounded by the confidence and directness found in Artemisia Gentileschi's correspondences (Solinas 2020: 48–59). Marchina's claim to lack training and polish (*indocta, parumque expolita*) also mimics misogynist complaints of the period when women speak or write Latin. See Sanson 2014.

Marchina's letters to her brother undermine the degree to which her modest stance can be believed, demonstrating her deep philological knowledge and ability to argue for proper Latin formations from Plautus and Cicero (pp. 139, 142, 143), as does her polymetric display of Horatian metres, Sapphics, epigrams and *versus rapportati* in the collection.[22] The funerary inscription the Oratorian Fathers dedicated to her also notes her wondrous love of knowledge, her skill in writing Latin poetry and her knowledge of Hebrew and Greek.[23]

From Marchina's letters and introductory material in the collection, we know that she became connected to Cardinal Spada because her poems on the plague at Bologna (1630/1) impressed him. We can also date some of her poems very precisely. *Musa Posthuma* contains a series of occasional poems in praise of her patron, Cardinal Bernardino Spada, and other members of the Spada family. Several of the Spada poems welcome Cardinal Spada back to Rome after his administrative work in Bologna, where he was a Papal Legate up until 1633. We also have the evidence of one of Spada's letters to Marchina herself, dated 2 October 1630, from Bologna (p. 104). This letter praises Martha for her deep literary talent and her piety (*et piam, et eruditam expertus, novissime te officiosam agnosco*), which, combined, make her a unique example for the ages of a woman whose skills reside in writing books, with pen and pencil rather than working wool (*raro saeculorum exemplo, ut pro lana librum, pro fuso calamum, stylum pro acu tractare noveris*, p. 104), and that positions her in the company of other learned women such as Cassandra Fedeli (1465–1558).[24] Thus, it is tempting to imagine that many of the poems collected in *Musa Posthuma* are a product of her writing in her thirties. Her poetry to Spada also suggests what may have been a truly close and friendly relationship between patron and poet.

The poems in *Musa Posthuma* reveal Martha's mastery of the epigram and a variety of polymetric lyric metres, her elegant classicising style and her authority as a religious guide. By claiming an authoritative position in largely Christian-focused poems, she advances a feminist agenda within a religious tradition that states that women deserve to be subordinate forever.[25] Throughout, Marchina

---

[22] The majority of Marchina's poems are elegiac. Pages 60–5 and elsewhere include odes in Horatian and Sapphic metres and acrostic poems, and page 69 includes *versus rapportati* on Mary.

[23] Stevenson 2022.

[24] Here, Spada articulates his praise through a quotation from Poliziano speaking about Cassandra Fedeli.

[25] The Council of Trent, in response to the Protestant Reformation, reinforced theological and philosophical traditions of female subjugation, responsibility for original sin, and the necessity for women to be obedient, silent and chaste while devoted to domestic matters (Price and Ristaino 2008: 14–16).

assumes a feminist, woman-centred standpoint that centres embodied affect as a site of knowledge, invites her readers to assume the *personae* of the women of the poems, and, typically, borrows from classical poetry via emulation to replace a patriarchal classical world of divinity with contemplation of Mary's immense power, or that of a woman saint. Marchina's poems give us a Baroque epistemology that also incorporates emerging science of the early modern period, to reject it in favour of Christian contemplation of miracles.[26] The standpoint of this poetry resonates with the 'mother of the mind' Collins outlines, and with Ruddick's maternal standpoint as a peacemaking perspective. I turn now to read several of Martha's religious poems – on Mary, on Saint Katherine of Alexandria and the Milky Way, and on Philip Neri.

In the first poem I read, we enter the manger scene, but now focused through a mother-centred, feminist perspective. Mary, so utterly exhausted from childbirth, wishes for the angels to stop singing their heavenly songs. This poem invites the reader to read as if she were Mary herself (p. 48):

Ad Pueri cunas properant e sedibus altis
    Concinit aethereum turba ministra melos.
Sed gemit heu puer: alterutrum cessare necesse est,
    Seu cantum Aligerum, seu gemitum pueri,
Vos ergo, o superi vestros rogo sistite cantus,   5
    Vox pueri in nostra dulcius aure sonat.
Ast ego quid volui? flebit mea sola voluptas?
    Siste Puer lacrymas, vos canite, ipse gemam.

They hasten to the boy's cradle from lofty seats
the crowd of attendants sings a heavenly melody in harmony.
But alas, the boy is crying: it is necessary for one of these two to stop,
whether it's the songs of the winged Angels, or the groaning of the boy,
well then, you, oh heavenly ones, I ask you, stop your songs,
My baby's voice sounds sweeter in my ear.
But, oh, what did I ask for? Will my only beloved weep?
Stop your tears, my boy, you all sing on, I shall groan.[27]

---

[26] Waller 2020: 17–70 reads the female Baroque in English early modern poetry inspired by Kristeva's 'intimate revolt'. I find a different aesthetic in Marchina's poetry: a matrocentric, care-centred and clearly articulated worldview that employs dominant masculinist, classical, scientific and imperial frameworks to reject them through *care*ful emulation and reception. See Shirley Chapter 2 for further discussion of Waller.

[27] All translations are my own.

In place of contemplating Jesus's birth, or the miraculous songs of angels surrounding the moment, Martha focuses completely on Mary's physical experience as a brand new mother, groaning from exhaustion, overstimulation and perhaps too many visitors. As readers, we sympathise with Mary, whose perspective shapes the poem (MMG). Mary is overwhelmed by too many sounds. She asks the angels (*Aligeri*) to stop singing because her baby boy is crying. Martha normalises a moment of divine epiphany into a fully embodied, utterly human response, and presents an incredibly familiar expression of a new mother's exhaustion. The baby cries (3), she prefers his voice to heavenly choruses (5), she comforts her child (6, 7), and she ends the poem in tears (8). Marchina richly captures a new mother's disorientation in the world, her sensory overload and her priority of the newborn over all else in the world, even when it is a chorus of angels.

Later epigrams echo this matrocentric view of the new baby and elevate a mother's understanding of the world over an authoritarian and patriarchal view of divinity. Even in poems where Mary no longer focalises a poem, we continue to hear a matrocentric view of the baby Jesus. In poem 11, Marchina's use of the diminutive to characterise the newborn baby, and repeated vocabulary for a baby's cries, comforts her audience and extends an ethics of care in place of fear (p. 50):

> Adam se nudum ut vidit, vocemque Tonantis
>   Audiit, heu culpae conscius extimuit.
> Sed nunc ne fugias nudus, timeasque vocantem:
>   En infans vagit nudulus ipse Deus.

> When Adam saw that he was naked, he heard
> the Thunderer's voice, alas, and aware of his sin, he grew afraid.
> But now, don't flee naked, and fear not the one who calls you:
> behold a wee naked babe cries, who is God himself.

The first couplet rehearses the well-known story of Adam's banishment from the Garden of Eden.[28] The Baroque epithet for god as *Tonans* in this poem evokes Jupiter Tonans – Jupiter both in his punitive form, as the one who conquered the Titans and Typhoeus, and in his manifestation as a patriarchal, ruling god of the Roman pantheon, to whom Augustus dedicated a temple of fully marble walls on the Palatine in 26 BCE (Suet. *Div. Aug.* 29). The second couplet resolves the audience's fears, stoked by a punitive, thundering god, and invites them instead to contemplate the divinity of a tiny naked newborn. Martha's diminutive *infans vagit nudulus* invites her readers to celebrate the miracle of babies and to treasure

---

[28] Eve does not appear in *Musa Posthuma*.

Jesus's cuteness (MMG).²⁹ Marchina's poems take an implicitly matrocentric, or better caregiver-centric view, even when Mary is obscured from the poem.

These first poems resonate with Ruddick's reading of maternal thinking as an epistemological standpoint she reads in Hartsock's feminist epistemology as 'caring labor', or 'maternal thinking':

> Caretakers are immersed in the materials of the physical world. The physical phenomena of human and other bodies must be interpreted in relation to the demands of caretaking. It is not useful to abstract to 'air, earth, fire, and water', let alone to electrons. Whether care workers are cleaning toilet bowls . . . whether they nurse a baby, invent a sauce, or mash potatoes thin enough to allow a toothless, elderly person to feed herself, care workers depend on a practical knowledge of the qualities of the material world, including the human bodily world, in which they deal. . . . Finally, caretakers work with subjects: they give birth to and tend self-generating, autonomously willing lives. A defining task of their work is to maintain mutually helpful connections with another person – or animal – whose separateness they create and respect. Hence they are continuously involved with issues of connection, separation, development, change, and the limits of control.³⁰

In these first two poems, Marchina thinks 'maternally', refocusing scenes often presented as sublime epiphanies by asking us to feel Mary the caregiver's physical exhaustion and her wonder at the perfection of a newborn baby, who is paradoxically both a crying, needy human child and a divinity. Her second poem teaches her audience to connect and marvel at the human bodily world as divine, not to fear an abstract and punishing god.

The next poem in my reading again concentrates on Mary's miraculous maternity and highlights a profound ambiguity that the paratext does not clarify. Macedo's extended paratextual material for this poem demonstrates Marchina's gift for profound ambiguity, and her editor's attempt to impose clarity on her ambiguous language and temporalities (p. 49).³¹

---

²⁹ In her use of *nudulus* in *Musa Posthuma* (pp. 50, 55), Marchina seems to get closest to the kitsch sentimentality Maravall 1986: 188 reads as a Baroque aesthetic, where 'the sublime and the anti-climactic, the divine, and the vulgar . . . share a common space'. Waller 2020: 37–9 defines how *kitsch* characterises English early modern women's writing.

³⁰ Ruddick 1989: 130.

³¹ See Jansen 2014 on paratext in classical texts. Wright's 2013: 200–46 study of English women's poetry (1600–1730) invites a comparative reading of Robert Molesworth's posthumous publication of his daughter Mary Molesworth Monck's poetry, where she demonstrates that his editorial agency is not only found in the prefatory material but also in the selection and arrangement of poems.

> *In Christi Natali.*
> *Exiit edictum, ut describeretur universus Orbis.*
> *Ad Romam.*
> *Felicior universi Orbis descriptio.*
>
> Immensus dum Roma tibi describitur Orbis,
>   Quis labor innumeros est numerare homines?
> Unam Virginibus divinam adscribere Matrem
>   Disce, interque homines adnumerare Deum.
>
> *On the birth of Christ*
> *'An edict went out, to take a census of the entire Empire'.*
> *To Rome.*
> *A more fortunate description of the whole world.*
>
> While the immense world is defined for you, Rome,
> What is the effort to count its countless people?
> Learn to assign a single Mother divine among maidens,
> learn to count God among humans.

Here, the poem itself may plausibly refer to the census P. Sulpicius Quirinus, governor of Syria, undertook in 6 CE (*Orbis describi*). The prefatory material to the poem quotes from Luke 2.1 in the Vulgate, <u>*exiit edictum* a Caesare Augusto *ut describeretur universus orbis*</u>, to reinforce this reading. Yet the first couplet may also plausibly refer to the age of discovery, as governments began to control the production of mapmaking and surveying in the age of European colonialism (*immensus describitur Orbis*) and to estimate the world's population (*numerare homines*).[32] The first couplet is inherently ambiguous, and this ambiguity invites Martha to claim the position of authority at Rome she takes up as the poem shifts into its second couplet, an exhortation to the reader.

The second half of the poem dispenses with Marchina's nationalism and her emulation of biblical texts, and carefully displaces the scientific fact of accounting all human lives, however countless they may be, as of less merit than contemplating Mary and Jesus. This poem relies on classical motifs of Roman imperial grandeur to imagine a new world in the age of European colonialism (*Immensus dum Roma tibi describitur Orbis*, 1). Marchina admits how difficult scientific efforts were to calculate the number of people living in the enormous world, made larger

---

[32] Phillip II of Spain, Habsburg emperor, commissioned a detailed survey of Habsburg possessions in southern Italy in 1575 (Wood 2010: 21); mapmaking boomed in mapping New Spain; and the mid-sixteenth century also saw a boom in mapmaking in Italy (Wood 2010: 30n61). Marchina's lifetime saw the invention of the telescope and Galileo's *Nuncius Sidereus* in 1610, and Gerardus Mercator produced the first cylindrical map projection of the world in 1569.

by knowledge of the Americas. Rather than attempting a count of all the people in the world, the poem bids us to learn to recognise that the divine Mother of God is a maiden, and God is a human man. Belief in the miraculous ambiguity of a divine mother and human god replaces scientific attempts at mastery and understanding.

Her four lines elegantly encapsulate the typical architecture of one of Marchina's epigrams. In the first two lines, readers praise Roman grandeur, evoking ancient and contemporary Roman geographical advances. The second couplet restores us to pious concentration on what is truly important, Christian practice and belief. Marchina exhorts her readers to belief and to individual contemplation and prayer. Many of her epigrams and lyrics advance this same argument, replacing scientific study of her moment with the primary importance of religious contemplation and awe. Martha's own second-person addresses to her readers and her characteristic rhetorical questions (MMG) invite the reader to believe Martha's own authority in placing the wonder of Christian devotion ahead of scientific discovery.

Marchina's poetry to Mary ends with a shift to Roman-specific patriotic poetry detailing the miracle of Our Lady of the Snows, or the foundation of Santa Maria Maggiore in Rome (pp. 68–70). The poem celebrates the foundation of the basilica in order to praise Mary as a special patron god of Rome. It may also be associated with the day of the Miracle of Our Lady of the Snows, celebrated annually in Rome on the fifth of August, when white rose petals are showered into the basilica to celebrate the original miracle.[33] In the fourth century, during Liberius's papacy (352–366 CE), John and his wife, a wealthy, childless patrician couple, decided to give their wealth to the Virgin Mary. Mary sent a miracle of snow in August, and the snow fell on the top of the Esquiline Hill, laying out the pattern for the foundation of Santa Maria Maggiore.

In Baroque Italy, women poets often celebrated Mary as a national symbol of pride and as a model for idealised femininity.[34] This poem accomplishes this, while elevating Mary to the highest status as divine saviour for Martha's Roman audience through emulation of classical and Christian epic poetry and hymns. In Martha's poem, she displaces a patriarchal Jupiter as saviour in favour of a conversation between two mother goddesses, *Tellus* or *Roma*, and Mary. Roman Jupiter *Tonans* is supplanted through reference to Lucretian and Vergilian Venus *Genetrix*, or reimagined as the child of Mary, and a patriarchal world of male salvation through destruction gives way to the nourishing, miraculous salvation of the Virgin Mary (p. 68).

---

[33] The *In Dedicatione Basilicae Sanctae Mariae ad Nives* was a local Roman festival from the mid-fourteenth century until Pius V made it part of broader Catholic celebrations in 1568 after the council of Trent.

[34] Cox 2011. See also Waller 2020: 51–8 on Mary in English women's Baroque poetry, and Haskins 2008 on Mary in Baroque Italian epic poetry by women.

Flammigeris Phoebi radiis percussa caloris,
Impatiens tellus, imbres rauco ore dehiscens
Invocat, atque imo depromit pectore voces.
O cui stellifero radiant diademate crines
Regnatrix Coeli, Virgo, summique Tonantis 5
Alma parens, superum decus, ex mortalibus una
Omnipotentis amor, hominum spes unica, vitae
Inventrix, genitrixque Dei, via regia Coeli,
Da pia Virgo nives, dum nos tibi vota, precesque,
Hic ubi consurgunt nivei fastigia templi, 10
Ore damus, dum Roma sacris advolvitur aris:
Roma nives orat: niveis Virgo annue votis.

Struck down by the fiery rays of the heat of Phoebus,
the suffering earth, gasping from her hoarse mouth, prays
for rains, and she pours out her voice from deep in her chest.
'Oh, she whose hair gleams below her starry diadem,
Queen of Heaven, Virgin, nourishing mother
of the high Thunderer, glory of the gods, lone among mortals,
love of the All-powerful, single hope of men,
Creator of life, mother of God, royal road to heaven,
give us snow, Virgin, while we make offerings and prayers to you,
here where the roofline of the snow-white temple rises up,
we pray with pious mouths, while Rome falls prostrate before sacred altars:
Rome prays for snow; to our snowy prayers, Virgin, consent'.

Marchina's ekphrastic description embodies the parched earth. Her language is rich with classical epic and Christian epic resonance, as is her representation of the earth as suffering and speaking. As Tellus suffers, she pours out her voice from deep in her chest (*imo pectore voces*), an epic *locus* found at Catullus 64, in the *Aeneid*, and *Argonautica* 6.496, and from its later reappearance in Christian poetry. The Latin version of *Paradise Lost* uses a similar phrase, but Marchina's text also parallels Aquilinus Juvencus's fourth-century *Evangeliorum libri*, composed in hexameters: *Christus item sancto depromit pectore vocem* (4.348).[35] The iconography of the earth gasping and crying out for rain, for me, most closely recalls the burning Earth's suffering prayer to Jupiter in Ovid's *Metamorphoses* (2.272–300), as Phaethon's cataclysmic ride in the chariot of the sun engulfs the world in fire. We hear the Roman land (*Tellus*) speaking for the Roman people

---

[35] See Cat. 64.125; *Aen.* 1.371, 5.409, 11.377, 11.840; Lucan 2.285; Paul. Nol. *Carm.* 6.42; and Avit. *Carm.* 5.576.

(*Roma*, 1), and praying to Mary for help ending a terrible heat and drought. Her prayer to Mary deploys the language of classical Roman epic to invoke Christian figures. Tellus or Roma's cultic epithets assimilate Mary to Venus *Genetrix*, especially as Aeneas's mother, and as Lucretius's cosmogonic force of creation. Mary is invoked as *alma parens*, using the Vergilian epithet (*Aen.* 2.591), and as the Lucretian *genetrix* (see Lucr. 1.1), and *vitae inventrix* (see Lucr. 1.4–5). These epithets blend ancient Roman epic names for Rome's nourishing patron goddess with the language of Catholic prayers such as the *Salve Regina* and the Litany of Loreto, where Mary is addressed as *Sancta Dei genetrix*.[36] Jesus takes on the name of Jupiter, as *summi Tonantis* (5). The image connects Marchina's Jesus not only to classical gods, but also may be an allusion to Lorenza Strozzi's *Ode in Purificationem Beatae Mariae Virginis*, a hymn by a woman poet published in Florence in 1588 and reprinted and translated across Europe, which begins with *Mater Tonantis Maximi | Virgo*, 'Mother of the greatest Thunderer, Maiden'.

Marchina's poem draws on classicising epithets, turns of phrase and scenes to transform patriarchal classical epic moments into a salvatory prayer between mother goddesses, both creators and nourishers of humanity, whose people are suffering. Where Ovid's *Tellus* sought help from Jupiter, whose lightning bolt will end Phaethon's fiery cataclysm (*Met.* 2.279, 308), Marchina's *Tellus* will be given a more peaceful end to heat and drought by the miraculous snowstorm that Mary sends to Rome in August. In the course of the poem, Marchina subverts a classical hierarchy of Olympian power, quelling the patriarchal power of the flaming sun god, *flammiger Phoebus* (1), under the power of a prayerful Mother Earth, and her appeal to all-powerful Mary, *hominum spes unica* (7), who becomes queen and ruler of heaven, *Regnatrix Coeli* (5), in place of a classical Jupiter. Marchina's poem fittingly places Mary as the source of celestial power in a poem in praise of a uniquely Roman miracle. A Marian-centred hymn draws from Marchina's classical epic sources to argue for Mary's unique power and to tantalisingly place Mary, as mother goddess and cosmogonic force, as the most significant god in Martha's Rome.

After reading these poems, our MMG noted that Marchina's epigrams often share a standard poetic architecture. The first couplet presents us with the ancient classical world, or the contemporary political situation of Rome at the head of a changing, expanding world. At times, contemporary Rome is evoked through classicising language that places Rome at the centre of a great world empire, in terms redolent of Horatian (*Carm.* 3.30) and Ovidian panegyric (*Met.* 15.871–

---

[36] The *Litaniae Lauretanae* are probably a French prayer c. 1150–1200. They were approved for public use by Pope Sixtus V in 1587, and the prayer is still developing: in 2020, Pope Francis added three additional epithets, *Mater misericordiae, Mater spei, Solacium migrantium*.

9) of Rome. The second couplet poses a rhetorical question, either explicitly or implicitly, or directly addresses the reader in a second-person imperative. This second couplet also then denies the epistemological frameworks of the classical world in favour of a Christian devotion to Mary and Jesus.

Musa Posthuma is also unique in Italian women's poetry of the Baroque period because of the number of women saints Martha celebrates. She focuses twenty-one of her poems explicitly on female saints and martyrs, and at least twenty on the Virgin Mary. This number of distinct women saints brings her attention to women saints beyond any of her contemporary Italian women writers, even as devotional literature exploded as a growth industry in printed texts in early modern Italy.[37] Her poem on Saint Catherine of Alexandria and the creation of the Milky Way is characteristic, focusing on a particularly emotionally charged moment in a saint's life, as the poem blurs the distinction between the human body of the saint, its experiences, feelings, and the natural world.

Saint Catherine of Alexandria, associated with the wheel, was martyred by the Emperor Maxentius in 305 CE. Catherine was a Christian living during Maxentius's persecutions, who asked Maxentius to stop torturing Christians and demonstrated her considerable skill as a philosopher and scholar. Maxentius is said to have brought pagan scholars to debate her; she not only won the debate but inspired several of these pagan philosophers to convert to Christianity, and later also converted many of her jailers. The emperor condemned Catherine to die on the wheel after she refused his attempt to seduce her, but by her request, an angel destroyed the wheel or wheels. Eventually, a *lictor* beheaded Catherine.[38] The tales of her *passio* include at least three moments of victimisation: imprisonment, intended torture by the spiked wheel, and eventual execution. Rather than detailing these elements of her life, and instead of calling attention to the gore of a beheading or to a sexualised representation of Catherine's beauty, Martha's poem focuses on a miracle that occurred during Catherine's execution.[39] Instead of blood, when the *lictor* decapitated her, milk flowed

---

[37] This devotional literature encouraged more religious individualism and greater piety. Many texts presented the lives of the saints, legends of the holy family, devotional texts to the virgin Mary, and the saying of the Rosary alongside an increasing number of vernacular editions of the Bible (Martin 2002: 33). Cox 2011: 69–71, on Lucrezia Marinella's 1603 *Rime Sacre*, notes that Marinella includes seventeen poems to women saints, as does Strozzi in her 1588 *Hymni*.

[38] See Jenkins and Lewis 2003: 7–10 on Saint Katherine in the west; this re-telling comes from the eleventh-century Vulgate version of Saint Katherine's legend, probably emerging in Normandy, and elaborated on in the *Legenda aurea*.

[39] Ferrari's c. 1525 *Martyrdom of Saint Catherine of Alexandria* at the Brera Pinacoteca, Hieronymus Franken II's 1607–23 *Martyrdom of Saint Catherine of Alexandria* at the Royal Museum of Fine Arts Antwerp and Signorelli's 1490 *Martyrdom of Saint Catherine of Alexandria* at the Clark Museum of Art offer several sensationalised versions of Catherine's martyrdom in European painting.

from her neck. Martha's poem invites her audience to contemplate this moment and to believe in this miracle. Further, Martha catasterises Catherine's bodily fluids, and then all of Catherine, during and after her martyrdom. According to this poem, the miracle of Catherine's milk that flowed from her body in place of blood will replace the astronomical phenomenon of the Milky Way and form a pathway to heaven for Catherine. As she has done in the Assumption of Mary poems, Marchina elevates Catherine to the heavens (p. 75).

> D. Catharinae V. & M.
> GALAXIA.
>
> Dum caput invictum crudeli abscinditur ense,
>   Gutture Virgineo flumina lactis eunt.
> Mirum hoc quis credat Virgo? Num sanguine ab ipso
>   Barbarica incessit Militis ora rubor?
> An tibi, dum dirae calcas pede limina mortis,   5
>   Panditur ad coeli sidera lactis iter?
> Vel potius coelo Virgo addis sidera, namque
>   Hoc quota fonte cadit guttula, stella cadit?
> Lacteus e mediis discedat circulus astris,
>   Hoc melius Coeli flumen in axe micat.   10

While the unconquered head is cut away by the cruel sword,
rivers of milk flow from the Virgin's neck.
Who could believe this miracle, Virgin? Was it from the blood itself
that the blush advanced on the barbarous face of the soldier?
Or for you, while you step over the threshold of this cruel death
does a milky path open up to the stars of heaven?
Or better you add stars to the heaven, Virgin, for
as many drops fall from this source, so many stars set?
Let the milky way yield its place from the midst of the stars,
better this river twinkles in the axes of Heaven.

Marchina's poem presents a new Christian aetiology for this galaxy and asks the classical world, and contemporary scientific interest in the stars, to yield to mystical Christian contemplation. Line 3, *Mirum hoc quis credat Virgo*, is a typical rhetorical question in Martha's poetry that asks audiences as much as the formal addressee to believe in Martha's epistemological position of authority. She presents us with a vivid, multi-sensory image that eschews gore or bodily objectification in favour of the miraculous: the blameless head is cut away (1), streams of milk flow from the neck (2), and there is no blood. The only blood in the poem is the blush that colours the executioner's face (3–4). Next Marchina's poem shifts to the cosmic: we move from Earth, humanity and an unjust state to the cosmic, divine and heavenly. Marchina imagines Catherine quite physically crossing the threshold of death and walking onto the streams of milk that create a pathway to heaven for her (5–7). This miracle will endure in perpetuity in the night sky. Martha Marchina's poem gives us a woman-authored, Christian reimagining of a catasterism, whence Catherine can intercede for humans as an eternal being among the stars.[40]

Marchina's etymological and exploratory riffing on names of the constellation and her claim for Catherine's primacy in establishing this celestial phenomenon displace ancient and contemporary scientific interest in the Milky Way. Marchina's word choices activate various terms that have been associated with the Milky Way, as the Galaxy (*Kuklos Galaxias*, in Eratosthenes), as a river (*flumina lactis*), as a path to heaven (*iter ad coeli sidera*, see Roman *via coeli regia*) and as the *circulus lacteus* (Plin. *HN* II.23.91).[41] In 1610, in the *Nuncius Sidereus*, Galileo had concluded that the Milky Way was 'nothing but a mass of countless stars planted together in clusters', *est enim GALAXIA nihil aliud, quam innumerarum Stellarum coacervatim consitarum congeries* (34). It is characteristic of Marchina's sacred poetry that she alludes to contemporary scientific breakthroughs while continuing to place her belief, and her advice to her readers, in Christian contemplation and faith. While the miracle of blood to milk is associated with other martyrs' lives, the poem connects to Marchina's broader interest in the particularity of female bodies' capacity to produce milk, become pregnant, and give birth, and in women saints and Mary as celestial sources of authority and of virtuous knowledge.[42]

In her poems on Mary and Catherine, Martha Marchina reaffirms the epistemological authority of 'caring labor' by valuing affect, sensation, mutual connection with others, and physical, embodied experiences as sources of knowing. Marchina's poems also 'mother the minds' of her audiences, inviting us in to empathise with the women who focalise these poems, to form a shared community which values these women's deeds, and to reinterpret ancient Roman poetic sources in light of Marchina's standpoint of care and connection.

Her architecture, shifting from ancient world to modern one, often looks like a shift from the classical world to a Christian worldview, as in the Catherine poem. Martha makes the same move in several poems focused on modern Roman contemporaries – as in her poem on Philip Neri, which will conclude my readings. These poems demonstrate Martha's wit, her capacity for wordplay, her deep

---

[40] Marchina's poem may allude to the classical myth of Juno, who nursed the infant Hercules. When he bit her, Juno released the nursing baby and sprayed breastmilk into the stars, forming the Milky Way.

[41] Allen 1963: 474–84.

[42] Indeed, Marchina's first poem on Catherine (*de Quinquaginta Viris*, p. 74) puns repeatedly on teaching and learning as childbirth and breastfeeding. Catherine birthed fifty Christians from her teachings (*partu, peperit*, 1, 4), her virgin body has a fertile womb (*sinus*, 2), and she did not nurse the converted philosophers with her breasts (*non nutriit ubere*, 4) but with her blood (*vulnere alit*, 5).

knowledge of the Roman poetic tradition and her focus on embodied sensation in her poetry (p. 91).

> Delicias Nerius divini ut sensit Amoris
>   In se de Cœli fontibus influere;
> Jam satis est, inquit, vestros rogo claudite fontes,
>   O Superi, angustos obruit unda sinus.
> Ipse ego, mutato fiam si nomine Nereus, 5
>   Non capit Oceanum hunc pectoris urna mei.
> Risit divus Amor, fractis dum pectore costis
>   Laxat, et in tales explicat ora sonos.
> Parva satis, nimiumque licet sit pectoris urna,
>   Hac tamen ex urna flumina mille fluent. 10

> When Neri felt the delights of divine love
> flow into him from the springs of heaven;
> that is enough already, he said, I ask you, close your streams,
> oh Heavenly ones, the surge overwhelms my narrow banks.
> Even if I should myself become Nereus, with my name changed,
> the vessel of my chest cannot contain this Ocean.
> Divine Love laughed, while he loosens
> the broken ribs in my chest, and he extends my mouth to such sounds.
> Small is enough, even if the vessel of my heart may be too small,
> still from this vessel a thousand rivers may flow.

In this poem for Philip Neri (1515–1595), the saint of joy and founder of the Congregation of the Oratory, an order of secular priests and laypeople, religious reverence for miracles in his life mingles with transformation, wordplay and Baroque corporealised religious experience, and demonstrates Marchina's skill in emulation.[43] Marchina's poem focuses on a miracle in the life of Neri. During

---

[43] Sor Juana Inés de la Cruz 1951: 170–1, a Mexican nun, writer, and feminist foremother, also demonstrates a Baroque interest in transformation, and wordplay in her poem about Mary:

> Nōmine māternō, mūtātā parte, Camilla
>   dīcitur ut Triviam, digna ministra, cōlat.
> Tōtum nōmen ego, Triados quae ancilla Parentis
>   mūtō: tōta in Avē vertitur Hēva mihi.
> Nec mūtāsse satis nōmen; mūtāsse parentem
>   gaudeō: mē prōlem Grātia māter habet.
> Namque Annae sum nāta, dēdit cui Grātia nōmen;
>   Grātia cui Prōlēs, cui sine lābe genus;
>
> flōs īdem hūmānō generī, vīvum decus. Inde
> prō Ancillā, Mātrem mē vocat ipse Deus.

the autopsy performed after his death, it was discovered Neri had broken several ribs and that his heart was enlarged. This was explained as a religious miracle, that he had been praying in 1545, and had been so filled with divine love that his heart had grown and his ribs had expanded to increase his capacity. As in Martha's Catherine poem, Martha brings us to the moment this miracle occurred and into the mystical physical experience of Neri. Divine love is embodied as the unconstrained flow of water through streams, waves, oceans and rivers (*fontes, unda, Oceanum, flumina*, 2, 3, 6, 10). Marchina continues the metaphor through her choice of ambiguous vocabulary, equating human bodies and objects that contain water, most conspicuously in the phrases *angustos sinus*, used both for the area of the ribcage in the human body and for a river bank, and in the repeated *urna*, vessel, in place of *cor*.

Marchina's poem exploits Ovidian amatory verse to describe Neri's experience of mystical, playful, religious joy. As in *Amores* 1.1, Amor laughs, and transforms the physical body of the one inspired by his divine love to create a body properly shaped for his new vocation, founding the Oratorians instead of writing as an elegiac poet-lover. As in *Amores* 1.1, Amor's love manifests in a violent incursion against the body: he expands Neri's broken ribs and stretches his face (or his mouth) to make it able to produce worshipful praise. Marchina's poem here best encapsulates the aesthetic that Jane Stevenson has termed 'the quasi-erotic pietism of the Baroque', where mystical religious fervour is figured in embodied language redolent of Roman love elegy.[44]

Throughout this chapter, I have sought to introduce readers to Martha Marchina's baroque Latin poetry and to highlight the many ways Marchina incorporates classical Latin poetry or emerging science of her period into her matrocentric, woman-focused religious poetry. Marchina's poetry operates, I have proposed, from an epistemology of care that interpolates its audience into a shared community that marvels at and values the knowledge the embodied experiences of Mary, women saints and Philip Neri can bring. The standpoint of Marchina's poems may emerge from her social position as a working-class, pious, unmarried, educated woman. Marchina's poetry performs the work of community othermothers in Collins's language, assuming a seat of power within an ethics of care that seeks to transform matrices of religious or social domination into relationships of mutual learning and joy from mind to mind.

---

[44] Stevenson 2005: 310.

CHAPTER 15

'Grey' Rape on the Silver Screen: Rapes of Enslaved People in Mass Media about the Ancient World

Anise K. Strong

While frequently depicting the ancient Mediterranean world as a sexually debauched society of wealthy elites dominating households full of submissive enslaved people, modern mass media often refuses to address the question of whether enslaved people can ever meaningfully consent to sex with their enslavers. Even more problematically, sex with enslaved women is often used in these films and television series as a means of softening or romanticising the treatment of slavery itself. Love and sex provides an easy means for such characters to escape the evils of forced labour and abuse, without consideration of the assault on their bodily integrity and their inability to consent. The multiple intersecting identities of such characters as enslaved people, as women and, frequently, as dark-skinned women are often inscribed on the screen to reinforce a visual representation of them as subordinate, inferior and willing.[1] Yet while they initially appear to serve as epistemic objects of a presumed male gaze, such women often, as theorised by Cahill and Pohlhaus Jr, instead follow the model of the derivatised. They may appear initially to exist only within the contexts that service and pleasure the male protagonist characters, yet they are capable of defying those limits, even if it then causes them to be perceived as 'dangerously rebellious'.[2]

Both eroticised, sentimentalised versions of forcible intercourse as well as violent, highly negative depictions of rape and sexual abuse form key parts of the

---

[1] On intersectionality theory, see Crenshaw 2017. As applied to film and television, see Sutherland and Feltey 2007.
[2] Cahill: 32; Pohlhaus Jr: 104–5.

reception of sexual violence and the ancient world. However, in this chapter I mostly focus on the depiction of allegedly romantic master–slave relationships and how such narratives complicate issues of the representation of consent, desire and objectification, both in antiquity and in modern understandings. It is harder to read between the lines to elicit the perspectives of fictional characters in these texts, as the modern creators were generally elite men. However, we can embark upon an examination of how these dominant external narratives of such relationships construct and offer frameworks for the audience's own self-understandings regarding sexual power dynamics, as well as their conceptions of ancient Roman societies.[3] This chapter listens to the silences of such enslaved women survivors and documents how their body languages tell different stories than the words of the men who sexually use them, by utilising Fricker and Medina's theories of pre-emptive silencing and epistemic objectification.[4]

In the early twenty-first century, two quite different television series about the ancient Roman world premiered on cable television: HBO's *Rome* (2005–7), about the fall of the Roman Republic, and STARZ's *Spartacus* (2010–14), about the slave revolt sparked in the Capuan gladiatorial school of Batiatus in 73–71 BCE. While these series differed substantially in their themes, budgets and artistic styles, both chose to begin their representation of Roman society with scenes involving sexual coercion. *Rome*'s first introduction to the major character of Mark Antony, at the beginning of its second episode, depicts him stopping on an urgent trip back to Rome to casually rape an anonymous, silent 'Peasant Woman' by the side of the road. Three other main characters, Octavian, Vorenus and Pullo, wait on the road for him to finish his assault. They seem mildly annoyed by the delay and Antony's fist-pumps of triumph but raise no objections or concerns about the actual act of violence. The audience is led to believe that, at a minimum, this act is simply standard behaviour for Antony, who does not even bother to remove his helmet. The anonymous peasant woman never appears again, nor is there ever any chance for her to offer her perspective.

In *Spartacus: Blood and Sand*, sexual assault is also featured in the audience's first substantial introduction to Batiatus and Lucretia, the married couple who own the gladiatorial school and whose workplace struggles form one major plot element of the first season.[5] While discussing their economic intrigues to expand their business, Lucretia suggests sex to Batiatus. At this point, her husband notes that he 'needs yet more stroking'. She gestures to a female enslaved woman of colour, who promptly drops to her knees to begin performing oral sex upon Batiatus, while a different enslaved woman of colour

---

[3] Thornham 2007: 19. See also Sutherland and Feltey 2007: 3.
[4] Fricker 2007: 141 and Medina 2013: 4–5.
[5] *Spartacus: Blood and Sand*. 2010. '*Sacramentum Gladiatorum*'. STARZ.

proceeds to massage Lucretia's own genitals underneath her dress. While the couple enthusiastically plans a future party, sharing their own narratives and dreams for the future, the silent enslaved women arouse them until, eventually, Lucretia and Batiatus brush aside their assistants and make passionate, consensual love with each other. This entire scene is presented from the elite couple's perspective, with the enslaved women being depicted and used as little more than sex toys. Although some of those enslaved women's stories were later developed and elaborated until they became central characters, they began the series as auxiliary accessories.

While themes of rape and consent form central concerns for the *Spartacus* series in general, this character introduction uses the coerced sexual acts of the enslaved women largely as set dressing to showcase the emotional and economic partnership of Lucretia and Batiatus. While not as obviously violent as Antony's rape of the peasant woman, I still describe these forced acts of arousal as rape, since the performers are enslaved women neither asked for their consent nor able to give it meaningfully. At the same time, these acts challenge the more traditional views of Roman – and often modern Western – sexuality as defined by the narrow roles of the active, superior partner and the passive, inferior partner, most typically a man penetrating a woman vaginally.[6] Lucretia and Batiatus possess all the power in this scene, but they use it to order others to take an active if traditionally humiliating sexual role and thus complicate and violate paradigmatic hierarchical axes of both power and gender.

These two relatively recent scenes of sex in the ancient Roman world, while quite distinct in their depiction and levels of eroticisation, both evoke the common popular belief that ancient Mediterranean societies were both dens of debauchery and societies with vastly unequal power structures in which elites used their power to control the bodies and actions of the disempowered. The combination of these tropes frequently leads to the depiction in mass media of scenes of sexual harassment and assault against enslaved or impoverished women and sometimes men, often as a metaphor for the larger evils of imperialism and slavery.

The ancient Mediterranean setting is often used as a justification for highly eroticised scenes of sexual coercion or assault, creating an impression that rape in the Roman Empire was a ubiquitous part of everyday life. This impression is often justified by reference to the fictive ideas of ancient culture established by earlier mass media, rather than to the historical record. Infamously, the *Game of Thrones* creators, Benioff, Weiss and George R. R. Martin, claimed that the frequent rapes in their medieval themed series were just an attempt to be historically accurate, despite the fact that the fantasy series also included dragons and magical

---

[6] The clips and images discussed in this paper are available at https://drive.google.com/drive/folders/1GU9cHmwQWlQgIDEOs7BNm1D4sZ-BbT6N?usp=sharing.

resurrection.⁷ Such false beliefs have actual consequences: 90 per cent of British teenagers surveyed by Kate Lister in 2017 believed that the depiction of ubiquitous sexual violence in *Game of Thrones* was historically accurate.⁸ Portraying the sexual assault of non-elites, especially enslaved people, in the ancient Roman world inevitably taints our understandings of complex and nuanced cultures. It also inextricably links rape with other major tropes associated with ancient Roman society, such as imperialism and luxury, and deprivileges the experiences and knowledge of enslaved people by rendering them as either helpless victims or as fully consenting lovers despite their inability to offer meaningful consent.

While historically accurate rape statistics for the ancient Mediterranean are impossible to calculate, legal texts make clear that rape of freeborn citizens was both an active concern and frequently prosecuted, while the rape of enslaved people is largely ignored. For instance, Ulpian describes sexual assault (*stuprum*) against either a man or woman as a public crime that, unlike other crimes, does not have a statute of limitations for prosecution (unlike modern American rape standards).⁹ One major distinction between ancient Roman perceptions of the likelihood of rape and modern American or British ones regards the gender of the victims; both Greek and Roman texts are particularly concerned about the vulnerability of young men and boys to sexual violence from other older men, a 'historical reality' that is almost never depicted in modern mass media, or, for that matter, much modern scholarship.¹⁰ While James Arieti, in 1997, could firmly declare while writing about rape in the works of the Roman historian Livy that 'rape is the sexual violation of a woman', Livy and other authors demonstrate clearly that young men and the parents of boys actively feared their sexual assault.¹¹

Before examining specific depictions of the rape of enslaved people in modern mass media about the ancient world, it is necessary to define what will count as 'rape'. What does it mean to sexually assault someone in the cinematic or historical Roman world? By one common feminist definition, any sexual act between a free person and a slave is rape since the slave cannot meaningfully consent. Furthermore, as generally accepted by most feminist scholars, the motive for rape is

---

⁷ Itzkoff 2014b, quoting Martin: 'An artist has an obligation to tell the truth. My novels are epic fantasy, but they are inspired by and grounded in history. Rape and sexual violence have been a part of every war ever fought, from the ancient Sumerians to our present day. To omit them from a narrative centred on war and power would have been fundamentally false and dishonest'.
⁸ Lister 2017: 3.
⁹ *Dig.* XLVIII 5, 30, 9. See Bauman 1993: 550–66.
¹⁰ Others in this volume who discuss the epistemological frameworks that underlie sexual and physical violence (especially the epistemology of rape) include McHardy (Chapter 4), Witzke (Chapter 7), Haley (Chapter 9), Bowen (Chapter 10) and Freas (Chapter 11).
¹¹ See Livy 8.28, Val. Max. 6.1 and Dion. Hal. 16.5.1–3. See also Richlin 1993b: 536; Marshall 2015: 124; and Strong 2021; contra Arieti 1997: 216–19.

patriarchal violence and domination, rather than desire for sexual intercourse.[12] However, such a perspective has not been the normative view among slaveholders in most historical slaveholding societies. Brownmiller notes that an 1851 Louisiana Supreme Court case alleged that in sexual relationships between male masters and female slaves, 'it is so rare in the case of concubinage that the seduction and temptation are not mutual', although the opinion does admit that female slaves are 'vulnerable to the seductions of an unprincipled master'.[13] Even American white abolitionists spoke of 'illicit passion' rather than 'sexual violence'.[14]

At the same time, there is obviously a strong argument against accepting the perspective of either slaveowners or modern elite men upon such sexual relations. What is clear is that masters' sexual abuse of their enslaved victims has been ubiquitous in every slave society, most certainly including the ancient Romans. While Roman slavery was not ethnically based, it was a dominant part of the Roman economy and society, both in history and in its depiction in mass media. We have little direct evidence of historical Roman masters sexually abusing their slaves, but the general omission from elite male-authored texts does not lead to the conclusion that it rarely happened. We do have substantial legal and literary evidence of intercourse between free people and their formerly enslaved freedmen and freedwomen, often with the presumption that a relationship began well before freedom was obtained, as well as the frequent presence of apparently enslaved people as observing servants in lovemaking scenes, even if there are few explicit references to free people having sex with enslaved people.[15] The surviving testimonies about such relationships reveal testimonial injustice themselves in focusing almost entirely on the perspectives either of the male enslaver or on the presumed jealousy of his wife, although some recent work attempts to read between the lines to consider how the enslaved people themselves might have understood their situations. Previous scholarship has, for instance, examined the tombstones honouring a favoured enslaved child, a '*delicatus*' or '*delicata*', while trying to imagine the perspective of that child, claiming that they were possibly although not necessarily a survivor of sexual abuse.[16] At the same time, regardless of age, both the

---

[12] Donat and d'Emilio 1992: 9–2.
[13] Brownmiller 1976: 153.
[14] Ibid. p. 154.
[15] Clarke 1998: 103; Perry 2014: 92.
[16] Laes 2003: 310–12; 2017: 61. While I include this scholarship as relevant, I note that Laes, some of whose theories are based heavily on the work of a scholar convicted on child pornography charges, repeatedly justifies these doubly imbalanced relationships (free/enslaved, adult/child) by arguing that modern norms cannot be applied to the ancient Mediterranean. That said, he does agree on the basic point that 'the use of young slaves for sex-ual purposes from the point of view of human rights is abuse' (2017: 63), while leaving open the possibility of praiseworthy consensual relationships between adult enslavers and enslaved, contrary to my argument above.

ancient Romans themselves and modern mass media often distinguish between forcible rape and the more commonplace master–slave sexual relations in which slaves could not meaningfully consent. Baird critiques this approach in modern scholarship as part of a general tendency to soften the representations of ancient Mediterranean slavery and accept an ancient elite devaluation of enslaved experiences.[17] Thus Peter Keegan, for instance, describes the 'little slave boys of Sulla's potent freedman' as well educated and elegant, echoing Cicero's words, without addressing the ways in which Cicero is rhetorically sexualising and objectifying these children to win his case.[18] However, he also traces the graffiti left by some of these 'page boys', whom he reads as choosing to celebrate their own attractiveness and roles as '*pueri*' in the admittedly extraordinarily privileged setting of the Imperial *familia*.[19] Irrespective of the arguments about changes between ancient and modern perspectives about ideas of sexual consent, this chapter illuminates how films and television created in the twentieth and twenty-first centuries, in full knowledge of modern American and British sexual norms during that period, choose to represent such relationships. In the process, it illustrates how the Othering of ancient Rome is used to justify transgressing those norms in favour of an erotic fantasy of 'authenticity'.

Unsurprisingly, representations have also changed over the last seventy-five years in both portrayal and level of explicitness, from the relatively demure depictions of the 1951 *Quo Vadis* to the full-frontal nudity and simulated sex of *Spartacus: Blood and Sand*. Such scenes are offered up for the viewing pleasure of the audience in different eras, although they also serve to condemn or celebrate both particular characters and classical Mediterranean society in general. Hollywood appears to generally be more indulgent of fantasies of sexual violence in the more permissible context of the ancient world, seemingly allowable due to their alleged 'historical accuracy'. As feminist and Marxist views have themselves become more prevalent over the last seventy years, so too do these films and television shows begin, grudgingly in some cases, to consider the unique perspective and standpoint of enslaved women themselves upon the institutions that oppress them as well as questions of false consciousness.[20] In particular, feminist postmodernist theory can be usefully applied to the depiction of enslaved Roman women who become free, demonstrating a radical change in social identity and status that nevertheless in these works does not usually alter their

---

[17] Baird 2015: 166.
[18] Keegan 2013: 74.
[19] Keegan: 82.
[20] Jost and Banaji 1994: 2–3. Others in this volume who give standpoint readings or use standpoint theory as an interpretative lens include Weiberg (Chapter 2), Gilbert (Chapter 3), Nally (Chapter 5), Witzke (Chapter 7), Haley (Chapter 9), Bowden (Chapter 12) and Zimmermann Damer (Chapter 14).

depiction as sexual objects but does offer a derivatisation of them that might complicate this picture.[21]

The following case studies analyse the depiction of non-violent sexual assault of enslaved people and non-elites by free Roman elites in order to consider how such scenes either normalise or problematise ancient Mediterranean slavery. Such romanticisation – both in terms of idealising and of adding romance – of ancient Roman slavery has a long history. For instance, in the 1951 hit *Quo Vadis*, one of the two 'healthy', positively depicted relationships involves Petronius, the historical famous Roman author and politician, and his enslaved woman Eunice. Petronius initially cheerfully offers Eunice as a sex slave to his relative Marcus, demanding that she turn around to display her body for Marcus's perusal and ordering that she be sent to Marcus's apartment for his pleasure.[22]

Eunice, however, speaks up in fervent protest of this gift, not because she is reluctant to have sex but because she is in love with Petronius himself, exclaiming, 'Whip me! Beat me! But don't send me from here, don't send me from you, my lord!'[23] Marcus refuses the offer of Eunice, since he has already developed a desire for the freeborn Christian hostage Lygia, whom he previously sexually harassed when he presumed her to be enslaved. However, Petronius insists on giving Eunice five lashes in any case 'for her impertinence'. Eunice enthusiastically agrees to the whipping as long as she can remain under Petronius's control. After she is dismissed and presumably beaten, Eunice finds a white marble bust of Petronius which she passionately kisses while proclaiming her love, thus temporarily reversing Petronius's explicit objectification of her. Later in the film, she eagerly dies by suicide along with Petronius even after he has freed her.

The entire relationship is portrayed as one of besotted devotion on Eunice's part and careless pleasure on that of Petronius, with no depiction of Eunice's inability to give any sort of meaningful consent given her servile status and explicit threats of corporal punishments or sale. No reason is ever given for why Eunice loves a much older enslaver who casually offers her body up to his friends, describes her in terms of the number of horses she is worth, and seems utterly unaware of her feelings. Even her momentary act of defiance in attempting to choose her preferred sexual partner is met with violent punishment, with no suggestion within the film of such treatment as immoral or unethical. Scodel and Bettenworth note that in the 1925 silent version of *Quo Vadis*, Petronius indeed only begins to desire Eunice when he watches her being beaten.[24] The music, dialogue and body language of these scenes in both versions all contrive to suggest that Petronius and Eunice have

[21] Hekman 1997: 358–9.
[22] Clip 1: https://drive.google.com/file/d/1_gQjyzpcScGRvJ1Wjv3iTW0Ti2YH8Y4d/view?usp=sharing.
[23] *Quo Vadis* 1951.
[24] Scodel and Bettenworth 2009: 60.

an admirable, epic romance marred only by their mutual suicide due to pressure from the evil Nero. At the same time, no hint of sexual acts take place on screen in the 1951 film, which carefully adheres to the Hays Production Code, so any actual rape remains merely implicit. Even the debauched Nero also has a devoted, besotted enslaved woman who loves him, the courtesan Acte, who is shown to be more loyal than his guards or his wife Poppaea Sabina; her devotion is depicted as admirable rather than insane.

The *Quo Vadis* relationship between Petronius and Eunice may be conceptualised as a classical case of what has often been labelled as 'grey rape', a term popularised mainly by antifeminist activists and scholars used to describe 'sex that is somewhere between consent and denial' or 'the ambiguous zone between sexual assault and bad sex'.[25] Alison Futrell notes that evil, decadent elites and virtuous Christian or enslaved Romans are often distinguished by whether they perform heteronormative, bland sex or 'bad sex' – decadent, oppressive, non-procreative intercourse with questionable consent.[26] 'Bad sex' can perhaps be expanded and elaborated here to any presumptively non-consensual intercourse between Roman elites and non-elites, yet not all relationships between elites and non-elites are depicted as 'bad'.

On one level, any implied sex between Petronius and Eunice appears to happen with the enthusiastic consent of both parties; this is true both for the 1951 film and earlier and later versions of the film and the book.[27] At the same time, Eunice in fact has no means to either affirmatively choose or refuse a relationship with Petronius, who as her enslaver explicitly controls her body. By depicting a mutually romantic relationship between enslaver and enslaved, while also paralleling such a romance with the one between the freeborn hostage Lygia and the Roman soldier Marcus Vinucius, *Quo Vadis* suggests that there is no meaningful distinction between such relationships and those between people without such disparate levels of power. In turn, the evils of slavery itself are also undercut, at least for women, as Eunice seems to be able to achieve her sole objective, a relationship with the man she loves, at the price of a few lashes which she happily accepts. While Petronius never commits violent sexual assault, this is not a healthy or functional romance.

As an audience, even an audience of the early 1950s, the knowledge of the harsh realities of ancient slavery is also undermined by this fiction in which an enslaved woman willingly trades abuse in return for affection. While Eunice's passionate monologue to Petronius's bust suggests that we are hearing her perspective, it remains the construction of male creators intended for a primarily male audience. It is difficult to read between the lines here to gain insight into

---

[25] Roiphe 1993: 54; Stepp 2007.
[26] Futrell 2001: 115.
[27] Scodel and Bettenworth 2009: 69–70.

this character's own desires, because she is so carefully constructed to appeal to male fantasies of a submissive woman. At the same time, denying this rare voice of an enslaved woman also perpetuates injustice by silencing her. Eunice, whose options are inherently restricted, risks her own suffering in order to demand her preferred sexual partner. Regardless of whether that relationship seems realistic or just to a modern audience, it is clearly better than being objectified as an extra pillow for a visiting house guest. Her act of rebellion, outside the derivatised world in which she exists only for Petronius's pleasure, is still an act that ultimately centres and gratifies Petronius.

Ancient material culture sheds only a small but revealing amount of light on actual sexual relations between enslavers and enslaved. Sarah Levin-Richardson notes that the famous Moregine gold bracelet, inscribed '*domnus ancillae suae*', or 'the master to his handmaid', appears to be decades old, despite being found on the skeleton of a comparatively young woman, and thus 'might have been passed down from an unnamed master to a series of female slaves, one after another'.[28] Yet this bracelet is repeatedly offered as evidence, even in its museum caption in Naples, of a loving, affectionate relationship between enslaver and enslaved, despite the reality that the bracelet both itself denotes the master's ownership and fails to even specifically name the allegedly beloved object.[29]

In this way, modern assumptions influenced by representations in mass media cause both scholars and audiences to romanticise the likely gritty and unpleasant reality of sex between Roman slaveowners and enslaved people. The same rose-coloured lens is not applied to either the archaeological evidence or mass media about slavery in the Americas. In that case, abundant evidence of mass rape of enslaved women has been, until recently, ignored or erased, rather than romanticised.[30] This distinction likely stems from cultural prejudices against interracial relationships as well as the temporal nearness of such rapes; it is ethically simpler to fantasise about Roman poets and 'enslaved Greek noblewomen' than about Great-Grandpappy and his housemaid.

While some might argue that this attitude that idealises romances with enslaved women was a result of conservative 1950s gender roles and morality, a closer examination of such treatment in movies and television over the last seventy-five years reveals startlingly inconsistent treatment of such relationships. For instance, in the 1960 Stanley Kubrick film *Spartacus*, the initial romantic 'meet-cute' of Spartacus and his love interest, Varinia, happens when she is thrust into the gladiator's cell as his sex slave for the night.[31] While a soft melody plays,

---

[28] Baird 2015: 165–70; Levin-Richardson 2019: 110.
[29] Licandro 2004: 293–302. See also Costabile 2001: 446–74.
[30] White 1999.
[31] Clip 2: https://drive.google.com/file/d/1yyjWVS6vMBMrgT_kJ6VSNDmxQF_iphCM/view?usp=sharing.

Spartacus (Kirk Douglas) objectifies and touches Varinia, exclaiming that he's 'never had a woman'. Varinia (Jean Simmons) reacts stoically and silently with the body language of a multiply traumatised rape victim, passively and unerotically removing her clothes as she has presumably done for other gladiators and enslavers for years. Simmons's facial expressions here form the unspoken text, allowing the audience to imagine this character's degradation and suffering despite its lack of depiction on screen. Varinia is epistemically objectified in that all three men – Spartacus, Batiatus and the Doctore – ignore her physical testimony of her unwillingness to have sex. At the same time, her communicative context, even if subject to epistemic injustice within the context of the gladiatorial barracks, is expressed to the audience.[32]

At this point in the scene, Batiatus (Peter Ustinov) and the Doctore of the gladiatorial school, gazing down at the pair from a barred skylight, mock Spartacus and egg him on to rape Varinia. Spartacus yells in rage that 'I am not an animal!' and Varinia echoes his sentiment, leading them to abandon any attempt at sex for conversation and, later, intrigue and romance. Yet the key object of sympathy in this scene, from the audience's perspective, remains Spartacus: it is his bodily integrity that is violated by Batiatus and Doctore's ogling gaze, not that of Varinia, who, after all, must be accustomed to such treatment. After Batiatus abandons his voyeurism, the romantic musical motif returns, suggesting that Spartacus's own pawing of Varinia was simply naïveté, not assault.

While W. Jeffrey Tatum suggests that this scene 'conveys Spartacus's self-control and gentleness', he also admits that Spartacus's hands clutching around Varinia's throat are 'difficult to watch for contemporary audiences'.[33] It seems unlikely that 1960 audiences would not have similarly viewed choking a woman as physical and sexual assault, given its prevalence in true crime stories of the time. However, Kubrick indicates to us through the musical and lighting cues that this scene is to be taken as ultimately romantic, not one of sexual assault, despite Varinia's implicit horrific lived experience of constant sexual assault. When Varinia is later taken captive by Crassus, she notes to Crassus that 'he can take her at any time', once again accepting and enduring her constant violability. Here Varinia becomes an epistemic subject; while she acknowledges Crassus's power, she does not justify it as morally acceptable. Kubrick's *Spartacus*, a film concerned with, along with many other themes, the nature of slavery and freedom, problematises the question of sex with enslaved people significantly more directly and deeply than *Quo Vadis*.

By 1966, however, Roman slavery and sexual assault was still a topic that could be viewed as prime material for the bawdy comedy *A Funny Thing Happened*

---

[32] Medina 2013: 5.
[33] Tatum 2008: 131.

on the Way to the Forum, directed by Richard Lester with music and lyrics by Stephen Sondheim. *Forum* is a pastiche of various ancient Roman comedies by the playwright Plautus, who often focused on the complex interactions between free and enslaved people and implicitly offered the 'hidden transcript' of enslaved women, especially those facing sexual subjugation.[34] However, Stephen Sondheim picked and chose which elements of Roman humour and plot he thought would be most palatable to modern American audiences, largely subverting the more complicated portrayals of enslaved viewpoints in the original texts. The most relevant and problematic number, for these purposes, is a joyous comic song called 'Everybody Ought to Have a Maid', in which the enslaved trickster Pseudolus explains to his older, married master Senex that they have acquired a new enslaved woman, the blonde, vapid Philia, as a combination of sex slave and housemaid.[35] (Pseudolus is hiding Philia's actual role as the love interest of the son of the household.) As more and more male characters are brought into this false narrative, they join into the chorus, singing and dancing through increasingly fantastical montages of Roman domestic life while women of all ages and skin tones perform menial domestic labour in the background:

> 'Everybody ought to have a maid
> Someone who you hire when you're short of help
> To offer you the sort of help
> You never get from a spouse'.[36]

All the male characters, whether free or enslaved, can agree humorously not only that having a domestic sex slave is entirely reasonable and ethical, but that, in fact, a normal Roman middle-class man deserves to have a sex slave, especially when forced to deal with a wealthy wife (*femina dotata*) who might use her financial power to exert sexual control in the marital relationship. Philia's own agency is never addressed in this song, yet in general she seems largely delighted by the thought of offering sexual services as an enslaved woman to whomever turns out to be her owner. Mostly, however, she, like the other enslaved women, is the object of male fantasies and affections.

Any question of consent is played in this song and entire film as a joke. While the courtesans of the neighbouring brothel eventually briefly escape from their enslavement due to the comic chaos, they are duly rounded up by the brothel eunuchs. The ethnically European remaining courtesans are handed out as consolation prizes to various characters at the end of the film, while all the dark-skinned

---

[34] Stewart 2012: 17–20.
[35] Clip 3: https://drive.google.com/file/d/1aCK0VWZv_1ctk1wVDV74rNG4ZHthE_AI/view?usp=sharing).
[36] *A Funny Thing Happened on the Way to the Forum*. 1966.

courtesans remain enslaved to work another day in the brothel. Meanwhile, much of the focus of *Forum* and plot is on the crucial quest of Pseudolus himself to achieve freedom, represented as the most desirable goal possible – for a man. The female characters' potential desire for freedom from sexual assault, however, remains unspoken, much like Pseudolus's own romantic interest, a mute courtesan from the 'Island of Silent Women' whose goals apart from a union with Pseudolus remain unknown.

Forum, like earlier mass media about the Roman world, again divorces virtuous Roman male pursuits of freedom and autonomy from any parallel goals for female characters, which are almost entirely relationship-centred and do not allow space for women to articulate their own identity as enslaved women, as survivors of sexual assault, or as bearers of their own pain. In doing so, it both reflects and shapes both contemporaneous and modern 'rape culture' in which both public and judicial focus is often on the potential harm to the career prospects of the alleged rapist, rather than the long-term trauma of the survivor.[37] Ann Hornaday of the *Washington Post*, after the 2014 mass murder of young women in Isla Vista, CA, wrote:

> For generations, mass entertainment has been overwhelmingly controlled by white men, whose escapist fantasies so often revolve around vigilantism and sexual wish-fulfilment (often, if not always, featuring a steady through-line of casual misogyny). Rodger's rampage ... shows how a sexist movie monoculture can be toxic for women and men alike.[38]

While Hornaday primarily indicted the role of contemporary 'frat bro' movies, the projection of these Roman fantasies of either eagerly submissive enslaved women or sexually traumatised women just looking for the right male hero to rekindle their hearts, has also had a significant long-term effect on modern attitudes towards sexual consent, as well as on modern American impressions of ancient Mediterranean sexual relations.

The two series which began this chapter, HBO's *Rome* and STARZ's *Spartacus: Blood and Sand*, also repeatedly address the issue of sexual relationships between enslaved and free Romans. One of the leading, largely ahistorical characters of HBO's *Rome* is the coarse ex-legionary Titus Pullo, played by the Northern Irish White actor Ray Stevenson. Pullo's major romantic arc involves an enslaved woman named Eirene, played by the olive-skinned Italian actress Chiara Mastalli, who is first depicted being summarily abducted by some of Pompey's fleeing troops and tied to a wagon like an animal. She is entirely mute for her

---

[37] Phillips 2016: 22 and following.
[38] Hornaday 2014.

first several appearances and does not know or understand Latin, echoing the 'Silent Woman' enslaved courtesan of *Forum*. The male fantasy of silent submission is a repetitive theme in these works, echoing broader themes of pre-emptive epistemic silencing that does not even ask for the woman's perspective, much less listen to it.[39] After Pullo belatedly rescues Eirene, he then promptly loses her to pay a bar bill before ultimately foisting her off as a housemaid upon his friend Vorenus's family. However, Pullo periodically returns to rape Eirene and ask for her comfort and emotional support for his own traumas:

> PULLO: 'You're a good girl. You don't smile much, though'.
> EIRENE: 'Do you want me to smile?'
> PULLO: 'I want you to be happy. <she forces a smile> That's better'.[40]

A slow romantic violin theme plays in this scene as Pullo demands that Eirene undress while she stands there with a fixed, suffering expression, much like that of Varinia, and he proceeds to nonviolently assault her.[41] In this scene even the ability to nonverbally communicate injustice, as Varinia did, is robbed from Eirene, who is forced to perform consensual and submissive body language in order to falsify willing and romantic consent.

After the Caesarian civil wars, Pullo returns to free Eirene, planning on marrying her, only to discover that she is already in love with a fellow enslaved man, Oedipus, who can now use their mutual savings to buy his own freedom and then marry Eirene. Pullo, enraged, promptly murders Oedipus, leaving Eirene distraught. By the end of the season, however, she has forgiven Pullo and agreed to marry him instead.

Their subsequent marriage is portrayed as more functional and mutually happy than any of the other relationships in the *Rome* series (which is an admittedly low bar). However, eventually another enslaved woman of the household, Gaia, who has fallen in love with Pullo, poisons Eirene and her unborn child. Gaia then succeeds in becoming Pullo's new lover, until, wounded in the civil wars, she confesses her crime to Pullo, who promptly murders her in turn and throws her body into the river. Kirsten Day notes that while Eirene continues to act subserviently and submissively to Pullo, calling him 'Master' even after her freedom, Gaia, 'despite her spunk', is still vulnerable to the violent whims and vengeance of her husband.[42]

---

[39] Fricker 2007: 133.
[40] *Rome*. 2005. 'Utica'. HBO.
[41] Clip 4: https://drive.google.com/file/d/126AlnWsXKB0FoYKJFBriqNIA1GYskC38/view?usp=sharing.
[42] Day 2016: 142.

To recap briefly, *Rome* depicts one enslaved woman first being explicitly kidnapped and implicitly gang raped, before finding a consensual, loving relationship with a fellow slave. However, although the free man who desires her murders her betrothed, all matters work out for the best when she marries her homicidal former owner. Gaia, the second enslaved woman in this messy family, murders her formerly enslaved mistress and replaces her but is ultimately herself a victim of domestic violence. Yet both of these relationships are fundamentally portrayed by *Rome* not as rape scenarios with extraordinarily problematic power dynamics but as the happiest, most normative, and most stable couples in the entire series – relationships with awkward beginnings and tragic endings but mutually satisfying middles. While *Rome* is notable among mass media set in the ancient world for spending substantial time focusing on the desires and perspectives of its elite female characters such as Atia, Servilia and Octavia, the same respect is not afforded to the enslaved women Eirene or Gaia, whose character arcs largely serve to further the pain and character development of Titus Pullo. At best, they are allowed a momentary consideration of agency, such as Eirene's brief attempt to kill Pullo, before reverting to romanticised tropes.

Steven DeKnight, the creator of *Spartacus: Blood and Sand*, enjoyed the privilege of being able to tell its extended stories of Batiatus's gladiatorial school and the subsequent slave revolt over four seasons, which offered opportunities for more nuance and complexity in the consideration of relationships between enslaved people and free elites. The relationship between the enslaved gladiator Crixus (played by Maori actor Manu Bennett) and the enslaver Lucretia (played by White New Zealand actress Lucy Lawless) forms one intriguing example of *Spartacus*'s depiction of non-violent rape, especially given Crixus's gender and his unusual role as one of only two characters who appear in every season of the series. In the prequel season, *Gods of the Arena*, Crixus is ordered by his domina, Lucretia, to have sex with her in order to produce a child, since she believes her beloved husband Batiatus to be infertile. Lucretia asserts her authority and control, ordering, 'You are never to speak of this – do you understand, slave? . . . I would not look at you – lest sight turn stomach. Enter me, and do not cease until you have spilled seed'.[43] At the same time, the scene is filmed as if it is a conventional rape of Lucretia herself; the camera focuses on her grimacing face while Crixus, relatively expressionless, enters her from behind, concealing his body. Despite Lucretia's expression, she is the one with the power and control, and thus the rapist. When Crixus later falls in love with his fellow slave Naevia, his reluctance to continue having sex with Lucretia becomes ever more obvious. Nevertheless, he has no choice but to continue his sexual services.

---

[43] *Spartacus: Blood and Sand*. 2011. 'Reckoning'. STARZ.

When the gladiators at last rebel violently against the House of Batiatus at the end of Season 1, Lucretia asks Crixus for mercy on the grounds of the foetus inside her belly, of whom he is the presumptive biological father, as well as appealing to the theoretically romantic nature of their relationship. Crixus responds by violently stabbing her belly and aborting the fetus. While this act is visually horrifying, it mirrors the right of some American rape victims to abort any offspring of an assault, a privilege supported by 75 per cent of Americans.[44] In this case, however, the male victim is enacting that right upon the female rapist's pregnant body. This act of violence confirms that, in Crixus's mind, his intercourse with Lucretia was indeed one of constant rape, even if Lucretia coloured it with false romantic overtones. Crixus perceives himself as a rape victim with no obligation or connection to any resulting foetus; he can begin to recover from his trauma by seeking revenge directly upon his attacker. The audience implicitly adopts his perspective on this incident, despite perhaps having some lingering sympathy for the complex character of Lucretia. He is repeatedly able to vocalise the injustices done to him and to his loved ones and reclaim agency through vengeance upon his oppressors.

In the third and fourth seasons, rape becomes a more dominant theme of the series, perhaps because the main characters are no longer living in a unified household of master and slave where more subtle dynamics of oppression are easily visible. In one of the early episodes of the *Vengeance* season, the Spartacani storm a house and attack an anonymous White *dominus* in the midst of his violent rape of an enslaved woman. The master is then interrogated about his former slave Naevia (played by Black actresses Lesley-Ann Brand and Cynthia Addai-Robinson in different seasons), whom he has also raped multiple times, and answers defensively, 'How could I know that she held meaning?' Crixus and Spartacus answer, 'You just saw something to be used'.[45]

From the *dominus*'s perspective, Naevia is not a creature of worth, nor human, and thus definitionally available for rape. In Season 4, *War of the Damned*, Julius Caesar similarly makes excuses to Crassus for having attempted to assault Crassus's slave Kore: 'Apologies. I did not know the girl held meaning'.[46] Kore is only protected from rape because of her emotional value to her *dominus*; otherwise, she would presumptively be readily available for sexual abuse.

DeKnight both highlights the trope of centring such media around male emotional narratives and undercuts it by illuminating the intrinsic dehumanisation and oppression underneath this perspective. The feminist series explicitly condemns the epistemic notion that enslaved women's value is determined by men's

---

[44] The Gallup Organization 2011.
[45] *Spartacus: Blood and Sand*. 2012. 'A Place in This World'. STARZ.
[46] *Spartacus: Blood and Sand*. 2013. 'Wolves at the Gate'. STARZ.

knowledge of them and of their relationships with other men, rather than by their own self-knowledge and self-worth. The villains' apologies express an assumption that they had no duty to either assume these women's inherent rights to bodily integrity or even to ask them if they 'belonged' to another man. They claim innocence through ignorance, but the Spartacani do not accept such ignorance as a defence. STARZ's *Spartacus* thus serves as one of the first works of classical reception to foreground the perspective and knowledge of enslaved women themselves.

In the last season of *Spartacus*, a new relationship specifically questions and highlights the standard tropes of early mass media about the ancient world. The season villain is Marcus Licinius Crassus, an extraordinarily wealthy and powerful Roman noble who is also depicted as generally compassionate and just, played by White English actor Simon Merrells. He appears to have few romantic feelings for his noble wife but carries on a lengthy and passionate relationship with his enslaved maid Kore, played by Australian White actress Jenna Lind. At the beginning of their sexual relationship, Crassus explicitly asks for her verbal consent, and Kore responds that she does indeed desire him. Crassus repeatedly demonstrates his trust in Kore and concern for her wellbeing, continued consent and affections. Kore uses her voice both to express her consent and as an authority figure within the household and family.

Unfortunately, this relationship is destroyed when Crassus's son Tiberius, seeking revenge on his father, violently rapes and terrorises Kore, telling her that 'You are yet a slave and you will do as I fucking command', despite Kore's attempt to take a pseudo-maternal role with him.[47] He redefines her social status as inferior and silences her, threatening Kore with death or worse if she tells his father. This rape is depicted according to conventional Hollywood standards, with Tiberius being shown only from behind and a focus on Kore's anguished face. Kore escapes to the Spartacani rebels but later returns to Crassus to assuage his anger over the death of Tiberius, which she has secretly caused.[48] Crassus and his right-hand man, Julius Caesar, eventually discover the truth of Kore's rape, and offer this verbal comfort to her:

CAESAR: You place blame upon victim. Your noble fucking son forced himself inside her, one of many acts that led to deserved fate . . .

CRASSUS: Apologies, apologies, apologies, for all you have suffered. Know that it shall end when Spartacus falls.

However, once Crassus has successfully quenched the slave rebellion, he still insists on crucifying Kore as a rebellious slave. In the final moments of *Spartacus*,

---

[47] *Spartacus: Blood and Sand*. 2013. 'Blood Brothers'. STARZ.
[48] Clip 5: https://drive.google.com/file/d/1F9jVFKuCkdWpsQ5yF0gMqAsqRGo_gt9E/view?usp=sharing.

she stands as the silent representative of all female victims of Roman oppression, echoing the earlier death of the traumatised escaped sex slave Dione, similarly executed for her resistance, as well as the brief triumphal revenges of Naevia, an enslaved rape survivor turned heroic warrior. Indeed, her crucifixion symbolically replaces that of Spartacus himself in the Kubrick film; her intersectional axes of oppression, despite her former comparatively privileged state as a beloved *ancilla*, represent all that is corrupt in the Roman system.[49]

At the same time, while the audience views Kore on the cross, we hear Crassus's voice speaking of a time 'when a man may find solace'; once again, the narrative focus is on a man's pain rather than a woman's suffering or her own voice.[50] By having Crassus crucify Kore, *Spartacus* demonstrates that, even if there is mutual love, respect and explicitly requested consent for intercourse, there is fundamentally no possible equality or meaningful consent in a relationship between an enslaved person and a free person in the ancient Mediterranean. DeKnight briefly tempts his audience with the traditional trope of the devoted, loving enslaved woman happy to do anything in return for a romance with her master, before effectively driving home the message that such stories are illusory fictions, innately epistemically unjust, and that happy endings to them are impossible. Even Eunice in *Quo Vadis* only equals her master by dying at his side. While Eirene in HBO's *Rome* does gain her freedom, she does so at the cost of marrying her lover's murderer. Kore remains sexually vulnerable to all the men in her lover–owner's household and fundamentally under his control even in matters of life or death.

There are very few works of mass media that have even dared to explore the murky waters of premodern – or modern – relationships between people of vastly different economic status or social standing. When such stories are depicted, they generally evoke the Cinderella motif: a woman of lowly status is able to find wealth and prestige through a romantic relationship with a powerful and wealthy man. Yet the reality of patriarchal societies is that, throughout history, millions of maids and servants and household cleaners, whether free or enslaved, have been sexually assaulted by their employers and enslavers.

Mass media about the ancient Mediterranean generally depicts a more complex, often gentler view of slavery than movies about American enslavement and less frequently invokes the other standardised taboo of interracial relationships, although it is notable that Eunice, Eirene and Naevia are all darker-skinned women assaulted by White men. The closest to a consensual relationship depicted

---

[49] See Augoustakis 2016: 155–6, who also notes that after her return to slavery, Crassus insists that Kore now call him 'Dominus' rather than 'Marcus'. On intersectional axes, see Crenshaw 2017.

[50] Daugherty 2016: 83.

in any of these media is that between the lighter-skinned Kore and the very light-skinned Crassus. These works thus form a unique subgenre to explore and often normalise such relationships by romanticising and eroticising their depiction. By focusing primarily on the elite male perspective in these couples, the viewpoint of the enslaved woman is mostly either silenced or imagined as motivated entirely by gentle affection. These female characters through sexual submission achieve both a relationship with a male protagonist and a rise in their own social status; they are generally portrayed as Cinderellas rather than survivors of assault.

Only a few works, like the varied representations of the story of *Spartacus*, consider whether these narratives themselves both reflect and shape the rape culture in the world around them. In the final episodes of *Spartacus*, Kore offers a blessing to a newborn baby boy, who is about to successfully escape into the Alps to be raised by a loving same-sex ex-gladiator male couple: 'I pray he uses his cock only upon the willing'. She offers her hard-won knowledge of systemic oppression in an attempt to shape positively the future of this free male child, and in doing so, she bends his path towards justice through her own words.

Selected Bibliography

Abramson, Kate. 2014. 'Turning up the Lights on Gaslighting'. *Philosophical Perspectives* 28: 1–30.

Achebe, Nwando. 2020. *Female Monarchs and Merchant Queens in Africa*. Ohio University Press.

Addelson, Kathryn Pyne. 1983. 'The Man of Professional Wisdom'. In Harding and Hintikka, eds. 165–86.

Ager, Sheila. 2013. 'Marriage or Mirage? The Phantom Wedding of Cleopatra and Antony'. *CP* 108.2: 139–55.

Agra, Kelly Louise Rexzy. 2020. 'Epistemic Injustice, Paralysis, and Resistance: A (Feminist) Liberatory Approach to Epistemology'. *Kritike* 14.1: 28–44.

Ahmed, Sara. 2017. *Living a Feminist Life*. Duke University Press.

Aikin, Scott. 2022. 'The Stoic Sage Does Not Err: An Error?' *Symposion* 9.1: 69–82.

Aikin, Scott and Emily McGill-Rutherford. 2014. 'Stoicism, Feminism and Autonomy'. *Symposion* 1.1: 9–22.

Alain of Lille. 1978. *De planctu Naturae*. In Nikolaus M. Häring, ed. *Stvdi medievali* 3.19: 797–879.

Alcoff, Linda Martín. 2006. *Visible Identities: Race, Gender, and the Self*. Oxford University Press.

———. 2008. 'How Is Epistemology Political?' In Bailey and Cuomo, eds. McGraw-Hill. 705–17.

Alcoff, Linda Martín and Elizabeth Potter, eds. 1993. *Feminist Epistemologies*. Routledge.

Allen, Danielle. 2000. *The World of Prometheus: The Politics of Punishing in Democratic Athens*. Princeton University Press.

Allen, Richard Hinkley. 1963. *Star Names: Their Lore and Meaning*. Dover.
Anderson, Elizabeth. 1995a. 'Knowledge, Human Interests, and Objectivity in Feminist Epistemology'. *Philosophical Topics* 23: 27–58.
_____. 1995b. 'Feminist Epistemology: An Interpretation and a Defense'. *Hypatia* 10.3: 50–84.
_____. 2020. 'Feminist Epistemology and Philosophy of Science'. In *Stanford Encyclopedia of Philosophy*. 13 February. https://plato.stanford.edu/entries/feminism-epistemology/.
Anderson, Graham. 1999. 'The Novella in Petronius'. In Heinz Hofmann, ed. *Latin Fiction*. Routledge. 52–63.
Anderson, William. 1993. *Barbarian Play: Plautus' Roman Comedy*. University of Toronto Press.
_____. 1997. *Ovid's* Metamorphoses. *Books 1–5*. University of Oklahoma Press.
_____. 2002. 'Resistance to Recognition and "Privileged Recognition" in Terence'. *CJ* 98.1: 1–8.
Anhalt, Emily K. 2015. 'The Tragic Io: Defining Identity in a Democratic Age'. *New England Classical Journal* 42.4: 246–60.
Annas, Julia. 1976. 'Plato's *Republic* and Feminism'. *Philosophy* 51.197: 307–21.
_____. 1990. 'Stoic Epistemology'. In Stephen Everson, ed. *Epistemology*. Cambridge University Press. 184–203.
Anzaldúa, Gloria E. 1987. *Borderlands/La Frontera: The New Mestiza*. Aunt Lute Books.
_____. 2015. *Light in the Dark/Luz en lo oscuro: Rewriting Identity, Spirituality, Reality*. Edited by Analouise Keating. Duke University Press.
Apostolakis, K. 2014. 'Ιδιωτικά σκάνδαλα και δημόσια εικόνα: ο Αριστογείτων στο στόχαστρο της δικανικής ρητορείας ([Δημ.] 25 και 26)'. In Loukia Athanasaki, Tasos Nikolaidis and Demos Spatharas, eds. Panepistimiakes Ekd. Kritis. Panepistimio Kritis, Filosofiki Scholi. 201–30.
Arduino, Anna Maria. 1697. *Rosa Parnassi plaudens triumpho imperiali S.M.C. invictissimi Leopoldi de Austria Romanorum Imperatoris etc., eiusque dignissimae uxoris Eleonorae Magdalenae Palatini Rheni*. S. Castaldun.
Arenson, Kelly, ed. *The Routledge Handbook of Hellenistic Philosophy*. Routledge.
Arieti, James A. 1997. 'Rape and Livy's View of Roman History'. In Deacy and Pierce, eds. 209–29.
Arnold, Edward V. 1911 [2014]. *Roman Stoicism*. Routledge.
Augoustakis, Antony. 2016. 'The Others'. In Augoustakis and Cyrino, eds. 148–60.
Augoustakis, Antony and Monica S. Cyrino, eds. 2016. *STARZ Spartacus: Reimagining an Icon on Screen*. Edinburgh University Press.
Augoustakis, Antony and Ariana Traill, eds. 2013. *Blackwell Companion to Terence*. Wiley-Blackwell.

Austin, Colin and Guido Bastianini, eds. 2002. *Posidippi Pellaei Quae Supersunt Omnia*. LED Edizioni Universitarie.

Austin, Lucy. 1946. 'The Caerellia of Cicero's Correspondence'. *CJ* 41.7: 305–9.

Bailey, Alison. 2018. 'On Anger, Silence, and Epistemic Injustice'. *Royal Institute of Philosophy Supplement* 84: 93–115.

Bailey, Alison and Chris Cuomo. 2008. *The Feminist Philosophy Reader*. McGraw-Hill.

Bailey, Lucy. 2021. 'Standpoint Theory'. In Kamden K. Strunk and Stephanie Anne Shelton, eds. *Encyclopedia of Queer Studies in Education*. Brill. 676–82.

Bakker, Egbert J., ed. 2017. *Authorship and Greek Song: Authority, Authenticity, and Performance*. Mnemosyne Supplement 402. Studies in Archaic and Classical Greek Song 3. Brill.

Balmaceda, Catalina. 2017. *Virtus Romana: Politics and Morality in the Roman Historians*. University of North Carolina Press.

Balsley, Kathryn. 2010. 'Between Two Lives: Tiresias and the Law in Ovid's *Metamorphoses*'. *Dictynna* 7: 13–31.

Bar On, Bat-Ami. 1993. 'Marginality and Epistemic Privilege'. In Alcoff and Potter, eds. 83–100.

Barfield, Wanda. 2022. 'When Women Speak, We Should All Listen'. *Centers for Disease Control and Prevention*. 16 February. https://www.cdc.gov/hearher/resources/news-media/when-women-speak.html.

Barletta, Mercedes, Rachel Beth Cunning, Elsbeth Currie, Claire Mieher, Océane Puche and Séverine Tarantino, eds. 2021. 'Martha Marchina, 50 Poems'. https://www.lupercallegit.org/martha-marchina.

Barsby, John. 2001. *Terence II: Phormio, The Mother-in-Law, The Brothers*. Harvard University Press.

Bassi, Karen. 2010. 'Making Prometheus Speak: Dialogue, Torture, and the Power of Secrets in *Prometheus Bound*'. In Karen Bassi and J. Peter Euben, eds. *When Worlds Elide: Classics, Politics, Culture*. Lexington Books. 77–110.

Bauman, Richard A. 1993. 'The Rape of Lucretia, "Quod metus causa" and the Criminal Law'. *Latomus* 52.3: 550–66.

Beard, Mary. 2006. 'Ciceronian Correspondence: Making a Book out of Letters'. In Timothy Peter Wiseman, ed. *Classics in Progress*. Oxford University Press. 103–44.

———. 2017. *Women and Power: A Manifesto*. Profile Books.

Beck, Roger. 1979. 'Eumolpus "Poeta", Eumolpus "Fabulator": A Study of Characterization in the *Satyricon*'. *Phoenix* 33: 239–53.

Becker, Hilary. 2016. 'Roman Women in the Urban Economy'. In Stephanie Lynn Budin and Jean Macintosh Turfa, eds. *Women in Antiquity*. Routledge. 915–31.

Begum-Lees, Rebecca. 2020. 'Que(e)r(y)ing Iphis' Transformation in Ovid's *Metamorphoses*'. In Allison Surtees and Jennifer Dyer, eds. *Exploring Gender Diversity in the Ancient World*. Edinburgh University Press. 106–17.

Belfiore, Elizabeth. 2005. Unpublished Abstract. 'Pregnant Men on Ladders: Comic Elements in Plato's *Symposium*'. https://camws.org/meeting/2005/abstracts2005/belfiore.html.

Berenstain, Nora. 2016. 'Epistemic Exploitation'. *Ergo* 3.22: 569–90.

Berlant, Lauren and Michael Warner. 1998. 'Sex in Public'. *Critical Inquiry* 24.2: 547–66.

Bernstein, Neil W. 2012. 'Torture Her Until She Lies: Torture, Testimony, and Social Status in Roman Rhetorical Education'. *G&R* 59.2: 165–77.

Bernstein, Rachel. 2015. 'Belief That Some Fields Require "Brilliance" May Keep Women Out'. *Science*. 15 January. https://www.science.org/content/article/belief-some-fields-require-brilliance-may-keep-women-out.

Bettcher, Talia Mae. 2018. '"When Tables Speak": On the Existence of Trans Philosophy (guest post by Talia Mae Bettcher)'. *Daily Nous*. 30 May. https://dailynous.com/2018/05/30/tables-speak-existence-trans-philosophy-guest-talia-mae-bettcher/.

Bierl, Anton. 2017. '*Melizein Pathe* or the Tonal Dimension in Aeschylus' *Agamemnon*: Voice, Song, and *Choreia* as Leitmotifs and Metatragic Signals for Expressing Suffering'. In Anton Bierl and Niall Slater, eds. *Voice and Voices in Antiquity*. Brill. 166–207.

Billings, Laurel. 2020. 'The Trans* Temporality of Lament: "Foolish" Hope and Trans* Survival in the *Ovide Moralisé's* "Iphis and Ianthe"'. In Traub, Badir and McKracken, eds. 60–79.

Blass, Friedrich. 1893. *Die Attische Beredsamkeit* III2/i. B. G. Teubner.

de Boer, Cornelis, Martina G. De Boer and Jeannette Th. M. Van, eds. 1931. '*Ovide moralisé:* Poème du commencement du quatorzième siècle publié d'après tous les manuscrits connus'. *Verhandelingen der Koninklijke Akademie van Wetenschapaen te Amsterdam, Afdeeling Letterkunde, nieuwe reeks*. 30.3. van de N.V Noord-Hollandsche Uitgevers-Maatschappi.

Bordo, Susan. 1987. *The Flight to Objectivity: Essays on Cartesianism and Culture*. State University of New York Press.

Boris, Eileen. 2003. 'From Gender to Racialized Gender: Laboring Bodies That Matter'. *International Labor and Working-Class History* 63: 9–13.

Borza, Eugene. 1990. *In the Shadow of Olympus: The Emergence of Macedon*. Princeton University Press.

Botta, Fabio. 1996. *Legittimazione, interesse ed incapacità all'accusa nei publica iudicia*. Edizioni AV.

_____. 2004. *Per vim inferre. Studi su stuprum violento e raptus nel diritto romano e bizantino*. Edizioni AV.

_____. 2011. '*Stuprum per vim illatum*. Violenza e crimini sessuali nel diritto classico e dell'occidente tardoantico'. In Francesco Lucrezi, Fabio Botta and Giunio Rizzelli, eds. *Violenza sessuale e società antiche*. Edizioni Grifo. 85–147.

Bowen, Megan Elena. 2018. *Prayer and Power in Ovid's* Metamorphoses. PhD diss. University of Virginia.
Bowie, Ewen. 2013. 'Milesian Tales'. In Whitmarsh and Thomson, eds. 243–58.
Brand, Peg. 2006. 'Feminism and Aesthetics'. In Eva Feder Kittay and Linda Martín Alcoff, eds. *The Blackwell Guide to Feminist Philosophy*. Wiley-Blackwell. 254–65.
Brazouski, Antoinette. 1998. '*Indicium* in the Works of Ovid'. *SyllClass* 9.1: 86–94.
Bremen, Riet van. 1996. *The Limits of Participation: Women and Civic Life in the Greek East in the Hellenistic and Roman Periods*. Dutch Monographs on Ancient History and Archaeology. Vol. 15. J. C. Gieben.
Brenk, Frederick. 2002–3. 'Sheer Doggedness or Love of Neighbor? Motives for Self-Sufficiency in the Cynics and Others'. *Illinois Classical Studies* 27/28: 77–96.
Brescia, Graziana. 2015. 'Ambiguous Silence: *Stuprum* and *Pudicitia* in Latin Declamation'. In Eugenio Amato, Francesco Citti and Bart Huelsenbeck, eds. *Law and Ethics in Greek and Roman Declamation*. De Gruyter. 75–94.
Brown, Carole Koepke. 'The Tale of Deianira and Nessus (CA, II, 2145–2307)'. In Peter G. Beidler, ed. *John Gower's Literary Transformations in the* Confessio Amantis *Original Articles and Translations*. University Press of America. 15–19.
Brownmiller, Susan. 1976. *Against Our Will: Men, Women and Rape*. Open Road Media.
Brundin, Abigail, Tatiana Crivelli and Maria Serena Sapegno. 2016. *A Companion to Vittoria Colonna*. Brill.
Burgess, Ann Wolbert and Carol R. Hartman. 2018. 'On the Origin of Grooming'. *Journal of Interpersonal Violence* 33: 17–23.
Burgwinkle, William E. 2009. *Sodomy, Masculinity and Law in Medieval Literature: France and England, 1050–1230*. Cambridge University Press.
Burnyeat, Myles and M. J. Levett, trans. 2015 [1990]. *The Theaetetus of Plato*. Hackett Publishing Company.
Burris, Simon, Jeffrey Fish and Dirk Obbink. 2014. 'New Fragments of Book 1 of Sappho'. *ZPE* 189: 1–28.
Bury, R. G., trans. 1932. *The Symposium of Plato*. Cambridge.
Butler, Judith. 1993. *Bodies That Matter: On the Discursive Limits of 'Sex'*. Routledge.
———. 2010. *Frames of War: When Is Life Grievable?* Verso.
Bychowski, M. W. 2016. 'Unconfessing Transgender: Dysphoric Youth and the Medicalization of Madness in John Gower's "Tale of Iphis and Ianthe"'. *Accessus: A Journal of Premodern Literature and New Media* 3.1: 1–38.
Byron, Gay L. 2002. *Symbolic Blackness and Ethnic Difference in Early Christian Literature*. Routledge.
Cahill, Anne J. 2011. *Overcoming Objectification: A Carnal Ethics*. Routledge.
Caldwell, Lauren. 2014. *Roman Girlhood and the Fashioning of Femininity*. Cambridge University Press.

Cameron, Averil. 1969. 'Petronius and Plato'. *CQ* 19: 367–70.
Campbell, David A. 1982a. *Greek Lyric Poetry: A Selection of Early Greek Lyric, Elegiac and Iambic Poetry*. Bristol Classical Press.
_____, ed. and trans. 1982b. *Greek Lyric: Sappho and Alcaeus*. Loeb Classical Library. Harvard University Press.
Cantarella, Eva. 2002. *Bisexuality in the Ancient World*. Yale University Press.
Carney, Elizabeth D. 2019. *Eurydice and the Birth of Macedonian Power*. Oxford University Press.
Carson, Anne, trans. 2002. *If Not, Winter: Fragments of Sappho*. Vintage Books.
Cartledge, Paul. 1987. *Agesilaos and the Crisis of Sparta*. Gerald Duckworth and Co., Ltd.
_____. 2003. *Spartan Reflections*. University of California Press.
Castro-Gómez, Santiago. 2007. 'The Missing Chapter of Empire'. *Cultural Studies* 21.2–3: 428–48.
Chae, Yung In. 2018. 'White People Explain Classics to Us: Epistemic Injustice in the Everyday Experiences of Racial Minorities'. *Eidolon*.
Chapleau, Kristine M., Debra L. Oswald and Brenda L. Russell. 2007. 'How Ambivalent Sexism toward Women and Men Support Rape Myth Acceptance'. *Sex Roles* 57: 131–6.
Choustoulaki, Georgia. 2019. '[Demosthenes] 25 *against Aristogeiton*: A Reconsideration'. *Rosetta* 24: 1–20.
Christ, Matthew R. 1998. *The Litigious Athenian*. The Johns Hopkins University Press.
_____. 2013. 'Demosthenes on Philanthrōpia as a Democratic Virtue'. *CPh* 108: 202–22.
Churchill, Laurie J., Phyllis Brown and Jane E. Jeffrey. 2002. *Women Writing Latin: From Roman Antiquity to Early Modern Europe*. Vol. 3. *Early Modern Women Writing Latin*. Routledge.
Cirillo, Thomas. 2009. 'Transferable Disgust in Demosthenes 54'. *SyllClass* 20: 1–30.
Clarke, John R. 1998. *Looking at Lovemaking. Constructions of Sexuality in Roman Art, 100 BC–AD 250*. University of California Press.
Clay, Jenny. 2003. *Hesiod's Cosmos*. Cambridge University Press.
Clayman, Dee. 2014. *Berenice II and the Golden Age of Ptolemaic Egypt*. Oxford University Press.
Cluett, Ronald G. 1998. 'Roman Women and Triumviral Politics, 43–37 BC'. *EMC* 42: 67–84.
Code, Lorraine. 1981. 'Is the Sex of the Knower Epistemologically Significant?' *Metaphilosophy* 12: 267–76.
_____. 1991. *What Can She Know?: Feminist Theory and the Construction of Knowledge*. Cornell University Press.
Coleman, Kathleen. 1990. 'Tiresias the Judge: Ovid *Metamorphoses* 3.322–38'. *CQ* 40: 571–7.

Collins, Patricia Hill. 1986. 'Learning from the Outsider Within: The Sociological Significance of Black Feminist Thought'. *Social Problems* 33.6: S14–S32.
_____. 1989. 'The Social Construction of Black Feminist Thought'. *Signs* 14.4: 745–73.
_____. 1990. *Black Feminist Thought: Knowledge, Consciousness, and the Politics of Empowerment*. Routledge.
_____. 2000. 'Black Women and Motherhood'. In Collins, *Black Feminist Thought. Knowledge, Consciousness, and the Politics of Empowerment*, 2nd edition. Routledge. 173–99.
Colonna, Vittoria, Chiara Matraini and Lucrezia Marinella. 2010. *Who Is Mary? Three Early Modern Women on the Idea of the Virgin Mary*. Trans. by Susan Haskins. University of Chicago Press.
Columbia Law School. 2017. 'Kimberlé Crenshaw on Intersectionality, More than Two Decades Later'. 8 June. law.columbia.edu/pt-br/news/2017/06/kimberle-crenshaw-intersectionality.
Combahee River Collective Statement. 1977. In Beverly Guy-Sheftall, ed. *Words of Fire*. The New Press. 232–40.
Conkey, Margaret. 2005. 'Dwelling at the Margins, Action at the Intersection? Feminist and Indigenous Archaeologies, 2005'. *Archaeologies* 1.1: 9–59.
Connelly, Joan Breton. 2007. *Portrait of a Priestess*. Princeton University Press.
Conte, Gian Biagio. 1996. *The Hidden Author: An Interpretation of Petronius' Satyricon*. Trans. by Elaine Fantham. University of California Press.
Coo, Lyndsay. 2021. 'Sappho in Fifth- and Fourth-Century Greek Literature'. In Finglass and Kelly, eds. 263–76.
Copeland, Rita. 2009. *Rhetoric, Hermeneutics, and Translation in the Middle Ages: Academic Traditions and Vernacular Texts*. Cambridge University Press.
Corbeill, Anthony. 2007. 'Rhetorical Education and Social Reproduction in the Republic and Early Empire'. In Hall and Dominik, eds. 69–82.
Costabile, Felice. 2001. 'Ancilla Domni: una nuova dedica su armilla aurea da Pompei'. *Minima Epigraphica et Papirologica* 4.6: 446–74.
Coulson, Frank T. 2007. 'Ovid's Transformations in Medieval France (ca. 1100–ca. 1350)'. In Alison Keith and Stephen Rupp, eds. *Metamorphosis. The Changing Face of Ovid in Medieval and Early Modern Europe*. University of Toronto Press. 33–61.
Courtney, Edward. 2001. *A Companion to Petronius*. Oxford University Press.
Cox, Virginia. 2000. 'Fiction 1560–1650'. In Letizia Panizza and Sharon Wood, eds. *A History of Women's Writing in Italy*. Cambridge University Press. 52–64.
_____. 2008. *Women's Writing in Italy, 1400–1650*. Johns Hopkins University Press.
_____. 2011. *The Prodigious Muse: Women's Writing in Counter-Reformation Italy*. Johns Hopkins University Press.

Craven, Samantha, Sarah Brown and Elizabeth Gilchrist. 2006. 'Sexual Grooming of Children: Review of Literature and Theoretical Considerations'. *Journal of Sexual Aggression* 12: 287–99.

Crease, Robert P., Joseph D. Martin and Peter Pesic. 2018. 'On "Minor" Scientists'. *Physics in Perspective* 20: 219–20.

Crenshaw, Kimberlé. 1989. 'Demarginalizing the Intersection of Race and Sex: A Black Feminist Critique of Antidiscrimination Doctrine, Feminist Theory and Antiracist Politics'. *University of Chicago Legal Forum* 1.8: 139–67.

———. 1991. 'Mapping the Margins: Intersectionality, Identity Politics, and Violence against Women of Color'. *Stanford Law Review* 43.6: 1241–99.

———. 2017. *On Intersectionality: Essential Writings*. The New Press.

Cuklanz, Lisa M. 2000. *Rape on Prime Time: Television, Masculinity, and Sexual Violence*. University of Pennsylvania Press.

Cunning, Rachel Beth. 2021. *Teacher's Guide to Martha Marchina. Italian Poet (1600–1646)*. Bombax Press. https://bombaxpress.com/teachers-guide-to-martha-marchina-2/.

Curran, Leo C. 1978. 'Rape and Rape Victims in Ovid's *Metamorphoses*'. *Arethusa* 11: 213–41.

Cyrino, Monica S. 2009. *Rome Season One*. Edinburgh University Press.

———, ed. 2013. *Screening Love and Sex in the Ancient World*. Palgrave Macmillan.

Cyrino, Monica S. and Lloyd Llewellyn-Jones, eds. 2016. *Rome Season Two: Trial and Triumph*. Edinburgh University Press.

D'Alessandro Behr, Francesca. 2018. *Arms and the Woman: Classical Tradition and Women Writers in the Venetian Renaissance*. Ohio State University Press.

Darcus, Shirley M. 1979. 'A Person's Relation to φρήν in Homer, Hesiod, and the Greek Lyric Poets'. *Glotta* 57.3/4: 159–73.

Daugherty, Greg. 2016. 'A New Crassus as Roman Villain'. In Augoustakis and Cyrino, eds. 69–83.

Daukas, Nancy. 2006. 'Epistemic Trust and Social Location'. *Episteme: A Journal of Social Epistemology* 3.1–2: 109–24.

Davis, Emmalon. 2016. 'Typecasts, Tokens, and Spokespersons: A Case for Credibility Excess as Testimonial Injustice'. *Hypatia* 31.3: 485–501.

———. 2018. 'On Epistemic Appropriation'. *Ethics* 128.4: 702–27.

Davis, Gregson. 1983. *The Death of Procris: 'Amor' and the Hunt in Ovid's Metamorphoses*. Edizioni dell'Ateneo.

Day, Kirsten. 2016. 'Windows and Mirrors'. In Cyrino and Llewellyn-Jones, eds. 141–54.

Deacy, Susan and Fiona McHardy. 2013. 'Uxoricide in Pregnancy: Ancient Greek Domestic Violence in Evolutionary Perspective'. *Evolutionary Psychology* 11.5: 994–1010.

Deacy, Susan and Karen F. Pierce, eds. 1997. *Rape in Antiquity: Sexual Violence in the Greek and Roman Worlds*. Duckworth.

Dean-Jones, Lesley. 1994. *Women's Bodies in Classical Greek Science*. Clarendon Press.

———. 1995. 'Autopsia, Historia and What Women Know: The Authority of Women in Hippocratic Gynaecology'. In Donald George Bates, ed. *Knowledge and the Scholarly Medical Traditions*. Cambridge University Press. 41–59.

De Forest, Mary. 1997. 'Female Choruses in Greek Tragedy'. *Didaskalia* 4.1.

DeKnight, Steven. 2010–14. *Spartacus: Blood and Sand*. STARZ.

de Melo, Wolfgang. 2013. *Plautus V: Stichus, Three-Dollar Day, Truculentus, The Tale of the Traveling Bag, Fragments*. Harvard University Press.

Desai, Murli. 2010. *A Rights-Based Preventative Approach for Psychosocial Well-Being in Childhood*. Springer Dordrecht.

Dessen, Cynthia S. 1977. 'Plautus' Satiric Comedy: The *Truculentus*'. *PhQ* 56.2: 145–68.

Destrée, Pierre and Zina Giannopoulou, eds. 2017. *Plato's Symposium: A Critical Guide*. Cambridge University Press.

De Vries, Kylan Mattias. 2015. 'Transgender People of Color at the Center: Conceptualizing a New Intersectional Model'. *Ethnicities* 15.1: 3–27.

Dillon, Matthew. 2003. *Girls and Women in Classical Greek Religion*. Routledge.

Dillon, Sheila. 2010. *The Female Portrait Statue in the Greek World*. Cambridge University Press.

Dimmick, Jeremy. 2002. 'Ovid in the Middle Ages: Authority and Poetry'. In Philip Hardie, ed. *The Cambridge Companion to Ovid*. Cambridge University Press. 264–87.

Dimundo, Rosalba. 1983. 'Da Socrate a Eumolpo. Degradazione dei personaggi e delle funzioni nella novella del fanciullo di Pergamo'. *MD* 10–11: 55–65.

———. 1986. 'La novella dell' efebo di Pergamo. Struttura del racconto'. *MCSN* 4: 83–94.

Dinshaw, Carolyn. 1999. *Getting Medieval: Sexualities and Communities, Pre- and Postmodern*. Duke University Press.

Dixon, Jessica Elizabeth. 2013. *The Language of Roman Adultery*. PhD diss. University of Manchester.

Dixon, Suzanne M. 2001. *Reading Roman Women: Sources, Genres and Real Life*. Duckworth.

Dotson, Kristie. 2011. 'Tracking Epistemic Violence, Tracking Practices of Silencing'. *Hypatia* 26.2: 236–57.

———. 2012. 'A Cautionary Tale: On Limiting Epistemic Oppression'. *Frontiers: A Journal of Women Studies* 33.1: 24–47.

Dover, Kenneth. 1978. *Greek Homosexuality*. Harvard University Press.

———, trans. 1980. Plato: *Symposium*. Cambridge University Press.

duBois, Page. 1988. *Sowing the Body: Psychoanalysis and Ancient Representations of Women*. University of Chicago Press.

———. 1995. *Sappho Is Burning*. University of Chicago Press.

Du Bois, W. E. B. 1994 [1903]. *The Souls of Black Folk*. Perfection Learning Corporation.
Ducat, Jean. 1998. 'La femme de Sparte et la cité'. *Ktema* 23: 385–406.
Duckworth, George E. 1952. *The Nature of Roman Comedy: A Study in Popular Entertainment*. Princeton: Princeton University Press.
Dugan, John. 2007. 'Modern Critical Approaches to Roman Rhetoric'. In Hall and Dominik, eds. 9–22.
Edmonds, Radcliffe G. III. 2000. 'Socrates the Beautiful: Role Reversal and Midwifery in Plato's *Symposium*'. *TAPA*. 130: 261–85.
―――. 2017. 'Alcibiades the Profane: Images of the Mysteries'. In Destrée and Giannopoulou, eds. 194–215.
Edmunds, Lowell. 2010. 'Toward a Minor Roman Poetry'. *Poetica* 42: 29–80.
Endres, Nikolai. 2014. 'Difficult Dialogues about a Difficult Dialogue: Plato's *Symposium* and Its Gay Tradition'. In Nancy Sorkin Rabinowitz and Fiona McHardy, eds. *From Abortion to Pederasty: Addressing Difficult Topics in the Classics Classroom*. The Ohio State University Press. 212–26.
Engel, David. 2003. 'Women's Role in the Home and the State: Stoic Theory Reconsidered'. *HSPh* 101: 267–88.
Enke, Finn. 2012. 'Introduction: Transfeminist Perspectives'. In Finn Enke, ed. *Transfeminist Perspectives in and beyond Transgender and Gender Studies*. Temple University Press. 1–15.
Enos, Richard Leo. 2005. 'Speaking of Cicero . . . and His Mother: A Research Note on an Ancient Greek Inscription and the Study of Classical Rhetoric'. *Rhetoric Review* 24.4: 457–65.
Eule, J. Cordelia. 2001. *Hellenistische Bürgerinnen aus Kleinasien. Weibliche Gewanstatuen in ihrem antiken Kontext*. TASK Foundation.
Evans, Nancy. 2006. 'Diotima and Demeter as Mystagogues in Plato's *Symposium*'. *Hypatia* 21.2: 1–27.
Fagan, Garrett G. 2011. 'Violence in Roman Social Relations'. In Michael Peachin, ed. *The Oxford Handbook of Social Relations in the Roman World*. Oxford University Press. 467–98.
Fantham, Elaine. 1975. 'Sex, Status, and Survival in Hellenistic Athens: A Study of Women in New Comedy'. *Phoenix* 29.1: 44–74.
―――. 1991. '*Stuprum*: Public Attitudes and Penalties for Sexual Offences in Republican Rome'. *EMC* 35.3: 267–91.
―――. 2000. 'DOMINA-tricks, or How to Construct a Good Whore from a Bad One'. *Dramatische Wäldchen* 80 (Festscrift für Eckard Lefèvre zum 65. Geburtstag): 287–99.
―――. 2009. 'Rhetoric and Ovid's Poetry', in Peter Knox, ed. *A Companion to Ovid*. Wiley-Blackwell. 26–44.
Fantuzzi, Marco. 2005. 'Posidippus at Court: The Contribution of the *hippika* of P. Mil. Vogl. VIII 309 to the Ideology of Ptolemaic Kingship'. In Kathryn

Gutzwiller, ed. *The New Posidippus: a New Poetry Book*. Oxford University Press. 249–68.

Farber, Paul M. and Ken Lum, eds. 2019. *Monument Lab: Creative Speculations for Philadelphia*. Temple University Press.

Farrow, Ronan. 2017. 'From Aggressive Overtures to Sexual Assault: Harvey Weinstein's Accusers Tell Their Stories'. *The New Yorker*. 23 October. https://www.newyorker.com/news/news-desk/from-aggressive-overtures-to-sexual-assault-harvey-weinsteins-accusers-tell-their-stories.

———. 2019. *Catch and Kill: Lies, Spies and a Conspiracy to Protect Predators*. Fleet.

Fedeli, Paolo and Rosalba Dimundo. 1988. *Petronio Arbitro: I racconti del Satyricon*. Salerno ed.

Feeney, Denis. 1991. *The Gods in Epic*. Oxford University Press.

Feldherr, Andrew. 2010. *Playing Gods: Ovid's* Metamorphoses *and the Politics of Fiction*. Princeton University Press.

Fetterley, Judith. 1978. *The Resisting Reader: A Feminist Approach to American Fiction*. Indiana University Press.

Fineberg, Stephen. 1986. 'The Unshod Maidens at Prometheus 135'. *The American Journal of Philology* 107.1: 95–8.

Finglass, P. J. and Adrian Kelly, eds. 2021. *The Cambridge Companion to Sappho*. Cambridge University Press.

Finley, Moses and Henri Willy Pleket. 1976. *The Olympic Games: The First Thousand Years*. Viking Press.

Fisher, Nick. 1998. 'Violence, Masculinity, and the Law in Classical Athens'. In Foxhall and Salmon, eds. 68–97.

Flemming, Rebecca. 2000. *Medicine and the Making of Roman Women: Gender, Nature, and Authority from Celsus to Galen*. Oxford University Press.

Foley, Helen P. 2002. *Female Acts in Greek Tragedy*. Princeton University Press.

Forché, Carolyn. 1993. *Against Forgetting: Twentieth-Century Poetry of Witness*. Norton.

Forché, Carolyn and Duncan Wu, eds. 2014. *Poetry of Witness: The Tradition in English, 1500–2001*. Norton.

Foss, Michael. 1998. *The Search for Cleopatra*. Arcade Publishing.

Foucault, Michel. 1985. *The Use of Pleasure. The History of Sexuality, Vol. 2*. Trans. by Robert Hurley. Vintage.

———. 1990. *The History of Sexuality. Vol. 1: An Introduction*. Trans. by Robert Hurley. Vintage Books.

Foxhall, Lin and John Salmon, eds. 1998. *Thinking Men: Masculinity and Its Self-Representation in the Classical Tradition*. Routledge.

Fraga, José Carracedo. 1997. 'El tópico literario de los grados hacia la culminación del amor y el cuento del muchacho de Pérgamo ("Satiricón" 85–87)'. *Latomus* 56: 554–66.

Frantzen, Allen J. 1996. 'The Disclosure of Sodomy in *Cleanness*'. *PMLA* 111.3: 451–64.

Freas, Debra. 2021. '*Fabula Muta*: Petronius, Poetry, and Rape'. *AJP* 142: 629–58.

Frede, Michael. 1999. 'Stoic Epistemology'. In Keimpe Algra, Jonathan Barnes, Jaap Mansfeld and Malcolm Schofield, eds. *The Cambridge History of Hellenistic Philosophy*. Cambridge University Press. 295–322.

Freedman, Karyn L. 2020. 'The Epistemic Significance of #MeToo'. *Feminist Philosophy Quarterly* 6.2.

Fricker, Miranda. 2007. *Epistemic Injustice: Power and the Ethics of Knowing*. Oxford University Press.

———. 2016. 'Epistemic Injustice and the Preservation of Ignorance'. In Rik Peels and Martijn Blaauw, eds. *The Epistemic Dimensions of Ignorance*. Cambridge University Press. 144–59.

———. 2017. 'Evolving Concepts of Epistemic Injustice'. In Kidd, Medina and Pohlhaus Jr, eds. 53–60.

Fricker, Miranda, Peter Graham, David Henderson and Nikolj Jang Lee Pedersen, eds. 2019. *The Routledge Handbook of Social Epistemology*. Routledge.

Fricker, Miranda and Katherine Jenkins. 2017. 'Epistemic Injustice, Ignorance, and Trans Experiences'. In Ann Garry, Serene J. Khader and Alison Stone, eds. *The Routledge Companion to Feminist Philosophy*. Routledge. 268–78.

Frost-Arnold, Karen. 2014. 'Imposters, Tricksters, and Trustworthiness as an Epistemic Virtue'. *Hypatia* 29.4: 790–807.

Frye, Marilyn. 1983. *The Politics of Reality: Essays in Feminist Theory*. Crossing Press.

Fulkerson, Laura. 2005. *The Ovidian Heroine as Author: Reading, Writing, and Community in the* Heroides. Cambridge University Press.

Futrell, Alison. 2001. 'Seeing Red: Spartacus as Domestic Economist'. In Joshel, Malamud and McGuire, eds. 77–118.

Gagarin, Michael. 1998. 'Women in Athenian Courts'. *Dike* 1: 39–51.

———. 2001. 'Women's Voices in Attic Oratory'. In André Lardinois and Laura McClure, eds. *Making Silence Speak: Women's Voices in Greek Literature and Society*. Princeton University Press. 161–76.

———. 2003. 'Telling Stories in Athenian Law'. *TAPA* 133: 197–207.

———. 2014. 'Aeschylus' *Prometheus*: Regress, Progress, and the Nature of Woman'. *Hyperboreus* 20.1–2: 92–100.

Galloway, Andrew. 2016. 'Gower's Ovids'. In Rita Copeland, ed. *The Oxford History of Classical Reception in English Literature: Vol. 1: 800–1558*. Oxford University Press. 435–64.

The Gallup Organization. 2011. Gallup US Poll. 9–12 June.

Gantz, Timothy. 1993. *Early Greek Myth: A Guide to Literary and Artistic Sources*. Johns Hopkins University Press.

Gardner, Jane F. 1986. *Women in Roman Law and Society*. Routledge.
_____. 1991. *Women in Roman Law and Society*. Vol. 635. Indiana University Press.
Garland-Thomson, Rosemarie. 2016. 'Becoming Disabled'. *The New York Times*. 19 August. https://www.nytimes.com/2016/08/21/opinion/sunday/becoming-disabled.html.
Gebhardt, Ulrich. 2009. *Sermo Iuris*: Rechtssprache und Recht in der augusteischen Dichtung. Leiden.
Gentilcore, Roxanne. 1995. 'The Landscape of Desire: The Tale of Pomona and Vertumnus in Ovid's *Metamorphoses*'. *Phoenix* 49.2: 110–20.
Gertz, Genelle. 2012. *Heresy Trials and English Women Writers, 1400–1670*. Cambridge University Press.
Gillespie, Vincent. 2005. 'From the Twelfth Century to *c.* 1450'. In Alastair Minnis and Ian Johnson, eds. *The Cambridge History of Literary Criticism*. Cambridge University Press. 145–236.
Gilligan, Carol. 1982. *In a Different Voice*. Harvard University Press.
Gilmore, Leigh. 2019. 'Frames of Witness: The Kavanaugh Hearings, Survivor Testimony, and #MeToo'. *Biography* 42.3: 610–23.
Gilula, Dwora. 1980. 'The Concept of the *Bona Meretrix*: A Study of Terence's Courtesans'. *RFIC* 108: 142–65.
_____. 2004. 'The *Cistellaria* Courtesans: Two Ways to Make a Living'. In Rolf Hartkamp and Florian Hurka, eds. *Studien zu Plautus'* Cistellaria. Gunter Narr Verlag. 239–46.
Gold, Barbara K. 2013. '"And I Became a Man": Gender Fluidity and Closure in Perpetua's Prison Narrative'. In Donald Lateiner, Barbara K. Gold and Judith Perkins, eds. *Roman Literature, Gender and Reception*. Routledge. 163–75.
_____. 2018. 'Remaking Perpetua: A Female Martyr Reconstructed'. In Mark Masterson, Nancy Sorkin Rabinowitz and James Robson, eds. *Sex in Antiquity*. Routledge. 502–19.
Goldberg, Sandy. 2011. 'The Division of Epistemic Labor'. *Episteme* 8.1: 112–25.
Golden, Mark. 1998. *Sport and Society in Ancient Greece*. Cambridge University Press.
Goldman, Alan and Dennis Whitcomb, eds. 2011. *Social Epistemology: Essential Readings*. Oxford University Press.
Goldman, Max. 2007. '*Anseres* [*sacri*]: Restrictions and Variations in Petronius' Narrative Technique'. In Maaike Zimmerman et al., eds. *Ancient Narrative, Vol. 5*. Barkhuis. 1–23.
Goodich, Michael. 1979. *The Unmentionable Vice: Homosexuality in the Later Medieval Period*. University of California Press.
Gosetti-Murrayjohn, Angela. 2006. 'Sappho as the Tenth Muse in Hellenistic Epigram'. *Arethusa* 39: 21–45.
Gower, John. 2006. In Russell A. Peck, ed. and Andrew Galloway, trans. *Confessio Amantis*. Rochester: TEAMS (The Consortium for the Teaching of the

Middle Ages) in Association with the University of Rochester by Medieval Institute Publications.

Graf, Fitzgerald. 1988. 'Ovide, les *Métamorphoses* et la véracité du mythe'. In Claude Calame, ed. *Métamorphoses du mythe en Grèce antique*. Labor et Fides. 57–70.

Grahn-Wilder, Malin. 2018. *Gender and Sexuality in Stoic Philosophy*. Palgrave Macmillan.

Grasswick, Heidi. 2004. 'Individuals-in-Communities: The Search for a Feminist Model of Epistemic Subjects'. *Hypatia* 19.3: 85–120.

———. 2018. 'Feminist Social Epistemology'. *The Stanford Encyclopedia of Philosophy*. 24 July. https://plato.stanford.edu/entries/feminist-social-epistemology/.

Grasswick, Heidi E. and Mark Owen Webb. 2002. 'Feminist Epistemology as Social Epistemology'. *Social Epistemology* 16.3: 185–96.

Gratwick, Adrian S. 1993. *Plautus: Menaechmi*. Cambridge University Press.

Graver, Margaret. 2007. *Stoicism and Emotion*. University of Chicago Press.

Griffin, Miranda. 2012. 'Translation and Transformation in the *Ovide moralisé*'. In Emma Campbell and Robert Mills, eds. *Rethinking Medieval Translation: Ethics, Politics, Theory*. Brewer. 41–60.

Griffith, Mark. 1977. 'The Authenticity of *Prometheus Bound*'. Cambridge University Press.

———. 1983. *Aeschylus Prometheus Bound: Text and Commentary*. Cambridge University Press.

———. 1984. 'The Vocabulary of *Prometheus Bound*'. *CQ* 34: 282–91.

Greene, Ellen, ed. 1996. *Reading Sappho: Contemporary Approaches*. University of California Press.

———. 1998. *The Erotics of Domination: Male Desire and the Mistress in Latin Love Poetry*. Johns Hopkins University Press.

———. 2002. 'Subjects, Objects, and Erotic Symmetry in Sappho's Fragments'. In Nancy Sorkin Rabinowitz and Lisa Auanger, eds. *Among Women: From the Homosocial to the Homoerotic in the Ancient World*. University of Texas Press. 82–105.

Guerrilla Girls. 2004. *The Guerrilla Girls' Art Museum Activity Book*. Printed Matter.

Gummere, Richard. 1963. *Seneca the Philosopher and His Modern Message*. Cooper Square.

Gunderson, Erik. 2007. 'S.V.B.; E.V'. *ClAnt* 26.1: 1–48.

Habermehl, Peter. 2006. *Petronius, Satyrica 79–141: Ein Philologisch-Literarischer Kommentar*. Walter de Gruyter.

Haley, Shelley P. 1989. 'Livy's Sophoniba'. *Classica et Mediaevalia* 40: 171–81.

———. 1993. 'Black Feminist Thought and Classics: Re-membering, Re-claiming, Re-empowering'. In Rabinowitz and Richlin, eds. 23–43.

———. 2021. 'Race and Gender'. In Denise Eileen McCoskey, ed. *A Cultural History of Race in Antiquity*. Bloomsbury Academic. 119–36.

Hall, Jon. 2009. *Politeness and Politics in Cicero's Letters*. Oxford University Press.

Hall, Jon and William Dominik. 2007. *A Companion to Roman Rhetoric*. Wiley-Blackwell.

Hall, Kim Q. 2017. 'Queer Epistemology and Epistemic Injustice'. In Kidd, Medina and Pohlhaus Jr, eds. 158–66.

Hallett, Judith P. 1989. 'Women as *Same* and *Other* in the Classical Roman Elite'. *Helios* 16.1: 59–78.

Halperin, David. 1990. 'Why is Diotima a Woman?' In Froma I. Zeitlin, John J. Winkler and David M. Halperin, eds. *Before Sexuality: The Construction of Erotic Experience in the Ancient Greek World*. Routledge. 113–51.

Hammer, Jessica. 2012. 'Greek Media – What's with All the Rape?' *Gaming As Women*. 31 May. https://web.archive.org/web/20120604230028/http://gamingaswomen.com/posts/2012/05/geek-media-whats-with-all-the-rape/.

Hänel, Hilkje. 2021. 'Who's to Blame? Hermeneutical Misfire, Forward-Looking Responsibility, and Collective Accountability'. *Social Epistemology* 35.2: 173–84.

Hansen, Mogens Herman. 1976. *Ἀπαγωγή, ἔνδειξις, and ἐφήγησις against κακούργοι, ἄτιμοι and φευγόντες. A Study in the Athenian Administration of Justice in the Fourth Century BC*. Odense University Press.

Hanses, Mathias. 2020. *The Life of Comedy after the Death of Plautus and Terence*. University of Michigan Press.

Haraway, Donna. 1988. 'Situated Knowledges: The Science Question in Feminism and the Privilege of Partial Perspective'. *Feminist Studies* 14.3: 575–99.

Harding, Sandra. 1982. 'Is Gender a Variable in Conceptions of Rationality? A Survey of Issues'. *Dialectica* 36.2–3: 225–42.

_____, ed. 1987. *Feminism and Methodology: Social Science Issues*. Indiana University Press.

_____. 1993. 'Rethinking Standpoint Epistemology: What Is "Strong Objectivity?"' In Alcoff and Potter, eds. 49–82.

_____. 1995. 'Strong Objectivity: A Response to the New Objectivity Question'. *Synthese* 104.3: 331–49.

_____. 2006. 'Two Influential Theories of Ignorance and Philosophy's Interests in Ignoring Them'. *Hypatia* 21.3: 20–36.

Harding, Sandra and Merrill Hintikka, eds. 1983. *Discovering Reality: Feminist Perspectives on Epistemology, Metaphysics, Methodology, and Philosophy of Science*. Reidel.

Harned, Melanie S. 2005. 'Understanding Women's Labeling of Unwanted Sexual Experiences with Dating Partners'. *Violence against Women* 11.3: 374–413.

Harris, Edward. 1997. 'Susan Deacy and Karen Peirce, eds. *Rape in Antiquity: Sexual Violence in the Greek and Roman Worlds*'. *EMC* 41.3: 483–96.

_____. 2018. *Demosthenes Speeches 23–26*. University of Texas Press.

Hartman, Saidiya. 2008. 'Venus in Two Acts'. *Small Axe* 26.12: 1–14.

Hartsock, Nancy. 1983a. 'The Feminist Standpoint: Developing the Ground for a Specifically Feminist Historical Materialism'. In Harding and Hintikka, eds. 283–310.

———. 1983b. *Money, Sex, and Power: Toward a Feminist Historical Materialism*. Longman.

Haselswerdt, Ella. 2016. 'Re-Queering Sappho'. *Eidolon*. https://eidolon.pub/re-queering-sappho-c6c05b6b9f0b.

———. 2020. 'Sappho's Body / Towards a Deep Lez Philology'. Queer and the Classical Seminar Series. https://queerandtheclassical.org/seminar-series-2020.

Haskins, Anne, trans. 2008. 'Introduction'. In Colonna, Matraini and Marinella, eds. 1–42.

Haslanger, Sally. 2012. 'What Are We Talking About? The Semantics and Politics of Social Kinds'. In Sally Haslanger, ed. *Resisting Reality: Social Construction and Social Critique*. Oxford University Press. 10–26.

Hayes, Sharon, Karyn Olivier and Paul M. Farber. 2020. 'Monument Exchange 2'. In Paul Farber and Ken Lum, eds., 258–79.

Heap, Angela. 1998. 'Understanding the Men in Menander'. In Foxhall and Salmon, eds. 114–29.

Heath, John. 1992. *Actaeon, the Unmannerly Intruder*. Peter Lang.

Hekman, Susan. 1997. 'Truth and Method: Feminist Standpoint Theory Revisited'. *Signs* 22.2: 341–65.

Hemelrijk, Emily A. 2015. 'The Education of Women in Ancient Rome'. In W. Martin Bloomer, ed. *A Companion to Ancient Education*. Wiley-Blackwell. 292–304.

Henderson, John. 2002. 'Columella's Living Hedge: The Roman Gardening Book'. *JRS* 92: 110–32.

Hensley, Ian. 2020. 'Stoic Epistemology'. In Arenson, ed. 137–47.

Hexter, Ralph. 2007. 'Ovid in Translation in Medieval Europe'. In Harald Kittel et al., eds. *Übersetzung-Translation-Traduction*. Vol. 2. De Gruyter. 1311–28.

Hill, Lisa. 2001. 'The First Wave of Feminism: Were the Stoics Feminists?' *History of Political Thought* 22.1: 13–40.

Hoagland, Sarah Lucia. 2001. 'Resisting Rationality'. In Nancy Tuana and Sandra Morgen, eds. *Engendering Rationalities*. SUNY Press. 125–50.

———. 2020. 'Feminism and Stoic Sagehood'. In Arenson, ed. 410–21.

Hobbs, Angela. 2007. 'Female Imagery in Plato'. In J. H. Lesher, Debra Nails and Frisbee C. C. Sheffield, eds. *Plato's Symposium: Issues in Interpretation and Reception*. Harvard University Press. 252–71.

Hodkinson, Stephen. 1989. 'Inheritance, Marriage and Demography: Perspectives upon the Success and Decline of Classical Sparta'. In Anton Powell, ed. *Classical Sparta*. University of Oklahoma Press. 79–121.

———. 1999. 'An Agonistic Culture? Athletic Competition in Archaic and Classical Sparta'. In Stephen Hodkinson and Anton Powell, eds. *Sparta: New Perspectives*. The Classical Press of Wales. 147–87.

———. 2000. *Property and Wealth in Classical Sparta*. Duckworth.
———. 2004. 'Female Property Ownership and Empowerment in Classical and Hellenistic Sparta'. In Thomas J. Figueira, ed. *Spartan Society*. The Classical Press of Wales. 103–36.
Holroyd, Jules, and Katherine Puddifoot. 2020. 'Epistemic Injustice and Implicit Bias'. In Erin Beeghly and Alex Madva, eds. *An Introduction to Implicit Bias: Knowledge, Justice, and the Social*. Routledge. 116–33.
Holst-Warhaft, Gail. 1992. *Dangerous Voices: Women's Laments and Greek Literature*. Routledge.
Holzberg, Niklas. 1999. 'Apollos erste Liebe und die Folgen. Ovids Daphne-Erzählung als Programm für Werk und Wirkung'. *Gymnasium* 106: 317–34.
Hong, Yurie. 2016. 'Playing Zeus: Reproductive Technology and Lessons from Hesiod'. *Eidolon*. 22 December. https://eidolon.pub/playing-zeus-reproductive-technology-and-lessons-from-hesiod-964a9d5bdb9a.
Hornaday, Ann. 2014. 'A Final Videotaped Message: A Sad Reflection of the Sexist Stories We See So Often on Screen'. 25 May. *Washington Post*.
Hornsby, Jennifer and Rae Langton. 1998. 'Free Speech and Illocution'. *Legal Theory* 4: 21–37.
Hubbard, Thomas K. 1986. 'The Narrative Architecture of Petronius' *Satyricon*'. *AC* 55: 190–212.
———, ed. 2013. *A Companion to Greek and Roman Sexualities*. Wiley-Blackwell.
Hunter, Richard. 1996. 'Response to Morgan'. In Alan H. Sommerstein and Catharine Atherton, eds. *Education in Greek Fiction*. Levante Editori. 191–205.
Hunter, Virginia. 1990. 'Gossip and the Politics of Reputation in Classical Athens'. *Phoenix* 44: 299–325.
Hurtado, Aida. 1996. 'Strategic Suspensions: Feminists of Color Theorize the Production of Knowledge'. In Jill Mattuck Traul, McVicker Blythe Clinchy and Mary Field Belensky, eds. *Knowledge, Difference and Power: Essays Inspired by Women's Ways of Knowing*. Basic Books. 372–92.
———. 2003. *Voicing Chicana Feminisms: Young Women Speak Out on Sexuality and Identity*. New York University Press.
Hutchins, Richard. 2020. 'Technology Won't Save Us: Why Promethean Problems Can't Have Promethean Solutions'. *Eidolon*. 24 February. https://eidolon.pub/technology-wont-save-us-1342a1d8163d.
Hutchinson, G. O. 1998. *Cicero's Correspondence: A Literary Study*. Clarendon Press.
Intemann, Kristen. 2010. '25 Years of Feminist Empiricism and Standpoint Theory: Where Are We Now?' *Hypatia* 25.4: 778–96.
———. 2016. 'Feminist Standpoint'. In Lisa Jane Disch and Mary E. Hawkesworth, eds. *The Oxford Handbook of Feminist Theory*. Oxford University Press. 261–82.
Irvin, Matthew W. 2014. *The Poetic Voices of John Gower: Politics and Personae in the* Confessio Amantis. Boydell and Brewer.

Itzkoff, Dave. 2014a. 'For "Game of Thrones", Rising Unease Over Rape's Recurring Role'. *The New York Times.* 3 May.

———. 2014b. 'George R. R. Martin on "Game of Thrones" and Sexual Violence'. *The New York Times.* 2 May.

Jackson, Debra L. 2019. 'Date Rape: The Intractability of Hermeneutical Injustice'. In Wanda Teays, ed. *Analyzing Violence against Women.* Springer. 39–50.

Jäger, Wolfgang. 1986. *Briefanalysen: Zum Zusammenhang von Realitätserfahrung und Sprache in Briefen Ciceros.* Peter Lang.

Jaggar, Alison. 1989. 'Love and Knowledge: Emotion in Feminist Epistemology'. *Inquiry* 32.2: 151–76.

James, Sharon L. 1998. 'From Boys to Men: Rape and Developing Masculinity in Terence's *Hecyra* and *Eunuchus*'. *Helios* 25.1: 31–47.

———. 2003. *Learned Girls and Male Persuasion: Gender and Reading in Roman Love Elegy.* University of California Press.

———. 2013a. 'Gender and Sexuality in Terence'. In Augoustakis and Traill, eds. 175–94.

———. 2013b. 'Reconsidering Rape in Menander's Comedy and Athenian Life: Modern Comparative Evidence'. In Sommerstein, ed. 24–39.

———. 2016. 'Rape and Repetition in Ovid's *Metamorphoses*: Myth, History, Structure, Rome'. In Laurel Fulkerson and Tim Stover, eds. *Repeat Performances: Ovidian Repetition and the* Metamorphoses. University of Wisconsin Press. 154–75.

———. 2019. 'Plautus and the Marriage Plot'. In Dorota M. Dutsch and George F. Franko, eds. *A Companion to Plautus.* Wiley-Blackwell. 109–22.

Janan, Micaela. 1994. '"There beneath the Roman Ruin where the Purple Flowers Grow": Ovid's Minyeides and the Feminine Imagination'. *AJPh* 115.3: 427–48.

Jansen, Laura, ed. 2014. *The Roman Paratext: Frame, Texts, Readers.* Cambridge University Press.

Jenkins, Jacqueline and Katherine J. Lewis. 2003. *St Katherine of Alexandria: Texts and Contexts in Western Medieval Europe.* Brepols.

Jenkins, Katharine. 2017. 'Rape Myths and Domestic Abuse Myths as Hermeneutical Injustices'. *Journal of Applied Philosophy* 34.2: 191–205.

Jennings, Thelma. 1990. '"Us Colored Women Had to Go Through a Plenty": Sexual Exploitation of African-American Slave Women'. *Journal of Women's History* 1.3: 45–74.

Jensson, Gottskálk. 2004. 'The Recollections of Encolpius: The *Satyrica* of Petronius as Milesian Fiction'. *Ancient Narrative Supplementum 2.* Barkhuis.

Johnson, Marguerite. 2016. 'Should academics cite those who have breached moral and humane borders?' *The Conversation.* 21 June. https://theconversation.com/should-academics-cite-those-who-have-breached-moral-and-humane-borders-60932.

Johnstone, Steven. 1998. 'Cracking the Code of Silence: Athenian Legal Oratory and the Histories of Slaves and Women'. In Sandra R. Joshel and Sheila Murnaghan, eds. *Women and Slaves in Greco-Roman Culture: Differential Equations*. Routledge. 227–41.
Jordan, Mark D. 1997. *The Invention of Sodomy in Christian Theology*. University of Chicago Press.
Joshel, Sandra R. 1992. 'The Body Female and the Body Politic: Livy's Lucretia and Verginia'. In Amy Richlin, ed. *Pornography and Representation in Greece and Rome*. Oxford University Press. 112–30.
Joshel, Sandra R., Margaret Malamud and Donald T. McGuire, eds. 2001. *Imperial Projections: Ancient Rome in Modern Popular Culture*. Johns Hopkins University Press.
Just, Roger. 1989. *Women in Athenian Law and Life*. Routledge.
Kahane, Ahuvia. 2005. *Diachronic Dialogues: Authority and Continuity in Homer and the Homeric Tradition*. Lexington Books.
Kamen, Deborah. 2013. *Status in Classical Athens*. Princeton University Press.
———. 2020. *Insults in Classical Athens*. University of Wisconsin Press.
Kamen, Deborah and C. W. Marshall. 2021. *Slavery and Sexuality in Classical Antiquity*. University of Wisconsin Press.
Karras, Ruth Mazo. 2017. *Sexuality in Medieval Europe: Doing Unto Others*. Routledge.
Kaster, Robert A. 2001. 'Controlling Reason: Declamation in Rhetorical Education at Rome'. In Yun Lee Too, ed. *Education in Greek and Roman Antiquity*. Brill. 317–37.
Keegan, Peter. 2013. 'Reading the "Pages" of the *Domus Caesaris: pueri delicati*, Slave Education, and the Graffiti of the Palatine Paedagogium'. In Michele George, ed. *Roman Slavery and Roman Material Culture*. University of Toronto Press: 69–98.
Keith, Alison M. 1992. *The Play of Fictions: Studies in Ovid's* Metamorphoses *Book 2*. University of Michigan Press.
———. 2000. *Engendering Rome: Women in Latin Epic*. Cambridge University Press.
———. 2002. 'Sources and Genres in Ovid's *Metamorphoses*'. In Barbara Weiden Boyd, ed. *Brill's Companion to Ovid*. Brill. 235–69.
———. 2010. 'Dionysiac Theme and Dramatic Allusion in Ovid's *Metamorphoses 4*'. In Ingo Gildenhard and Martin Revermann, eds. *Beyond the Fifth Century: Interactions with Greek Tragedy from the Fourth Century BCE to the Middle Ages*. 187–218. De Gruyter.
Keller, Evelyn Fox. 1985. *Reflections on Gender and Science*. Yale University Press.
Kenney, Edward J. 1969. 'Ovid and the Law'. *Yale Classical Studies* 21: 241–63.
Kennedy, Rebecca Futo. 2014. *Immigrant Women in Athens: Gender, Ethnicity, and Citizenship in the Classical City*. Routledge.

Kidd, Ian James. 2020. 'Epistemic Corruption and Social Oppression'. In Ian James Kidd, Heather Battaly and Quassim Cassam, eds. *Vice Epistemology*. Routledge. 69–86.
Kidd, Ian James, José Medina and Gaile Pohlhaus Jr, eds. 2017. *The Routledge Handbook of Epistemic Injustice*. Routledge.
King, Helen. 2002. *Hippocrates' Woman: Reading the Female Body in Ancient Greece*. Routledge.
Knorr, Ortwin. 1995. 'The Character of Bacchis in Terence's *Heauton Timorumenos*'. *AJP* 116: 221–35.
_____. 2013. 'Terence's *Hecyra:* Farce or Failure?' In Augoustakis and Traill, eds. 296–317.
Knox, Peter E. 1986. *Ovid's* Metamorphoses *and the Traditions of Augustan Poetry*. Cambridge University Press.
Kokkiou, Chara. 2014. 'Choral Self-Referentiality in the *Prometheus Bound*: Song, Dance, and the Emotions'. *Logeion: A Journal of Ancient Theatre* 4: 127–43.
Konstan, David. 1983. *Roman Comedy*. Cornell University Press.
Kraemer, Ross. 2010. *Unreliable Witnesses: Religion, Gender, and History in the Greco-Roman Mediterranean*. Oxford University Press.
Kron, Uta. 1996. 'Priesthoods, Dedications and Euergetism'. In Riet van Bremen, ed. *Religion and Power in the Ancient Greek World*. Gieben. 139–82.
Kukla, Rebecca. 2006. 'Objectivity and Perspective in Empirical Knowledge'. *Episteme* 3.1: 80–95.
Kurke, Leslie. 1993. 'The Economy of *Kudos*'. In Carol Dougherty and Leslie Kurke, eds. *Cultural Poetics in Archaic Greece: Cult, Performance, Politics*. Cambridge University Press. 131–63.
Kyle, Donald. 2003. '"The Only Woman in All Greece": Kyniska, Agesilaus, Alcibiades and Olympia'. *Journal of Sport History* 30.2: 183–203.
Lackey, Jennifer. 2021. *The Epistemology of Groups*. Oxford University Press.
Laes, Christian. 2003. 'Desperately Different? *Delicia* Children in the Roman Household'. In D. Balch and Carolyn Osiek, eds. *Early Christian Families in Context: An Interdisciplinary Dialogue*. Wm. B. Eerdmans Publishing. 298–324.
_____. 2016. 'Touching Children in Roman Antiquity'. In Christian Laes and Ville Vuolanto, eds. *Children and Everyday Life in the Roman and Late Antique World*. Routledge. 60–78.
_____. 2019. '"Stay Away from My Children!": Educators and the Accusation of Sexual Abuse in Roman Antiquity'. In Shawn W. Flynn, ed. *Children in the Bible and the Ancient World*. Routledge. 115–33.
Lämmer, Manfred. 1981. 'Women and Sport in Ancient Greece: A Plea for a Critical and Objective Approach'. In Jan Borms, Marcel Hebbelinck and Antonio Venerando, eds. *Women and Sport*. Karger. 16–23.

Lange, Dorothy. 1972. 'Two Financial Maneuvers of Cicero'. *CW* 65.5: 152–5.
Lape, Susan. 2004. *Reproducing Athens: Menander's Comedy, Democratic Culture, and the Hellenistic City*. Princeton University Press.
———. 2010. *Race and Citizen Identity in the Classical Athenian Democracy*. Cambridge University Press.
Larson, Bridget A. and Stanley L. Brodsky. 2010. 'When Cross-Examination Offends: How Men and Women Assess Intrusive Questioning of Male and Female Expert Witnesses'. *Journal of Applied Social Psychology* 40.4: 811–30.
Larson, Jennifer. 2001. *Greek Nymphs: Myth, Cult, Lore*. Oxford University Press.
———. 2012. *Greek and Roman Sexualities: A Sourcebook*. Bloomsbury.
Lardinois, André. 2021. 'Sappho's Personal Poetry'. In Finglass and Kelly, eds. 163–74.
Lear, Andrew. 2013. 'Ancient Pederasty: An Introduction'. In Hubbard, ed. 106–31.
Lefèvre, Eckard. 1997. *Studien zur Struktur der 'Milesischen' Novelle bei Petron und Apuleius*. Franz Steiner.
Lefkowitz, Mary R. 1996. 'Critical Stereotypes and the Poetry of Sappho'. In Greene, ed. 26–34.
Leitao, David D. 2012. *The Pregnant Male as Myth and Metaphor in Classical Greek Literature*. Cambridge University Press.
Lenski, Noel. 2016. 'Violence and the Roman Slave'. In Riess and Fagan, eds. 275–98.
Lesser, Rachel H. 2021. 'Sappho's Mythic Models for Female Homoeroticism'. *Arethusa* 54.2: 121–61.
Levin-Richardson, Sarah. 2019. *The Brothel of Pompeii: Sex, Class, and Gender at the Margins of Roman Society*. Cambridge University Press.
Lewis, Juan P. 2013. 'Did Varro Think That Slaves Were Talking Tools?' *Mnemosyne* 66: 634–48.
Licandro, Orazio. 2004. 'The Slave of Moregine: Between Prostitution and *Affectio Domini*'. In *Minima epigraphica et papyrologica*. 293–302.
Lipsius, Justus Hermann. 1883. 'Über die Unechtheit der ersten Rede gegen Aristogeiton'. *Leipziger Studien* 6: 319–31.
Lister, Kate. 2017. 'Medievalism and Sexual Violence: Representations of Rape in Game of Thrones'. In Bettina Bildhauer and Chris Jones, eds. *The Middle Ages in the Modern World: Twenty-first Century Perspectives*. Oxford University Press.
Litaniae Lauretanae. 1998–2023. Michael W. Martin. *Thesaurus Precum Latinarum*. https://www.preces-latinae.org/thesaurus/BVM/Laurentanae.html.
Llewellyn-Jones, Lloyd. 2011. 'Domestic Abuse and Violence against Women in Ancient Greece'. In Stephen D. Lambert, ed. *Sociable Man: Essays on Ancient Greek Social Behaviour*. Classical Press of Wales. 231–66.
———. 2020. '"Knocking Her Teeth Out with a Stone": Violence against Women in Ancient Greece'. In Garrett G. Fagan, Linda Fibiger, Mark Hudson and

Matthew Trundle, eds. *The Cambridge World History of Violence: Vol. 1.* Cambridge University Press. 380–99.

Lloyd, E. Paige, Gina A. Paganini and Leanne ten Brinke. 2020. 'Gender Stereotypes Explain Disparities in Pain Care and Inform Equitable Policies' *Sage Publications* 7.2: 198–204.

Lloyd, Genevieve. 1979. 'The Man of Reason'. *Metaphilosophy* 10.1: 18–37.

———. 1984. *The Man of Reason: 'Male' and 'Female' in Western Philosophy.* University of Minnesota Press.

Lochrie, Karma. 2005. *Heterosyncracies: Female Sexuality When Normal Wasn't.* University of Minnesota Press.

———. 2012. *Covert Operations: The Medieval Uses of Secrecy.* Philadelphia: University of Pennsylvania Press.

———. 2020. 'Gower's Riddles in "Iphis and Iante"'. In Traub, Badir and McKracken, eds. 80–98.

Lofgreen, Ashton M., Richard E. Mattson, Samantha A. Wagner, Edwin G. Ortiz and Matthew D. Johnson. 2017. 'Situational and Dispositional Determinants of College Men's Perception of Women's Sexual Desire and Consent to Sex: A Factorial Vignette Analysis'. *Journal of Interpersonal Violence* 36.1–2.

Longino, Helen. 1990. *Science as Social Knowledge.* Princeton University Press.

Loraux, Nicole. 1993. *The Children of Athena: Athenian Ideas about Citizenship and the Division Between the Sexes.* Trans. by Caroline Levine. Princeton University Press.

Lorde, Audre. 1984. *Sister Outsider: Essays and Speeches.* Crossing Press.

Lowe, Nick J. 2007. *Comedy.* Vol. 37. Cambridge University Press.

Ludwig, Walther. 1965. *Struktur und Einheit der* Metamorphosen *Ovids.* De Gruyter.

Lugones, Maria. 2010. 'Toward a Decolonial Feminism'. *Hypatia* 25: 742–59.

Lunt, David. 2009. 'The Heroic Athlete in Ancient Greece'. *Journal of Sport History* 36.3: 375–92.

Lutz, Cora. 1947. 'Musonius Rufus: "The Roman Socrates"'. *YCIS* 10: 3–147.

MacDowell, Douglas M. 2009. *Demosthenes the Orator.* Oxford University Press.

Maguire, Kate. 2015. *Margaret Mead.* Springer Dordrecht.

Mainzer, Conrad. 1972. 'John Gower's Use of the "Mediaeval Ovid" in the *Confessio Amantis*'. *Medium Ævum* 45: 215–22.

Maitra, Ishani. 2010. 'The Nature of Epistemic Injustice'. *Philosophical Books* 51.4: 195–211.

Malpezzi Price, Paola and Christine Ristaino. 2008. *Lucrezia Marinella and the 'Querelle des Femmes' in Seventeenth-Century Italy.* Fairleigh Dickinson University Press.

Manning, Charles E. 1973. 'Seneca and the Stoics on the Equality of the Sexes'. *Mnemosyne* 26.2: 170–7.

Maravall, José Antonio. 1986. *Culture of the Baroque: Analysis of a Historical Structure*. Trans. by Terry Cochran. Manchester University Press.

Marchina, Martha. 1662. *Marthae Marchinae virginis Neapolitanae Musa posthuma*. Filippo Maria Mancini.

———. 1701. *Marthae Marchinae virginis Neapolitanae Musa posthuma*. Antonio Bulifon.

Marder, Elissa. 1992. 'Disarticulated Voices: Feminism and Philomela'. *Hypatia* 7.2: 148–66.

Marinella, Lucrezia. 1999. *The Nobility and Excellence of Women and the Defects and Vices of Men*. Trans. by Anne Dunhill. University of Chicago Press.

Marino, John A. 2002. *Early Modern Italy, 1550–1796*. Oxford University Press.

Marshall, Christopher W. 2015. 'Domestic Sexual Labor in Plautus'. *Helios* 42.1: 123–41.

Martínez, Theresa A. 1996. 'Toward a Chicana Feminist Epistemological Standpoint: Theory at the Intersection of Race, Class, and Gender'. *Race, Gender and Class* 3.3: 107–28.

Mason, Rebecca. 2011. 'Two Kinds of Unknowing'. *Hypatia* 26: 294–307.

———. 2021. 'Hermeneutical Injustice'. In Justin Khoo and Rachel Sterken, eds. *The Routledge Handbook of Social and Political Philosophy of Language*. Routledge. 247–58.

Masterson, Mark. 2013. 'Studies of Ancient Masculinity'. In Hubbard, ed. 19–32.

Mathieu, Georges. 1947. *Démosthène: Plaidoyers politiques Vol. IV*. Les Belles Lettres.

Matlock, Andres. 2020. 'Relationality, Fidelity, and the Event in Sappho'. *CA* 39.1: 29–56.

May, Vivian. 2014. '"Speaking into the Void"? Intersectionality Critiques and Epistemic Backlash'. *Hypatia* 29.1: 94–112.

McAlinden, Anne-Marie. 2012. *'Grooming' and the Sexual Abuse of Children: Institutional, Internet, and Familial Dimensions*. Oxford University Press.

———. 2014. 'Deconstructing Victim and Offender Identities in Discourses on Child Sexual Abuse: Hierarchies, Blame and the Good/Evil Dialectic'. *The British Journal of Criminology* 54: 180–98.

McCarter, Stephanie. 2019. 'Seneca's "Lost Cause": The Myth of the Noble Stoic/Southern Slave Owner'. *Eidolon*. 1 February. https://eidolon.pub/senecas-lost-cause-cfcbb5d15d32.

McCarthy, Kathleen. 2000. *Slaves, Masters, and the Art of Authority*. Princeton University Press.

McClure, Laura. 1999. *Spoken Like a Woman: Speech and Gender in Athenian Drama*. Princeton University Press.

McCutcheon, R. W. 2016. 'Cicero's Textual Relations: the Gendered Circulation of *de Finibus*'. *Helios* 43.1: 21–53.

McDermott, William C. 1972. 'M. Cicero and M. Tiro'. *Historia* 21.1: 259–86.
McGarrity, Terry. 1980–1. 'Reputation vs. Reality in Terence's *Hecyra*'. *CJ* 76.2: 149–56.
McGill, Emily. 2022. '*Prohairesis* and a Stoic-Inspired Feminist Autonomy'. *Symposion* 9.1: 83–104.
McGinn, Thomas A. J. 1998. *Prostitution, Sexuality, and the Law in Ancient Rome*. Oxford University Press.
McGlathery, Daniel Beyer. 1998a. 'Reversals of Platonic Love in Petronius' *Satyricon*'. In David H. J. Larmour, Paul Allen Miller and Charles Platter, eds. *Rethinking Sexuality: Foulcault and Classical Antiquity*. Princeton University Press. 204–27.
———. 1998b. '"*Commendatam Bonitatem*": Sexual Spectacle and Linguistic Deception in the Philomela's Daughter Episode of Petronius' *Satyricon*'. *Pacific Coast Philology* 33: 1–14.
McGowan, Mary K. 2014. 'Sincerity Silencing'. *Hypatia* 29.2: 458–73.
McHardy, Fiona. 2004. 'Women's Influence on Revenge in Ancient Greece'. In Fiona McHardy and Eireann Marshall, eds. *Women's Influence on Classical Civilization*. Routledge. 92–114.
———. 2018. '"The Power of Our Mouths": Gossip as a Female Mode of Revenge'. In Lesel Dawson and Fiona McHardy, eds. *Revenge and Gender in Classical, Medieval and Renaissance Literature*. Edinburgh University Press. 160–80.
———. 2021. 'The Risk of Violence towards Motherless Children in Ancient Greece'. In Sabine R. Huebner, ed. *Missing Mothers: Maternal Absence in Antiquity*. Peeters Press. 71–88.
McKinley, Kathryn L. 2011. 'Gower and Chaucer: Reading of Ovid in Late Medieval England'. In James G. Clark, Frank T. Coulson and Kathryn L. McKinley, eds. *Ovid in the Middle Ages*. Cambridge University Press. 197–230.
McMillan, Lesley. 2018. 'Police Officers' Perceptions of False Allegations of Rape'. *Journal of Gender Studies* 27.1: 9–21.
McWhorter, Ladelle. 1999. *Bodies and Pleasures: Foucault and the Politics of Sexual Normalization*. Indiana University Press.
Medina, José. 2012. 'Hermeneutical Injustice and Polyphonic Contextualism: Social Silences and Shared Hermeneutical Responsibilities'. *Social Epistemology: A Journal of Knowledge, Culture and Policy* 26: 201–20.
———. 2013. *The Epistemology of Resistance: Gender and Racial Oppression, Epistemic Injustice, and Resistant Imaginations*. Oxford University Press.
———. 2017. 'Varieties of Hermeneutical Injustice'. In Kidd, Medina and Pohlhaus Jr, eds. 41–52.
Medina-Minton, Natalie. 2019. 'Are Children an Oppressed Group? Positing a Child Standpoint Theory'. *Child and Adolescent Social Work Journal* 36.5: 439–47.

Meyer, Michael. 1987. 'Stoics, Rights, and Autonomy'. *APhQ* 24.3: 267–71.
Mignolo, Walter. 2009. 'Epistemic Disobedience, Independent Thought and Decolonial Freedom'. *Theory, Culture and Society* 26.7–8: 159–81.
———. 2010. 'Cosmopolitanism and the De-colonial Option'. *Studies in Philosophy and Education* 29.2: 111–27.
Miller, Andrew M., trans. 1996. *Greek Lyric: An Anthology in Translation*. Hackett Publishing Company, Inc.
Miller, Frank Justus, ed. and trans. Revised by G. P. Goold. 1977–84. *Ovid. Metamorphoses*. Vols I–II. Loeb Classical Library. Harvard University Press.
Miller, John F. 2009. *Apollo, Augustus, and the Poets*. Cambridge University Press.
Mills, Charles W. 1988. 'Alternative Epistemologies'. *Social Theory and Practice* 14.3: 237–63.
———. 1997. *The Racial Contract*. Cornell University Press.
———. 2007. 'White Ignorance'. In Tuana and Sullivan, eds.
———. 2015. 'Global White Ignorance'. In Matthias Gross and Linsey McGoey, eds. *Routledge International Handbook of Ignorance Studies*. Routledge.
Mills, Robert. 2015. *Seeing Sodomy in the Middle Ages*. University of Chicago Press.
Milnor, Kristina. 2005. *Gender, Domesticity, and the Age of Augustus*. Oxford University Press.
Minnis, Alastair J. 2001. *Magister Amoris: The 'Roman De La Rose' and Vernacular Hermeneutics*. Oxford University Press.
Mohanty, Chandra Talpade. 1984. 'Under Western Eyes: Feminist Scholarship and Colonial Discourses'. *Boundary* 2: 333–58.
Mommsen, Theodor, Paul Krueger and Alan Watson. 1985. *The Digest of Justinian IV*. University of Pennsylvania Press.
Monument Lab. 2021. *The National Monument Audit*. Produced in partnership with the Andrew W. Mellon Foundation. Monument Lab.
Moore, Timothy J. 1998. *The Theatre of Plautus: Playing to the Audience*. University of Texas Press.
Moreno Soldevila, Rosario. 2011. *Diccionario de motivos amatorios en la literatura latina*. University of Huelva.
Moretti, Luigi. 1953. *Iscrizioni agonistiche greche*. A. Signorelli.
Morgan, John R. 2009. 'Petronius and Greek Literature'. In Prag and Repath, eds. 32–47.
Morrison, John S. 1964. 'Four Notes on Plato's *Symposium*'. *CQ* 14.1: 42–55.
Most, Glenn W. 1995. 'Reflecting Sappho'. *BICS* 40: 15–38.
Motto, Anna Lydia. 1972. 'Seneca on Women's Liberation'. *CW* 65.5: 155–7.
Mueller, Melissa. 2021. 'Sappho and Sexuality'. In Finglass and Kelly, eds. 36–52.
Müller, Konrad. 2003. *Petronii Arbitri Satyricon Reliquiae*. Karl G. Saur Verglag.

Muñoz, José Esteban. 1999. *Disidentifications: Queers of Color and the Performance of Politics*. University of Minnesota Press.

Myers, K. Sara. 1994. '*Ultimus Ardor*: Pomona and Vertumnus in Ovid's *Met.* 14.623–771'. *CJ* 89.3: 225–50.

Nagel, Thomas. 1986. *The View from Nowhere*. Oxford University Press.

Nagle, Betty Rose. 1984. '*Amor, Ira*, and Sexual Identity in Ovid's *Metamorphoses*'. *ClAnt* 3.2: 236–55.

———. 1988. 'Erotic Pursuit and Narrative Seduction in Ovid's *Metamorphoses*'. *Ramus* 17.1: 32–51.

Najmabadi, Asfaneh. 2006. 'Beyond the Americas: Are Gender and Sexuality Useful Categories of Historical Analysis?' *Journal of Women's History* 18: 11–21.

Nakata, Martin. 2007. *Disciplining the Savages: Savaging the Disciplines*. Aboriginal Studies Press.

Narayan, Uma. 1989. 'The Project of Feminist Epistemology: Perspectives from a Nonwestern Feminist'. In Alison M. Jaggar and Susan Bordo, eds. *Gender/Body/Knowledge: Feminist Reconstructions of Being and Knowing*. Rutgers University Press. 256–69.

Nardal, Paulette. 2002 [1932]. 'The Awakening of Race Consciousness among Black Students'. Trans. and reprinted in T. Denean Sharpley-Whiting. *Negritude Women*. University of Minnesota Press. 119–24.

Nawar, Tamer. 2014. 'The Stoic Account of Apprehension'. *Philosophers' Imprint* 14.29: 1–21.

Nehamas, Alexander and Paul Woodruff, trans. 1989. *Plato's Symposium*. Hackett Publishing Company.

Neils, Jenifer. 2012. 'Spartan Girls and the Athenian Gaze'. In Sharon L. James and Sheila Dillon, eds. *A Companion to Women in the Ancient World*. John Wiley and Sons. 153–84.

Nelson, Lynn Hankinson. 1990. *Who Knows: From Quine to a Feminist Empiricism*. Temple University Press.

Nguyen, Nghiem L. 2006. 'Roman Rape: An Overview of Roman Rape Laws from the Republican Period to Justinian's Reign'. *Michigan Journal of Gender and Law* 13.1: 75–112.

Nightingale, Andrea. 2017. 'The Mortal Soul and Immortal Happiness'. In Destrée and Giannopoulou, eds. 142–59.

Nochlin, Linda. 1988. 'Why Have There Been No Great Women Artists?' In Linda Nochlin. Harper and Row. 1–36.

Noddings, Nel. 1988. 'An Ethic of Caring and Its Implications for Instructional Arrangements'. *American Journal of Education* 96.2: 215–30.

Nordmarken, Sonny. 2014. 'Becoming Ever More Monstrous: Feeling Transgender In-Betweenness'. *Qualitative Inquiry* 20.1: 37–50.

Noy, David. 2008. 'Review of Terentia, Tullia, and Publilia'. *BMCR* 2008. 07. 06

Nussbaum, Martha. 1986. *The Fragility of Goodness: Luck and Ethics in Greek Tragedy and Philosophy.* Cambridge University Press.

———. 2002. 'The Incomplete Feminism of Musonius Rufus: Platonist, Stoic, and Roman'. In Martha Nussbaum and Juha Sihvola, eds. *The Sleep of Reason: Erotic Experience and Sexual Ethics in Ancient Greece and Rome.* University of Chicago Press. 283–316.

Obbink, Dirk. 2016. 'The Newest Sappho: Text, Apparatus Criticus, and Translation'. In Anton Bierl and André Lardinois, eds. *The Newest Sappho.* Brill. 13–33.

Ober, Josiah. 1989. *Mass and Elite.* Princeton University Press.

Obermayer, Hans Peter. 1998. *Martial und der Diskurs über männliche 'Homosexualität' in der Literatur der frühen Kaiserzeit.* Gunter Narr Verlag.

Ohlheiser, Abby. 2017. 'The Woman Behind "Me Too" Knew the Power of the Phrase When She Created It – 10 Years Ago'. *The Washington Post.* 19 October. https://www.washingtonpost.com/news/the-intersect/wp/2017/10/19/the-woman-behind-me-too-knew-the-power-of-the-phrase-when-she-created-it-10-years-ago/.

Okin, Susan Moller. 1979. *Women in Western Political Thought.* Princeton University Press.

Olsen, Glenn Warren. 2011. *Of Sodomites, Effeminates, Hermaphrodites, and Androgynes Sodomy in the Age of Peter Damian.* Pontifical Institute of Mediaeval Studies.

Olson, Greta. 2022. 'Harvey Weinstein and #MeToo'. In Maria Mäkelä and Paul Dawson, eds. *The Routledge Companion to Narrative Theory.* Taylor & Francis.

Olson, Philip and Laura Gillman. 2013. 'Combating Racialized and Gendered Ignorance: Theorizing a Transactional Pedagogy of Friendship'. *Feminist Formations* 25.1: 59–83.

Omitowoju, Rosanna. 2016. 'The Crime that Dare not Speak its Name: Violence against Women in the Athenian Courts'. In Riess and Fagan, eds. 113–35.

Ortega, Mariana. 2006. 'Being Lovingly, Knowingly Ignorant: White Feminism and Women of Color'. *Hypatia* 21.3: 56–74.

Packman, Zola M. 1993. 'Call It Rape: A Motif in Roman Comedy and its Suppression in English-Speaking Publications'. *Helios* 20: 42–55.

———. 1999. 'Rape and Consequences in the Latin Declamations'. *Scholia* 8.: 17–36.

Padel, Ruth. 1992. *In and Out of the Mind: Greek Images of the Tragic Self.* Princeton University Press.

Padilla Peralta, Dan-el. 2019. 'Some thoughts on AIA-SCS 2019'. *Medium.* 7 January. https://medium.com/@danelpadillaperalta/some-thoughts-on-aia-scs-2019-d6a480a1812a.

———. 2020. 'Epistemicide: The Roman Case'. *Classica: Revista Brasileira de Estudos Clássicos* 33.2: 151–86.

Panayotakis, Costas. 2019. 'Slavery and Beauty in Petronius'. In Stelios Panayotakis, Michael Paschalis and Costas Panayotakis, eds. *Masters and Slaves in the Ancient Novel*. Barkhuis. 181–202.
Parker, Holt. 2005. 'Sappho's Public World'. In Ellen Greene, ed. *Women Poets in Ancient Greece and Rome*. University of Oklahoma Press. 3–24.
Parry, Hugh. 1964. 'Ovid's *Metamorphoses*: Violence in a Pastoral Landscape'. *TAPA* 95: 268–82.
Pender, Elizabeth E. 1992. 'Spiritual Pregnancy in Plato's *Symposium*'. *CQ* 42.1: 72–86.
Penwill, John L. 2004. 'The Unlovely Lover of Terence's *Hecyra*'. *Ramus* 33: 130–49.
Perry, Matthew J. 2014. *Gender, Manumission, and the Roman Freedwoman*. Cambridge University Press.
Peterson, Zoë D. and Charlene L. Muehlenhard. 2004. 'Was It Rape? The Function of Women's Rape Myth Acceptance and Definitions of Sex in Labeling Their Own Experiences'. *Sex Roles* 51.3: 129–44.
Phillips, Lynne M. 2000. *Flirting with Danger: Young Women's Reflections on Sexuality and Domination*. New York University Press.
Phillips, Nickie D. 2016. *Beyond Blurred Lines: Rape Culture in Popular Media*. Rowman and Littlefield Publishers.
Pierce, Karen F. 1997. 'The Portrayal of Rape in New Comedy'. In Deacy and Pierce, eds. 163–83.
Pitts, Andrea J. 2016. 'Gloria E. Anzaldúa's *Autohistoria-teoría* as an Epistemology of Self-Knowledge/Ignorance'. *Hypatia* 31.2: 352–69.
Plancarte, Alfonso Méndez, ed. 1951. *Obras completas de Sor Juana Inés de la Cruz*. 4 vols. Fondo de Cultura Económico.
Platt, Verity. 2011. *Facing the Gods: Epiphany and Representation in Graeco-Roman Art, Literature and Religion*. Oxford University Press.
Pletcher, Mark J., Stefan G. Kertesz, Michael A. Kohn and Ralph Gonzales. 2008. 'Trends in Opioid Prescribing by Race/Ethnicity for Patients Seeking Care in US Emergency Departments'. *JAMA* 299.1: 70–8.
Podosky, Paul-Mikhail Catapang. 2021. 'Rethinking Epistemic Appropriation' *Episteme* 1: 1–21.
Pohlhaus Jr, Gaile. 2011. 'Wrongful Requests and Strategic Refusals to Understand'. In Heidi Grasswick, ed. *Feminist Epistemology and Philosophy of Science: Power in Knowledge*. Springer. 223–40.
———. 2012. 'Relational Knowing and Epistemic Injustice: Toward a Theory of Willful Hermeneutical Ignorance'. *Hypatia* 27.4: 715–35.
———. 2014. 'Discerning the Primary Epistemic Harm in Cases of Testimonial Injustice'. *Social Epistemology* 28.2: 99–114.
———. 2017. 'Varieties of Epistemic Injustice'. In Kidd, Medina and Pohlhaus Jr, eds. 13–26.
Pomeroy, Sarah B. 2002. *Spartan Women*. Oxford University Press.

———. 2013. *Pythagorean Women: Their History and Writings*. Johns Hopkins University Press.
Poole, Monica. 2021. 'Feminist Epistemologies'. In Brian C. Barnett, ed. www.press.rebus.community/intro-to-phil-epistemology/chapter/feminist-epistemologies.
Porter, John R. 1997. 'Adultery by the Book: Lysias I (*On the murder of Eratosthenes*) and Comic Diegesis'. *EMC* 16: 421–53.
Poser, Rachel. 2021. 'He Wants to Save Classics From Whiteness. Can the Field Survive?' *The New York Times*. 25 April. https://www.nytimes.com/2021/02/02/magazine/classics-greece-rome-whiteness.html.
Possamaï-Pérez, Marylène. 2006. L'Ovide moralisé: *Essai d'interprétation*. Champion.
Prag, Jonathan and Ian Repath, eds. 2009. *Petronius: A Handbook*. Wiley-Blackwell.
Price, Anthony W. 2017. 'Generating in Beauty for the Sake of Immortality: Personal Love and the Goals of the Lover'. In Destrée and Giannopoulou, eds. 184–5.
Prior, William J. 2006. 'The Portrait of Socrates in Plato's *Symposium*'. *OSAPh* Winter: 137–66.
Projansky, Sarah. 2001. *Watching Rape: Film and Television in Postfeminist Culture*. NYU Press.
Project Nota with Lupercal. 2022. https://www.projectnotalatin.org/.
Quijano, Anibal. 2000. 'Coloniality of Power and Eurocentrism in Latin America'. *International Sociology* 15.2: 215–32.
Rabinowitz, Nancy Sorkin. 1993. 'Introduction'. In Rabinowitz and Richlin, eds. 1–22.
———. 2001. 'Personal Voice/Feminist Voice'. *Arethusa* 34.2: 191–210.
Rabinowitz, Nancy Sorkin and Amy Richlin, eds. 1993. *Feminist Theory and the Classics*. Routledge.
Race, William H. 1989. 'Sappho, Fr. 16 L-P. and Alkaios, Fr. 42 L-P.: Romantic and Classical Strains in Lesbian Lyric'. *CJ* 85.1: 16–33.
———, ed. and trans. 1997. *Pindar: Olympian Odes and Pythian Odes*. Vol. I. Loeb Classical Library. Harvard University Press.
Rader, Richard. 2014. 'The Radical Theology of *Prometheus Bound*; or, on Prometheus' God Problem'. *Ramus* 42.1–2: 162–82.
Ramelli, Ilaria. 2009. *Hierocles the Stoic: Elements of Ethics, Fragments, and Excerpts*. Society of Biblical Literature.
Reed, Rebecca A., et al. 2020. 'Higher Rates of Unacknowledged Rape among Men: The Role of Rape Myth Acceptance'. *Psychology of Men and Masculinities* 21.1: 162.
Reeve, Charles David Chanel. 2012. 'Plato on Begetting in Beauty'. In Alison Denham, ed. *Plato on Art and Beauty*. Palgrave Macmillan. 142–72.
Repath, Ian D. 2010. 'Plato in Petronius: Petronius *In Platanona*'. *CQ* 60: 577–95.
Rich, Adrienne. 1980. 'Compulsory Heterosexuality and Lesbian Existence'. *Signs* 5.4: 631–60.

Richardson, T. Wade. 1984. 'Homosexuality in the *Satyricon*'. *C&M* 35: 105–27.
Richlin, Amy. 1981. 'Approaches to the Sources on Adultery at Rome'. *Women's Studies* 8.1–2: 225–50.
———. 1992. 'Reading Ovid's Rapes'. In Amy Richlin, ed. *Pornography and Representation in Greece and Rome*. Oxford University Press. 158–79.
———. 1993a. 'The Ethnographer's Dilemma and the Dream of a Lost Golden Age'. In Rabinowitz and Richlin, eds. 272–303.
———. 1993b. 'Not Before Homosexuality: The Materiality of the *Cinaedus* and the Roman Law against Love between Men'. *JHSex* 3: 523–73.
———. 2009. 'Sex in the *Satyrica*: Outlaws in Literatureland'. In Prag and Repath, eds. 82–100.
———. 2014. *Arguments with Silence*. University of Michigan Press.
———. 2017. *Slave Theater in the Roman Republic: Plautus and Popular Comedy*. Cambridge University Press.
Riess, Werner and Garrett G. Fagan, eds. 2016. *The Topography of Violence in the Greco-Roman World*. University of Michigan Press.
Roach, Imani. 2017. 'Sharon Hayes for Monument Lab'. *The Art Blog*. 5 October. https://www.theartblog.org/2017/10/sharon-hayes-for-monument-lab.
Robinson, Olivia F. 1995. *The Criminal Law of Ancient Rome*. Duckworth.
Roiphe, Katie. 1993. *The Morning After: Sex, Fear, and Feminism on Campus*. Little, Brown and Company.
Roisman, Joseph. 2005. *The Rhetoric of Manhood*. University of California Press.
Roller, Duane. 2010. *OUP Blog*. 6 December. https://blog.oup.com/2010/12/cleopatra-2/.
Rollero, Chiara and Stefano Tartaglia. 2019. 'The Effect of Sexism and Rape Myths on Victim Blame'. *Sexuality and Culture* 23: 209–19.
Romei, Danilo, ed. 2018. *Galileo Galilei. Sidereus Nuncius*. Nuovo Rinascimento. http://www.nuovorinascimento.org/n-rinasc/astrit/pdf/galilei/sidereus_nuncius.pdf.
Rooney, Phyllis. 1991. 'Gendered Reason: Sex Metaphor and Conceptions of Reason'. *Hypatia* 6: 77–103.
Rosati, Gianpiero. 1999. 'Form in Motion: Weaving the Text in the *Metamorphoses*'. In Philip Hardie, Alessandro Barchiesi and Stephen Hinds, eds. *Ovidian Transformations: Essays on the* Metamorphoses *and its Reception*. Cambridge University Press. 240–53.
———, ed. 2007. *Ovidio Metamorfosi: Vol. II (Libri III–IV)*. Milan: Fondazione Lorenzo Valla.
Rose, Hilary. 1983. 'Hand, Brain, and Heart: A Feminist Epistemology for the Natural Sciences'. *Women and Religion* 9.1: 73–90.
Rosen, Jeremy. 2016. *Minor Characters Have Their Day: Genre and the Contemporary Literary Marketplace*. Columbia University Press.

Rosenbloom, David S. 2003. 'Aristogeiton Son of Cydimachus and the Scoundrel's Drama'. In John Davidson and Arthur Pomeroy, eds. *Theatres of Action. Papers for Chris Dearden*. Polygraphia. 88–117.

Rosenzweig, Rachel. 2004. *Worshiping Aphrodite: Art and Cult in Classical Athens*. University of Michigan Press.

Rossi, Gian Vittorio. 1643. *Pinacotheca imaginum illustrium doctrinae vel ingenii laude virorum (etc.)*. Judocus Kalcovius.

Roth, Ulrike. 2021. 'Speaking Out?: Child Sexual Abuse and the Enslaved Voice in the *Cena Trimalchionis*'. In Kamen and Marshall, eds. 211–38.

Rubinstein, Lene. 2000. *Litigation and Cooperation: Supporting Speakers in the Courts of Classical Athens*. Steiner.

Ruden, Sarah. 2000. *Petronius. Satyricon*. Hackett.

Ruddick, Sara. 1989. 'Maternal Thinking as a Feminist Standpoint'. In Sara Ruddick, *Maternal Thinking*. Beacon Press. 127–39.

Saatsoglou-Paliadeli, Chrysoula. 2000. 'Queenly Appearances at Vergina-Aegae. Old and New Epigraphic and Literary Evidence'. *AA* 3: 387–403.

Salamon, Gayle. 2010. *Assuming a Body: Transgender and Rhetorics of Materiality*. Columbia University Press.

Saller, Richard. 1991. 'Corporal Punishment, Authority, and Obedience in the Roman Household'. In Beryl Rawson, ed. *Marriage, Divorce, and Children in Ancient Rome*. Clarendon Press. 144–65.

———. 1999. 'Pater Familias, Mater Familias, and the Gendered Semantics of the Roman Household'. *CP* 94: 182–97.

Salzman-Mitchell, Patricia. 2005. *A Web of Fantasies: Gaze, Image, and Gender in Ovid's* Metamorphoses. Ohio State University Press.

Sanders, G. D. R. 2009. 'Platanistas, The Course and Carneus: Their Places in the Topography of Sparta'. In William G. Cavanagh, Chrysanthi Gallou and Mercourios Georgiadis, eds. *Sparta and Laconia from Prehistory to Pre-modern*. The British School at Athens Studies. 195–203.

Sanson, Helena. 2014. '"Femina proterva, rude, indocta [. . .], chi t'ha insegnato a parlar in questo modo?" Women's "Voices" and Linguistic Varieties in Sixteenth- and Seventeenth-Century Written Texts'. *The Italianist* 34: 400–17.

Santos, Boaventura de Sousa. 2016. 'Epistemologies of the South and the Future'. *From the European South: A Transdisciplinary Journal of Postcolonial Humanities* 1: 17–29.

Scafuro, Adele C. 2011. *Demosthenes, Speeches 39–49*. University of Texas Press.

Scanlon, Larry. 1995. 'Unspeakable Pleasures: Alain de Lille, Sexual Regulation, and the Priesthood of Genius'. *Romanic Review* 86.2: 213–42.

Scanlon, Thomas F. 2002. *Eros and Greek Athletics*. Oxford University Press.

Schaefer, Arnold. 1887. *Demosthenes und seine Zeit*. Gg Olms.

Schaps, David M. 1998. 'What was Free about a Free Athenian Woman?' *TAPA* 128: 161–88.

———. 2006. 'Zeus the Wife-Beater'. *SCI* 25: 1–24.

Schiff, Stacy. 2009. 'Who's Buried in Cleopatra's Tomb?' *The New York Times*. 21 April. https://www.nytimes.com/2009/04/22/opinion/22schiff.html.

Schmeling, Gareth. 2011. *A Commentary on the Satyrica of Petronius*. Oxford University Press.

Schmitt, Frederick. 2017. 'Social Epistemology'. In John Greco and Ernest Sosa, eds. *The Blackwell Guide to Epistemology*. Blackwell. 354–82.

Schofield, Malcolm. 1991. *The Stoic Idea of the City*. Cambridge University Press.

Scodel, Ruth and Anja Bettenworth. 2009. *Whither Quo Vadis? Sienkiewicz's Novel in Film and Television*. John Wiley and Sons.

Scott, William C. 1987. 'The Development of the Chorus in *Prometheus Bound*'. *TAPA* 117: 85–96.

Scourfield, J. H. David. 2003. 'Anger and Gender in Chariton's *Chaereas and Callirhoe*'. In Susanna Braund and Glen W. Most, eds. *Ancient Anger: Perspectives from Homer to Galen*. Cambridge University Press. 163–84.

Scullin, Sarah. 2016. 'Making a Monster'. *Eidolon*. 24 March. https://eidolon.pub/making-a-monster-3cd90135ef3f.

Sealey, Raphael. 1960. 'Who was Aristogeiton?' *BICS* 7: 33–43.

———. 1967. 'Pseudo-Demosthenes XIII and XXV', *Revue des Études Grecques* 80: 250–5.

Sedgwick, Eve Kosofsky. 1990. *Epistemology of the Closet*. University of California Press.

Sega, Giovanni. 1986. 'Due milesie: La matrona di Efeso e l'efebo di Pergamo'. *MCSN* 4: 37–81.

Segal, Charles P. 1969. *Landscape in Ovid's Metamorphoses*. Franz Steiner Verlag.

———. 1998. 'Ovid's Metamorphic Bodies: Art, Gender, and Violence in the *Metamorphoses*'. *Arion* 5: 9–41.

Segal, Erich. 1968. *Roman Laughter: The Comedy of Plautus*. Oxford University Press.

Sellars, John. 2006. *Stoicism*. University of California Press.

Seung, Thomas Kaehao. 1982. *Structuralism and Hermeneutics*. Columbia University Press.

Shackleton Bailey, David R., ed. 1965. *Cicero's Letters to Atticus*. 8 vols. Cambridge University Press.

———, ed. 1977. *Cicero: Epistulae ad Familiares*. 2 vols. Cambridge University Press.

Shade, Barbara J. 1982. 'Afro-American Cognitive Style: A Variable in School Success?' *Review of Educational Research* 52.2: 219–44.

Sharrock, Alison. 2019. 'An Introduction to Roman Comedy'. In Martin Dinter, ed. *The Cambridge Companion to Roman Comedy*. Cambridge University Press. 1–14.

———. 2020. 'Gender and Transformation: Reading, Women, and Gender in Ovid's *Metamorphoses*'. In Mats Malm, Alison Sharrock and Daniel Möller, eds. *Metamorphic Readings: Transformation, Language, and Gender in the Interpretation of Ovid's* Metamorphoses. Oxford University Press. 33–53.

Sheffield, Frisbee C.C. 2006. *Plato's* Symposium: *The Ethics of Desire*. Oxford University Press.

———. 2012. 'The *Symposium* and Platonic Ethics: Plato, Vlastos, and a Misguided Debate'. *Phronesis* 57.2: 117–41.

———. 2017. '*Erōs* and the Pursuit of Form'. In Destrée and Giannopoulou, eds. 125–41.

Shirley, Skye. Forthcoming. *Three Collections of Latin Poetry by Women from the 17th Century*. PhD diss. University College London.

Shotwell, Alexis. 2011. *Knowing Otherwise: Race, Gender, and Implicit Understanding*. Penn State University Press.

Silvers, Anita. 2013. 'Feminist Perspectives on Disability'. *The Stanford Encyclopedia of Philosophy*. 29 August. https://plato.stanford.edu/entries/feminism-disability/.

Simson, Rosalind S. 2005. 'Feminine Thinking'. *Social Theory and Practice* 31.1: 1–26.

Skinner, Marilyn B. 1996. 'Woman and Language in Archaic Greece, or, Why Is Sappho a Woman?' In Greene, ed. 175–92.

———. 2011. *Clodia Metelli: The Tribune's Sister*. Oxford University Press.

———. 2013. *Sexuality in Greek and Roman Culture*. Wiley-Blackwell.

Slater, Niall W. 1990. *Reading Petronius*. Johns Hopkins University Press.

———. 2009. 'Reading the *Satyrica*'. In Prag and Repath, eds. 16–31.

Slings, Simon Roelof. 1990. 'The I in Personal Archaic Lyric: An Introduction'. In Simon Roelof Slings, ed. *The Poet's I in Archaic Greek Lyric*. VU University Press. 1–30.

Smith, Dorothy E. 1974. 'Women's Perspective as a Radical Critique of Sociology'. *Sociological Inquirer* 44.1: 7–13.

———. 1991. *The Conceptual Practices of Power: A Feminist Sociology of Knowledge*. Northeastern University Press.

———. 1997. 'Comment on Hekman's "Truth and Method: Feminist Standpoint Theory Revisited"'. *Signs* 22.2: 392–8.

Smith, Linda T. 1999. *Decolonizing Methodologies: Research and Indigenous Peoples*. Zed Books.

Smith, Louise P. 1994. 'Audience Response to Rape: Chaerea in Terence's *Eunuchus*'. *Helios* 21.1: 21–38.

Solinas, Francesco. 2020. '"Bella, pulita, e senza macchia": Artemisia and Her Letters'. In Letizia Treves, ed. *Artemisia*. National Gallery. 46–63.
Sommerstein, Alan H. 1998. 'Rape and Young Manhood in Athenian Comedy'. In Foxhall and Salmon, eds. 100–13.
———, ed. and trans. 2009. *Aeschylus I: Persians. Seven against Thebes. Suppliants. Prometheus Bound*. Loeb Classical Library. Harvard University Press.
———, ed. 2014. *Menander in Contexts*. Routledge.
Spelman, Elizabeth V. 1982. 'Woman as Body: Ancient and Contemporary Views'. *Feminist Studies* 8.1: 109–31.
Spentzou, Efrossini. 2003. *Readers and Writers in Ovid's* Heroides*: Transgressions of Genre and Gender*. Oxford University Press.
Spivak, Gayatri Chakravorty. 1988. 'Can the Subaltern Speak?' In Cary Nelson and Lawrence Grossberg, eds. *Marxism and the Interpretation of Culture*. Macmillan Education. 271–313.
———. 1999. *A Critique of Postcolonial Reason: Toward a History of the Vanishing Present*. Harvard University Press.
Stamatopoulou, Zoe. 2017. *Hesiod and Classical Greek Poetry: Reception and Transformation in the Fifth Century BCE*. Cambridge University Press.
Staples, Ariadne. 1998. *From Good Goddess to Vestal Virgins: Sex and Category in Roman Religion*. Routledge.
Steele, Laura. 2019. 'From Aristotle to Artificial Intelligence: Can Ancient Theories be Applied to Modern Ethical Challenges?' *The QMS Ethics, Responsibility, Sustainability Blog*. https://www.qub.ac.uk/schools/Queens-ManagementSchool/About/Ethics/FileUpload/Filetoupload,895822,en.pdf.
Stehle [Stigers], Eva. 1981. 'Sappho's Private World'. *Women's Studies* 8: 47–63.
Stepp, Laura Sessions. 2007. 'A New Kind of Date Rape'. *Cosmopolitan*. 11 September.
Stetz, Margaret D. 2001. 'Listening "With Serious Intent": Feminist Pedagogical Practice and Social Transformation'. *Transformations: The Journal of Inclusive Scholarship and Pedagogy* 12.1: 7–27.
Stevenson, Jane. 2005. *Women Latin Poets: Language, Gender, and Authority, from Antiquity to the Eighteenth Century*. Oxford University Press.
———. 2022. 'Marta Marchina, Poetry and Social Mobility in Baroque Rome'. In Neil Kenny, ed. *Literature, Learning, and Social Hierarchy in Early Modern Europe*. Oxford University Press. 139–60.
Stewart, Roberta. 2012. *Plautus and Roman Slavery*. Wiley-Blackwell.
Stirrup, B. E. 1977. 'Techniques of Rape: Variety of Wit in Ovid's *Metamorphoses*'. *G&R* 24.2: 170–84.
Stokes, Michael C. 1986. *Plato's Socratic Conversations: Drama and Dialectic in Three Dialogues*. Johns Hopkins University Press.

Strong, Anise K. 2016. *Prostitutes and Matrons in the Roman World*. Cambridge University Press.
———. 2021. 'Male Slave Rape and Victims' Agency in Roman Society'. In Kamen and Marshall, eds. 174–87.
Strozzi, Lorenza. 1588. *Venerabilis Laurentiae Stroziae Monialis S. Dominici in monasterio divi Nicholaie de Prato, in singula totius Anni solemnia, Hymni*. Filippo Giunta.
Stryker, Susan and Aren Z. Aizura. 2013. *The Transgender Studies Reader 2*. Routledge.
Sullivan, John Patrick. 1968. *The* Satyricon *of Petronius: A Literary Study*. Indiana University Press.
Sussman, David. 2005. 'What's Wrong with Torture?' *Philosophy and Public Affairs* 33.1: 1–33.
Sutherland, Jean-Anne and Kathryn M. Feltey. 2017. 'Here's Looking at Her: An Intersectional Analysis of Women, Power and Feminism in Film'. *Journal of Gender Studies* 26.6: 618–31.
Swanson, Judith A. 1994–5. 'The Political Philosophy of Aeschylus' *Prometheus Bound*: Justice as Seen by Prometheus, Zeus, and Io'. *Interpretation* 22.2: 215–45.
Synodinou, Katerina. 1987. 'The Threats of Physical Abuse of Hera by Zeus in the *Iliad*'. *WS* 100: 13–22.
Tanesini, Alessandra. 1999. *An Introduction to Feminist Epistemologies*. Blackwell.
———. 2018. 'Epistemic Vice and Motivation'. *Metaphilosophy* 49.3: 350–67.
———. 2020. *Ignorance, Arrogance, and Privilege: Vice Epistemology and the Epistemology of Ignorance*. Routledge.
Tarn, William W. and Martin P. Charlesworth. 1967. *Octavian, Antony and Cleopatra*. Cambridge University Press.
Tarrant, Richard J. 1995. 'The *Narrationes* of "Lactantius" and the Transmission of Ovid's *Metamorphoses*'. In Oronzo Pecere and Michael D. Reeve, eds. *Formative Stages of Classical Tradition*. Centro italiano di studi sull'Alto medioevo. 83–115.
Tatum, James. 1983. *Plautus: The Darker Comedies*. Johns Hopkins Press.
Taylor, Rabun. 1997. 'Two Pathic Subcultures in Ancient Rome'. *JHSex* 7: 319–71.
Tentler, Thomas N. 2015. *Sin and Confession on the Eve of the Reformation*. Princeton University Press.
Thornham, Sue. 2007. *Women, Feminism and Media*. Edinburgh University Press.
Tilton, Emily C. 2022. 'Rape Myths, Catastrophe, and Credibility'. *Episteme* 1–17.
Tod, Marcus. 1949. 'Greek Record-Keeping and Record-Breaking'. *CQ* 43: 105–12.
Todd, Stephen. 1990. 'The Purpose of Evidence in Athenian Courts'. In Paul Cartledge, Paul Millett and Stephen Todd, eds. Nomos: *Essays in Athenian Law, Politics and Society*. Cambridge University Press.
———. 1993. *The Shape of Athenian Law*. Oxford University Press.

Tomes, Yuma I. 2008. 'Ethnicity, Cognitive Styles, and Math Achievement: Variability within African-American Post-Secondary Students'. *Multicultural Perspectives* 10: 17–23.
Toole, Briana. 2019. 'From Standpoint Epistemology to Epistemic Oppression'. *Hypatia* 34.4: 598–619.
Traub, Valerie. 2002. *The Renaissance of Lesbianism in Early Modern England*. Cambridge University Press.
——. 2020. 'Introduction: Transversions of "Iphis and Ianthe"'. In Traub, Badir and McKracken, eds. 1–41.
Traub, Valerie, Patricia Badir and Peggy McKracken. 2020. *Ovidian Transversions: 'Iphis and Ianthe', 1300–1650*. Edinburgh University Press.
Treggiari, Susan. 1991. *Roman Marriage. Iusti Coniuges from the Time of Cicero to the Time of Ulpian*. Oxford University Press.
——. 2007. *Terentia, Tullia, and Publilia: The Women of Cicero's Family*. Routledge.
Treves, Piero. 1936. 'Apocrifi demostenici'. *Athenaeum* 14: 252–8.
Trouillot, Michel-Rolph. 1995. *Silencing the Past: Power and the Production of History*. Beacon Press.
Tuana, Nancy. 1993. 'With Many Voices: Feminism and Theoretical Pluralism'. In Paula England, ed. *Theory on Gender/Feminism on Theory*. De Gruyter. 281–89.
——, ed. 1994. *Feminist Interpretations of Plato*. Penn State Press.
——. 2004. 'Coming to Understand: Orgasm and the Epistemology of Ignorance'. *Hypatia* 19.1: 194–232.
——. 2006. 'The Speculum of Ignorance: The Women's Health Movement and Epistemologies of Ignorance'. *Hypatia* 21.3: 1–19.
——. 2017. 'Feminist Epistemology: The Subject of Knowledge'. In Kidd, Medina and Pohlhaus Jr, eds. 125–38.
Tuana, Nancy and Shannon Sullivan. 2006. 'Introduction: Feminist Epistemologies of Ignorance' *Hypatia* 21.3: 1–19.
——. 2007. *Race and Epistemologies of Ignorance*. SUNY Press.
Tuerkheimer, Deborah. 2017. 'Incredible Women: Sexual Violence and the Credibility Discount'. *University of Pennsylvania Law Review* 166.1.
Umachandran, Mathura. 2022. 'Disciplinecraft: Towards an Anti-racist Classics' *TAPA* 152.1: 25–31.
Vandvik, Eirik. 1943. *The Prometheus of Hesiod and Aeschylus*. Dybwad.
Veyne, Paul. 1985. 'Homosexuality in Ancient Rome'. In Philippe Ariès and André Béjin, eds. *Western Sexuality: Practice and Precept in Past and Present Times*. Trans. by Anthony Forster. Basil Blackwell. 26–35.
Vidal-Naquet, Pierre. 1986. *The Black Hunter: Forms of Thought and Forms of Society in the Greek World*. Trans. by Andrew Szegedy-Maszak. Johns Hopkins University Press.

Vlastos, Gregory. 1981 [1973]. 'The Individual as an Object of Love in Plato'. In Gregory Vlastos, *Platonic Studies*. Princeton University Press. 3–42.
Voigt, Eva-Maria, ed. 1971. *Sappho et Alcaeus: Fragmenta*. Athenaeum.
Waithe, Mary Ellen, ed. 1987–1991. *A History of Women Philosophers*. Vols. 1–3. Kluwer Academic Publishing.
Waller, Gary. 2020. *The Female Baroque in Early Modern English Literary Culture from Mary Sidney to Aphra Behn*. Amsterdam University Press.
Warshaw, Robin. 1988. *'I Never Called It Rape': The Ms. Report on Recognizing, Fighting, and Surviving Date and Acquaintance Rape*. Ms. Foundation.
Watt, Diane. 2003. *Amoral Gower Language, Sex, and Politics*. University of Minnesota Press.
Weil, Henri. 1887. 'L'auteur du premier discours *contre Aristogiton* est-il bien informé des institutions d'Athènes?' *Melagnes Renier*: 17–25.
White, Deborah Gray. 1999. *Ar'n't I a Woman?: Female Slaves in the Plantation South*. Norton.
White, Hugh. 2008. *Nature, Sex, and Goodness in a Medieval Literary Tradition*. Oxford University Press.
White, Peter. 2010. *Cicero in Letters: Epistolary Relations of the Late Republic*. Oxford University Press.
White, Stephen Augustus. 2001. 'Io's World: Intimations of Theodicy in *Prometheus Bound*'. *JHS* 121: 107–40.
Whitmarsh, Tim and Stuart Thomson. 2013. *The Romance between Greece and the East*. Cambridge University Press.
Wilamowitz-Moellendorf, Ulrich von. 1913. *Sappho und Simonides: Untersuchungen über griechische Lyriker*. Wiedmann.
Williams, Craig A. 1995. 'Greek Love at Rome'. *CQ* 45: 517–39.
_____. 2010. *Roman Homosexuality*, 2nd edition. Oxford University Press.
Williamson, Jacquelyn. 2015. 'Alone before the God: Gender, Status, and Nefertiti's Image'. *JARCE* 51: 179–92.
Wills, Garry. 1967. 'The Sapphic "Umwertung aller Werte"'. *AJP* 88.4: 434–42.
Wills, Jeffrey. 1990. 'Callimachean Models for Ovid's "Apollo-Daphne"'. *MD* 24: 143–56.
Wing, Adrien K. 2003. *Critical Race Feminism: A Reader*. New York University Press.
Winkler, Jack. 1981. 'Gardens of Nymphs: Public and Private in Sappho's Lyrics'. *Women's Studies* 8: 65–91.
Winnington-Ingram, R. P. 1983. *Studies in Aeschylus*. Cambridge University Press.
Winters, Georgia M. and Elizabeth L. Jeglic. 2017. 'Stages of Sexual Grooming: Recognizing Potentially Predatory Behaviors of Child Molesters'. *Deviant Behavior* 38: 724–33.

Wiseman, Timothy P. 1985. *Catullus and His World: A Reappraisal*. Cambridge University Press.
Wistrand, Erik. 1976. *The So-Called Laudatio Turiae*. Acta Universitatis Gothoburgensis.
Witzke, Serena S. 2014. 'An Ideal Reception: Oscar Wilde, Menander's Comedy, and the Context of Victorian Classical Studies'. In Sommerstein, ed. 215–32.
———. 2015. 'Harlots, Tarts, and Hussies? A Problem of Terminology for Sex Labor in Roman Comedy'. *Helios* 42.1: 7–27.
———. 2016. 'Violence against Women in Ancient Rome: Ideology versus Reality'. In Riess and Fagan, eds. 248–74.
———. 2020. 'Ethics in Roman New Comedy'. In Michael Ewans, ed. *Antiquity*. Vol. 1. Bloomsbury. 165–74.
———. 2022. 'Reading from Outside: Revealing and Teaching Violence and Oppression in Our Texts'. *Classical Outlook* 97.1: 10–15.
Wohl, Victoria. 2010. *Law's Cosmos: Juridical Discourse in Athenian Forensic Oratory*. Cambridge University Press.
Woloch, Alex. 2003. *The One vs. the Many: Minor Characters and the Space of the Protagonist in the Novel*. Princeton University Press.
Wolpert, Andrew. 2000–1. 'Lysias 1 and the Politics of the οἶκος'. *CJ* 96: 415–24.
Wood, Denis. 2010. *Rethinking the Power of Maps*. Guilford Press.
Worman, Nancy. 2008. *Abusive Mouths in Classical Athens*. Cambridge University Press.
Worthington, Ian, Craig Cooper and Edward M. Harris, eds. 2001. *Dinarchus Hyperides and Lycurgus*. University of Texas Press.
Wright, Gillian. 2013. *Producing Women's Poetry, 1600–1730: Text and Paratext, Manuscript and Print*. Cambridge University Press.
Wyke, Maria. 1994. 'Taking the Woman's Part: Engendering Roman Love Elegy'. *Ramus* 23.1–2: 110–28.
Yarrow, Liv Mariah. 2020. 'On Controversies in the Classics – with Updates'. *Liv Mariah Yarrow: Adventures in My Head*. September 29. https://livyarrow.org/2020/09/29/on-controversies-and-classics/.
Yatromanolakis, Dimitrios. 2007. *Sappho in the Making: The Early Reception*. Center for Hellenic Studies.
Young, David. 1996. '"First with the Most": Greek Athletic Records and Specialization'. *Nikephoros* 9: 175–97.
Young, Iris Marion. 2006. 'Responsibility and Global Justice: A Social Connection Model'. *Social Philosophy and Policy* 23.1: 102–30.
Zeitlin, Froma I. 1985. 'Playing the Other: Theater, Theatricality, and the Feminine in Greek Drama'. *Representations* 11: 63–94.

Ziogas, Ioannis. 2021. *Law and Love in Ovid: Courting Justice in the Age of Augustus*. Oxford University Press.

Zmigrod, Leor. 2018. 'Brexit Psychology: Cognitive Styles and Their Relationship to Nationalistic Attitudes'. *The London School of Economics and Political Science*. 17 September. https://blogs.lse.ac.uk/brexit/2018/11/27/brexit-psychology-cognitive-styles-and-their-relationship-to-nationalistic-attitudes/.

Index

Note: The index is ordered using the word-by-word method.

#MeToo (#MeToo Movement), 1, 24, 61,
    68–9, 71, 134–5, 169
#classicssowhite, 11

abuse, 50, 55, 60–2, 70–3, 79, 81,
    121, 128, 132, 134–5, 168, 170,
    186, 198–201, 262, 266, 268–9,
    278
Achebe, N., 156, 168
Acte (character in *Quo Vadis* 1951), 239
active ignorance *see* epistemologies of
    ignorance
Acts of Peter (*Actus Petri*), 156–7,
    160, 168
Adam (biblical), 251
adulterium, 173–9
Aeneas, 160–3, 256
Aeschylus, 48, 112
    Prometheus Bound (*Prometheus
    Vinctus*), 48–50, 54, 59, 63,
    65–6
Alain de Lille
    The Complaint of Nature (*De planctu
    Naturae*), 226

Alcaeus
    Fragment 117b, 43
    Fragment 344, 43
Alcibiades, 70n, 190, 197
Alcman
    Partheneion, 108
Altis, 103, 111
Amans, 234–5
amica, 121–2
Amor, 261
amor impossibilis, 227, 229, 232,
    237–8
Antony (Marcus Antonius), 147, 161–5,
    263–4
anti-atomism, 15–16
Apelleas, 102–3; *see also* Cynisca
Aphrodite, 38; *see also* Venus
Aphrodite Ourania, 89, 92
Aphrodite Pandemos, 89
Apollo, 179; *see also* Phoebus; *see also*
    Daphne and Apollo
Apollonius
    Argonautica, 255
Adruino, A. M., 245

Aristophanes, 74, 78, 90
  Knights (*Equites*), 74
  Lysistrata, 78
Aristotle, 3
  Poetics (*Poetica*), 158n
  Politics (*Politica*), 80, 131
  Rhetoric (*Rhetorica*), 80
Astaphium, 126–8
atomism, 13–17
atomistic model of knowers (atomistic knower), 13, 16, 83, 100, 203, 208–9, 211–12, 219
Atticus (Titus Pomponius), 140, 146–50, 152–4, 161
Augustus (Caesar Augustus, Octavian), 161–3, 166, 251, 253
Aulus Gellius, 148
autarkeia (autonomy) 207–8, 211–12

Bacchis, 123–4, 127–9, 133–6
Bacchus (Dionysus), 171, 172n
Batiatus (character in Spartacus 2010–14), 263–4, 275–6
Batiatus (character in Spartacus 1960), 271
Bernini, G. L., 246
Bersuire, P.
  Ovidius moralizatus, 225; see also *Ovide moralisé*
Bible/biblical, 250–61
Black feminist standpoint *see* feminist standpoint theory
Black identity/Blackness, 8–9, 11–12, 17–18, 21, 55, 156–7, 160, 168, 243
body *see* embodiment
Bona Dea scandal, 149
breastfeeding/breastmilk, 91–2, 99, 250, 252, 257–9

Caerellia, 140, 150
Caesar (Julius Caesar), 144, 152–4, 276–7
Callicles (father of Apelleas), 102
Callicles (character), 123–4, 130, 132–3, 135

Callisto, 183
care ethics *see* ethics of care
Catherine of Alexandria, 257–9, 261
Catiline, 146
Cato the Elder, 144
Catullus, 255
Chiesa Nuova, 246–7
child grooming, 186, 199–201
childbirth, 10, 82–3, 86–91, 210, 259n; *see also* pregnancy and breastfeeding
Christian/Christianity, 168, 223–41, 246–61, 259, 269
Cicero (Marcus Tullius Cicero) 139–44, 146–54, 267
  De Finibus, 140, 150n
  Letters to Atticus (*Epistulae ad Atticus*), 144n, 146–50, 161
  Letters to Family (*Epistulae ad Familiares*), 141, 146
Cinderella motif, 278–9
class, 3, 5, 6, 8, 28, 33n, 34, 55, 90, 104–5, 124, 141, 145, 149–50, 155n, 159–61, 169n, 202, 206–10, 212, 219, 228, 242–3, 245–6, 254, 261, 262, 272, 277–8
Cleopatra VII, 161, 163, 165–67
Clodia (wife of Metellus), 153–4
Clytie, 171–82
Collins, P. H., 8–9, 18, 55–6, 243, 247, 250, 261; *see also* othermothers
colonialism, 14n, 19–20, 113, 116, 167, 253; *see also* imperialism
Columella
  De Re Rustica, 144
Combahee River Collective Statement (B. Smith, B. Smith, and D. Frazier), 157
consent, 22, 56, 172–3, 175–7, 179–80, 182–3, 196–201, 255, 262, 264–5, 267–9, 272, 274, 277–8
contributory injustice, 18–19, 20–2, 25, 185–6, 191–2, 199, 201; *see also* epistemic injustice
Crassus (character in Spartacus 1960), 271, 276–8

Crenshaw, K., 68, 157–8
Creolisation, 158
critical race feminism (CRF), 158
critical race theory (CRT), 158
Crixus (character in Spartacus 2010–14), 275
cross-dressing, 172n
Cupid, 236–40; *see also* Eros
Cynisca, 102–14, 116, 120

Daphne and Apollo, 179
De Morel, C., 245
Demosthenes, 60, 68, 72–3, 80
    Against Aristogeiton, 72, 80
    Against Evergus and Mnesibulus, 109
    Against Meidias, 73
desire, 22, 31–47, 58–9, 83–92, 100, 162, 164, 166–7, 176n, 171, 177, 189–90, 198, 207, 222–41, 263, 266, 268, 275, 277
Dido, 156, 160–3, 168
Diniarchus (character), 122–4, 126–8, 130, 135
Diogenes Laertius, 203, 216n
Diotima, 82–101
Dotson, K., 17–19, 22, 186, 191, 199
drag, 224n

Egeria
    Peregrinatio, 242
Eirene (character in Rome 2005–7), 273–6; *see also* Pullo, T.
Elizabeth I of England, 245
embodiment, 4, 11, 14, 31–2, 34, 35, 39, 42–7, 56, 66, 83n, 86–7, 90, 97–100, 132–3, 167–8, 182, 192, 223–39, 257–9, 261, 263, 268–9, 274–6.
emotion/emotions, 5, 9, 14, 15, 19n, 27, 39, 41–4, 208, 213, 215–20, 257, 264, 274, 276
emotional residue *see* queer epistemology
Encolpius, 185, 188–9, 198

enslavement, 2, 3, 4, 16, 66n, 69–70, 72, 76–80, 118, 123, 125–6, 130–3, 135–6, 141, 143, 145, 148, 158n, 174, 206, 262–79
Epictetus, 204–5, 212
epistemic injustice, 17–21, 23–6, 29–34, 40, 47, 68–9, 71–2, 122, 125, 131, 136–7, 171, 178, 181, 185–7, 197, 210, 223, 226, 271
    epistemic appropriation, 19
    epistemic objectification, 71, 81, 263
    epistemic paralysis, 19
    epistemic violence, 19, 23–4, 30, 31n, 41, 71, 129–30, 168
    epistemic resistance, 23–4, 31–3, 47, 49, 50n, 60, 69n, 132
    epistemic vice, 23, 54, 49, 118; *see also* active ignorance
    epistemicide, 19, 20, 23–4, 119
    epistemologies of ignorance, 7, 37, 41
    active ignorance, 3, 21, 23
erastes, 89–90, 93n, 94, 95n, 190, 196n
Eros (Cupid), 38, 44, 86, 89, 236–8, 240
eros (desire), 44, 85–7, 89–93, 97, 99, 100, 107
eromenos, 94–5, 190, 194–5, 196n, 201
ethics of care (care ethics), 85, 100, 243, 246, 252; *see also* feminist epistemologies of care
Eumolpus, 185–201
Eunice (character in *Quo Vadis* 1951), 268–70; *see also* Petronius (character in *Quo Vadis* 1951)
Eurydice I of Macedon (Eurydice), 109, 111
evidentiary injustice, 20, 24, 104n, 139n

Fedeli, C., 249; *see also* Marchina, M.
female portrait statue, 109
feminist epistemology, 2, 3, 5, 6–8, 12–13, 17, 19, 21, 25–8, 30, 48–9, 68, 81, 94, 122, 124–5, 129, 136, 187–8, 201–3, 206, 208–13, 217–20, 242–3, 252
    feminist epistemologies of care, 251–2

feminist standpoint theory, 8–12, 41, 49, 55, 84, 125, 245
  Black feminist standpoint, 8, 10, 12, 55, 157, 243; *see also* standpoint theory
feminist Stoicism, 202–3, 206n, 220
Ford, C., 174
Fricker, M., 17–19, 22–3, 49, 71, 170, 186, 223; *see also* epistemic injustice
A Funny Thing Happened on the Way to the Forum see Sondheim, S.

Gaia (character in *Rome* 2005–7), 275
Game of Thrones (2011–19), 264–5
Ganymede, 188–9
Garden of Eden, 251
gender, 2, 5, 6, 7, 15, 17, 22, 27, 28, 31–7, 39–41, 47, 48–52, 55–6, 65, 68, 79, 83–6, 88–101, 107–8, 110–11, 113–14, 122, 129–30, 134, 157, 158–68, 183–4, 188, 202, 205, 207–9, 212, 219, 222–3, 226, 228–9, 231–4, 237–40, 243, 245, 264–5, 270, 275
gender identity, 15, 31, 41, 55, 59, 85, 98, 105, 108, 157, 159, 163, 228, 238, 273
gender performance, 163, 167, 223, 226, 231–2, 237, 240
gender transformation, 229–31, 233, 234n
gendered pronouns, 37, 222n, 238
Genius (character), 234–5
Gentileschi, A., 246
Giton, 188
Gower, J., 221, 223, 234–40
  Confessio Amantis, 221, 223, 234–5
  see also Ovide moralisé
grey rape, 269; *see also* rape and consent

Hannibal, 161
Hasdrubal, 165
Helen, 37–9, 108
Helvia, 142–6, 151–2, 155
Hephaestus, 53

Hera (Juno), 62, 78, 103, 105, 107
Heracles (Hercules), 108, 259n
Hermaphroditus, 171; *see also* Salamacis and Hermaphroditus
hermeneutical injustice, 18, 22, 169–72, 180, 186, 223, 225–6, 228, 238; *see also* epistemic injustice
  manifest concept, 170, 178, 181
  operative concept, 170, 178–81, 183
Hermes, 56, 63–6
Herodotus, 77
Hesiod, 54, 66–7, 87
heterosexuality/heterosexualism/heteronormativity, 22, 37–8, 38n, 40, 223, 239n, 269; *see also* sexual orientation/identity
Hilarus, 149
Hippocrates
  On Airs, Waters, Places, 131
Homer, 53n, 56n, 68n, 78, 87, 171
  Iliad, 139n
homoeroticism/homosexuality, 16, 22, 91, 95n, 191n, 193n, 194n, 196n, 222–8, 231–3, 236–9, 240; *see also* sexual orientation/identity
Horace/Horatian, 144, 249, 256
Hortensia, 138n
Hyacinthus, 188
Hyenté, 229–32
Hylas, 188
Hymenaeus, 230

Ianthe, 222, 228n, 230, 234, 237; *see also* Iphis
Iarbas, 160–2
If They Should Ask (S. Hayes), 104, 115–20
imperialism, 23, 118, 168, 250n, 253, 264–5, 267; *see also* colonialism
implicit understanding *see* queer epistemology
intersectionality, 9, 68, 157–8, 243, 278
Io, 49–67

Iphis, 221–5, 227, 229–31, 233–40
Isis, 222, 229, 231–2, 237
Isomachus's wife, 2, 3, 5

Jesus Christ, 78n, 157, 251–3, 256–7
Juno, 163, 180n, 183, 230, 259n; see also Hera
Jupiter 183, 251, 254–6; see also Zeus
Juvenal, 144
Juvencus, A.
  Evangeliorum libri, 255

Kavanaugh, B., 174
knowing otherwise see queer epistemology
knowing resistant anger, 24, 69, 81; see also epistemic resistance
Kore (character in *Spartacus* 2010–14), 276–7
Kratos, 50n, 54n
Kubrick, S., 270–1, 278
  Spartacus (1960), 263, 270–1, 278
kudos, 107, 110n, 111

Leuconoe, 171, 178–9
Leucothoe, 24, 169–84; see also Ovid's *Metamorphoses*
Ligdus, 228, 232
Litany of Loreto, 256
Livia, 138
Livy (Titus Livius), 138–9, 160–7, 265
  Ab Urbe Condita, 139
Lorde, A., 32, 41–2, 46–7, 156
Lucretia, 138, 162, 167
Lucretia (character in *Spartacus* 2010–14), 263, 271
Lucretius, 159–60, 256

Macedo, F., 245, 247–8, 252; see also Marchina, M.
malitia (badness), 121, 129, 136
manifest concept see hermeneutical injustice
Marcellus, 156

Marchina, G. (brother of Martha), 246, 248
Marchina, M., 242, 247–56, 258–61
  Musa Posthuma, 242–57
Marchina, M. (sister of Martha), 246
marriage, 40, 62–3, 92–3, 121–3, 131, 134–5, 162–3, 166, 175, 222, 230–4, 240, 245, 274
Mars, 171
Martha Marchina Group (MMG), 244, 251–2, 254, 256
Marx, K., 8, 10
Marxism, 125, 267
Marxist feminism, 8, 84, 159, 267
Mary (mother of Jesus Christ), 251–7
Masinissa, 163–7
maternal standpoint, 250–1; see also standpoint theory and feminist standpoint theory
Maxentius, 257
Medina, J., 3–4, 17, 20, 23, 51, 180, 263; see also epistemologies of ignorance
Menander, 122, 148
meretrix, 121–4, 127–31, 133, 136
Metellus, L., 153
metic, 68–9, 72, 76, 79, 81
Milky Way, 259; see also Marchina, M.
Milton, J.
  Paradise Lost, 255
Minyads (daughters of Minyas), 171
mothers/motherhood, 38, 69n, 72, 75–6, 85n, 91, 93, 96–7, 100, 109–10, 113, 123–4, 128, 142–6, 172, 222, 243, 247, 250–6, 259; see also feminist ethics of care; feminist standpoint theory; othermothers
Musonius Rufus
  Lecture 3, 204
  Lecture 4, 205

Naevia (character in *Spartacus* 2010–14), 275–8
Neri, P., 250, 259–61
Nero (character in *Quo Vadis* 1951), 269–70

Numidia/Numidians, 163–7
nursing *see* breastfeeding
nymphs, 55–6

objectification (including epistemic objectification), 33, 71, 81, 199n, 258, 261, 263, 267–8, 270–2
objectivity, 5–6, 9–11, 13–16, 83, 216–18
Ocean, 50–1, 53–4, 56n, 57–8, 66
Oceanids, 12, 16, 48–67
Octavian *see* Augustus
Olympia (location), 36, 103, 106–8, 110–11
operative concept *see* hermeneutical injustice
Oratorians, 246–9
othermother, 243, 247, 261
others/othering, 23, 130, 163, 267
Oticilia, 149
Our Lady of the Snows (miracle), 254; *see also* Marchina, M.
Ovid
   Amores, 261
   Art of Love (*Ars Amatoria*), 179n, 180, 197, 235n
   Metamorphoses, 161, 171, 173, 178–9, 184, 224–5, 228–9, 235, 255–6
Ovide moralisé, 221, 223–5, 228

Padilla Peralta, D., 11–12, 23, 118
Palatine Hill, 148
Paris, 37–8
pathe, 215–20
Paulus
   Digest, 194
Pausanias (Historian), 103, 107–8, 111
Pausanias (of Athens), 89–90, 92, 190
pederasty, 26, 85, 89–94, 97, 185–97, 201; *see also erastes, eromenos*
Pergamene Boy, 185–201; *see also* Petronius
Perpetua *see* Vibia Perpetua
Peter (the Apostle) *see Acts of Peter*

Petronius, 185, 198
   Satyrica, 185, 188
   (character in *Quo Vadis* 1951), 268–70
Phaedrus, 89, 96–7; *see also* Plato's *Symposium*
Phaethon, 255
phantasiai, 207, 213, 219
Philadelphia (Pennsylvania), 115–17, 119
Phoebus, 255, 256; *see also* Apollo
Phronesium (character), 121–4, 126–9, 132–3
Piscopia, E. C., 244
Plancina, 138
Plato, 16, 94, 198
   Menexenus, 84
   Republic (*Respublica*), 82, 91
   Symposium, 83–5, 88, 90–2, 94–8, 185, 190
   Theaetetus, 82–4
Plautus, 12, 24, 122, 124–5, 131, 136, 150
   The Little Carthaginian (*Poenulus*), 150
   The Mother-in-law (*Hecyra*), 24, 121–4, 127–8, 130, 133, 135
   The Woman Money Lender (*Faeneratrix*), 148–9
   The Surly Man (*Truculentus*), 121–4, 126, 130–3, 135
Plutarch, 142
   Agesilaus, 105–6
   Cicero, 142
   Antony (*Antonius*), 165
Pohlhaus Jr, G., 35, 60, 182, 186, 262
Polybius, 163–4
Pompey, 152–3
Pomponia, 152
Poppaea Sabina (character in *Quo Vadis* 1951), 269–70
Porcia (sister of Cato the Younger), 144
pregnancy, 1, 10, 68n, 83–4, 86–95, 100, 121, 123, 133, 259, 276
priamel, 35–6, 38, 40
Prometheus *see* Aeschylus

propositional knowledge *see* queer
    epistemology
Pulcher, P. Clodius, 149
Pullo, T. (character in *Rome* 2005–7),
    273–6; *see also* Vorenus and Pullo
    (characters in *Rome* 2005–7)
Pyramus and Thisbe, 171

Queen Kristina of Sweden, 247
queer epistemology, 9, 31–2, 34, 41
    emotional residue, 41–2
    implicit understanding, 42–3, 46–7
    knowing otherwise, 32, 34, 40, 42,
        44–6
    propositional knowledge, 42–3, 45–7,
        209
queer theory/queer studies, 9n, 22, 31–2,
    38, 40–1, 239
Quintus (brother of Cicero), 142–6, 152;
    see also Cicero
Quirinus, P. S., 253
Quo Vadis (1925), 268
Quo Vadis (1951), 267–71, 278

racialised gender, 157, 159–65,
    167–8
race, 1, 5, 6, 11, 15n, 28, 55, 157–62,
    166–7, 168n, 208–9, 243, 273, 275,
    277–8
rape, 1, 18, 22, 24, 55, 121–37, 138,
    169–84, 187n, 193n, 196–7,
    263–79
rape myths, 25, 134, 169–84, 196–7
Respublica litterarum, 244–5
Roma (goddess), 254–6
Rome (2005–7), 254–78

Saint Catherine of Alexandria
    see Catherine of Alexandria
Santa Maria Maggiore, 254; *see also*
    Marchina, M.
Salamacis and Hermaphroditus, 171
Sallust
    Bellum Catilinae, 139
Salve Regina, 256

same-sex relationships, 91n, 227, 279;
    see also homoeroticism/
    homosexuality and pederasty
Santolino, Fr. L., 246, 248
Sappho
    Fragment 16, 34–6, 38, 40
    Fragment 31, 34, 39, 40
    Fragment 47, 44
    Fragment 48, 44
    Fragment 51, 42
    Fragment 88, 43
    Fragment 95, 46
Sapphics, 249
science, 6, 9, 14, 22, 209, 218, 243, 246,
    250, 253–4, 258–9, 261
Scipio Africanus, 163–8
Sedgwick, E. K., 138, 141, 155, 226
Seneca
    Consolation of Marcia (*De
        Consolatione ad Marciam*), 204–5
    Moral Letters to Lucilius (*Epistulae
        Morales ad Lucilium*), 204, 206
Sestius, P., 146
sex (act), 22, 25, 43, 91n, 93, 95n, 100,
    128–9, 169, 173–7, 179, 182, 185,
    187n, 188n, 189–201, 224, 226–8,
    236–8, 262–78
sex (biological/bodily), 5, 10, 28, 83n,
    88–91, 93–4, 98, 100–1, 159,
    185n, 192n, 210, 223, 229n, 233–4,
    237–41
sex labour/sex work, 43, 121, 126,
    128–9, 131
Sextus Empiricus, 214
sexual abuse, 55, 131, 134, 170, 199, 262,
    266, 276
sexual assault, 17, 134–5, 263, 265, 268,
    269, 271, 273
sexual harassment, 18, 170, 198, 264
sexual orientation/sexual identity, 6,
    28, 47, 162, 187, 223, 227,
    238, 241
sexual violence, 1, 7, 55, 66n, 68, 134,
    169, 172n, 179n, 183–7, 193, 197,
    201, 263, 265–7

sexuality, 5, 22, 26, 31, 34–5, 41, 47, 162, 193n, 237–9, 243, 264
silence/silencing, 19, 20, 29, 30, 40, 50n, 65, 67, 69–70, 79, 81, 112–13, 118, 125n, 129–36, 156, 168, 186, 200, 223, 226–8, 232, 234, 237–8, 240, 263, 270, 274, 279; *see also* epistemic injustice
situated knowledge *see* standpoint theory
slavery *see* enslavement
Socrates (in Petronius), 190, 197
Socrates (in Plato's *Theaetetus*), 82–3
Socrates (in Plato's *Symposium*), 83–4, 86, 91, 95–7
Socrates (in Xenophon's *Oeconomicus*), 2
sodomy, 22, 224–41
Sol, 171–2, 174–6, 178–83
Sondheim, S., 271–3
Sophoniba, 160, 163–8; *see also* racialised gender
Spada (Cardinal Bernadino), 246–9
Spada (Family), 246–7
Sparta, 38, 102–4, 109–13, 120
Spartacus (2010–14), 263–77
Spartacus (1960) see Kubrick, S.
standpoint theory, 8–9, 49n, 210–12, 250
  situated knowledge, 9, 210–12, 219; *see also* feminist standpoint theory, standpoint theory
Stoics/Stoicism, 202–20
Stratophanes, 128
Strozzi, L., 245
stuprum, 173, 175–6, 178, 185, 187–9, 191–2, 194, 198, 201, 265
suicide, 167–8, 269
Sulla, P., 146, 267
Syphax, 163–7
Syra, 127–8

Tacitus
  Annals, 138–9
Telethusa, 222–40; *see also* Iphis
Tellus (*Tellus Mater*), 254–6

Terence, 124, 136
  Brothers (*Adelphoe*), 135
  The Eunuch (*Eunuchus*), 135
  The Mother-in-Law (*Hecyra*), 121–2, 128, 136
Terentia, 140, 147, 152
Tertia, 141
testimonial injustice, 17–18, 130–2, 134, 136, 180n, 210, 266; *see also* epistemic injustice
testimonial quieting, 18
testimonial silencing, 18, 20
testimonial smothering, 18
Teucris (Cornelia), 146–52, 155
Theogenes, 106–7, 111
Thisbe, 171; *see also* Pyramus and Thisbe
Tiro, 142–3, 145–6, 150
Titans, 52, 251
To Kill a Mockingbird (Lee, H.), 17, 186n
trans/trans-/trans* discourse, 9, 13n, 22, 116–17, 227, 228n, 232–3
Traub, V., 227, 233, 239
Troy, 37–8, 148
Trump, D., 174
Tullia, 140
Typhoeus, 251

Valerius Maximus
  Memorable Words and Deeds, 149
Varinia (character in *Spartacus* 1960), 271
Varro, C. Visellius, 132, 149
Velleius Paterculus
  Historia Romana, 139
Venus, 161, 163, 171, 195, 230, 254, 256; *see also* Aphrodite
Vergil
  Aeneid, 160–3, 255–6
Vibia Perpetua, 4, 5, 242
virtue, 6, 23, 84–8, 93, 97–101, 105, 151, 163, 166–7, 204–5, 208, 216–17, 219–20
Vorenus and Pullo (characters in *Rome* 2005–7), 263

Vulcan, 171

Weinstein, H., 134, 169n
white ignorance, 8, 22
white supremacy, 3, 9, 11–12,
    17–18, 21, 115–16, 118, 159–61,
    273
Widow of Ephesus, 188; *see also*
    Petronius

Xenophon
    Agesilaus, 105–6
    Economics (*Oeconomicus*), 2–3, 144

Yphis *see* Iphis

Zeus, 49, 50–5, 57–8, 60–6, 78, 95, 103,
    204; *see also* Jupiter
Zobia, 68–9, 72, 76–8

EU representative:
Easy Access System Europe
Mustamäe tee 50, 10621 Tallinn, Estonia
Gpsr.requests@easproject.com

www.ingramcontent.com/pod-product-compliance
Lightning Source LLC
Chambersburg PA
CBHW050201240426
43671CB00013B/2211